Quaker Records of Northern Maryland

Births, Deaths, Marriages, and Abstracts from the Minutes

1716-1800

Henry C. Peden, Jr., M.A.

WILLOW BEND BOOKS
2006

WILLOW BEND BOOKS
AN IMPRINT OF HERITAGE BOOKS, INC.

Books, CDs, and more—Worldwide

For our listing of thousands of titles see our website at
www.HeritageBooks.com

Published 2006 by
HERITAGE BOOKS, INC.
Publishing Division
65 East Main Street
Westminster, Maryland 21157-5026

Copyright © 1993 Henry C. Peden, Jr.

All rights reserved. No part of this book may be reproduced or transmitted in any form or by any means, electronic or mechanical, including photocopying, recording or by any information storage and retrieval system without written permission from the author, except for the inclusion of brief quotations in a review.

International Standard Book Number: 978-1-58549-249-3

CONTENTS

FORWARD..v
MAP OF QUAKER MEETINGS IN NORTHERN MARYLAND...............ix
GUNPOWDER MONTHLY MEETINGS, BIRTHS AND DEATHS..........1
GUNPOWDER MONTHLY MEETING: MINUTES AND MARRIAGES...26
ABSTRACTS OF GUNPOWDER MONTHLY MEETING MINUTES....58
GUNPOWDER MONTHLY MEETING, CERTIFICATES OF REMOVAL..99
DEER CREEK MONTHLY MEETING, BIRTHS AND DEATHS..........103
DEER CREEK MONTHLY MEETING MARRIAGE CERTIFICATES...108
ABSTRACTS OF DEER CREEK MONTHLY MEETING MINUTES...127
DECEASED MEMBERS OF BALTIMORE MONTHLY MEETING....163
BALTIMORE MONTHLY MEETING CERTIFICATES OF REMOVAL..171
ABSTRACTS OF BALTIMORE MONTHLY MEETING MEMORIALS..174
BALTIMORE MONTHLY MEETING, EASTERN DISTRICT - BIRTHS, DEATHS, DISOWNMENTS AND REMOVALS...................175
BALTIMORE MONTHLY MEETING, EASTERN DISTRICT - MARRIAGE CERTIFICATES..211
ABSTRACT OF BALTIMORE MONTHLY MEETING MINUTES.......218
LITTLE FALLS MONTHLY MEETING, BIRTHS AND DEATHS........239
PIPE CREEK MONTHLY MEETING - WOMEN'S MINUTES.................247
PIPE CREEK MONTHLY MEETING - MARRIAGES...........................264
PIPE CREEK MONTHLY MEETING - BIRTHS....................................279
INDEX..289

FORWARD

Quakers (or Society of Friends) first settled in Maryland in 1658, primarily in southern Maryland. Those records through 1800 have been abstracted by the author in *Quaker Records of Southern Maryland: Births, Deaths, Marriages and Abstracts from the Minutes, 1658-1800*. On Maryland's Eastern Shore, the first Monthly Meetings were established between 1672 and 1698. Abstracts of the Eastern Shore Quaker records are included in the series, *Maryland Eastern Shore Vital Records*, 5 volumes, by F. Edward Wright. They are also contained in Kenneth Carroll's *Quakerism on the Eastern Shore*.

As a sequel, the Quaker records through 1800 in northern Maryland have been abstracted for those meetings held in Baltimore City and the counties of Baltimore, Harford, Carroll, Howard and Frederick. These records begin in 1716 for the most part, although there are references within the records as early as 1674.

Gunpowder Monthly Meeting records begin in 1716 and include Patapsco and early Elk Ridge Meetings. Baltimore Monthly Meeting separated from Gunpowder in 1792 and its records begin that year (although there is a record of deceased members which goes as far back as 1674) and include Patapsco and early Elk Ridge Meetings. Little Falls Monthly Meeting records begin in 1738, and include Forrest Meeting early in its history, but there are no monthly minutes until 1815. Deer Creek Monthly Meeting records begin in 1761, with some references back to 1741, and refer to meetings at Bush River and Susquehanna (or Bayside).

Pipe Creek Monthly Meetings consisted of the two Preparative Meetings, one called Pipe Creek near present-day Union Bridge in Carroll County and Bush Creek Meeting in Frederick County. Both Meetings were initially formed as Preparative Meetings of Fairfax (Waterford) Monthly Meeting in Loudoun County, Virginia. The first Pipe Creek Monthly Meeting was held at Bush Creek in 1772, alternating thereafter between that site and Pipe Creek.

This book is based on the earliest records at the Maryland State Archives up through 1800 (and in some cases to 1820 if the children's dates of birth started prior to 1800 and ended thereafter), as follows, with the microfilm numbers shown:

(1) Gunpowder Monthly Meeting, Register, 1716-1800 (M626)
(2) Gunpowder Monthly Meeting, Marriages, 1740-1779 (M627)
(3) Gunpowder Monthly Meeting, Minutes, 1739-1800 (M627A)
(4) Gunpowder Monthly Meeting, Removals, 1794-1800 (M629)
(5) Baltimore Monthly Meeting, Register, 1793-1800 (M593)
(6) Baltimore Monthly Meeting, Marriages, 1794-1800 (M577)
(7) Baltimore Monthly Meeting, Memorials, 1783-1800 (M594)
(8) Baltimore Monthly Meeting, Removals, 1796-1800 (M579)
(9) Baltimore Monthly Meeting, Decedents, 1674-1800 (M577A)
(10) Baltimore Monthly Meeting, Minutes, 1792-1800 (M591)
(11) Little Falls Monthly Meeting Register, 1738-1800 (M645)
(12) Deer Creek Monthly Meeting, Register, 1761-1800 (M609)
(13) Deer Creek Monthly Meeting, Marriages, 1761-1800 (M609)
(14) Deer Creek Monthly Meeting, Minutes, 1761-1800 (M607)
(15) Pipe Creek Monthly Meeting, Register, 1737-1800, Marriages, 1773-1800, and Removals, 1794-1800 (M665)

Henry C. Peden, Jr.
Bel Air, Maryland
November 4, 1992

MONTHLY MEETINGS MENTIONED IN THE MINUTES

Abbington Meeting, Montgomery Co., PA.

Amawalk Meeting, NY.

Baltimore Meeting, Baltimore Co., now Baltimore City, MD.

Blackwater Meeting, Surry Co., VA.

Bradford Meeting, Chester Co., PA.

Buckingham Meeting, Bucks Co., Pa.

Burlington Meeting, Burlington Co., NJ.

Bush River Meeting, SC.

Bush Creek Meeting, Frederick Co., MD

Cane Creek Meeting, NC.

Cecil Meeting, Kent Co., Md.

Cedar Creek Meeting, Hanover Co., VA.

Center Meeting, Winchester, Frederick Co., VA.

Chester Meeting, Chester Co. before 1789, now Delaware Co., PA.

Chesterfield Meeting, Mercer Co., NJ.

Concord Meeting, Chester Co., before 1789, now Delaware Co., PA.

Crooked Run Meeting, Warren Co., VA.

Darby Meeting, Chester Co. before 1789, now Delaware Co., PA.

Deer Creek Meeting, Harford Co., MD.

Dover Meeting, NJ.

East Caln Meeting, Chester Co., PA.

East Nottingham Meeting (Brick Meeting House), Cecil Co., MD.

Elk Ridge Meeting, Howard Co., MD.

Evesham Meeting, Burlington Co., NJ.

Exeter Meeting, Berks Co., PA.

Fairfax Meeting (Waterford), Loudoun Co., VA.

Falls Meeting, Bucks Co., PA. [Falls Meeting sometimes refers to Little Falls Meeting in Harford Co., MD.]

Fawn Meeting, York Co., PA.

Goose Creek Meeting, VA. There were two Goose Creek Meetings in Virginia, one in Bedford Co. and the other in Loudoun Co.

Goshen (Gishen) Meeting, Chester Co., PA.

Greenwich Meeting, West NJ.

Gunpowder Meeting, Baltimore Co., MD.

Gwynedd Meeting, Philadelphia Co., now Montgomery Co., PA.

Haddonfield Meeting, Camden Co., NJ.

Haverford Meeting, PA.

Hopewell Meeting, Frederick Co., VA.

Horsham (Horshan, Harsham) Meeting, PA.

Indian Spring Meeting, Anne Arundel Co., MD.

Kennet Meeting, Chester Co., PA.

Kingwood Meeting, Hunterdon Co., NJ.

Little Falls Meeting, Harford Co., MD.

London Grove Meeting, Chester Co., PA.

Maiden Creek Meeting, Bucks Co., PA.

Menallen Meeting (Monallin, Monallen) Adams Co., PA.

Middletown Meeting, Bucks Co., PA.

Motherkill (Motherkiln) Meeting, Kent Co., DE.

New Cornwell Meeting, NY.

New Garden Meeting, NC.

New Garden Meeting, Chester Co., PA.

New Hope Meeting, Western Territory.

New York Meeting, NY.

Nottingham Meeting, Chester Co., PA, until 1769, now Cecil Co., MD. There was also a Nottingham Meeting in Northampton Co., VA.

Patapsco Meeting, Baltimore Co., MD.

Philadelphia Meeting, Philadelphia, PA.

Pipe Creek Meeting, near Union Bridge, in present-day Carroll Co., MD.

Providence Meeting, RI.

Redstone Meeting, Fayette Co., Pa.

Richland Meeting, Bucks Co., PA.

Sadsbury Meeting, Lancaster Co., PA.

Salem Meeting, Salem, MA. There was also a Salem Monthly Meeting in Salem Co., NJ.

Sandy Spring Meeting, Montgomery Co., MD.

South River Meeting, Anne Arundel Co., MD.

South River Meeting, VA. There were South River Meetings in Albemarle Co., VA and Campbell Co., VA.

Southland Meeting, VA.

Sutton Creek, Perquimans Co., NC.

Third Haven Meeting, Talbot Co., MD.

Uwchlan Meeting, Chester Co., PA.

Warrington Meeting, York Co., PA.

West River Meeting, Anne Arundel Co., MD.

Western Branch Meeting, Isle of Wight Co., VA.

Westland Meeting, Washington Co., PA.

White Oak Swamp Meeting, Henrico Co., VA.

Wilmington Meeting, Wilmington, DE.

Woodbury Meeting, Gloucester Co., NJ.

Wrightstown (Rights Town) Meeting, Bucks Co., PA.

York Meeting, York Co., PA.

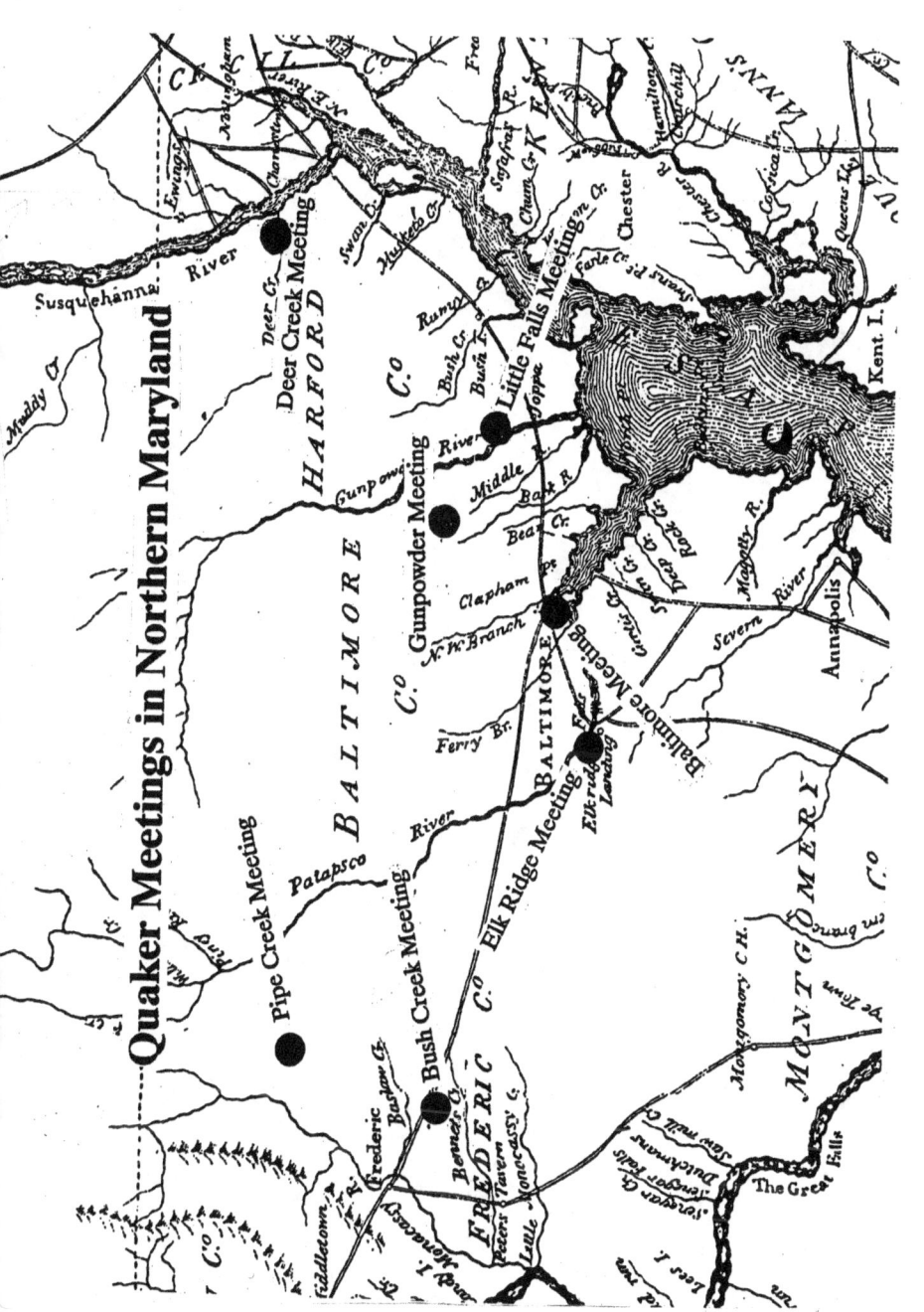

GUNPOWDER MONTHLY MEETING, BIRTHS AND DEATHS, 1716-1800

Joseph England, son of Lewis and Sarah, b. 11th day of 4th month, 1716, at Burton upon Trout in Stafford Shear in old England.

Elizabeth England, dau. of Joseph and Elizabeth, b. 26th day of 6th month, 1760.

Ann Underhill, b. 1st day of 10th month, 1687.

Sarah Wagstaff, wife of Richard Wagstaff and dau. of John and Ann Yarnal of Willis Town, Chester County, Pa., b. 24th day of 2nd month, 1724.

John Forman, first son of Robert and Mary, b. 24th[?] day of 1st month, 1767.

Samuel England, son of Joseph and Elizabeth, b. 23rd day of 7th month, 1757.

William Wheeler, son of William and Susan, b. 8th day of 1st month called March in "oald stile" 1693/4.

Rachel Malsby, dau. of John and Mary, b. 3rd day of 2nd month, 1782, and d. 26th day of 7th month, 1783.

David Malsby, son of John and Mary, b. 10th day of 5th month, 1784.

Mary Malsby, dau. of John and Mary, b. 28th day of 2nd month, 1786.

John Malsby, father of said children, d. 10th day of 9th month, 1785, and was interred at Friends Burying Ground in Baltimore the day following.

Joseph England, son of Lewis and ---- [Sarah], d. 26th day of ---- [torn page], 1761, at about two in the afternoon.

Ann Underhill, d. 15th day of 8th month, 17-- [torn page].

Sarah Wagstaff, wife of Richard Wagstaff of Baltimore Town, and dau. of John and Ann Yarnal of Willis Town, Chester County, Pa., d. 31st day of 7th month, 1763, and was interred at Friends Burying Ground at Patapsco.

Jacob Scott, Sr., d. 11th day of 12th month, 1766, and was bur. at Friends Burying Ground at Gunpowder on the 13th.

William Wheeler, d. 3rd day of 1st month, ---- [torn page].

Sarah Dukehart, dau. of Volerius and Margaret [torn page], b. 21st day of 9th month, 1767.

Margaret and Elizabeth Dukehart, twin dau. of Volerius and Margaret, b. 29th day of 1st month, 1771.

John Dukehart, son of Volerius and Margaret, b. 8th day of 3rd month, 1775.

Catharine Dukehart, dau. of Volerius and Margaret, b. 28th day of -- [torn page], 1779.

Volerius Dukehart, son of Volerius and Margaret, b. 11th day of 9th month, 1783.

Rachel Price, dau. of John, Jr. and Urath, b. 13th day of 6th month, 1758.

Lucey Belt, dau. of John and Lucey, b. 25th day of 9th month, 1744.

Mary Belt, dau. of John and Lucey, b. 30th day of 4th month, 1747.

Joseph Belt, son of John and Lucey, b. 10th day of 4th month, 1750.

Esther Price, dau. of Mordecai (of John) and Mary, b. 28th day of 11th month, 1755.

Ruth Price, dau. of Mordecai (of John) and Mary, b. 21st day of 2nd month, 1758.

John Price, son of Mordecai (of John) and Mary, b. 26th day of 2nd month, 1760.

Mary Price, dau. of Mordecai (of John) and Mary, b. 2nd day of 5th month, 1762.

Jesse Price, son of Mordecai (of John) and Mary, b. 14th day of 12th month, 1763.

Phebe Price, dau. of Mordecai (of John) and Mary, b. 12th day of 10th month, 1765.

Ann Price, dau. of Mordecai (of John) and Mary, b. 27th day of 2nd month, 1768.

John Price, son of Mordecai (of John) and Mary, d. 28th day of 6th month, 1786, aged 26 years, 5 months and 2 days.

John Belt (an Elder), d. 1st of 10th month, 1788, in the 85th year of his age.

Rachel Price, dau. of John, Jr. and Urath, d. 21st day of 4th month, 1761.

William Parrish, d. 5th day of 7th month, 1788, about the 4th hour afternoon, in the 70th year of his age, and was interred in the Friends Burying Ground the day following.

Keturah Parrish, widow of William, d. 22nd day of 2nd month, 1789, about 9 o'clock in the morning, and was interred in Friends Burying Ground at Gunpowder the 24th following, being in the 72nd year of her age.

Jacob Johnson (an Elder), d. 24th day of 1st month, 1792, aged about 74 years, and was interred the day following at Gunpowder Meeting House.

Cassandra Hopkins, dau. of Samuel and Sarah, b. 17th day of 1st month, 1755.

Richard Hopkins, son of Samuel and Sarah, b. 31st day of 8th month, 1756.

Joseph Hopkins, son of Samuel and Sarah, b. 2nd day of 9th month, 1758.

William Hopkins, son of Samuel and Sarah, b. 23rd day of 7th month, 1760.

Sarah Coale, first dau. of William and Sarah, b. 21st day of 3rd month, 1759, between one and two in the afternoon.

Samuel Robertson Coale, first son of William and Sarah, b. 10th day of 1st month, 1761, on the 7th day of the week, about 10 o'clock in the morning.

Elizabeth Coale, second dau. of William and Sarah, b. 5th day of 6th month, 1763, in the evening on the 1st day of the week.

Ann Jackson, dau. of Isaiah and Margaret, b. 9th day of 7th month, 1774.

Sarah Jackson, dau. of Isaiah and Margaret, b. 21st day of 7th month, 1776.

Thomas Lewis Jackson, son of Isaiah and Margaret, b. 10th day of 9th month, 1778.

Mary Jackson, dau. of Isaiah and Margaret, b. 29th day of 10th month, 1780, and d. 7th day of 12th month, 1782.

Mary Jackson (2nd), dau. of Isaiah and Margaret, b. 10th day of 12th month, 1782.

Frances Jackson, dau. of Isaiah and Margaret, b. 24th day of 6th month, 1785.

John Jackson, son of Isaiah and Margaret, b. 31st day of 5th month, 1788.

Sarah Coale, wife of William Coale and dau. of Samuel and Elizabeth Robertson, d. 28th day of 1st month, 1766, after 10 days illness with the flux.

William Riley, son of Benjamin and Hannah, b. 25th day of 9th month, 1762.

Benjamin Riley, son of aforesaid William and Sarah, b. 22nd day of 9th month, 1785.

Ann Riley, dau. of William and Sarah, b. 6th day of 8th month, 1787.

William Riley, son of William and Sarah, b. 25th day of 7th month, 1789.

John Parrish, b. 30th day of 4th month, 1723.

Mary Parrish, "before marriage Price," b. 20th day of 1st month, 1726.

Mordecai Parrish, son of John and Mary, b. 3rd day of 2nd month, 1755.

Aquilla Parrish, son of John and Mary, b. 15th day of 8th month, 1757.

Mary Parrish, mother of the above children, d. 21st day of 8th month, 1793.

John Parrish, father of the above children, d. 2nd day of 8th month, 1796.

Nicholas Hopkins, first son of Richard and Katherine, b. 12th day of 3rd month, 1747, "oald stile".

Rachel Hopkins, first dau. of Richard and Katherine, b. 31st day of 11th month, 1749, "oald stile".

Richard Hopkins, second son of Richard and Katherine, b. 17th day of 12th month, 1750, "oald stile".

Sarah Hopkins, second dau. of Richard and Katherine, b. 20th day of 7th month, 1751, "oald stile".

Katherine Hopkins, third dau. of Richard and Katherine, b. 20th day of 1st month, 1753, "new stile".

Gerrard Hopkins, third son of Richard and Katherine, b. 21st day of 2nd month, 1754.

Samuel Hopkins, fourth son of Richard and Katherine, b,. 25th day of 9th month, 1756.

Elizabeth Hopkins, fourth dau. of Richard and Katherine, b. 17th day of 9th month, 1758.

Joseph Hopkins, fifth son of Richard and Katherine, b. 9th day of 4th month, 1761.

Katherine Hopkins, Jr., third dau. of Richard and Katherine, d. 27th day of 9th month, 1763, at one o'clock in the morning.

Samuel Hopkins, fourth son of Richard and Katherine, d. 2nd day of 12th month, 1757, at 9 o'clock in the morning.

Mary Harris, first dau. of George and Susanna, b. 13th day of 8th month, 1790, about 6 o'clock in the evening.

Beulah Harris, second dau. of George and Susanna, b. 6th day of 8th month, 1792, about one o'clock in the morning.

Lemuel Howard, Sr., d. 17th day of 5th month, 1759, age 63.

Anne Howard, wife of Lemuel, d. 26th day of 6th month, 1771, between one and two o'clock in the morning, age 74.

Mary Price, wife of Mordecai (of John), d. 2nd day of 9th month, 1770, aged about 45 years and a wife of 16 years.

Aquila Price, d. 28th day of 2nd month, 1773, who appeared for some time zealously concerned with the promotion of truth.

Leah Price, dau. of the abovesaid Aquila and Ann Price, b. 10th day of 12th month, 1772.

Mary Howard, second wife of Benjamin Howard, d. 20th day of 6th month, 1777, between 3 and 4 o'clock in the afternoon, a religious woman, a good wife, a fine mother in law, and a servisable neighbour.

Susanna Howard, dau. of Benjamin and Sarah, b. 1st day of 7th month, 1756.

Anne Howard, dau. of Benjamin and Sarah, b. 7th day of 6th month, 1758.

Benjamin Howard, son of Benjamin and Sarah, b. 8th day of 9th month, 1760.

Elizabeth Howard, dau. of abovesaid Benjamin and Mary, b. 13th day of 12th month, 1767.

Lemuel Howard, son of Benjamin and Mary, b. 7th day of 9th month, 1769.

Mary Howard, dau. of Benjamin and Mary, b. 1st day of 2nd month, 1772.

Sarah Howard, dau. of Benjamin and Mary, b. 10th day of 3rd month, 1774.

Sarah Howard, first wife of Benjamin Howard, d. 24th day of 4th month, 1763, in the morning, a good wife, a loving mother, a kind neighbour, and a fine mistress.

Susanna Dutton, wife of Robert Dutton, d. 25th day of 11th month, 1769.

Sarah Dutton, dau. of Robert, d. 19th day of 6th month, 1770.

Robert Dutton, Sr., d. 13th day of 9th month, 1770.

Robert Dutton, Jr., son of Robert, Sr. and Susanna, b. 24th day of 12th month, 1759.

John Dutton, son of Robert, Sr. and Susanna, b. 23rd day of 12th month, 1761.

Anne Dutton, dau. of Robert, Sr. and Susanna, b. 19th day of 6th month, 1764.

Mary Browne, wife of George Browne, d. 3rd day of 5th month, 1769.

William Schofield, b. 14th day of 12th month, 1752.

Ann Schofield, b. 2nd day of 6th month, 1757.

Joseph Leonard Schofield, b. 18th day of 8th month, 1760.
Andrew Schofield, b. 11th day of 9th month, 1762.
Issachar Schofield, b. 17th day of 6th month, 1765.
Mahlen Schofield, b. 2nd day of 10th month, 1769.
John Stockdale, son of Thomas and Mary, b. 2nd day of 8th month, 1777.
William Stockdale, son of Thomas and Mary, b. 31st day of 8th month, 1779.
Thomas Stockdale, son of Thomas and Mary, b. 22nd day of 8th month, 1781.
Mary Stockdale, wife of Thomas, d. 10th day of 3rd month, 1782.
Elizabeth Ellicott, dau. of Elias and Mary, b. 17th day of 2nd month, 1787.
Evan Thomas Ellicott, son of Elias and Mary, b. 17th day of 9th month, 1788.
Rachel Ellicott, dau. of Elias and Mary, b. 17th day of 2nd month, 1792.
Evan T. Ellicott, above mentioned, d. 19th day of 8th month, 1791, aged 3 years, 11 months and 1 day.
William Matthews, son of George and Dorothy, b. 6th day of 3rd month, 1753.
Elizabeth Matthews, dau. of George and Dorothy, b. 11th day of 3rd month, 1755.
Samuel Matthews, second son of George and Dorothy, b. 14th day of 11th month, 1756.
George Matthews, Jr., third son of George and Dorothy, b. 14th day of 6th month, 1762.
Mary Matthews, second dau. of George and Dorothy, b. 30th day of 4th month, 1764.
Dorothy Matthews, third dau. of George and Dorothy, b. 19th day of 10th month, 1769.
Dorothy Matthews, wife of George and mother of the above, d. 11th day of 1st month, 1770, "after a weeks illness of a violent nerviss fever," and was interred on the 13th of same month in the burying ground on the plantation near Patapsco Falls in Baltimore County, where the above George and Dorothy Matthews formerly lived.
Susanna Hicks, dau. of James and Mary, b. 22nd day of 2nd month, 1762.
Ann Hicks, second dau. of James and Mary, b. 31st day of 12th month, 1763.

GUNPOWDER MONTHLY MEETING

Mary Hicks, third dau. of James and Mary, b. 31st day of 3rd month, 1766.

James Hicks, first son of James and Mary, b. 26th day of 6th month, 1767.

Jane Hicks, fourth dau. of James and Mary, b. 15th day of 2nd month, 1770.

David Hicks, second son of James and Mary, b. 15th day of the 3rd month, 1774.

Bathsheba Hicks, fifth dau. of James and Mary, b. 15th day of 4th month, 1776.

Henry Hicks, third son of James and Mary, b. 6th day of 5th month, 1779.

Ruth Price, dau. of Mordecai and Mary, d. 2nd day of 8th month, 1775, about sunrise, in the 17th year of her age.

Rebecca Price, d. 4th day of 2nd month, 1788, aged upwards of 78 years, and was buried in Friends Burying Ground at Gunpowder Meeting House.

Thomas Matthews, d. 19th day of 11th month, 1766.

Samuel Naylor, son of John, Jr. and Mary, b. 9th day of 9th month, 1771.

Ann Naylor, son of John, Jr. and Mary, b. 7th day of 6th month, 1773.

John Naylor, son of John, Jr. and Mary, b. 31st day of 7th month, 1775.

James Naylor, son of John, Jr. and Mary, b. 24th day of 4th month, 1777.

Isaac Naylor, son of John, Jr. and Mary, b. 25th day of 4th month, 1780.

Levinah Naylor, dau. of John, Jr. and Mary, b. 24th day of 4th month, 1782.

Jane Naylor, dau. of John, Jr. and Mary, b. 24th day of 10th month, 1784.

Elizabeth Naylor, dau. of John, Jr. and Mary, b. 6th day of 6th month, 1787.

Mary Naylor, dau. of John, Jr. and Mary, b. 15th day of 6th month, 1789.

William Naylor, son of John, Jr. and Mary, b. 8th day of 4th month, 1791.

Abraham Naylor, son of John, Jr. and Mary, b. 15th day of 6th month, 1793.

Daniel Matthews, son of Oliver and Hannah, b. 5th day of 7th month, 1763.

Hannah Matthews, son of Oliver and Hannah, b. 7th day of 7th month, 1767.

Daniel Price, son of Samuel and Ann, b. 22nd day of 10th month, 1761.

Elizabeth Price, dau. of Samuel and Ann, b. 20th day of 5th month, 1764.

Samuel Price, Jr., son of Samuel and Ann, b. 23rd day of 11th month, 1766.

Worrick Price, son of Samuel and Ann, b. 10th day of 6th month, 1769.

Israel Price, son of Samuel and Ann, b. 30th day of 5th month, 1772.

Mordecai Price, son of Samuel and Ann, b. 16th day of 3rd month, 1775.

Richard Price, son of Samuel and Ann, b. 5th day of 11th month, 1777.

John Price, son of Samuel and Ann, b. 29th day of 12th month, 1779.

Ann Price, dau. of Samuel and Ann, b. 27th day of 2nd month, 1784.

Ann Price, wife of Samuel Price, d. 16th day of 9th month, 1785.

Sarah Matthews, dau. of Thomas and Rachel, b. 12th day of 10th month, 1752.

Mordecai Matthews, son of Thomas and Rachel, b. 12th day of 9th month, 1755.

Daniel Matthews, son of Thomas and Rachel, b. 8th day of 2nd month, 1758.

John Matthews, son of Thomas and Rachel, b. 22nd day of 2nd month, 1760.

Jesse Matthews, son of Thomas and Rachel, b. 17th day of 10th month, 1762.

Rachel Matthews, dau. of Thomas and Rachel, b. 19th day of 4th month, 1765.

Eli Matthews, son of Thomas and Rachel, b. 21st day of 2nd month, 1767.

Elizabeth Matthews, dau. of Thomas and Rachel, b. 3rd day of 4th month, 1769.

Thomas Matthews, son of Thomas and Rachel, b. 7th day of 9th month, 1771.

William Matthews, son of Thomas and Rachel, b. 26th day of 1st month, 1774.

Thomas Matthews, father to the above said children, d. 12th day of 8th month, 1774.

Frances Brown, dau. of David and Elizabeth, b. 24th day of 1st month, 1777, and d. 26th day of 8th month, 1778, aged 1 year, 7 months and 2 days.

Elizabeth Brown, dau. of David and Elizabeth, b. 15th day of 11th month, 1778.

Mary Brown, dau. of David and Elizabeth, b. 6th day of 2nd month, 1781, and d. 28th day of 9th month following, aged 7 months and 22 days.

David Brown, son of David and Elizabeth, b. 25th day of 10th month, 1782.

George Brown, son of David and Elizabeth, b. 25th day of 4th month, 1785.

John Brown, son of David and Elizabeth, b. 28th day of 3rd month, 1788.

William Brown, son of David and Elizabeth, b. 2nd day of 12th month, 1791.

Oliver Matthews, son of William and Ann, b. 4th day of 5th month, 1775.
Hannah Matthews, dau. of William and Ann, b. 25th day of 11th month, 1776.
Mary Matthews, dau. of William and Ann, b. 3rd day of 12th month, 1778.
Ann Matthews, dau. of William and Ann, b. 5th day of 10th month, 1780.
Elizabeth Matthews, dau. of William and Ann, b. 19th day of 7th month, 1782.
William Matthews, son of William and Ann, b. 19th day of 1st month, 1784, and d. 20th day of 2nd month following, aged 1 month and 1 day, and was interred at Gunpowder.
Rebecca Matthews, son of William and Ann, b. 3rd day of 3rd month, 1785.
Miriam Matthews, dau. of William and Ann, b. 20th day of 11th month, 1786.
Sarah Matthews, dau. of William and Ann, b. 16th day of 12th month, 1788.
Rachel Matthews, dau. of William and Ann, b. 7th day of 2nd month, 1791, and d. 18th day of 8th month following, aged 6 months and 11 days, and was interred at Gunpowder.
Ruth Matthews, dau. of William and Ann, b. 7th day of 1st month, 1792, and d. 1st day of 2nd month following, aged 25 days, and was interred at Gunpowder.
Ann Matthews, wife of the above William Matthews and dau. of Isaac Griffith, d. 6th day of 7th month, 1792, between 12 and 1 o'clock in the morning and was interred at Gunpowder the next day following, in the 39th year of her age.
Ann Matthews, dau. of George and Sarah, b. 26th day of 9th month, 1778.
James Amos, son of William, Sr. and Hannah [sic], b. 31st day of 1st month, 1764.
Luke Amos, son of William, Sr. and Martha [sic], b. 20th day of 5th month, 1766.
Ann Amos, dau. of William, Sr. and Martha, b. 12th day of 4th month, 1771.
Benjamin Amos, son of William, Sr. and Martha, b. 29th day of 8th month, 1773.
Abraham Griffith, son of Isaac and Ann, b. 2nd day of 4th month, 1746, and married Mary Moore, dau. of Walter and Ann, on 3rd day of 4th month, 1771.

Ann Griffith, dau. of Abraham and Mary, b. 16th day of 12th month, 1771, on the 2nd day of the week.

Reuben Griffith, son of Abraham and Mary, b. 3rd day of 2nd month, 1774, on the 5th day of the week, about 10 o'clock in the morning.

Isaac Griffith, son of Abraham and Mary, b. 25th day of 8th month, 1776, on the 1st day of the week, between 7 and 8 o'clock in the morning.

Miriam Griffith, dau. of Abraham and Mary, b. 10th day of 4th month, 1779, on the 7th day of the week, between 10 and 11 o'clock in the morning.

Sophia Griffith, dau. of Abraham and Mary, b. 28th day of 5th month, 1782, on the 2nd day of the week, 28 minutes after 8 o'clock in the evening.

Mary Griffith, mother of the above named children, d. 13th day of 9th month, 1784, and was buried in Friends Burial Ground at Gunpowder Meeting House on the 14th of same.

Mary Cornthwait, d. 6th day of 2nd month, 1781, and was buried the 8th day of said month.

Hannah Cornthwait, dau. of John and Mary, b. 26th day of 5th month, 1775, and d. 10th day of 10th month, 1778.

John Cornthwait, son of John and Mary, b. 26th day of 7th month, 1777.

Robert Cornthwait, son of John and Mary, b. 16th day of 7th month, 1780.

John Cornthwait, Sr., d. 8th day of 9th month, 1782.

John Trimble, son of William, b. 27th day of 10th month, 1775.

Sarah Trimble, dau. of William, b. 9th day of 8th month, 1778.

James Trimble, son of William, b. 20th day of 11th month, 1782.

Hannah Trimble, second wife of the aforesaid William Trimble, b. 1st day of 1st month, 1745.

William Trimble, son of William and Hannah, b. 13th day of 11th month, 1789.

Sarah Mason, dau. of John and Ann, b. 26th day of 10th month, 1777.

Benjamin Mason, son of John and Ann, b. 6th day of 6th month, 1779.

George Mason, son of John and Ann, b. 7th day of 9th month, 1781.

John Mason, son of John and Ann, b. 22nd day of 12th month, 1783, and d. 30th day of 12th month, 1783.

John Mason, son of John and Ann, b. 21st day of 2nd month, 1785.

Lemuel Mason, son of John and Ann, b. 6th day of 6th month, 1787.

Howard Mason, son of John and Ann, b. 12th day of 10th month, 1789.

James Mason, son of John and Ann, "no date and deceased."

Susanna Mason, dau. of John and Ann, b. 2nd day of 2nd month, 1792.

Mary Mason, dau. of John and Ann, b. 17th day of 10th month, 1795, and d. 14th day of 11th month, 1802.

Elizabeth Dillon, dau. of Moses and Hannah, b. 12th day of 2nd month, 1773.

Ann Dillon, dau. of Moses and Hannah, b. 29th day of 10th month, 1774.

John Dillon, son of Moses and Hannah, b. 29th day of 9th month, 1776.

Rebecka Dillon, dau. of Moses and Hannah, b. 8th day of 11th month, 1778, and d. 16th day of 3rd month, 1782, at 10 o'clock.

Mary Dillon, dau. of Moses and Hannah, b. 26th day of 11th month, 1780.

Rebecka Dillon, dau. of Moses and Hannah, b. 28th day of 4th month, 1783.

Moses Dillon, son of Moses and Hannah, b. 30th day of 1st month, 1785.

Hannah Dillon, dau. of Moses and Hannah, b. 14th day of 7th month, 1787.

Martha Dillon, dau. of Moses and Hannah, b. 28th day of 10th month, 1789.

Loyd Dillon, son of Moses and Hannah, b. 3rd day of 2nd month, 1792.

Isaac Dillon, son of Moses and Hannah, b. 4th day of 10th month, 1794, and d. 7th day of 5th month, 1794 [sic].

Moses Dillon, d. 23rd day of 2nd month, 1800? [unclear].

Gravener Jefferis, son of William and Priscilia, b. 16th day of 8th month, 1784.

Samuel Jefferis, son of William and Priscilia, b. 11th day of 3rd month, 1786.

Sarah Amoss, dau. of William, Jr. and Susanna, b. 15th day of 4th month, 1774.

Benjamin Amoss, son of William, Jr. and Susanna, b. 8th day of 10th month, 1775.

Ann Amoss, dau. of William, Jr. and Susanna, b. 25th day of 5th month, 1777.

Hannah Amoss, dau. of William, Jr. and Susanna, b. 21st day of 5th month, 1779.

William Amoss, son of William, Jr. and Susanna, b. 26th day of 2nd month, 1782.

Martha Amoss, dau. of William, Jr. and Susanna, b. 7th day of 10th month, 1784.

Thomas Amoss, son of William, Jr. and Susanna, b. 10th day of 12th month, 1786.

Susanna Amoss, dau. of William, Jr. and Susanna, b. 3rd day of 6th month, 1789.

Elizabeth Amoss, dau. of William, Jr. and Susanna, b. 8th day of 6th month, 1791.

Lemuel Howard Amoss, son of William, Jr. and Susanna, b. 25th day of 2nd month, 1793.

John Amoss, son of William, Jr. and Susanna, b. 25th day of 1st month, 1795, and d. 30th day of 1st month, 1795.

Susanna Amoss, mother of the above named children, d. 28th day of 1st month, 1795.

Benjamin Amoss, son of above William, "deceased, no date."

Samuel Price, son of Daniel and Betty, b. 11th day of 11th month, 1784.

Jesse Price, son of Daniel and Betty, b. 25th day of 9th month, 1786.

Caleb Price, son of Daniel and Betty, b. 13th day of 5th month, 1788.

Mary Price, dau. of Daniel and Betty, b. 15th dau of 8th month, 1790.

John Hussey Price, son of Daniel and Betty, b. 19th day of 3rd month, 1792.

Nathan Price, son of Daniel and Betty, b. 26th day of 9th month, 1794.

Daniel Price, son of Daniel and Betty, b. 16th day of 12th month, 1796.

George Price, son of Daniel and Betty, b. 3rd day of 1st month, 1799.

Edith Price, dau. of Daniel and Betty, b. 9th day of 5th month, 1801.

Joel Price, son of Daniel and Betty, b. 26th day of 7th month, 1803.

Nathan Price, son of Daniel and Betty, d. in his 11th year.

Thomas Brown, son of John and Mary, b. 22nd day of 10th month, 1774, and d. 23rd day of 10th month, 1789.

James Brown, son of John and Mary, b. 26th day of 9th month, 1776.

Frances Brown, dau. of John and Mary, b. 21st day of 11th month, 1780, and d. 21st day of 7th month, 1783.

Esther Brown, dau. of William and Elizabeth, b. 30th day of 12th month, 1775.

Hannah Brown, dau. of William and Elizabeth, b. 21st day of 9th month, 1777.

Joseph Brown, son of William and Elizabeth, b. 13th day of 7th month, 1779.

Thomas Brown, son of William and Elizabeth, b. 23rd day of 6th month, 1782, and d. 29th day of 7th month, 1784.

John Brown, son of William and Elizabeth, b. 29th day of 1st month, 1784, and d. 12th day of 8th month, 1784.

Ann Brown, dau. of William and Elizabeth, b. 30th day of 5th month, 1785.

Elizabeth Brown, dau. of William and Elizabeth, b. 17th day of 8th month, 1788.

Hannah Painter Towsend, dau. of Joseph and Mary, b. 3rd day of 2nd month, 1789, at Baltimore, about half past the 2nd hour in the morning.

Nicholas Waln Townsend, son of Joseph and Mary, b. 30th day of 10th month, 1790, at Baltimore, near the 3rd hour in the afternoon.

George Dent Scott, son of Thomas and Elizabeth, b. 1st day of 12th month, 1793, and d. 1st day of 9th month, 1794, aged 9 months.

Eli Scott, son of Thomas and Elizabeth, b. 11th day of 6th month, 1795.

John Scott, son of Thomas and Elizabeth, b. 1st day of 6th month, 1798.

Elizabeth Scott, dau. of Thomas and Elizabeth, b. 29th day of 9th month, 1801, and d. 16th day of 7th month, 1807, and was buried at Friends Burial Ground at Gunpowder.

Rachel and Eliza, twin daus. of Thomas and Elizabeth, b. 4th day of 7th month, 1807.

Rachel Price, dau. of Thomas and Elizabeth, d. 11th day of 8th month, 1807, and was buried at Friends Burial Ground at Gunpowder.

Isabel Price, dau. of Mordecai and Tabitha, b. 22nd day of 10th month, 1772.

Joshua Price, son of Mordecai and Tabitha, b. 2nd day of 7th month, 1774, and d. 23rd day of 2nd month, 1802.

Aquila Price, son of Mordecai and Tabitha, b. 24th day of 10th month, 1778, and d. 27th day of 8th month, 1797.

William Price, son of Mordecai and Tabitha, b. 22nd day of 10th month, 1780.

Rachel Price, dau. of Mordecai and Tabitha, b. 9th day of 7th month, 1782, and d. 11th day of 7th month, 1800.

Benjamin Price, son of Mordecai and Tabitha, b. 23rd day of 8th month, 1784.

Elizabeth Price, dau. of Mordecai and Tabitha, b. 25th day of 8th month, 1786.

John Price, son of Mordecai and Tabitha, b. 23rd day of 5th month, 1791.

Kitturah Price, dau. of Mordecai and Tabitha, b. 2nd day of 6th month, 1792.

Rebecca Price, dau. of Mordecai and Tabitha, d. 22nd day of 9th month, 1785, aged 2 years and 12 days, "her birth is not recorded."

Nicholas Tipton, son of William and Angelica, b. 9th day of 1st month, 1753.

Micajah Tipton, son of aforesaid Nicholas and Esther, b. 2nd day of 9th month, 1776.

Mary Tipton, dau. of Nicholas and Esther, b. 5th day of 12th month, 1778.

Sarah Tipton, dau. of Nicholas and Esther, b. 28th day of 3rd month, 1781, and d. 20th day of 7th month, 1782, and was interred at Friends Burying Ground at Gunpowder.

Rebecca Tipton, dau. of Nicholas and Esther, b. 8th day of 1st month, 1784.

John Tipton, son of Nicholas and Esther, b. 8th day of 11th month, 1786.

Luke Tipton, son of Nicholas and Esther, b. 22nd day of 4th month, 1789.

Nicholas Tipton, father of the aforesaid children, d. 26th day of 11th month, 1789, and was interred on the 28th following at Friends Burying Ground at Gunpowder.

George Hussey, b. 4th day of 3rd month, 1758.

Rachel Hussey (formerly Hayward), wife of George Hussey, b. 19th day of 9th month, 1758.

Joseph Hussey, son of George and Rachel, b. 15th day of 6th month, 1781.

John Hussey, son of George and Rachel, b. 8th day of 9th month, 1782, and d. 27th day of 8th month, 1783.

George Hussey, son of George and Rachel, b. 13th day of 2nd month, 1784.

Rachel Hussey, dau. of George and Rachel, b. 19th day of 10th month, 1785, and d. 1st day of 11th month, 1785.

Rachel Hussey, dau. of George and Rachel, b. 29th day of 10th month, 1786.

William Hussey, son of George and Rachel, b. 12th day of 9th month, 1788.

Rebecca Hussey, dau. of George and Rachel, b. 9th day of 9th month, 1790.

Ennion Hussey, son of George and Rachel, b. 20th day of 5th month, 1792.

William Tipton, father of Nicholas Tipton, d. 14th day of 2nd month, 1797.

Susannah Jones, dau. of Aquila and Elizabeth, b. 24th day of 12th month, 1791.

Hannah Jones, dau. of Aquila and Elizabeth, b. 4th day of 8th month, 1793.

Daniel Tredway, d. 25th day of 5th month, 1810, age 86.

Jesse Carr, son of William and Sarah, b. 10th day of 5th month, 1792.

Paul Pennington, son of Daniel and Martha, b. 9th day of 11th month, 1769.

Sarah Pennington, dau. of Daniel and Martha, b. 30th day of 11th month, 1771.

Mary Pennington, dau. of Daniel and Martha, b. 30th day of 7th month, 1775.

John Pennington, son of Daniel and Martha, b. 31st day of 7th month, 1777.

Josiah Pennington, son of Daniel and Martha, b. 17th day of 2nd month, 1780.

Levi Pennington, son of Daniel and Martha, b. 20th day of 6th month, 1784.

Thomas Matthews, son of Oliver Matthews, d. 7th day of 2nd month, 1792, about sunrise, and was interred the 9th of the same at Gunpowder Meeting House.

Hannah (Johns) Matthews, wife of Oliver Matthews, d. 15th day of 11th month, 1791, and was interred at Gunpowder, "concering whom a memorial is approved by the Monthly, Quarterly and Yearly Meetings of which she was an Elder."

John Matthews m. Leah Price, 8th day of 12th month, 1790.

Matilda Matthews, dau. of John and Leah, b. 18th day of 9th month, 1791.

Aquila Matthews, son of John and Leah, b. 16th day of 12th month, 1792, and d. 19th day of 6th month, 1793.

Leah Matthews, mother of the above, d. 27th day of 3rd month, 1793, and was interred the 29th at Gunpowder.

John Matthews m. Martha Yarnall, 8th day of 9th month, 1794, "being his second wife."

Samuel Hanway Matthews, son of William and Elizabeth, b. 3rd day of 11th month, 1794, between 9 and 10 o'clock in the morning.

Benjamin Lukins, son of Moses and Sarah, b. 30th day of 3rd month, 1794.

Rachel Lukins, dau. of Moses and Sarah, b. 27th day of 12th month, 1795.

Mary Lancaster, dau. of Jesse and Mary, b. 20th day of 3rd month, 1777, on fifth day, and d. 22nd day of 6th month, 1792, aged 15 years, 3 months and 2 days.

Isaiah Lancaster, son of Jesse and Mary, b. 23rd day of 10th month, 1780.

John Lancaster, son of Jesse and Mary, b. 16th day of 5th month, 1782.

Benjamin Lancaster, son of Jesse and Mary, b. 24th day of 11th month, 1784.

Phebe Lancaster, dau. of Jesse and Mary, b. 11th day of 12th month, 1787.

Rachel Lancaster, dau. of Jesse and Mary, b. 27th day of 5th month, 1788.

Mary Lancaster, mother of the above, d. 31st[?] day of 12th month, 1783, and was interred at Little Falls on the 1st day of 1st month, 1784.

John Lancaster, d. 27th day of 7th month, 1803, and was buried in Friends Burying Ground in Munsey, Pennsylvania.

Joannah Lancaster, dau. of Jesse and Elizabeth his 2nd wife, b. 12th day of 7th month, 1796.

Joseph Lancaster, dau. of Jesse and Elizabeth his 2nd wife, b. 10th day of 5th month, 1798.

Mary Lancaster, dau. of Jesse and Elizabeth his 2nd wife, b. 30th day of 7th month, 1800.

Esther Lancaster, dau. of Jesse and Elizabeth his 2nd wife, b. 2nd day of 6th month, 1802.

John Lancaster, son of Jesse and Elizabeth his 2nd wife, b. 28th day of 6th month, 1804.

Julia Lancaster, dau. of Jesse and Elizabeth his 2nd wife, b. 14th day of 2nd month, 1807.

Elizabeth Parsons, dau. of Abner and Rachel, b. 5th day of 2nd month, 1791.

Joseph Dyer Parsons, son of Abner and Rachel, b. 1st day of 2nd month, 1793.

Abraham Parsons, son of Abner and Rachel, b. 1st day of 2nd month, 1795.

Honner Parsons, dau. of Abner and Rachel, b. 17th day of 1st month, 1798, and d. 25th day of same month.

Rachel Parsons, mother of the above named children, d. 23rd day of 1st month, 1798.

Thomas Price, son of Benjamin and Temperance, b. 1st day of 12th month, 1755.

James Price, son of Benjamin and Temperance, b. 14th day of 6th month, 1757, and d. 15th day of 12th month, 1802.

Joshua Price, son of Benjamin and Temperance, b. 15th day of 1st month, 1759.

Jarrett Price, son of Benjamin and Temperance, b. 27th day of 12th month, 1760.

Keturah Price, dau. of Benjamin and Temperance, b. in 1762.

Elizabeth Price, dau. of Benjamin and Temperance, b. in 1764.

Rebecca Price, dau. of Benjamin and Temperance, b. 18th day of 11th month, 1769.

Beal Price, son of Benjamin and Temperance, b. 4th day of 10th month, 1772.

Temperance Price, mother of the above named children, d. 27th day of 1st month, 1798, aged about 58 years, and buried at Gunpowder Meeting House.

Benjamin Price, father of the above named children, d. 2nd day of 12th month, 1794, aged about 60 years, 9 months and 24 days, and buried at Gunpowder Meeting House.

Samuel Wilson, son of John and Deborah, b. 26th day of 2nd month, 1772.

Elizabeth Wilson, dau. of John and Deborah, b. 8th day of 2nd month, 1774.

Kathrine Wilson, dau. of John and Deborah, b. 11th day of 2nd month, 1777.

Grace Wilson, dau. of John and Deborah, b. 15th day of 2nd month, 1780.

William Wilson, son of John and Deborah, b. 6th day of 6th month, 1782.
John Wilson, son of John and Deborah, b. 11th day of 6th month, 1784.
Anna Wilson, dau. of John and Deborah, b. 5th day of 11th month, 1786.
Thomas Wilson, son of John and Deborah, b. 5th day of 2nd month, 1789.
David Wilson, son of John and Deborah, b. 31st day of 7th month, 1791.
Jessee Parsons, son of John and Susanna, b. 24th day of 11th month, 1791.
Susanna Parsons, dau. of John and Susanna, b. 14th day of 7th month, 1794.
Susanna Parsons, mother of the above named children, d. 14th day of 7th month, 1794.
Ellen Williams, dau. of Enoch and Ann, b. 10th day of 3rd month, 1781.
David Harry, our esteemed Friend, d. 11th day of 8th month, 1800, aged 50 years, 8 months and 4 days.
Margaret Tyson, dau. of Jacob and Ann, b. 13th day of 12th month, 1794.
Sarah Tyson, dau. of Jacob and Ann, b. 17th day of 7th month, 1796.
George Tyson, son of Jacob and Ann, b. 6th day of 6th month, 1798.
Ann Tyson, dau. of Jacob and Ann, b. 8th day of 11th month, 1800.
Jonathan Tyson, son of Jacob and Ann, b. 8th day of 9th month, 1802.
William Amos Tyson, son of Jacob and Ann, b. 12th day of 6th month, 1805.
Enos West, son of Thomas and Elizabeth, b. 23rd day of 11th month, 1777.
Stacy West, son of Thomas and Elizabeth, b. 15th day of 11th month, 1779.
Amos West, son of Thomas and Elizabeth, b. 29th day of 9th month, 1781.
Rebecca West, dau. of Thomas and Elizabeth, b. 26th day of 8th month, 1784.
Eli West, son of Thomas and Elizabeth, b. 28th day of 12th month, 1786, and d. 13th day of 2nd month, 1801.
Amos Scott, son of Abraham and Elizabeth, b. 26th day of 9th month, 1759.
Levi Scott, son of Amos and Rachel, b. 5th day of 5th month, 1790.
Mordecai Scott, son of Amos and Rachel, b. 7th day of 1st month, 1792, and d. 17th day of 1st month, 1793.
Esther Scott, dau. of Amos and Rachel, b. 11th day of 1st month, 1794.
William Scott, son of Amos and Rachel, b. 20th day of 1st month, 1796.

Amos Scott, son of Amos and Rachel, b. 21st day of 3rd month, 1798, and died the same year.

Rachel Scott, dau. of Amos and Rachel, b. 9th day of 10th month, 1799.

Rachel Scott, mother of the above named children, d. 25th of 10th month, 1799, aged 32 years, 8 months and 6[?] days.

Rachel Matthews, dau. of John and Martha, b. 29th day of 11th month, 1794[?].

John Matthews, son of John and Martha, b. 28th day of 8th month, 1797.

Uriah Matthews, son of John and Martha, b. 1st day of 10th month, 1799.

Martha Matthews, another of the above named children, d. 27th day of 6th month, 1802, and was interred the 28th of same in the afternoon at Gunpowder Meeting House.

John Matthews m. Alice Kinsey, 7th day of 9th month, 1805, being his third wife.

David Harding, son of Charles and Elizabeth, b. 20th day of 6th month, 1796.

Mary Harding, dau. of Charles and Elizabeth, b. 2nd day of 11th month, 1798.

Thomas Harding, son of Charles and Elizabeth, b. 27th day of 7th month, 1801.

George Harding, son of Charles and Elizabeth, b. 6th day of 10th month, 1804.

Lydia Harding, dau. of Charles and Elizabeth, b. 14th day of 9th month, 1807.

Milcah Belt, dau. of Richard and Keturah, b. 12th day of 1st month, 1765.

Sarah Matthews, dau. of Jesse and Milcah, b. 17th day of 12th month, 1794, about one o'clock in the morning.

Jesse Matthews, son of Jesse and Milcah, b. 29th day of 7th month, 1796, about 9 o'clock at night.

Milcah Matthews, dau. of Jesse and Milcah, b. 9th day of 8th month, 1798, about 9 o'clock at night, and d. 4th day of 7th[?] month, 1808, and buried at Gunpowder Meeting House.

Thomas Matthews, son of Jesse and Milcah, b. 12th day of 3rd month, 1800, about 3 o'clock in the morning.

Rachel Matthews, dau. of Jesse and Milcah, b. 5th day of 5th month, 1802, about 20 minutes after 3 o'clock in the morning.

Richard Matthews, son of Jesse and Milcah, b. 26th day of 10th month, 1804, about 15 minutes after 2 o'clock in the morning.

Benjamin Matthews, son of Jesse and Milcah, b. 18th day of 12th month, 1806[?], about half after 10 o'clock at night.

Rhoda Matthews, dau. of Mordecai and Ruth, b. 28th day of 11th month, 1789.

Edith Matthews, dau. of Mordecai and Ruth, b. 23rd day of 9th month, 1791.

Eliza Matthews, dau. of Mordecai and Ruth, b. 4th day of 11th month, 1793.

Mariah Matthews, dau. of Mordecai and Ruth, b. 17th day of 10th month, 1795.

Mordecai Matthews, son of Mordecai and Ruth, b. 12th day of 10th month, 1797.

Amos Matthews, son of Mordecai and Ruth, b. 17th day of 4th month, 1800.

Rachel Matthews, dau. of Mordecai and Ruth, b. 22nd day of 8th month, 1802.

Edward Matthews, son of Mordecai and Ruth, b. 28th day of 11th month, 1805[?].

Eli Matthews, son of Thomas and Ann, b. 16th day of 8th month, 1795.

Susanna Matthews, dau. of Thomas and Ann, b. 9th day of 10th month, 1796.

Mary Matthews, dau. of Thomas and Ann, b. 25th day of 2nd month, 1798.

Daniel Matthews, son of Thomas and Ann, b. 5th day of 9th month, 1799.

John Matthews, son of Thomas and Ann, b. 13th day of 12th month, 1800.

Rachel Matthews, dau. of Thomas and Ann, b. 20th day of 11th month, 1802.

Ann Matthews, dau. of Thomas and Ann, b. 10th day of 2nd month, 1804.

Elizabeth Matthews, dau. of Thomas and Ann, b. 17th day of 5th month, 1805.

Thomas Matthews, son of Thomas and Ann, b. 10th day of 2nd month, 1807.

Hannah Matthews, dau. of Thomas and Ann, b. 14th day of 5th month, 1808.

Rebecca Matthews, dau. of Thomas and Ann, b. 26th day of 10th month, 1809.

Rhoda Matthews, dau. of Thomas and Ann, b. 31st day of 1st month, 1811.

George Matthews, son of Thomas and Ann, b. 10th day of 6th month, 1812.

Ariana Matthews, dau. of Thomas and Ann, b. 20th day of 5th month, 1813[?].

Joshua Matthews, son of Thomas and Ann, b. 5th day of 1st month, 1814.

Jonathan Jones Scott, son of Jessee and Rebekah, b. 9th day of 7th month, 1789.

Elizabeth Scott, dau. of Jessee and Rebekah, b. 19th day of 12th month, 1792.

Jane Scott, dau. of Jessee and Rebekah, b. 1st day of 10th month, 1794.

Abraham Scott, son of Jessee and Rebekah, b. 15th day of 2nd month, 1797.

Jessee Scott, son of Jessee and Rebekah, b. 7th day of 10th month, 1799.

Elizabeth Scott, dau. of Jessee and Rebekah, b. 28th day of 6th month, 1801.

Rebekah Scott, dau. of Jessee and Rebekah, b. 29th day of 7th month, 1803.

----- Scott, dau. of Jessee and Rebekah, b. 3rd day of 3rd month, 1807, and died the same day.

Abraham Griffith m. Rachel Taylor, dau. of Thomas and Calip, 30th day of 12th month, 1788.

Thomas Taylor Griffith, son of Abraham and Rachel, b. 26th day of 9th month, 1789.

Mary Griffith, dau. of Abraham and Rachel, b. 21st day of 10th month, 1790.

Rachel and Sarah Griffith, twin daus. of Abraham and Rachel, b. 3rd day of 11th month, 1791.

Abraham Griffith, father of the above named children, d. 26th day of 5th month, 1800, and was buried the 27th in Friends Burying Ground at Gunpowder Meeting House.

Benjamin Matthews, son of William and Rebecca, b. 16th day of 12th month, 1800.

Elizabeth Matthews, dau. of William and Rebecca, b. 19th day of 7th month, 1802.

Thomas Matthews, son of William and Rebecca, b. 24th day of 12th month, 1804, and d. 23rd day of 8th month, 1806.

Evan Matthews, son of William and Rebecca, b. 20th day of 1st month, 1807.

Rachel Matthews, dau. of William and Rebecca, b. 22nd day of 4th month, 1809.

Mary Ann Amoss, dau. of James and Hannah, b. 2nd day of 3rd month, 1792.

David Lee Amoss, son of James and Hannah, b. 26th day of 9th month, 1794, and "deceased, no date."

William Lee Amoss, son of James and Hannah, b. 26th day of 7th month, 1796.

Elias Ellicott Amoss, son of James and Hannah, b. 18th day of 10th month, 1799.

Oliver Hough Amoss, son of James and Hannah, b. 18th day of 8th month, 1801.

Matilda Reed, dau. of Samuel and Elizabeth, b. 17th day of 3rd month, 1797.

Eveline Reed, dau. of Samuel and Elizabeth, b. 24th day of 3rd month, 1800.

Deborah Reed, dau. of Samuel and Elizabeth, b. 11th day of 3rd month, 1802.

William Reed, son of Samuel and Elizabeth, b. 22nd day of 7th month, 1804.

Anna Reed, dau. of Samuel and Elizabeth, b. 13th day of 4th month, 1806.

Harriett Reed, dau. of Samuel and Elizabeth, b. 10th day of 4th month, 1808.

John Wilson Reed, son of Samuel and Elizabeth, b. 11th day of 4th month, 1810.

Sarah Spencer, dau. of Mahlon and Eleanor, b. 22nd day of 12th month, 1798.

Ann Spencer, dau. of Mahlon and Eleanor, b. 2nd day of 5th month, 1800.

William Spencer, son of Mahlon and Eleanor, b. 21st day of 5th month, 1802, and died the 8th month following.

William Lee Spencer, son of Mahlon and Eleanor, b. 13th day of 9th month, 1803.

Mahala Spencer, dau. of Mahlon and Eleanor, b. 23rd day of 10th month, 1805.

Enoch Lucas Spencer, son of Mahlon and Eleanor, b. 15th day of 1st month, 1808.

Elizabeth Spencer, dau. of Mahlon and Eleanor, b. 9th day of 2nd month, 1810.

Makton Atkinson Spencer, son of Mahlon and Eleanor, b. 1st day of 2nd month, 1812.

Sarah Hooker England, dau. of George and Catharine, b. 3rd day of 10th month, 1800.

Thomas Hooker England, son of George and Catharine, b. 5th day of 1st month, 1803.

Elizabeth Dutton England, dau. of George and Catharine, b. 16th day of 4th month, 1805.

Mary McConnell, dau. of Samuel and Frances, b. 24th day of 1st month, 1799.

James Orr McConnell, son of Samuel and Frances, b. 14th day of 10th month, 1801.

Mordecai Price, son of Mordecai and Elizabeth, b. 28th day of 1st month, 1753.

Ann Price, dau. of Mordecai and Elizabeth, b. 25th day of 9th month, 1760.

Mordecai Price, son of Mordecai and Elizabeth, b. 31st day of 7th month, 1762.

Sophia Price, dau. of Mordecai and Elizabeth, b. 12th day of 2nd month, 1764, and d. 22nd day of 4th month, 1783.

Rachel Price, dau. of Mordecai and Elizabeth, b. 22nd day of 2nd month, 1767.

Sarah Price, dau. of Mordecai and Elizabeth, 17th day of 2nd month, 1769.

Elizabeth Price, dau. of Mordecai and Elizabeth, b. 2nd day of 12th month, 1771.

Joseph Price, son of Mordecai and Elizabeth, b. 28th day of 10th month, 1774.

Levi Price, son of Mordecai and Elizabeth, b. 6th day of 11th month, 1777, and d. 27th day of 8th month, 1785.

Elijah Price, son of Mordecai and Elizabeth, b. 26th day of 4th month, 1780.

Mordecai Price, father of the above named children, d. 5th day of 5th month, 1796.

Mahlon Price, son of Mordecai, Jr. and Charity, b. 26th day of 9th month, 1795.

Levi Price, son of Mordecai, Jr. and Charity, b. 22nd day of 9th month, 1797.

Amos Price, son of Mordecai, Jr. and Charity, b. 10th day of 11th month, 1799.

Eli Price, son of Mordecai, Jr. and Charity, b. 3rd day of 10th month, 1801, and d. 24th day of 11th month, 1805.

Rachel Price, dau. of Mordecai, Jr. and Charity, b. 9th day of 10th month, 1803.

Ann Price, dau. of Mordecai, Jr. and Charity, b. 25th day of 4th month, 1806.

Mary Price, dau. of Mordecai, Jr. and Charity, b. 18th day of 11th month, 1808, and died in 7th month, 1816[?].

Joshua C. Price, son of Mordecai, Jr. and Charity, b. 26th day of 8th month, 1811.

Mordecai C. Price, son of Mordecai, Jr. and Charity, b. 27th day of 3rd month, 1814, and d. 6th day of -- month, 1820.

Morris Malsby, son of David and Sarah, b. 24th day of 12th month, 1779.

Mary Malsby, dau. of David and Sarah, b. 22nd day of 6th month, 1781.

Katharine Malsby, dau. of David and Sarah, b. 25th day of 6th month, 1783.

Pamala Malsby, dau. of David and Sarah, b. 10th day of 6th month, 1785.

Sarah Malsby, dau. of David and Sarah, b. 1st day of 7th month, 1787.

John Malsby, son of David and Sarah, b. 19th day of 4th month, 1789, and d. 31st day of 11th month, 1798.

Frances Malsby, dau. of David and Sarah, b. 11th day of 12th month, 1794.

Jehu Price, son of Samuel, Jr. and Frances, b. 21st day of 11th month, 1795.

Jared Price, son of Samuel, Jr. and Frances, b. 19th day of 2nd month, 1798.

John Price, son of Samuel, Jr. and Frances, b. 30th day of 11th month, 1800.

David Price, son of Samuel, Jr. and Frances, b. 9th day of 7th month, 1803.

Frances Price, mother of the above named children, d. 14th day of 7th month, 1803, and buried at Gunpowder Meeting.

Jeminah Hair, dau. of John and Elizabeth, b. 14th day of 6th month, 1770.

Elizabeth Hair, dau. of John and Elizabeth, b. 18th day of 1st month, 1772, and d. 13th day of 7th month, 1777.

Rachel Hair, dau. of John and Elizabeth, b. 29th day of 9th month, 1774, and d. 9th day of 7th month, 1777.

Mary Hair, dau. of John and Elizabeth, b. 3rd day of 3rd month, 1777.

Sarah Hair, dau. of John and Elizabeth, d. 20th day of 3rd month, 1779, and d. 7th day of 7th month, 1794.

Hannah Hair, dau. of John and Elizabeth, b. 28th day of 8th month, 1781.

Elennor Hair, dau. of John and Elizabeth, b. 13th day of 5th month, 1784.

Phebe Hair, dau. of John and Elizabeth, b. 7th day of 9th month, 1786.

Rebekah Hair, dau. of John and Elizabeth, b. 14th day of 9th month, 1788, and d. 23rd day of 8th month, 1795.

Tamar Hair, dau. of John and Elizabeth, b. 26th day of 9th month, 1791.

James Spicer, Sr., d. 17th day of 5th month, 1799.

Isaiah Spicer, d. in 10th month, 1793.

Reuben Benson, son of James and Elizabeth, b. 17th day of 12th month, 1795.

Elijah Benson, son of James and Elizabeth, b. 28th day of 12th month, 1797.

Rachel Benson, dau. of James and Elizabeth, b. 4th day of 1st month, 1800.

Benjamin Benson, son of James and Elizabeth, b. 25th day of 10th month, 1801.

John Benson, son of James and Elizabeth, b. 27th day of 9th month, 1802.

William Benson, son of James and Elizabeth, b. 23rd day of 11th month, 1803.

James Benson, son of James and Elizabeth, b. 29th day of 10th month, 1807.

Elizabeth Benson, dau. of James and Elizabeth, b. 10th day of 11th month, 1809.

Mordecai Benson, son of James and Elizabeth, b. 26th day of 4th month, 1812.

Sarah Ann Benson, dau. of James and Elizabeth, b. 15th day of 7th month, 1814.

Amos Benson, son of James and Elizabeth, b. 13th day of 10th month, 1817, and d. 30th day of 10th month, 1818.

Mary Parrish, dau. of Mordecai and Rachel, b. 14th day of 7th month, 1776.

Edieth Parrish, dau. of Mordecai and Rachel, b. 26th day of 10th month, 1778.

Benjamin Parrish, son of Mordecai and Rachel, b. 9th day of 2nd month, 1800[sic]. [Note: It appears that "1800" should be "1780" since the births were written down in order].

Peter Parrish, son of Mordecai and Rachel, b. 10th day of 3rd month, 1782.

John Parrish, son of Mordecai and Rachel, b. 28th day of 7th month, 1784.

Mordecai Parrish, son of Mordecai and Rachel, b. 22nd day of 4th month, 1787.

Uareth Parrish, dau. of Mordecai and Rachel, b. 30th day of 5th month, 1790.

Leonard Parrish, son of Mordecai and Rachel, b. 28th day of 5th month, 1793.

Jaret Parrish, son of Mordecai and Rachel, b. 16th day of 1st month, 1795.

Abraham Tudor, son of William and Martha, b. 3rd day of 7th month, 1797.

Martha Tudor, dau. of William and Martha, b. 26th day of 8th month, 1799.

Hannah Tudor, dau. of William and Martha, b. 7th day of 9th month, 1801.

Ruth Tudor, dau. of William and Martha, b. 5th day of 10th month, 1803, and d. 5th day of 8th month, 1805.

Benjamin Price, of Thomas, d. 3rd day of 12th month, 1794, aged 61 years.

Temperance Price, wife of Benjamin, d. 27th day of 1st month, 1793, aged about 58.

John Price, Jr., b. 2nd day of 3rd month, 1728, d. 14th day of 4th month, 1809.

Urith Price, wife of John, Jr., d. 2nd day of 10th month, 1811, aged 83 years.

GUNPOWDER MONTHLY MEETING: MINUTES AND MARRIAGES, 1739-1800

Joseph Taylor appointed Clerk, 9th day of 4th month, 1739.

Samuel Hopkins, of Baltimore County, m. Sarah Giles, 2nd day of 7th month, 1740. Witnesses: Edward Fell, Aquilia Carr, William Hammond, Richard Croxall, Richard Gott, John Hammond Dorsey, Thomas Colegate, John

Colegate, John Redgely, Joseph Tayler, Casandro Giles, Rachel Hopkins, Elizabeth Giles, Betty Lewis, Elizabeth Parrish, Sarah Fell, Mary Hanson, Sarah Hammond, Dorothy Lawson, Pleasents Redgely, Elizabeth Rogers, Mary Johnson, William Hopkins, Richard Richardson, Nathan Richardson, John Parrish.

William Parrish, Jr., of Baltimore County, m. Keturah Price, 25th day of 12th month, 1742. Witnesses: Samuel Underwood, Thomas Carr, Rees Bowen, John Colegate, Benjamin Bowen, Elexeious Lemond, Joseph Tayler, Richard Chenowth, Susanah Parrish, Mary Parrish, Mary Foard, Mary Carr, Rebeckah Price, Elizabeth Bauzley, Mary Price, Elizabeth Underwood, William Parrish, Samuel Merryman, Sr.[?], John Parrish, Moses Merryman, John Price, James Bauzley.

Norton Groves Baker, of Baltimore County, m. Mary Rawlings, 23rd day of 1st month, 1742. Witnesses: Samuel Underwood, Thomas Carr, William Parrish, Sr., John Price, William Parrish, Jr., John Parrish, Denis Garrot Coal, Danil Stansbury, John Ashman, William Wheeler, Richard Hooker, George Ashman, Rees Bowen, Augustine Hawkins, Christofer Randall, Beniamin Bowen, Joseph Tayler, Keturah Parrish, Sarah Price, Daniel Rawlings, Sr., Daniel Rawlings, Jr., Dorothy Rawlings, Rachel Price, Rebeckah Price, Mary Carr, Mary Price, Ruth Morray, Franis Daughaday, Patiance Ashman.

John Parrish, son of William, of Baltimore County, m. Mary Price, dau. of John, 30th day of 1st month, 1744. Witnesses: Edward Talbott, Thomas Colegate, Rees Bowen, Thomas Hooker, Denis Garrott Cole, Richard Chenowth, William Tipton, John Tipton, Jr., Joseph Tayler, Aquila Carr, Nicholas Merryman, Mordica Price, Jr., Mordica Price (of John), Mary Carr, Elizabeth Price, Sarah Price, Rachel Price, Susanah Parrish, Sr., Susanah Parrish, Jr., Casiah Chenowth, Hanah Hooker, Mary Parrish, Leah Price, Elizebeth Underwood, Elizebeth Tipton, Jane Marryman, William Parrish, Sr., John Price, William Parrish, Jr., Thomas Carr, Mordica Price, Sr., Beniamin Price, Samuel Marryman, Jr., John Price, Jr., Joseph Parrish, Denis Cole, Ureth Cole.

Beniamin Bowen, of Baltimore County, m. Mary Carr, 4th day of 8th month, 1744. Witnesses: Samuel Hopkins, Samuel Underwood, John Parrish, Samuel Gott, Thomas Colegate, John Sollers, Mordica Price, Sr., Mordica Price, Jr., John Willmott, Jr., Moses Galloway, Mary Parrish, Elizabeth Underwood, Joseph Tayler, Averilla Wilmott[?], Tabitha Bowen, Mary

Walker, Mary Hanson, Agness Walker, Elizabeth Price, Mary Parrish, Rebecker Price, Sarah Price, Rachel Price, Keturah Parrish, Sarah Hopkins, Nathan Bowen, Solomon Bowen, Josias Bowen, Thomas Carr, Aquila Carr, John Price, Beniamin Foard, Susanah Parrish, Elizabeth Gott, Martha Wheeler.

Aquila Carr, of Baltimore County, m. Susanah Parrish, 21st day of 2nd month, 1745. Witnesses: Susanah Parrish, Sr., Keturah Parrish, Mary Parrish, Sarah Price, Rachel Price, Edward Talbott, Samuel Underwood, John Hooker, Richard Cross, Abraham Galloway, Thomas Carr, John Willmott [Sr.?], Richard Chenowth, Rees Bowen, Joseph Tayler, William Parrish, Sr., Edward Parrish, William Parrish, Jr., John Parrish, Joseph Parrish.

John Price, son of John and Rebeckah, b. 26th day of 1st month, 1729.

Mordica Price, his brother, b. 27th day of 12th month, 1731.

Aquila Price, their brother, b. 27th day of 9th month, 1735.

Elizabeth Price, their sister, b. 25th day of 12th month, 1737.

Keturah Price, their sister, b. 21st day of 2nd month, 1739.

Elizabeth Price, their sister, b. 4th day of 6th month, 1742.

Thomas Mathews, son of Thomas, b. 16th day of 4th month, 1725.

George Mathews, his brother, b. 19th day of 7th month, 1729.

Sarah Mathews their sister, b. 15th day of 8th month, 1731.

Margaret Hooker, dau. of Richard, b. 15th day of 9th month, 1732.

Barny Hooker, her brother, b. 28th day of 9th month, 1734.

Eurath Hooker, their sister, b. 6th day of 10th month, 1736.

Charity Hooker, their sister, b. 11th day of 1st month, 1739.

Aquila Hooker, their brother, b. 22nd day of 12th month, 1741.

Sarah Hooker, their sister, b. 28th day of 3rd month, 1742.

Mary Hooker, their sister, b. 1st day of 11th month, 1744.

Robert Parrish, son of John and Elizabeth, b. 12th day of 8th month, 1727.

John Parrish, his brother, b. 25th day of 11th month, 1729.

Edward Parrish, their brother, b. 20th day of 12th month, 1731.

Isaac Parrish, their brother, b. 9th day of 8th month, 1734.

Mary Parrish, their sister, b. 8th day of 6th month, 1738.

Elizabeth Parrish, their sister, b. 16th day of 8th month, 1740.

Ann Parrish, their sister, b. 10th day of 11th month, 1745.

Solomon Wheeler, of Baltimore County, m. Rachel Tayler, in 11th month, 1745. Witnesses: Joh. Tayler, El. Gott, Joh. Matthews, M. Bowen, H. Wheeler, K. Parrish, S. Price, R. Haile, A. Cromwell, ----[?] Morray, ----[?] Morray, ----[?] Price, Rees Bowen, Benimin Foard, Thomas Colegate, Benemin Hooker, Thomas Hooker, John Green, Richard Gott, Martha Boreing, Beniamin Bowen, Samuel Hopkins, Thomas Cockey Dye, Samuel Gott, Richard Cross, Thomas Mathews, Jr., John Clausy, Thomas Carr, Aquilia Carr, Mordica Price, John Price, William Parrish, Jr., John Parrish, Edward Talbott, Thomas Mathews, Sr., William Wheeler, Thomas Wheeler, Samuel Wheeler, Moses Wheeler, Joseph Tayler.

Samuel Hooker, son of Samuel, b. 8th day of 2nd month, 1724.

Lovely Hooker, his sister, b. 27th day of 1st month, 1727.

Richard Hooker, their brother, b. 3rd day of 8th month, 1730.

Thomas Hooker, their brother, b. 17th day of 2nd month, 1733.

Sarah Hooker, their sister, b. 19th day of 6th month, 1735.

Thomas Cole, Jr., of Baltimore County, m. Sarah Price, 23rd day of 2nd month, 1747. Witnesses: Rachel Price, Hannah Wheeler, John Green, Thomas Mathews, Benjamin Wheeler, Teague Tracey, Moses Merryman, Mordica Price, Benjamin Price, Thomas Carr, Aquila Carr, Mordica Tipton, Thomas (his "T" mark) Cole, Christofer Cole, Abraham Cole.

Nicholas Gassaway, of Anne Arundel County, and Margaret Peirpoint, of same county, having appeared at two monthly meetings in Gunpowder in Baltimore County, were married 4th day of 9th month, 1747, at Elk Ridge in Anne Arundel County. Witnesses: Margret Richardson, Mary Ridgway, Sarah Brown, Zeporh Baker, Elinor Todd, Frances Todd, --opocia Owings, Eliza. Sellmon, Richard Ridgway, Basel Dever, John Roberson, Rebeca Dorsey, Richard Reynolds, Betty Reynolds, Priscilla Dorsey, Eliza. Talbott, Sidney Peirpoint, Chew Peirpoint, Calib Peirpoint, Faithfull Peirpoint, Mary Peirpoint, Sidney Peirpoint, Bershaba Peirpoint, Sarah Peirpoint, Ann Peirpoint, Johanna Peirpoint, Charles Peirpoint, John Peirpoint, Francis Peirpoint, Henry Peirpoint, Joseph Peirpoint, Misial Peirpoint, Charles Peirpoint, Abraham Peirpoint.

Danil Mathews, from Manocqusy, visited this meeting with his neighbor and friend Eleaser Hunt, in the 12th month, 1747.

Michel Huff and family, having removed from Nottingham to these parts, "who being very weak of body and sickly," desired to be taken under the care of Friends, on 22nd day of 4th month, 1748.

Jennet Huff, widow of Michel Huff, with some of her family, were present at this meeting "in a sober Christian professing faith," on the 24th day of 1st month, 1748.

John Price, Jr., of Baltimore County, m. Mary Parrish, 26th day of 6th month, 1748. Witnesses: Susanah Parrish, Mary Parrish, Rebh. Price, Rlear[?] Maccubins, Susanah Carr, Keturah Parrish, Richard Chinowth, Rees Bowen, Aquila Price, Aquila Carr, Edward Parrish, John Parrish, Mordica Price, Joseph Parrish, John Price, William Price, William Price, Jr.

Elizabeth Carr, dau. of Aquila and Susan, b. 22nd day of 1st month, 1745.

Rachel Carr, her sister, b. 13th day of 3rd month, 1747.

Basil Deaver, of Annarendel [Ann Arundel] County, m. Chew Peirpoint, 25th day of 11th month, 1748. Witnesses: John Parrish, Thomas Huff, William Tipton, Michel Huff, Benjamin Bowen, John Price, Samuel Hopkins, George Mathews, Thomas Colegate, William Parrish, William Parrish, Jr., Rees Bowen, Susanah Carr, Thomas Carr, Aquila Carr, Thomas Mathews, Thomas Mathews, Jr., Mordica Price, Joseph Tayler, Casandrew Talbott, Charles Peirpoint, Misel Peirpoint, Abraham Peirpoint, Calib Peirpoint, Sidney Peirpoint, Rachel Price, Rebecah Price.

Dutton Lane, Jr. and Margret Hooker were charged with having "gone to the hireling priest in case of marriage." Thomas Carr and his son Aquilla Carr were appointed to visit with them and their parents, the 25th day of 11th month, 1749.

Robert Parrish, of Philadelphia, requested lines from this meeting by way of cert., the 25th day of 2nd month, 1750.

Francis Peirpoint, by a friend, signified his intention to remove to dwell in Fradrick [Frederick] County, on 24th day of 8th month, 1750.

Thomas Carr, son of Benjamin, signified his convincement to join amongst Friends, the 5th day of 10th month, 1750.

Zepporiah Baker, widow of Elexander Baker, signified her desire for herself and her children to be taken under care of Friends, the 23rd day of 11th month, 1750.

Thomas Tayler, of Farefax Meeting in Frederick County, Maryland, and Caleb Peirpoint, dau. of Charles, deceased, and Sidney Peirpoint, of Elk Ridge Meeting in Anne Arundel County, Maryland, having appeared at two monthly meetings at Gunpowder in Baltimore County, were married in Elk Ridge on 28th day of 12th month, 1750. Witnesses: Elizabeth Hayward, John Peirpoint, Samuel Peirpoint, Obed Peirpoint, John Poyd [Poyel?], Sidney Peirpoint, Chew Deaver, Sidney Peirpoint, Mary Peirpoint, Johanna Peirpoint, Ann Peirpoint, Hanah Brown, Faithfull Peirpoint, Barsheba Peirpoint, Nicholas Gassaway, Basel Deaver, Thomas Mathews, Rees Bowen, George Mathews, Thomas Mathews, Jr., William Mathews, Joseph Hayward, Joshua Brown, Sr., Oliver Mathews, Roger Randall, George Mathews, Jr., John Peirpoint, Francis Peirpoint, Misel Peirpoint, Henry Peirpoint, Joseph Peirpoint, Charles Peirpoint, Abraham Peirpoint.

Solomon Miller, of Frederick County, Maryland, son of Robert and Ruth Miller of Chester County, Pennsylvania, and Sarah Mathews, dau. of Thomas and Sarah Mathews of Baltimore County, Maryland, having appeared before several meetings of the Gunpowder Meeting, were married 26th day of 2nd month, 1751. Witnesses: Sarah Mathews, Dorthy Miller, Mary Mathews, Jennat Huff, Love Hooker, Sarah Hooker, Faithfull Peirpoint, Bershaba Peirpoint, Mary Morray, Tulatha Carr, Ruth Morray, Cherrity Lane, Margret Lane, Urith Hooker, Sufirah Chinouth, M. Price, Rees Bowen, William Tipton, Michel Huff, John Price, John Price, Jr., Mordica Price, Jr., John Parrish, Mordica Price, Sr., Richard Hooker, Jr., Art. Chinouth, Joseph Parrish, Augustine Hawkins, Thomas Hooker, Thomas Hooker, Shedrick Morray, Thomas Carr, Jr., William Harguer, William Harguer, Jr., Allin Harguer, Francis Carter, Thomas Carr, Mordica Carr, Samuel Hooker, Richard Hooker, John Carter, Thomas Mathews, Oliver Mathews, Danil Mathews, Thomas Mathews, Jr., George Mathewss, William Mathews, Edward Mathews, John Thomas, Thomas Bond.

Thomas Mathews, of Baltimore County, m. Rachel Price, on the 26th day of 12th month, 1751. Witnesses: Sufiah Price, Keturah Parrish, Mary Parrish, Thomas Cole, Jr., Beniamin Price, Beniamin Wheeler, Joseph Bausly, Jr., William Parrish, Jr., Charles Gorsuch, John Lane, Rees Bowen, Thomas Cole, Sr., Samuel Price, Joseph Bausly, William Cole, Joseph Parrish,

Thomas Mathews, Mordica Price, Sr., Mordica Price, Jr., Oliver Mathews, George Mathews, Edward Mathews, Thomas Carr.

Limuel Howard and his son John Howard, and Stephen Roberts, applied for membership on 25th day of 2nd month, 1752.

Meeting was informed on 22nd day of 4th month, 1752, that "John Peirpoint, by his brother, removed from Elk Ridge to dwell among friends in Frederick County."

Meeting was informed on 29th day of 6th month, 1752, that "Richard Richardson, with his family, removed Aquila and Jonathan Massey to dwell in Frederick County."

Meeting was informed on 27th day of 10th month, 1752, that "Thomas Carr, Jr. intended in a few days to [go to] North Carolina to visit some relations."

John Price, of Baltimore County, son of John, m. Urith Cole, 26th day of 1st month, 1753. Witnesses: Rees Bowen, Richard Hooker, Jr., William Tipton, Thomas Colegate, John Cross, Jr., Anthony Gott, Richard Chinoath, Joseph Tayler, John Mellonee, Joseph Parrish, Mordica Tipton, John Tipton, John Fraisor, Rebecca Price, Keturah Price, Sarah Tayler, Mary Tayler, Hanah Gott, Jemina Tracey, Rebecca Price, Mary Ford, Ann Grant, Casa. Gott, John Price, Sr., Mordica Price (son of John), Aquila Price, Stephen Price, Nicholas Merryman, John Parrish, Denis Cole, William Cole (son of John).

William Willson and Henry Willson, their wives and children, were accepted by certificate from East Nottingham to the care of this meeting, 27th day of 6th month, 1753.

Thomas Bond, Sr., and his sons Thomas and John, by a friend, produced a Deed of Gift dated 2nd day of 6th month, 1749, for one acre of land, part of a tract called "Bond's Forest" for use of Friends forever, whereon Friends Meeting house is built near the Little Falls of Gunpowder River, at a meeting held 22nd day of 8th month, 1753.

Daniel Tredaway, "having for some time frequently attended the meetings of Friends for public worship" is taken into membership at a meeting held 22nd day of 8th month, 1753.

John Sheepherd, "having some time desired to be taken into this meeting, produced some lines from his former neighbours friends of Nottingham of Pennsylvania showing he had been educated in that neighbourhood and behaved honestly and quietly," was accepted into membership on 26th day of 9th month, 1753.

Ann Moore, "having removed from amongst Friends of Abington Monthly Meeting in Philadelphia County, Pennsylvania, with four children: Elizabeth, Rachel, Ann and John, dwell amongst Friends here," were accepted into membership on 23rd day of 1st month, 1754.

Mary Peseley "from the monthly meeting at Mountmetick in Ireland, in company with Catheren Payton from the monthly meeting at County Worchestershair of old England" were accepted into membership on 22nd day of 5th month, 1754.

Samuel Hopkins and Sarah his wife, "in membership with the Society of Friends, 24th day of 4th month, 1754," reported their children's births: Margret Hopkins, b. 2nd day of 7th month, 1747; Philip Hopkins, b. 30th day of 7th month, 1749; Elizabeth Hopkins, b. 17th day of 6th month, 1751; and "Garrard, Samuel and John, brothers, entered before."

Children of Richard Hopkins (in membership with the Society of Friends) entered in register in 1754 [and then crossed out with three large X's]: Nicholos Hopkins, b. 12th day of 3rd month, 1747; Rachel Hopkins, b. 31st day of 4th month, 1749; Richard Hopkins, b. 17th day of 12th month, 1750; Sarah Hopkins, b. 20th day of 7th month, 1751; Cathern Hopkins, b. 20th day of 1st month, 1753; and, Gerrard Hopkins, b. 21st day of 2nd month, 1754.

Children of Solomon Wheeler and Rachel his wife: Agness Wheeler, b. 5th day of 11th month, 1746; Sarahanna Wheeler, b. 1st day of 9th month, 1748; Rachel Wheeler, b. 19th day of 9th[?] month, 1749; and, Tabitha Wheeler, b. 6th day of 12th month, 1751.

Children of Benjamin Bowen and Mary his wife: Benjamin Bowen, b. 28th day of 5th month, 1746; Elizabeth Bowen, b. 7th day of 5th month, 1748; Joshua Bowen, b. 13th day of 10th month, 1750; and, Aquila Bowen, b. 26th day of 10th month, 1753.

Joseph Tayler accepted into membership with Friends in 1754, along with: Richard Tayler, his cousin, b. 16th day of 12th month, 1738; Richard Daughaday, his cousin, b. 28th day of 9th month, 1736; Joseph Daughaday, his brother, b. 26th day of 12th month, 1738; and, Rachel Daughaday, his sister, b. 26th day of 10th month, 1740.

Thomas Carr and Elizabeth his wife were accepted into membership with Friends in 1754.

William Parrish and Susannah his wife were accepted into membership with Friends in 1754.

Children of John Price and Rebecca his wife: Agness Price, b. 28th day of 11th month, 1745; Benjamin Price, b. 5th day of 11th month, 1747; Rachel Price, b. 2nd day of 2nd month, 1751; and, "also has six children formerly entered on record of Friends in this book."

Children of Mordecai Price and Elizabeth his wife: Mordecai Price, b. 28th day of 11th month, 1733; Sophia Price, b. 28th day of 12th month, 1736; Samuel Price, b. 28th day of 12th month, 1739' Elizabeth Price, b. 22nd day of 8th month, 1741; and, Mary Price, b. 9th day of 12th month, 1744.

Children of Thomas Coal, Jr. and Sarah his wife: Salathiel Coal (his son by his first wife Elizabeth), b. 7th day of 8th month, 17--[blank]; Elizabeth Coal (by Sarah, his second wife), b. 31st day of 11th month, 1747; Sophia Coal, b. 8th day of 9th month, 1751; and, Rachel Coal, b. 19th day of 11th month, 1753.

Children of John Parrish and Mary his wife: Hanah Parrish, b. 16th day of 5th month, 1748; Mordecai Parrish, b. 3rd day of 12th month, 1750; and, Annmaria Parrish, b. 3rd day of 6th month, 1753.

Children of John Price, Jr. and Urith his wife: Leah Price (by Mary his first wife), b. 1st day of 7th month, 1749; and, Rebeckah Price (by Urith his second wife), b. 25th day of 11th month, 1753.

Children of Ann Moor: Elizabeth Moor, b. 19th day of 10th month, 1738; Rachel Moor, b. 17th dy of 5th month, 1741; Ann Moore, b. 16th day of 2nd month, 1744; John Moore, b. 21st day of 8th month, 1746; and, Mary Moore, b. 28th day of 9th month, 1754.

Children of John Chalke and Mary his wife: Margret Chalke, b. 19th day of 5th month, 1736; Mary Chalke, b. 30th day of 12th month, 1737; Elizabeth Chalke, b. 23rd day of 12th month, 1739; Sarah Chalke, b. 10th day of 1st month, 1741; George Chalke, b. 1st day of 11th month, 1744; Martha Chalke, b. 24th day of 1st month, 1747; John and Joshua Chalke (twins), b. 23rd day of 8th month, 1749; and, Tudor Chalke, b. 25th day of 10th month, 1752.

Rachel Willson and her son Kid Willson were accepted into membership in 1754.

Richard Roads was accepted into membership in 1754.

Children of William Willson and ----[blank] his wife: Rachel Willson, b. 19th day of 4th month, 1741; William Willson, b. 14th day of 9th month, 1747; Gover Willson, b. 3rd day of 1st month, 1749; and, Samuel Willson, b. 11th day of 2nd month, 1752.

Children of Henry Willson and Presilla his wife: Henry Willson, b. 19th day of 4th month, 1747; Presilla Willson, b. 29th day of 8th month, 1749; Rachel Willson, b. 9th day of 9th month, 1751; and. Elizabeth Willson, b. 13th day of 3rd month, 1754.

Children of William Amos and Hannah his wife: Ann Amos, b. 22nd day of 12th month, 1740; Hannah Amos, b. 27th day of 10th month, 1747; William Amos, b. 26th day of 6th month, 1749; and, Elizabeth Amos, b. 21st day of 10th month, 1752.

Accepted into membership and care of Friends in 1754: Thomas Miles; Stephen Robers; George Brown and wife Mary; Thomas Bond, Jr.; Lemuel Howard; John Howard; Joseph Ingland and wife Elizabeth; John Willson; Peter Miles; Rees Bowen; Henry Peirpoint, his brother Abraham Peirpoint, and their sister Faithfull Peirpoint; Joseph Peirpoint, his sister Sidney Peirpoint, their sister Barshaba Peirpoint, their sister Mary Peirpoint, and their cousin Samuel Peirpoint (son of John); Dutto [Dutton?] Lane, Jr. and his wife Mary[?]; Aquila Carr and his wife Susanna; Thomas Mathews, Jr. and wife Rachel; Thomas Mathews and his son George Mathews; Edward Talbott; Michel Huff; William Coal; William Wheeler and his wife Constant; William Tipton; and, John Colegate and his wife Honner.

Nicholas Gassaway and Margret his wife, were accepted in marriage, and recorded that their daughter Rachel Gassaway was born 15th day of 12th month, 1750.

Children of Basel Deaver and Chew his wife, accepted in marriage: Abraham Deaver, b. 13th day of 11th month, 1749; Misal Deaver, b. 6th day of 6th month, 1751; and, Mary Deaver, b. 15th day of 9th month, 1753.

Children of Richard Hooker: Ruth Hooker, born 27th day of 7th month, 1751; and, Susanah Hooker, b. 17th day of 3rd month, 1753.

Samuel Hooker accepted into membership in 1754 with "his children before entered being: Lovely, Richard, Thomas, and Sarah Hooker, all 4 alive at this visit."

Mordica Price, of Baltimore County, son of John, m. Mary Hyatt, 30th day of 8th month, 1754. Witnesses: Martha West, Urith Price, Mary Peirpoint, Sidney Peirpoint, Rachel Daughaday, Sarah Tayler, Keturah Price, Anjalico Tipton, Sarah Coale, Ann Moor, Keturah Parrish, Mary Parrish, Elizabeth Moore, Rachel Moore, Ann Moore, Jr., Ann Boreing, Rachel Coale, Susana Dean, Susana Carr, Walter Moore, William Coale, Jr., Rees Bowen, John Floyd, Samuel Price, Richard Tayler, Joseph Bozley, Jr., William Tipton, Dennis Coale, Beniamin Powell, Jacob Cox, George Hyatt, John Price, John Price, Jr., Aquila Price, William Parrish, Jr., Thomas Coale, Jr., Aquila Carr.

Robert Dutton "produced some lines from Friends at their monthly meeting at East Nottingham" and was accepted into membership on 23rd day of 10th month, 1754.

Beniamin Powell, "having for some considerable time attended frequently the meetings of Friends" was accepted into membership on 25th day of 12th month, 1754.

Beniamin Powell, of Baltimore County, m. Mary Peirpoint, of Ann Arundel County, on the 24th day of 1st month, 1755. Witnesses: Samuel Rullay, Edward Talbott, Richard Talbott, Jeremiah Talbott, Henry Bateman, Burrage Nott, William Haywood, John Peirpoint, Jno. Gowsry, Rachel Moore, Joseph Tayler, Rees Bowen, Thomas Mathews, John Floyd, Joseph Haywood, Benjamin Brown, William Coale, Thomas Floyd, Faithfull Peirpoint, Margret Gassaway, Barsheba Peirpoint, Johanna Peirpoint, Rebecca Gott, Elizabeth Bolman, Zeporah Baker, Mary Price, Keturah Price, Thomas Colegate, Charles Peirpoint, Abraham Peirpoint, Joseph Peirpoint, Samuel Peirpoint, Richard Gassaway, Jr.

Beniamin Price, son of Thomas Price, and Aaron Rawlings, applied for membership on 26th day of 2nd month, 1755.

John Belt applied for membership on 23rd day of 4th month, 1755, and Daniel Treadaway was accepted into membership.

Thomas Floyd, of Baltimore County, m. Rachel Daughaday, on the 23rd day of 4th month, 1755. Witnesses: Henry Willson, John Willson, John Chalke, Aquila Carr, William Amos, Rees Bowen, John Price, Aquila Price, Joshua Cockey, Sidney Peirpoint, Honnour Colegate, Samuel Hopkins, Joseph Peirpoint, George Brown, Joseph Ingland, Misel Peirpoint, Abraham Peirpoint, William Mathews, William Coale, Richard Hopkins, George Mathews, John Belt, Danil Rawlings, Zeporah Baker, Nichles

Baker, John Daughaday, Richard Daughaday, Joseph Daughaday, Joseph Tayler, Richard Tayler.

John Colegate and William Tipton expressed their desire to be joined in membership, on 28th day of 5th month, 1755.

Richard Hooker, Thomas Hooker, Dutton Lane, Jr., and Aquila Price applied for membership, 25th day of 6th month, 1755.

Oliver Matthews and wife Hannah, produced a certificate from Fairfax Monthly Meeting for themselves and their children, Mary, Thomas, and William, on 25th day of 6th month, 1755.

Samuel Peirpoint produced a certificate from Fairfax or Monockosy Monthly Meeting for himself and his brothers and sisters, whose names are John, Henry, Rachel and Ann, on 25th day of 6th month, 1755.

William Hayward and Richard Belt applied for membership on 25th day of 6th month, 1755.

Dennis Cole and Samuel Price applied for membership on 27th day of 8th month, 1755.

A certificate for Barney Hoker "on account of the melitia" was read and signed on 24th day of 9th month, 1755.

Joseph Tayler charged with "his disorderly and opposite appearence against Friends...saying Ann Moor was an ill natured creture and took things into the gallery, and signified she spoke there in a revengefull spirit, and that Catherine Paton and Mary Peasly were under a cloud or vail of darkness," on the 24th day of 9th month, 1755.

Thomas Bosley requested to be joined in membership on the 24th day of 9th month, 1755.

Oliver Matthews was appointed Elder for Gunpowder Weekly Meeting, Samuel Hopkins appointed Elder for Patapsco Meeting, Joseph England appointed Elder for Little Falls Meeting, and George Matthews appointed Elder for Patapsco Forrest Meeting, on the 24th day of 9th month, 1755.

Nathan Hains produced a certificate from East Nottingham on 22nd day of 10th month, 1755, and he and Sophia Price declared their intention to marry. [Note: The marriage is noted as having been accomplished in an orderly manner in the minutes of the 26th day of 11th month, 1755, but there is no record of the marriage date, place and witnesses]. On the 25th day of 2nd month, 1756, Nathan Hanes and wife requested a certificate to Fairfax Monthly Meeting.

Ben Kid Willson "requested a certificate on account of marriage" on 26th day of 11th month, 1755.

Children of Thomas and Rachel Mathews: Sarah Mathews, b. 12th day of 10th month, 1752; Mordica Mathews, b. 12th day of 9th month, 1755; Daniel Mathews, b. 8th day of 2nd month, 1758.

Children of Joseph and Eliza. England: Robart England, b. 7th day of 7th month, 1743; Hannah England, b. 21st day of 9th month, 1746; Joseph England, b. 11th day of 5th month, 1749; George England, b. 3rd day of 9th month, 1751; John England, b. 20th day of 2nd month, 1755; and, Samuel England, b. 23rd day of 7th month, 1757.

Thomas Bosley was accepted into membership on the 25th day of 8th month, 1756, having for some time been under the care of friends.

Thomas Sharp was accepted into membership on the 22nd day of 9th month, 1756, having for some time been under the care of friends.

Thomas James was accepted into membership on the 27th day of 19th month, 1756, having for some time been under the care of friends.

Michael Hoof was disowned on the 24th day of 11th month, 1756, for "keeping unprofitable company and hath appeared several times under arms at the place of training" and "he rather justifies his practice therein."

Robert Dutton and Sussa [also written "Sussy" and "Suse"] Howard declared their intention to marry, on 26th day of 1st month, 1757, and the meeting requested his mother's consent in writing or in person. [Note: The minutes of 23rd day of 3rd month, 1757, record the marriage was accomplished in an orderly manner, but no record was made of the marriage date, place and witnesses].

Joseph Hayward and Rebecca Scott declared their intention to marry, on 27th day of 4th month, 1757. [Note: The minutes of 22nd day of 6th month, 1757, record the marriage was accomplished in an orderly manner, but no record was made of the marriage date, place and witnesses].

Benjaman Buffinton visited from Swaney Monthly Meeting in New England on the 27th day of 4th month, 1757.

Garrard Hopkins, son of Samuel Hopkins, is removed to live in Philadelphia, his father requested a certificate to join him in Philadelphia, on 27th day of 4th month, 1757.

John Bond produced a certificate from Nottingham Monthly Meeting on 27th day of 4th month, 1757, "recommending him and family, Samuel excepted, members of our Christian Society, which is excepted only his daughter Hannah which between the making out of the certificate and the delivery of it to our meeting, went in marriage for which we see cause to refuse and leave to Nottingham to deal with."

Isaac Andrews produced a certificate from Haddonfield Monthly Meeting in the Province of Westiersay [West Jersey] on a religious visit, on 25th day of 5th month, 1757.

George Matthews produced a certificate from Cane Creek Monthly Meeting in North Carolina signifying their unity with him, on 25th day of 5th month, 1757.

John Peirpoint removed under the verge of Farefax Monthly Meeting and was granted a certificate on 25th day of 5th month, 1757.

Joshua Lard visited from Haddonfield Monthly Meeting in Gloster County in Westgersey [West Jersey] on the 22nd day of 6th month, 1757.

William Haywart [Hayward] and Sidney Peirpoint declared their intention to marry, on 16th day of 10th month, 1757. [Note: The minutes of 28th day of 12th month, 1757, record the marriage was accomplished in an orderly manner, but there is no record of the marriage date, place and witnesses].

John Naylor produced a certificate from Middletown Monthly Meeting in the County of Bux [Bucks] in Pennsylvania, on the 22nd day of 3rd month, 1758.

Daniel Robertson was received by certificate from West River Monthly Meeting, on the 22nd day of 3rd month, 1758.

Abraham Peirpoint charged with "fighting in a publick company" on the 24th day of 5th month, 1758.

James Comly and Mary his wife, "a well approved minister," with their children: Jacob, James, Jonathan, David, Rachel and John; plus Sarah, daughter of Joseph Comly, in Abington Monthly Meeting in Pennsylvania, were accepted in membership in Baltimore County on 28th day of 6th month, 1758.

Joseph Haywart [Hayward] removed within the verge of the Nottingham Monthly Meeting on 28th day of 6th month, 1758.

Daniel Rawlings accepted into membership on 27th day of 9th month, 1758, having been for some time under the care of Friends.

Samuel Hopkins requested a certificate for his son Samuel to join in Philadelphia, on 25th day of 10th month, 1758.

William Willson requested a certificate on account of his removal to reside within the verge of Nottingham Monthly Meeting, on 25th day of 10th month, 1758.

Joseph Parrish charged with "neglecting attending meetings and being part of a prise and lending his cretor for the same," on the 27th day of 12th month, 1758.

Benjamin Howard accepted into membership on 28th day of 2nd month, 1759, having for some time been under their care.

Thomas Cole, Jr. disowned in 6th month, 1759, "having taken liberty to drink to excess and fight with his neighbor."

Richard Hooker disowned in 9th month, 1759, for misconduct in "having taken the liberty to wrassel for a prize."

John Stores [Storer?] produced certificates for religious visits made to Nottingham in old England, dated 6th day of 3rd month, 1758, and to Mansfield in old England, dated 3rd day of 7th month, 1758.

John Loid [Loyd] produced a copy of the minutes from the Abington Monthly Meeting of 29th day of 10th month, 1759.

Daniel Brown produced a certificate from Goshom [?] Monthly Meeting in Chester County, Pennsylvania, dated 17th day of 12th month, 1759.

Barney Hooker disowned on 23rd day of 1st month, 1760, for "going to shooting matches and shooting for prizes."

John Colegate, Samuel Coale, Samuel Price and Richard Daughaday were charged with "going out in marriage," on the 6th day of 3rd month, 1760.

Abraham Peirpoint charged with misconduct and "being accused with drinking to access and gaming, also foul language and a child laid to him, and fighting" in 1760.

Mary Thomson, formerly Choalk, charged with misconduct in 1760.

Thomas Hooker accepted into membership, 28th day of 1st month, 1761.

Ann Harbert, formerly Nailor, disowned on 25th day of 2nd month, 1761, for having been "married by a priest."

Thomas Hooker, son of Samuel, disowned on 27th day of 3rd month, 1761, for "going out in marriage to a young woman of this Society."

Peter Ball produced a certificate for himself, his wife and children, from Rightstown in Bucks County, Pennsylvania, on 27th day of 3rd month, 1761.

Samuel Coale was disowned in 1761 because "some considerable time ago [he] was married contrary to our principles."

Daniel Hains and Mary Price declared their intention to marry on 24th day of 3rd month, 1762. [Note: The minutes of the 28th day of 4th month, 1762, record it was accomplished in an orderly manner, but no record is made of the marriage date, place and witnesses].

Joseph Scott requested some lines to Deer Creek Monthly Meeting on the 24th day of 3rd month, 1762, as he intended to marry Ann Haywart [Hayward] of that meeting.

Hugh Burges produced a certificate from Buckingham Monthly Meeting in Bucks County, Pennsylvania, recommending him as a member of this meeting, on 26th day of 5th month, 1762.

Mry Tucker produced a certificate from Buckingham Monthly Meeting in Bucks County, Pennsylvania, for herself and her three children, Robert, Nicholas, and Elizabeth, on the 26th day of 5th month, 1762.

Thomas Matthews, Sr. condemned his own actions and being "guilty of taking too much strong drink and too frequently attending places of diversion to my own shame and trouble of friends," on the 24th day of 6th month, 1762.

Certificate ordered sent to Bassel Deaver's wife Chew and her children at Farefax Monthly Meeting, 28th day of 7th month, 1762.

David Humphrey produced a certificate from the monthly meeting held in the County of Philadelphia for himself and his wife Elizabeth and their children, Margaret, Elenor, Robert, Anna, Catharener, Jeane, Joshua and Elizabeth, on the 27th day of 10th month, 1762.

Henry Willson, son of Henry, being bound to Stevens Collins, merchant of Philadelphia, "in order to learn the bisnes of a merchant," was granted a certificate to that monthly meeting on the 25th day of 11th month, 1762.

On 27th day of 1st month, 1763, Rees Bowen condemned his actions for "his drinking too much strong licker." At the same meeting, Thomas Hooker, son of Samuel, acknowledged his "outgoing in marriage with one not of our society." Also, William Amos produced a certificate from Seader Creek Quarterly Meeting in the Colony of Verjaney [Virginia] signifiying their unity with him and companion Joseph Jones from Deer Creek Monthly Meeting.

Frances Brown produced a certificate from Haddonfield in West Jersey for herself and her three children, Mary, David, and James, on 25th day of 5th month, 1763. Also, Hannah Johns produced a certificate from Deer Creek. And Benjamin Powel condemned his own actions "for drinking too much strong liquor."

Sarah Wagstaff, wife of Richard, produced a certificate from Philadelphia Monthly Meeting on 22nd day of 6th month, 1763. Also, John Nalor and Thomas Hooker, son of Samuel, condemned themselves for drinking too much strong liquor.

Patrick Dunkin produced a certificate from Abbington Monthly Meeting in Pennsylvania for himself and his children, Benjaman, Margreat, Jean, and James, on 22nd day of 7th month, 1763.

Jacob Comly, Thomas Hooker (of Samuel), and William Parrish (son of William, Jr.) were disowned for "accompanying divers people which mostly took guns, they also bore arms themselves, and in the time of engagement with the said negroes one was killed and two wounded," on 28th day of 9th month, 1763.

Certificate for Jacob Scott, Jr. was produced on 28th day of 9th month, 1763, "on account of marriage to Elizabeth Hayward, a member of Salsbery Monthly Meeting in Pennsylvania."

Leonard Belt was disowned on 26th day of 10th month, 1763, for "having married a young woman of our Society by a priest."

George Briggs produced a certificate from Burlington Monthly Meeting to this meeting on 26th day of 10th month, 1763.

On the 28th day of the 12th month, 1763, a complaint was made againt Thomas Bond (son of John) "relating to a young woman laying a bastard child to the said Bond."

Mordecai Price (son of John) charged in 1st month, 1764, with "a difference with one of his neighbors which led to blows."

John Moore produced a certificate from Kennet Monthly Meeting for himself and his children, David, John, Jehu, Mary and Abigal, on 28th day of 3rd month, 1764. John Moore also declared his intention to marry Rebecah Price. [Note: The minutes on the 23rd day of 5th month, 1764, record the marriage was accomplished in an orderly manner, but no record was made of the marriage date, place, and witnesses].

Samuel Hopkins requested a certificate on 26th day of 4th month, 1764, for his son Philip to Philadelphia Monthly Meeting, where he is bound as an apprentice to Isaac Parrish to learn the business of a hatter.

Reported on 25th day of 7th month, 1764, that Basel Deaver "some time ago removed from amongst us and settled in Farefax Monthly Meeting."

Samuel Day condemned on 22nd day of 8th month, 1764, "for playing cards."

John Schofield condemned on 22nd day of 8th month, 1764, "for taking an oath."

James Conley condemned on 22nd day of 8th month, 1764, "for taking of negroes."

George Mathews condemned his own actions on 23rd day of 11th month, 1764, for having "been led into the vane evils of the world such as fighting, gaming, and in some measures drinking to excess, and in some sort been active in too many other of the folleys of this life." Aquila Price also condemned himself for having "fell into the scandulas practise of fighting."

Josiah Diah [Dyer?] produced a certificate from Buckingham Monthly Meeting on 23rd day of 11th month, 1764, for himself, wife Esther and three children, Esther, Pheby and Rachel.

On 23rd day of 1st month, 1765, Thomas James and William Everit were charged with "both gone out in marriage and both married by a priest or priests."

On 27th day of 2nd month, 1765, it was reported that Daniel Rawlings and Basil Deaver "a considerable time past removed from us and left their affairs unsettled."

Isaac Daws was received into membership from Little Falls Preparative meeting on 27th day of 2nd month, 1765.

On 27th day of 3rd month, 1765, John Ward and wife Rachel were recommended as members in unity from West River.

Henry Peirpoint (son of John) condemned on 24th day of 4th month, 1765, with "drinking to excess and unseamly keeping company with a young woman so as to have a child by her."

Elizabeth England, widow of Joseph, requested a certificate on 24th day of 4th month, 1765, to London Grove Monthly Meeting in Chester County, Pennsylvania, for her son Joseph who was bound as an apprentice to David England to "learn the bisness of a shop jiner."

James Comley, son of James, on 26th day of 6th month, 1765, was reported by David Humphrey for having been married by a priest. Also, David Humphrey condemned his own actions by having "been overtaken with drinking of strong drink."

Robert Foreman produced a certificate on 26th day of 6th month, 1765, from Wilmington Monthly Meeting. Peter Perine, long under the care of Little Falls Preparative Meeting, was accepted into membership at Gunpowder Monthly Meeting.

John Gibbons produced a certificate on 25th day of 9th month, 1765, from Salsbury Monthly Meeting in Pennsylvania for his wife, Martha, and children Joseph and Ann, "tho it hath pleased devine providence to remove one of the children by death, to wit, Ann."

Richard Hopkins requested a certificate "for his son Richard to Philadelphia Monthly Meeting as he is bound an aprintis in that city to Samuel Hopkins to larn the bisness of a carpenter," on 27th day of 11th month, 1765.

On 27th day of 11th month, 1765, Jeremiah Belt condemned his "misconduct in accompanying his brother [Richard] to be married by a priest which is contrary to the good order."

Even Griffith produced a certificate on 27th day of 11th month, 1765, from Sadsbury Monthly Meeting, for himself and wife Rebecckah.

Abraham Huff produced a certificate on 25th day of 12th month, 1765, from East Notangham Monthly Meeting.

On 22nd day of 1st month, 1766, Robert Foreman and Mary Nailor declared their intention to marry. [Note: The minutes of 26th day of 3rd month, 1766, record the marriage had been accomplished in an orderly manner, but there is no record of the marriage date, place and witnesses].

John Gibbons requested a certificate on 22nd day of 1st month, 1766, to Philadelphia Monthly Meeting for himself and wife and child.

On 26th day of 3rd month, 1766, John Moore and Phebe Dyer declared their intention to marry. [Note: The Minutes of 28th day of 5th month, 1766, record the marriage had been accomplished in an orderly manner, but there is no record of the marriage date, place and witnesses].

William Highat, "in these parts for some time," produced a certificate on 23rd day of 7th month, 1766, from New Garden Monthly Meeting in North Carolina and stated "he intends to return there again."

On 27th day of 8th month, 1766, it was reported that Joshua Carr and Thomas Hooker, Jr. "hath differed with one of their neighbors so far as to fight him."

On 24th day of 9th month, 1766, John Maleny [Malenee] was charged with "being married by a priest, and suffering musick, and dancing, and gaming in his house."

On 22nd day of 10th month, 1766, Benjamin Howard and Mary Dutton declared their intention to marry.

Francis Daws produced a certificate from Buckingham Monthly Meeting in Pennsylvania, on 22nd day of 10th month, 1766, recommending him as a member. Also, Francis Daws and Mary Scott declared their intention to marry. [Note: The minutes of 20th day of 1st month, 1767, indicate the marriage was accomplished in an orderly manner, but there is no record of the marriage date, place, and witnesses].

On 26th day of 11th month, 1766, "a certificate from Kings Wood Monthly Meeting in the Jarsies [Jersey] was produced at this meeting recommending Josiah Dyer, his wife and children, as members of society, and as he is settled within the verge of Fairfax Monthly Meeting, we have put it in the hands of Oliver Mathews to send it."

On 25th day of 2nd month, 1767, Benjamin Price (of John) was found "guilty of dancing, playing cards, and using unsavory language."

Thomas Gothrop, from Old England, and Paul Osburn, from the Government of New York, visited this meeting on the 25th day of 2nd month, 1767.

On 24th day of 6th month, 1767, Jeremiah Belt was guilty of "having repeatedly taken the oath in open court."

On 22nd day of 7th month, 1767, George Mason attended this meeting "with some lines of recommendation from Friends of Plastow in Old England....also a certificate for his wife Jean and children, George, John, James, Jean and Grace."

Elizabeth Smith, widow of John, produced a certificate on 23rd day of 10th month, 1767, from Wilmington Monthly Meeting for herself and her children, Joshua, John, Mary, and Peter.

On 25th day of 11th month, 1767, William Moore, John Moore, David Humphries, and Henry Burges [Note: There is a later entry that gives his name as "Hugh Burgess"] were charged with "being concerned in a lottery."

Robert Dutton, son of Robert Dutton, of Northeast in Cecil County, Maryland, deceased, m. Susanna Howard, dau. of Lemuel Howard, of Winters Run in Baltimore County, on 24th day of 2nd month, 1757. Witnesses: John Talberd, Thomas Bond, Jr., William Maccomas, Philip Jackson, Elizabeth Jackson, Daniel Tredaway, Peter Miles, Richard Ross, Samuel Day, Margrett Chalke, Anna[?] Amos, Mary Chalk, Hannah Amoss, Hannah Roads, Henry Wilson, Jr., James Bond, Prisilla Wilson, Jr., Mary Dutton, Martha Bond, Mary Green, Robert England, William Amoss, John Chocke, Rachal Willson, Prisilla Willson, Mary Chalk, Hannah Amoss, William Wilson, Rachel Willson, Francis Bond, Henry Wilson, B.Kid Wilson, Aquila Johns, George Brown, Ann Howard, Elisebeth England, Lemuel Howard [Jr.?], Joseph England, J. Bond, Hannah Bond, Josa. Bond, Jea.[?] Bond, John Bond, Jr., Anne Bond.

Joseph Hayward, of Baltimore County, m. Rebeckah Scott, dau. of Jacob and Hannah Scott, on 9th day of 6th month, 1757. Witnesses: Mary Parrish, Keturah Parrish, Benjamin Powell, John Parrish, Joseph Comly, William Parrish, Jr., Jane Naylor, John Naylor, Mary Price, Sarah Scott, Elizabeth Moor, Sidney Peirpoint, Rebekah Price, Ann Naylor, Keturah Price, Isabella Price, Ann Moor, Mordeca Price, Sarah Hopkins, Honour Colegate, Thomas Matthews, Jr., Hannah Matthews, John Colegate, John Price, Sr., Aquila Carr, Aquila Price, Samuell Peirpoint, Abram. Peirpoint, Ann Moor, Jacob Scott, Hannah Scott, Jacob Scott, Jr., Joseph Scott, William Hayward, Elizabeth Hayward, Ann Hayward.

Nathan Hains, son of Joseph Hains, of the Township of West Notingham in the County of Chester, Pennsylvania, m. Sophia Price, dau. of Mordeca Price, of Baltimore County, Maryland, on 23rd day of 10th month, 1755 [sic] at Gunpowder Meeting House. Witnesses: Elizabeth Moor, Rachel Moor, Rachel Gorsuch, Sarah Gorsuch, Elizabeth Price, Mary Price, Walter Moor, William Cole, Jr., Aquila Price, Mordeca Price, Jr., Thomas Cole, Jr., Ann Moor, Hannah Matthews, Susana Carr, Keturah Parrish, Samuel Price, Keturah Price, Samuel Price, William Hains, Lydia Hains, Thomas Matthews, Solomon Miller, Aquila Carr, George Mathews, Thomas Matthews, Jr., Oliver Matthews, Joseph Hains, Jr., Elizabeth Hains, Mordeca Price, Sr., Daniel Hains, Jacob Hains, Deborah Hains, John Price, William Parrish.

William Hayward, of Anne Arundel County, m. Sidney Peirpoint, dau. of Charles and Sidney Peirpoint, deceased, on 29th day of 11th month, 1757, at Elk Ridge Meeting House in Anne Arundel County. Witnesses: Jeremiah Talbott, Mary Talbott, Benjamin Hoker, William Tipton, Rees Bowen, Ann Peirpoint, Rachel Gassaway, Henry Peirpoint, Henry Dorsey, Samuell Peirpoint, Rachel Peirpoint, Benjamin Powell, Isabela Price, Richard Talbott, Rebecca Dorsey, Bethsheba Peirpoint, Elizabeth Hayward, Nicholas Gassaway, Johanna Peirpoint, Rebecca Price, Joseph Peirpoint, Margret Gassaway, Mary Powell.

Mordeca Price, son of Mordeca and Elizabeth Price, of Baltimore County, m. Rachel Moore, dau. of Walter and Ann Moore, deceased, on 27th day of 12th month, 1759, at Gunpowder Meeting House. Witnesses: Hannah Amus, Isabel Price, Rachel Gorsuch, Rebecca Price, Oliver Matthews, Daniel Robetson, John Hooker, Charles Gorsuch, William Parrish, Jr., Ann Colgate, Hannah Matthews, Mary Matthews, Mary Powel, Thomas Hooker, Joseph Scott, Joseph Hayward, Aquila Price, John Colgate, Joseph England, Allen Farquer, Jr., William Amus, Benjaman Powel, Benjaman Hooker, Richard Colgate, Thomas Price, Walter Bozley, Rachel Matthewss, Ann Moore, Jr., John More, Thomas Matthews, Jr., Aquila Carr, Benjamin Price, William Coale, Jr., Keturak Parish, Thomas Cole, Jacob Scott, Walter Moore, Ann Moore, Elizabeth Price, Elizabeth Price, Sarah Cole, Samuel Price.

Richard Belt, son of John Belt, of Gunpowder in Baltimore County, m. Keturah Price, dau. of John Price of Gunpowder in Baltimore County, on 24th day of the 1st month called January, 1760. Witnesses: Susann Price, Mary Parrish, Hannah Parrish, Jane Naylor, Casa: Cockey Colgate, Colegate Colegate, Charcila Ford, Rachel Maryman, Oliver Matthews, Joseph England, Lemuel Saunders, William Tipton, Jr., George Tye, Thomas Johnson, Anne Amos, Rebekah Price, Mary Parrish, Ketturah

Parrish, Elizabeth Price, Benoni Belt, Thomas Mathews, William Parrish, Jr., William Tipton, Daniel Rallings, Robert England, Jacob Scott, Rees Bowen, John Mallonee, Thomas Cockey Deye, John Price, John Price, Jr., Mordeca Price, Acquila Price, John Belt, Jr., Nathan Belt, Jeremiah Belt, Samuel Meryman, Nich: Meryman, Samuel Price, Benjamin Price, Thomas Price, Samuel Price.

Samuel Price, son of Mordica and Elizabeth, of Baltimore County, m. Ann Moore, dau. of Walter and Anne, on 26th day of 12th month, 1760. Witnesses: Thomas Bozley, Eligah Bosley, Green Bozley, Thomas Matthews, Sr., Allen Farquer, Jr., Charles Gorsuch, James Comley, Jr., John Scholfield, Thomas Sheridine, Jacob Comley, Tego Tracey, John Price, Jr., Mary Comley, Rachel Scholfield, Keturah Parrish, John Naylor, James Comley, Daniel Rawlings, Isabel Price, Rebecca Price, Ann Price, Mary Parrish, Jane Naylor, Ann Naylor, Oliver Matthews, John Gorsuch, Mordica Price, Walter Moore, Rachel Price, Rachel Matthews, Elizabeth Price, Mary Price, Thomas Matthews, Jr., Thomas Cole, Jr., Thomas Price, Mordica Price (son of Jno.).

Thomas James, of Baltimore County, m. Ann Amos, dau. of William and Hannah, on 27th day of 8th month, 1761, at Little Falls Meeting House. Witnesses: Joseph England, Elizabeth England, Prissella Wilson, Charles Bkaer, Temperence Roberson, Mary Choake, Alsann Bond, Susanna Dutton, Hannah Johns, Elizabeth Wilson, Hannah Day, Alasanna Bond, Martha Bond, Sarah Bond, Henry Wilson, Prissella Wilson, Susannah Sharp, Rachel Wilson, Solomon Maccomas, Stephen Roberts, David Carlisle, Mary Tredway, Sarah Tredway, John Bond, Joseph Jones, Richard Everit, Rachal Wilson, Henry Wilson, John Chocke, Daniel Tredway, Aquila Thompson, John Tredway, Isaac Milner, Richard Rhoads, Sarah Rhoads, Benkid Wilson, William Amos, Hannah Amos, Thomas Amos, Daniel Maccomas (son of William), Moses Maccomas, James Amos, Benjamin Amos, Thomas Tredway, Ann Amos, Joshua Amos, Petter Miles, Peter Perine, Hannah Perine, Sarah Amos, Martha Amos.

Daniel Haines, son of Joseph and Elisabeth Haines, of West Nottingham Township in Chester County, Pennsylvania, m. Mary Price, dau. of Mordecai (deceased) and Elizabeth Price, of Baltimore County, on 25th day of 3rd month, 1762, at Gunpowder Meeting House. Witnesses: Temperence Price, Elizabeth Taylor, Mary Comley, Hannah Matthews, Daniel Rawlings, Jr., Jacob Comley, Isabel Price, Aggnis Price, William Parrish, Jr., Mordica

Price, Benjaman Wheeler, Thomas Cole, Aquila Price, James Comley, Mary Matthews, Bellenda Bozley, Joseph Haines, William Haines, Nathan Haines, Warrick Miller, Mordica Price, Samuel Price, Sarah Cole, Elizabeth Price, Rachel Price, Ann Price, Rebeccah Price, Rebeccah Price.

Warrick Miller, son of Robert (deceased) and Ruth Miller, of East Caln Township in Chester County, Pennsylvania, m. Elizabeth Price, dau. of Mordica (deceased) and Elizabeth Price, of Baltimore County, at Gunpowder Meeting on 29th day of 6th month, 1762. Witnesses: Isable Price, John Gorsuch, Thomas Hoker, Mary Matthews, Ann Price, Thomas Matthews, Sr., Charles Gorsuch, Rachel Scholfield, Jos. Bozley, Jr., Oliver Matthews, Thomas Matthews (son of Oliver), Jane Haines, Allen Farquar, Jr., Aquila Price, Mordica Price, Thomas Cole, Jr., Benjamin Price, Samuel Price, Thomas Price, Rebecca Price, Susannah Price, Hannah Matthews, Solomon Miller, Sarah Cole, Rachel Matthews, Mordica Price, Samuel Price, Jacob Miller, Mary Haines, Daniel Haines, George Matthews, Sarah Miller, Lydia Haines.

Hugh Burges, of Baltimore County, m. Ailse More [Ailce Moore] at Patapsco Meeting House on 6th[?] day of 2nd month, 1764. Witnesses: Elizabeth Humphrey, Sarah Hopkins, Rachel Floyd, Nicholas Merimon, Jonathan Humphrey, Benjamin Griffith, Alisana Hanson, John Hopkins, Mark Alexander, David Shields, Fanney Brigs, John Bond, Thomas Price, William Coale, Thomas Floyd, Samuel Hopkins, Richard Hopkins, David Humphrey, John Deaver, Ann Moore, Mary Comley, Kiturah Parrish, Alesanna Bond, Richard Hopkins, James Coox [sic], Rachel Hopkins, Margreat Hopkins, Mary Frazer, William Moore, John Burges, John Moore, Mary Moore, Sarah Burges.

Benjamin Howard, son of Lamuel [Lemuel] Howard (deceased), of Baltimore County, m. Mary Dutton, dau. of Robert Dutton, at Little Falls Meeting House on 4th day of 12th month, 1766. Witnesses: Edward Cripple, Rachel Wilson, Priscilla Wilson, Mary Daws, Sarah Rodes, Elisabeth Amos, Ellener Amos, Martha Amos, Rachel Bull, Henry Wilson, Rachel Willson, Priscilla Wilson, Benkid Wilson, John Bond, Jr., Isaac Dawes, Richard Bond, Thomas Hutchins, Robert Dutton, Lemuel Howard, Mary Brown, Robert England, Charity Bond, Ann Howard, William Amus.

William Amos, son of William Amos (deceased), m. Martha Bull, dau. of Luke Wiley, both of Baltimore County, on 4th day of 7th month, 1765, at Little Falls Meeting House. Witnesses: Mary Willson, Margaret Robinson,

Elizabeth Willson, Ellener Amos, Joseph Jones, Henry Willson, John Willson, Richard Roades, Isaac Dawes, John Bond, Jr., Edward Norris, Priscilla Willson, Rachel Willson, Elizabeth Willson, Sarah Bond, Priscilla Willson, Rachel Willson, Jr., Sarah Roades, Elizabeth England, Ann Amos, Thomas Amos, Benjaman Amos, Sarah Amos, Thomas James, Peter Perine, William Amos, William Perine, Peter Miles, Rinnis Bull, Sarah Bull, Simon Perrine, Hannah Miles.

Robert Forman, son of John and Elizabeth Forman, of Bucks County, Pennsylvania, m. Mary Naylor, dau. of John and Jane Nalor [sic], of Baltimore County, at Gunpowder Meeting House on 18th day of 3rd month, 1766. Witnesses: Rachel Price, William Price, John Ensor, Rebeckah Price (daughter of J. Price), Ann Colegate, Rebeckah Colegate, Mordica Price, Mary Matthews, Aquila Price, Isabel Price, Hester Dyer, Phebe Dyer, Benjamin Price, Francis Daws, Ann Price, Rachel Price, Mordica Price, Ester Dyer, Thomas Moore, Ann Price, Josiah Dyer, John Price, Jr., Ureth Price, John Nalor, Jane Nalor, Ann Moore, Sarah Nalor, Samuel Price, Jacob Scott, John Moore, Eliz: Colegate.

John Worthington, son of Charles Worthington, of Deer Creek, m. Priscilla Willson, dau. of Henry Willson, of Little Falls, on 7th day of 11th month, 1769, at Little Falls Meeting House. Witnesses: William Willson, Jr., Joseph Fenley, William Amos, Peter Perine, Robert Dutton, B: Howard, Hannah Fulton, Mary Howard, Hannah Bull, Elizabeth Dutton, Martha Amos, Cassander Gover, Ann Hopkins, Sarah Coale, Mary Lee, Elizabeth Amos, Joseph Hopkins, Elihu Hall, Jr., Joseph Hall, Skipwith Coale, James Giles, Sarah Basey, Mary Daws, Priscilla Willson, Henry Willson, Jr., Cassander Willson, Charles Worthington, Samuel Worthington, Mary Willson, Rachel Willson, Cassander Lee.

Samuel Harris, son of William Harris, of Calvert County, m. Rachel Willson, dau. of Henry Willson, of Baltimore County, at Little Falls Meeting House on 2nd day of 4th month, commonly called April, 1771. Witnesses: William Willson, William Willson, Benjamin Willson, Thomas Morgan, John Hopkins, William Amos, Hannah Bull, Samuel Young, Edward Norris, John Smith, Thomas Hutchins, James Amos, John Bond, Jr., John Hutchens, Edward Bussey, Edward Bull, Sarah Bond, Ann Bond, Elizabeth Bond, Rebeca Yong [sic], John Worthington, Rachel Willson, Cassand. Willson, Eliza. Willson, Prisa. Gover, Mary Hopkins, William Willson, Jr., Samuel Willson, Elizabeth Amos, William Amos, Ann Thomas, Elizabeth Johns,

Gittings Willson, Johnkid Willson, Henry Willson, Prisilla Willson, Henry Willson, Jr., Priscilla Worthington, Eliza. Willson, Margaret Willson, Eliza. Harris, William Willson, John Willson, Samuel Harris, Benkid Willson.

Joseph Burges, of Baltimore County, m. Mary Moore, dau. of William and Mary Moore, at Patapsco Meeting House on 1st day of 10th month, 1770. Witnesses: David Rusk, Nathan Griffith, Mary Cox, Mary Rusk, Miriam Hopkins, Elizabeth Hopkins, Elizabeth Griffith, Garrard Hopkins, Elizabeth James, Rachel Hopkins, Sarah Hopkins, Nicholas Hopkins, Margaret Hopkins, John Hopkins, Samuel Moore, James Giles, Elizabeth Aisquith, Susannah Chew, Ann Humphrey, Sarah Frazer, Cassandra Hopkins, Mary Bankson, Achsah Cockey, Thomas Floyd, George Daffin, Thomas Towson, Joseph Daffin, William Moore, John Moore, Richard Hopkins, William Coale, Beng. Griffith, James Cox, William Aisquith, Josep [sic] Hayward, Josias Penington.

Mordica Price, of Baltimore County, son of John and Rebecca Price, m. Tabitha Tipton, dau. of William and Angilico Tipton, at Gunpowder Meeting House on 1st day of 1st month, 1772. Witnesses: Luke Tipton, Esther Price, Ruth Price, John Belt, Jr., Aquila Carr, Jr., Mary Bond, Joshua Jones, Rebeckah Price, John Tipton, Nicholas Tipton, Jane Naylor, Thomas Price, Mary Tipton, Rachel Wooden, Rachel Colgate, John Tipton, Jabus M:y Tipton, Stepton Wooden, William Parrish, John Belt, Samuel Price, Tabitha Tipton, Robert Foreman, Mary Foreman, Anna Price, Mary Powel, Ureth Price, Samuel Merryman, Benj. Powel, George Tye, Jonathan Tipton, John Price, William Tipton, Rebeccah Price, John Price, Jr., Aquila Price, Aquila Tipton, Isabel Price, Benjamin Price, Richard Belt.

Aquila Price, of Baltimore County, son of John and Rebecca Price, m. Ann Griffith, dau. of Isaac and Ann (deceased), at Gunpowder Meeting House on 27th day of 2nd month, 1772. Witnesses: John Naylor, Henry Coale, Thomas Price, Mordica Parrish, George Ensor, Benjamin Hooker, John Moore, Jane Naylor, Tabitha Price, James Lawler, Joseph Melein [?], Rachel Wooden, Richard Belt, Thomas Moore, Asaph Colegate, Mordica Cole, Mordica Matthews, Mordica Price, Jr., Rachel Price, Mary Griffith, Thomas Morford, Aquila Tipton, Mordica Price, Sr., Bale Owings, Joseph Shaw, Samuel Price, Robart Foreman, Elizabeth Matthews, Rachel Dyer, Elizabeth Sott [Scott?], Richard Colgate, Elizabeth Colgate, John Price, Sr., Isaac Griffith, John Price, Jr., Mordica Price, William Tipton, Abraham Griffith, Hannah Griffith, Isable Price, Mary Nalor, Rebeckah Price.

John Cornthwait, of Baltimore Town, merchant, son of Thomas and Elizabeth Cornthwait, of the Fals[?] Township in Bucks County, Pennsylvania, m. Mary Matthews, dau. of Oliver and Hannah Matthews, of Baltimore County, at Gunpowder Meeting House on 17th day of 4th month, 1771. Witnesses: Sarah Meryman, Mary Gorsuch, Ann Griffith, Rachel Dyer, Charlote Deye Colegate, Elizabeth Lacey, Penelope Deye Cockey, Nancy Wells, Mary Griffith, Eliz. Hopkins, Rachel Hopkins, Susanna Chew, John Griffith, Jos. Elgar, Eliz. Colegate, Rachel Price, Ann Price, Mary Powell, Hannah Griffith, Sarah Naylor, Thomas Cockey Deye, John Hopkins, Isaac Griffith, James Naylor, Isabel Price, Constant Price, Nicholas Hopkins, Ann Moore, Mary Hervey, Jacob Johnson, Mordica Price, John Price, Jr., Benj. Price, Mordica Price (son of J.), Samuel Price, Frances Matthews, Robert Foreman, Joseph Griffith, Thomas Morford, Aquila Tipton, William Tipton, Thomas Lacey, Aquila Price, Oliver Matthews, Hannah Matthews, Thomas Matthews, Jr., William Matthews, Thomas Matthews, Sr., George Matthews, Sarah Matthews, Elizabeth Bond, Rachel Price, Benjamin Price, Elextious (his "EL" mark) Lemmon, John Bond.

William Amos, Jr., of Baltimore County, son of William Amos, Sr., m. Susanna Howard, dau. of Benjamin Howard, on 1st day of 7th month, 1773, at Little Falls Meeting House. Witnesses: Tuder Cholk, Lancelot Carlile, Mathew Talbott, Benjamin Howard, Jr., John Dutton, Walter Bull, Mary Dimmet, Martha Howard, Robert Dutton, Bukler Bond, Rachel Lancaster, Rachel Amos, Stanchy[?] Lancaster, Elisabeth Harklee, David Malsby, Amos Lacey, Mary Daws, Mary Richardson, Ruth Howard, Elisabeth Smith, Sarah Bull, William Smitson, Simon Perine, John McComas, Edward Cripple, Joshua Cholk, Benkid Wilson, Alley Bond, Rachal Bull, Ellen Jarrett, Thomas Bond (of John), John Taylor, Isaac Daws, Susanna Bond, Alesanna Johns, Aquila Norris, Rebecca Bond, Greenbury Chany, Elisabeth Askew, Elisabeth Jones, Sr., Prisilla Wilson, Ann Bond, Elisabeth Beaver, Elisabeth England, Elisabeth Jones, Jr., John Malsby, William Amos, Sr., Benjamin Howard, Mary Howard, Martha Amos, Mauldon Amos, Moses McComas, Lemuel Howard, Elisabeth Norris, Eleanor Amos, Anne Howard, Mary Amos, Benjamin Amos, Edward Norris, Peter Perine, Martha Amos, Hannah Bull, Henry Wilson, William Bull.

Jacob Radd [Read?], of Baltimore County, m. Ann Peirpoint, dau. of Charles and Johannah, at Elk Ridge Meeting House on 6th day of 10th month, 1773. Witnesses: John Hayward, William Wilson, Mary Hayward,

Margaret Deavor, Elisabeth Hayward, Rachel Hayward, Elisabeth Hayward, Rebecca Hayward, Charles Peirpoint, Jr., William Hayward, John Peirpoint, Joseph Hayward, Sidney Peirpoint, Chue [Chew] Peirpoint, Bathsheba Peirpoint, Miscal Peirpoint, Jacob Scott, Charles Peirpoint, Henry Peirpoint, Joseph Peirpoint, Nicholas Gassaway, Rebecca Hayward, Rachel Gassaway, Faithfull Peirpoint, Jonas Deavor, William Hayward, Jr.

William Brown, of Harford County, son of Joseph and Hannah Brown, pf West Nottingham Township in Chester County, Pennsylvania, m. Elizabeth Lacy, dau. of Thomas and Esther Lacey, of Harford County, at Little Falls Meeting on 23d day of 2nd month, 1775. Witnesses: Rachel Bull, Sarah Bull, Elener Bull, Elizabeth Daws, Margaret Jinkins, Tabitha Thorn, Martha Amos, William Brown, David Malsbey, Mary Patrick, Robert Smith, Mary Dimmit, Jonathan Jinkins, William Jinkins, Mary Amos, William Lewin, Jas.[Jos.?] Lancaster, Ann Lacey, Deborah Wilson, Thomas Lacey, Jr., David Smith, David Lacey, Amos Lacey, Samuel Lacey, Henry Wilson, William Amos, Sr., Benjamin Howard, Isaac Daws, Jesse Lancaster, James Hicks, William Amos, Jr., Benjamin Lancaster, John Malsbey, Joseph Brown, Thomas Lacey, Esther Lacey, William Lacey, Ann Smith, Samuel Smith, Esther Lacey, Jr.

Nicholas Tipton, son of William and Anjillico Tipton, of Baltimore County, m. Esther Price, dau. of Mordecai and Mary Price, at Gunpowder Meeting House on 25th day of 5th month, 1775. Witnesses: Elizabeth Scott, Mary Powel, Ann Tipton, Rebekah Tipton, Colegate Deye Owings, Rachel Cole, Mary Cole, Ann Meryah Parish, Rachel Scott, John Belt, Thomas Price, John Cromwell, Jehu Moore, Edward Hall, Aquila Parish, Thomas Hale, Charles Stevenson, Jesse Price, Rebekah Belt, Mary Parish, Henry Cromwell, Ruth Bond, Ann Moore, Isabel Price, Mordecai Price, Joshua Tipton, Benjamin Price, John Price, Jr., Mordecai Price, Benjamin Price, Benjamin Powel, Jno. Cockey Owings, Daniel Penington, Richard Belt, John Bond, Jr., Thomas Price.

Mordecai Price, son of John and Mary Price, of Baltimore County, m. Rachel Malone, dau. of John and Edif[?] Malone, at Gunpowder Meeting House on 28th day of 9th month, 1775. Witnesses: Edward Gill, Amos Scott, Leod. Belt, Peter Mallone, John Mallone, Edward Barret, Vensent Cole, John Cole, Thomas Cromwell, R. N. Carnan, Mordecai Matthews, John Hair, Jeremiah Belt, Jr., William Matthews, Benjamin Price, Stephen Gill (of John), Cassandry Gill, Rachel Scott, Mary Ambrose, Isabel Price, Ann

Ambrose, Sarah Matthews, Catherine Gill, William Ambrose, James Bosley, Aquila Parrish, Dennis Mallone, John Mallone, John Price, Jr., Mary Carr, Rebekah Belt, Cassandry Mallone, Mordecai Price, Ann Moore, Rachel Price, Tabitha Price, Ann Parrish.

David Brown, of Baltimore Town, potter, son of Thomas Brown, deceased, and Francess Brown, of Baltimore Town, m. Elizabeth Matthews, dau. of George Matthews and wife Dorothy, deceased, at Patapsco Meeting House on 29th day of 2nd month, 1776. Witnesses: Mordecai Matthews, Elizabeth Humphreys, Natl. Humphreys, Richard Hopkins, Joseph Burgess, Margaret Buchanan, William Matthews, Daniel Matthews, Daniel Matthews (son of --), Caleb Gough, Mary Cornthwait, Mary Hollingsworth, Mary Smith, Elizabeth Cornthwait, Elizabeth Cornthwait, Jr., Catharine Ricketts, Ann Matthews, Mary Dukehart, Mary Burgess, Sidney Buchanan, Francess Brown, George Matthews, John Brown, James Brown, Oliver Matthews, Rachel Matthews, Ann Moore, John Cornthwait, Mary Brown, Jane Humphreys, Martha Davis.

John Mason, of Harford County, son of George Mason, deceased, and his wife Jane of Kennit Township in Chester County, Pennsylvania, m. Ann Howard, dau. of Benjamin Howard and his wife Sarah, deceased, of Harford County, at Little Falls Meeting House on 3rd day of 10th month, 1776. Witnesses: Isaiah Ratcliff, Joshua Chalk, Elisabeth Bond, Robert Dutton, John Dutton, Ruth Hayhurst, Jacob Bond, Jr., Jennet Patrick, David Malsby, Mary Amos, Priscilla Amos, Edward Cunnard, David Lee, Deborah Wilson, John Wilson, Jr., Rebekah Lee, Thomas Stockdale, Elisabeth Hayhurst, John Paul, Cassandra Fulton, Elisabeth Bond, Sarah Bull, Tamer Hayhurst, William Wilson, Mary Patrick, William Amos, Sr., Henry Wilson, Sr., Priscilla Wilson, Daniel Bond, Patience Bond, Martha Bond, Sarah Bond, John Malsbey, Charles Baker, Jr., Moses Dillon, Elisha Tyson, John England, Judith Cunnard, Jesse Lancaster, Benjamin Lancaster, Benjamin Howard, Mary Howard, Jane Mason, Thomas Bond, Benjamin Mason, George Mason, William Amos, Jr., Susanna Amos, Grace Mason, James Mason, Elisabeth Bond, Lemuel Howard, Benjamin Howard, Jr.

Elisha Tyson, son of Isaac and Esther Tyson, of Philadelphia County, Pennsylvania, m. Mary Amos, dau. of William Amos and his wife Hannah, deceased, of Harford County, at Little Falls Meeting House on 5th day of 11th month called November, 1776. Witnesses: B. Lancaster, Jr., Thomas Lacy, Thomas Lacey, Jr., William Lewen, Charles Herbert, William Mc-

Comas, Mary Patrick, Martha Bond, Elisabeth Gilbert, Sarah Norris, Elisabeth Norris, Mordecai Daws, John Wyle, Margaret Jinkins, Judith Cunnard, Rebekah Lee, Hannah Bull, Catherine Amos, Rachel Amos, Rebekah Parsons, Mary Lancaster, Elisabeth Bond, Mary Richardson, B. Howard, Jr., Mary Daws, Nathl. Lancaster, Jesse Lancaster, Joseph Lancaster, Thomas Stockdale, William Jinkins, Benjamin Lancaster, Jonathan Jinkins, Jacob Bull, William Hutchins, Daniel Bond, John Taylor, Jr., Thomas Ford, L. Onion, David Lee, James Amos, Jr., John Parsons, Benjamin Daws, Thomas Hutchins, Edward Parker, Thomas Norris, Hannah Fulton, Rinnis Bull, Cassandra Fulton, Buckler Bond, Benjamin Amos, Edward Cunnard, John Benire [?], William Amos, Sr., Martha Amos, Maulden Amos, William Amos, Jr., Enos Tyson, Jacob Tyson, Tacy Tyson, Moses McComas, Thomas Bond, Sr., Henry Wilson, Sr., Priscilla Wilson, Edward Norris, Margaret Wilson, B. Howard, John Taylor, Enoch Williams, Elenar Bull, Susanna Amos, Mary Dimmet, Mary Brown, Martha Norris, William Bull, Cumfort Wiley, Joseph Norris.

John Wells, of Baltimore Town, son of William and Ann Wells of Baltimore County, m. Rachel Gassaway, dau. of Nicholas and Margaret Gassaway, of Anne Arundel County, at Elk Ridge Meeting House on 29th day of 10th month, 1776. Witnesses: William Hayward, Elizabeth Hayward, Rebeckah Hayward, Rachel Hayward, Alexander Cohoon, Jacob Read, Henry Pierpoint, Jr., Benjamin Powell, Ann Pierpoint, Sidney Hayward, Molley Hayward, Joseph Pierpoint, John Hayward, Eli Pierpoint, Nicholas Gassaway, Francis Pierpoint, Joseph Pierpoint, Susanna Wells, John Pierpoint.

Thomas Stockdale, son of William Stockdale, late of Wrights Town, Bucks County, Pennsylvania, deceased, m. Mary Patrick, dau. of John Patrick, of Baltimore County, at Little Falls of Gunpowder Meeting House on 5th day of 12th month, 1776. Witnesses: Aquila Thomson, Sarah Matthews, Jesse Lancaster, Mordecai Matthews, Natl. Thomson, Tacy Tyson, Thomas Bond, Mary Tyson, Isaiah Ratcliff, James Spicer, Christn. Mutchner, William Linton, John Mason, Moses Dillon, Isaac Daws, Elizabeth Bond, William Amos, Jr., Priscilla Wilson, Benja. Howard, Mary Howard, Elizabeth Wilmoth, Rachel Bull, Sarah Mutchner, Elizabeth Thomson, Robert Smith, Ann Mason, Patience Bond, John Paul, Hannah Fitzwater, Henry Wilson, William Amos, Thomas Hughes, Elizabeth Spicer, Ann Stewart, John Malsby, David Wilson, Elizabeth Smith, Cathe. Bond, Thomas Hutchons, Elizabeth Slade, Elizabeth Hutchins, William Hutchins, John Patrick, Mary

Patrick, Abel Fitzwater, John Patrick, Jr., Jennet Patrick, Daniel Bond, Jacob Hutchins, Sarah Ryon, Ann Amos, Mary Smith, John Wilson [Jr.?], Ann Price, George Patrick.

Thomas Lacey, of Harford County, m. Elizabeth Hayhurst, of Harford County, at Little Falls of Gunpowder Meeting House on 18th day of 12th month, 1777. Witnesses: Ann Lacey, Priscilla Amos, Sarah Ryon, Rachel Bull, Abraham Bull, Sarah Bull, Sarah Willmott, James Beard, Mary Dubry [Dulery?], Mary Smith, Elizabeth Wilmott, Amos Scott, John Mason, Ann Mason, Enoch Williams, John Smith, William Briggs, Robert England, Walter Bull, William Baldw[?], Samuel Garrison, Benja. Howard, Jr., William Sharp, James Garrison, Joseph Dubry [Dulery?], William Bull, Wheeler Malsby, Jesse Lancaster, John Wiles, Esther Lacey, William Brown, James Hicks, William Amos, Jr., Aseph Warner, Isaiah Jackson, William Amos, Sr., Benjamin Howard, Catron Thomson, David Smith, Eliner Bull, Rachel Scott, Joshua Smith, Thomas Lacey, Sr., James Hayhurst, Sr., Ann Hayhurst, James Hayhurst, Jr., Samuel Lacey, Enoch Spencer, Sarah Spencer, Job Spencer, Ruth Hayhurst, Sarah Hayhurst, Elizabeth Brown.

George Matthews, of Baltimore County, son of Thomas and Sarah Matthews, both deceased, m. Sarah Nailor, dau. of John and Jane Nailor, at Gunpowder Meeting House on 3rd day of 12th month, 1777. Witnesses: Mordecai Price, Mordecai Matthews, Ann Price, Jesse Matthews, Thomas Price, Daniel Thomas, James Price, John Thomas, Elizabeth Price, Rachel Scott, Asaph Colegate, Michael Ceath, Abraham Griffith, Daniel Price, Jesse Scott, Rositer Scott, Amos Scott, Daniel Matthews, Sophia Price, Jacob Johnson, John Price, Jr., Samuel Nailor, John Belt, Mordecai Price, Rachel Matthews, Sarah Matthews, Mary Griffith, Hannah Johnson, Richard Belt, Daniel Penington, Samuel Price, William Matthews, Francis Matthews, John Nailor, Jane Mailor, Oliver Matthews, Ann Moore, John Thomas, Elizabeth Brown, David Brown, Samuel Matthews, Elizabeth Nailor, Rachel Nailor, Hannah Matthews, Ann Matthews, Elizabeth Colegate, Thomas Matthews.

Enoch Williams, of Harford County, son of William Williams of Gwynedd Township in Philadelphia County, Philadelphia, and his wife Ellenor, deceased, m. Ann Weeks, widow of Daniel Weeks, deceased, and dau. of Benjamin and Rachel Lancaster, of Harford County, at Little Falls Meeting House on 5th day of 11th month, 1778. Witnesses: Rebeckah Norrinton,

Sarah Norris, William Bull, Ann Weeks, Daniel Weels, B. Howard, Jr., Walter Bull, Mary Lancaster, William James, Amos James, Griffith Evans, Elizabeth Evans, William Jinkins, Mary Tyson, Ann Mason, Ezekiel Weeks, B. Howard, John Malsby, Benjamin Lancaster, Maulden Amos, Susanna Taylor, Mary Norris, Susanna Brown, Elizabeth Smith, Precilla Wilson, Susanna Norris, Israel Morris, Samuel Bond, William Amos, Elisha Tyson, Frances Everitt, John Bleany, Joshua Smith, William Brown, William Amos, Jr., Edward Norris, Benjamin Lancaster, Rachel Lancaster, Jesse Lancaster, Jos. Lancaster, Thomas Norris, Aquila Norris, Peter Williams, John Garrett, John Norris, David Malsby, Rachel Everit, Jonathan Jinkins, John Smith, Elizabeth Norris, Sarah Bond, Susanna Morris.

William Matthews, of Baltimore County, yeoman, son of Oliver and Hannah Matthews, m. Ann Price, widow of Aquila Price, and dau. of Isaac Griffith in the Colony of Virginia, at Gunpowder Meeting House on 3rd day of 9th month, 1774 [sic]. Witnesses: ---illh.[?] Belt, Rebeckah Belt, John Belt, Aquila Parrish, John Thomas, Daniel Matthews, Mary Ball, Stephen Price, John Nailor, Jr., David Armstrong, James Trapnall, Robert Parker, Mordecai Coale, Moses Dillon, Joshua Tipton, Robert Penrose, Rachel Coale, Rebeckah Price, Ann Price, Mary Cole, Thomas Morford, William Harvey, George Armstrong, Jr., Susanna Parrish, Elen. Humphry, William Lester, Daniel Thomas, Benjamin Price, Mordecai Parrish, William Tipton, John Bond, Jr., Aquila Tipton, Jacob Johnson, Richard Belt, Nicholas Tipton, Mary Parrish, Ann Moore, Rachel Mallonee, Mordecai Price, William Herbert, Joseph Ball, Abram. Scott, Oliver Matthews, Hannah Matthews, Thomas Matthews, Abrm. Griffith, Mary Nailor, Mary Griffith, Mary Cornthwait, Hannah Dillon, John Price, Jr., Mordecai Price, Isabel Price, Kitturah Parrish.

Aaron Dyer, son of Joseph and Joanna Dyer of Harford County, m. Elizabeth Dawes, dau. of Isaac and Mary Dawes of Harford County, at Little Falls Meeting House on 29th day of 4th month, 1779. Witnesses: Thomas Norris, Benjamin Dawes. Judith Cunard, B. Howard, Amos Scott, B. Howard, Jr., William Brown, William Amos, Enoch Williams, Israel Williams, William Amos, Jr., Jesse Lancaster, Joseph Lancaster, Joshua Smith, Samuel Howell, Francis[?] Frazer[illegible?], Prisa. Wilson, Mary Patrick, Sarah Bull, Elizabeth Smith, Sarah Bond, Mary Smith, Ann Bond, Ann Mason, Ann Lacey, Aseth. Billingslea, Mordecai Dawes, Rachel Bull, Sarah Billingslea, Edward Cunard, William Bull[illegible?], Isaac Dawes, Joseph

Dyer, Mary Daws, Joanna Dyer, Rachel Scott, David Gallaway, Susanna Gallaway, Phebe Dyer, John Dyer, Mary Dyer, Elizabeth Dyer, John Mason, Henry Wilson.

ABSTRACTS OF GUNPOWDER MONTHLY MEETING MINUTES, 1767-1796

Daniel Penington presented a certificate from Buckingham Monthly Meeting in Pennsylvania, dated 5th day of 10th month, 1767, with his wife Martha and children, Israel, Amos, Elizabeth and Harris[?], and they were received.

Reported on 24th day of 2nd month, 1768, that Rachel Parish, formerly Carr, "is married unto her cousin by a priest."

David Humphrey charged on 23rd day of 3rd month, 1768, with "drinking to excess and being concerned in a lottery."

Isabel Price asked forgiveness on 23rd day of 3rd month, 1768, for going with her sister to see her married by a priest.

Peter Miles was disowned on 23rd day of 6th month, 1768, for "severely whipping a neighbor woman while in a rage."

Elizabeth Carr was disowned on 29th day of 7th month, 1768, for "accompanying her brother to his marriage contrary to the good order of Friends and having a bastard child, to her, and Friends dishonor."

John Cornthwaite presented a certificate from Philadelphia Monthly Meeting, dated 20th day of 8th month, 1768, and he was received.

On 28th day of 9th month, 1768, Aquila Carr was charged with selling a negro. Benjamin Bowen, Jr. was charged with horse racing and dancing.

Reported on 26th day of 10th month, 1768, that George Mason and family were about to remove to New Garden Monthly Meeting in Pennsylvania.

On 23rd day of 11th month, 1768, George Matthews requested a certificate for his sons William and Samuel Matthews to East Nottingham Monthly Meeting, as William is with Benjamin Chandly, and Samuel with Joseph Hains, within the verge of said meeting.

Thomas Lacy and wife attended a meeting on 23rd day of 11th month, 1768, and presented a certificate from Buckingham Monthly Meeting in Pennsylvania, for themselves and their children, Thomas, Samuel, William, Elizabeth, David, Ann, Esther, Ephraim and Ralph, and they were received.

Reported on 22nd day of 2nd month, 1769, that Michael Hough had removed within the verge of Warrington Monthly Meeting in Pennsylvania, and has requested a certificate.

On 11th day of 2nd month, 1769, Sophia Coale was charged with "disorderly walking."

On 24th day of 5th month, 1769, Isaac Griffith presented a certificate from Richland Monthly Meeting for himself and his wife Anne and their children, Abraham, Hannah, Mary, Ann, Sarah, Joseph, Martha, Elizabeth, Isaac, John and James, and they were received into membership.

On 20th day of 6th month, 1769, Oliver Matthews reported that he was about to place his son William Matthews to James Gillingham of the City of Philadelphia to learn the business of cabinetmaker, and requested a certificate.

William Moore, Jr. was charged with frequent dancing, and was disowned "until he comes to a sense of his errors."

On 26th day of 7th month, 1769, Paul Penington was received by a certificate from Middletown Monthly Meeting in Pennsylvania, and Francis Matthews, son of Daniel, was received by a certificate from Fairfax Monthly Meeting.

On 23rd day of 8th month, 1769, Rachel Hooker (formerly Comley), dau. of James and Mary Comley, was charged with "being married outside of the society by a priest."

On 27th day of 12th month, 1769, Jacob Comley was disowned for "marrying contrary to the approved rule for Friends."

On 24th day of 1st month, 1770, Mary Hopkins (formerly Wilson) was charged with marrying outside the society. Leah Gill (formerly Price) was charged for "going out in marriage contrary to rules."

On 28th day of 3rd month, 1770, John Browne was charged with being married by a priest. Priscilla Worthington, wife of John Worthington, requested a certificate to Deer Creek Monthly Meeting since she had settled within their verge.

On 24th day of 4th month, 1770, Mary Patrick was received into membership by a certificate from Buckingham Monthly Meeting in Bucks County, Pennsylvania. James Spicer and wife Rachel and their children, Sarah, James, Ann, Yeaman, Gulim, Uriah and John, were received into membership by a certificate from Rightstown Monthly Meeting in Bucks County, Pennsylvania.

On 23rd day of 5th month, 1770, George Matthews was disowned "for frequenting taverns, drinking to excess, gaming, fighting, and dancing, evil practices inconsistent with the society's principles." John Paul attended the meeting with a certificate from Richland Monthly Meeting in Pennsylvania.

On 27th day of 6th month, 1770, Croasdale Warner and wife Mary and six of their children, Hannah, Mary, Aaron, Amos, Croasdale, and Sarah, were received into membership by a certificate from Wrights Town Monthly Meeting in Pennsylvania. Edward Talbott was disowned for "excessive drinking, unsavory language, fighting, allowing of music, and dancing." Maulden Amos, son of William Amos, was charged with "outgoing in marriage by a priest." Hannah Tanner (before marriage Scott) reportedly had been "before a magistrate and made oath that she was with child by George Tannner, and since was married to said Tanner by a priest." Robert Smith and wife Elizabeth were received into membership by a certificate from Buckingham Monthly Meeting in Pennsylvania. Henry Wilson, Jr. was received from the Philadelphia Monthly Meeting.

On 22nd day of 8th month, 1770, Margaret Pritchert was condemned for outgoing in marriage.

On 26th day of 9th month, 1770, Margaret McKey (before marriage Dunkin) was reportedly married by a priest.

"Ancient Friend" Hannah Griffith, a minister in unity with Friends, attended the meeting with a certificate from the Richland Monthly Meeting in Pennsylvania, dated 16th day of 8th month, 1770.

John Wilson attended a meeting with a certificate from East Nottingham Monthly Meeting, dated 20th day of 7th month, 1770.

On 23rd day of 11th month, 1770, Benkid Wilson was appointed overseer of Little Falls Meeting in the room of Robert Dutton, deceased. Elizabeth Wheeler (before marriage Dutton) had reportedly gone out in marriage.

On 26th day of 12th month, 1770, Susanna Bond, dau. of John Bond, was charged with "dancing and frequenting places of vain diversion."

On 23rd day of 1st month, 1771, Margaret Dukehart was condemned for going out in marriage. Nicholas Gassaway was found guilty of banishing a negro to the West Indies. Joseph Howard and wife Rebecca and children,

Rachel, William, Hannah and Mary, were received by a certificate from Deer Creek Monthly Meeting, dated 2nd day of 8th month, 1770.

On 28th day of 2nd month, 1771, Elizabeth Polton (before marriage Dyer) and Margaret Hunt (before marriage Hopkins) had reportedly gone out in marriage. Samuel Price (son of Thomas) was charged with "drinking to excess, using unsavory language, and differing with one of his neighbors."

On 27th day of 3rd month, 1771, Samuel Harris produced a certificate from West River Monthly Meeting and his father's consent to his marrying Rachel Wilson. Joseph England produced a certificate from New Garden Monthly Meeting in Chester County, Pennsylvania, dated 3rd day of 11th month, 1770. John Wilson (joiner) requested a certificate to Nottingham Monthly Meeting so he could join in marriage to a Friend of that meeting. Rachel Lancaster, wife of Benjamin Lancaster, and four of her children, Jesse, Joseph, Benjamin and Nathan, were received into membership by a certificate from Deer Creek Monthly Meeting, dated 29th day of [no month given], 1770.

On 24th day of 4th month, 1771, George Choake reportedly "went out in marriage with a woman of another society."

On 22nd day of 5th month, 1771, William Bull and wife Sarah and their children, John and William, having been under the care of Little Falls Preparative Meeting, were received into membership at Gunpowder Monthly Meeting.

On 27th day of 6th month, 1771, Nicholas Gassaway was charged with "giving orders to shoot one of his negroes on the legs....and banishing a negro to the West Indies." David Scholfield and wife Rachel and their children, Samuel, John, Enoch and Benjamin, were received into membership by a certificate from Deer Creek Monthly Meeting. Edward Cunnard and Judith Hurst were received into membership by certificates from Rights Town Monthly Meeting in Bucks County, Pennsylvania. Greenberry Bosley was charged with "neglecting meetings, going to places of diversion, and disusing the plain language." Ann Pierpoint "guilty of having a child before marriage."

On 24th day of 7th month, 1771, Aquila Carr was disowned for "falling into the evil practice of selling negroes, upon which his public testimony as a minister became burdensome to Friends." Jane Cross (before marriage Dunkin) charged with "having gone out in marriage with a man of another society."

On 25th day of 8th month, 1771, a certificate was produced for Elizabeth Matthews and directed to the Fairfax Monthly Meeting in Virginia.

On 23rd day of 10th month, 1771, Jacob Linton received into membership by a certificate from Rights Town Monthly Meeting in Bucks County, Pennsylvania.

On 27th day of 11th month, William Tipton reported that when "his family had been taken into membership the name of his daughter Tabitha Tipton had been omitted from the records." Our Friend Zachariah Pharris attended this meeting with a certificate from Wilmington Monthly Meeting, dated 11th day of 9th month, 1770. William Brown (son of Joseph) attended this meeting with a certificate from Nottingham Monthly Meeting, dated 5th day of 10th month, 1771.

On 25th day of 12th month, 1771, Rachel Cole (daughter of Thomas Cole) was charged with "infrequently attending church and meetings, and dancing." Elizabeth Norris (before marriage Amos) and Hannah Miles (before marriage Thomson) were charged with marrying outside the society.

On 22nd day of 1st month, 1772, James Dunkin was charged with being married by a priest, and Rebecca Murray (before marriage Colegate) was also charged with that violation.

On 26th day of 2nd month, 1772, John Nailor, Jr. and wife Mary were charged with "having a child born too soon after marriage." Thomas and William Bond (sons of John) were charged with going out in marriage contrary to the order. Abraham Scott [Scotten?] and wife Elizabeth and children, Rachel, Amos, Jesse, Roserter[?], Heather and Thomas, were received into membership by certificate from Rights Town Monthly Meeting.

On 25th day of 3rd month, 1772, Benjamin Price (son of John) charged with "dancing and frequenting places of diversion." Elizabeth Colegate was received into membership by a certificate from Wilmington Monthly Meeting. Samuel Day reportedly "guilty of taking of oaths."

On 22nd day of 4th month, 1772, Annmariah Parish admitted she was "guilty of the evil practice of dancing and for attending marriages contrary to the discipline of Friends, and she hoped to be more careful for the time to come." Lucy Belt, daughter of John and Milcah Belt, charged with having "sworn a child to a man and have got one unmarried." Robert Foreman requested a certificate for himself, wife and children to go to Gwynded Monthly Meeting in Pennsylvania. Nicholas Tucker requested a certificate to go to Fairfax Monthly Meeting in Virginia. A deed of conveyance was obtained for one acre of land for the use of Friends of Gunpowder Meeting House and Graveyard, and recorded by Oliver Matthews. Benjamin Brown received into membership by a certificate from Nottingham Monthly Meeting, dated 29th day of 2nd month, 1772.

On 27th day of 5th month, 1772, Edward Cunnard and Judith Hurst, with his[her?] mother's consent, declared their intention to marry. Sarah Hopkins made a request to this meeting for "some lines for her son Richard Hopkins by way of certificate to Philadelphia Monthly Meeting." Benjamin Howard appointed overseer in stead of Henry Wilson.

On 24th day of 6th month, 1772, Rachel Colegate was charged with "under dealing for some time." William Matthews was received into membership by certificate from Philadelphia Monthly Meeting, dated --[?] day of 4th month, 1777.

On 23rd day of 9th month, 1772, John Moore (son of Walter) charged with "leaving his wife and children, and we have great reason to think he intends to take a young woman with him on a private and scandalous manner."

On 25th day of 11th month, 1772, Ura[?] Butler (before marriage Burgess) charged with marriage outside the society. Sarah Griffith charged with "keeping unseeming company with a married man of her neighborhood."

On 23rd day of 12th month, 1772, Rebecka Pitts (before marriage Price) charged with having "gone out in marriage to a man of another society."

On 27th day of 1st month, 1773, Sarah Ryan (before marriage Spicer) charged with having gone out in marriage. Certificate given to Elizabeth Colegate to go to East Caln Monthly Meeting in Chester County, Pennsylvania.

On 24th day of 2nd month, 1773, agreed to build a meeting house on this place, 40 feet by 30 feet, with convenient galleries, with good cedar roof of three feet shingles, and Abraham Scott, Jacob Johnson, Aquila Price, and Oliver Matthews appointed to have the said house built."

On 28th day of 4th month, 1773, David Moore (son of John) charged with "frequenting places of diversion." Hannah Johns charged with "dancing and attending with her children places of vain diversion." John Cornthwait appointed overseer of the Patapsco Meeting. Crosdale Warner requested a certificate to Deer Creek Monthly Meeting for himself, wife and children, Hannah, Mary, Aaron, Amos, Crosedale, Sarah and Agness.

On 26th day of 5th month, 1773, William Amos, Jr. and Susanna Howard declared their intention to marry. Certificate produced for John Moore, his wife and five children to go to Pipe Creek Monthly Meeting.

On --[?] day of 6th month, 1773, Robert Humphreys charged with "drinking to excess." Certificate from Herring Creek Monthly Meeting produced for Margaret Wilson, wife of Henry Wilson, Jr., recommending her as a member in unity, and was received.

On 23rd day of 8th month, 1773, Jacob Red received into membership by a certificate from Kennet Monthly Meeting in Pennsylvania. Jacob Red and Ann Pierpoint declared their intention to marry.

On 22nd day of 9th month, 1773, Samson Kirk reportedly "appeared some time ago with a certificate from Nottingham Monthly Meeting, dated 30th day of 5th month, 1772, but is not received because he had since been married by a priest."

On 27th day of 10th month, 1773, Henry Cunnard (son of Henry) was received into membership by a certificate from Abington Monthly Meeting in Pennsylvania, dated 31st day of 5th month, 1773. Josiah Dyer requested a certificate for himself, his wife Hester[?] and daughters, Phebe Moore (wife of John Moore) and Rachel Dyer, to go to Buckingham Monthly Meeting in Bucks County, Pennsylvania.

On 24th day of 11th month, 1773, Peter Perine charged with "having sold a negro contrary to the discipline of Friends." Isaac Griffith reportedly "married outside the good order."

On 22nd day of 12th month, 1773, Joseph Shaw charged with "drinking, gaming, and using unsavory language."

On 25th day of 5th month, 1774, Eleanor Bull (before marriage Amos) reportedly married by a priest. Jaminna Grilse[?] (formerly Ball) also married by a priest. Enoch Spencer and wife Sarah and children, Hannah and Mahlon, were received into membership by a certificate from Abington Monthly Meeting, dated 25th of 1st month, 1773. Job Spencer was also received by a certificate dated 31st day of 5th month, 1773, from Abington Monthly Meeting. Certificate was produced for Josiah Dyer, his wife, two daughters, and Phebe Moore's children, directed to Buckingham Monthly Meeting in Bucks County, Pennsylvania.

On 22nd day of 6th month, 1774, Samuel Fisher and wife Margaret and children Ruth, Unice, Samuel, Josiah and Joseph, were received into membership by a certificate from Buckingham Monthly Meeting in Pennsylvania. Johns Hopkins presented a certificate from Philadelphia Monthly Meeting, dated 28th day of 1st month, 1774, and was received into membership.

On 27th day of 7th month, 1774, Benjamin Brown reportedly "hath taken the oath, and hath a child laid to his charge by a young woman."

On 23rd day of 11th month, 1774, Tacy Tyson was received into membership by a certificate from Abington Monthly Meeting, dated 29th day of 9th month, 1774.

On 25th day of 1st month, 1775, William Brown and Elizabeth Lacy declared their intention to marry.

On 6th day of 4th month, 1775, Nicholas Tipton and Esther Price declared their intention to marry. Johns Hopkins requested a certificate to West[?] River Monthly Meeting "in order for marriage to a woman of that meeting." Philip Hopkins charged with marrying a woman outside of the society. Joseph Burgess [of Baltimore Town] and wife Deborah and children, Elizabeth, Jonathan, Tacey, Jesse, Thomas, Sarah, Martha, John, Daniel, Leticia, Joseph and Grace, were received into membership by a certificate from Buckingham Monthly Meeting in Pennsylvania. Joseph Kall [Ball?] and wife Mary were received into membership by a certificate from Richland Monthly Meeting. John Tyson was received into membership by a certificate from Abington Monthly Meeting.

On 28th day of 6th month, 1775, Samuel Price (son of John) charged with "evil practice of drunkness and making use of much unsavory language." Benkid Wilson excused from being overseer and Henry Wilson was appointed in his stead. Elizabeth Adair (formerly Wilson) reportedly married contrary to the good order.

On 26th day of 7th month, 1775, Mary Patrick, Jr., for some time under the care of Little Falls Preparative Meeting, was received into membership at Gunpowder Monthly Meeting. Sarah Bull was appointed an Elder to Little Falls Monthly Meeting, and Jane Nailor an Elder to Gunpowder Meeting.

On 27th[?] day of 8th month, 1775, George Matthews requested certificates for his two daughters, Mary Matthews at New Garden Monthly Meeting in Chester County, Pennsylvania, and Dorothy Matthews at Sadsbury Monthly Meeting in same county. Jacob Tyson was received into membership by a certificate from Abington Monthly Meeting, dated 20th day of 3rd month, 1775. William Briggs was received into membership by a certificate from Wrights Town Monthly Meeting. A collection of 109 pounds and 19 shillings was provided by Friends of Gunpowder Monthly Meeting in Baltimore County, Maryland, "for the unhappy sufferers of Massachusetts Bay and other parts of New England, and put in the hands of John Cornthwait to forward to John Reynolds of Philadelphia, who was appointed by the Meeting of Sufferings to superintend and distribute it in accordance with the Rhode Island Quarterly Meeting."

On 27th day of 9th month, 1775, Thomas Matthews and Ann Humphries declared their intention to marry. Mordecai Parrish and Rachel Malloney declared their intention to marry. Stephen Moore charged with being married by a priest. Nathan Tyson presented a certificate from Abington Monthly Meeting, dated 28th day of 3rd month, 1775, and was received. Jesse Trump presented a certificate from Abington Monthly Meeting, dated 28th day of 8th month, 1775, and was received.

On 25th day of 10th month, 1775, Mary Ambrose (formerly Parrish) reportedly married by a priest.

On 22nd day of 11th month, 1775, Joseph Ball charged with "drinking to excess and disorderly conduct in his family." Mary Ball "found guilty of adultery" and Elizabeth Spicer "hath had a base born child." Mordecai Cole charged with "the practice of using unsavory language and frequenting places of diversion."

On 30th day of 12th month, 1775, William Matthews (son of George) presented a certificate from Nottingham Monthly Meeting, dated 26th day of 8th month, 1775, and was received. Isaac Griffith requested a certificate for himself and daughter Martha Griffith to Fairfax Monthly Meeting in Virginia. Sarah Linton requested a certificate for herself and children to Wrights Town Monthly Meeting in Bucks County, Pennsylvania.

On 27th day of 1st month, 1776, David Brown and Elizabeth Matthews declared their intention to marry. John Wells presented a certificate from Philadelphia Monthly Meeting and was received into membership. John Comley charged with "going out in marriage with a young woman of a different persuasion." William Bull appointed an Elder of the Little Falls Preparative Meeting.

On 24th day of 2nd month, 1776, Daniel Matthews and Martha Davis declared their intention to marry. Elizabeth Bowen reportedly had gone out in marriage.

On 30th day of 3rd month, 1776, John Colegate, Jr. "hath taken up arms and joined with the military." Joseph Ball requested a certificate to Richland Monthly Meeting in Bucks County, Pennsylvania. James Hicks appointed overseer in stead of William Bull. Thomas Hughs presented a certificate from Buckingham Monthly Meeting, dated 3rd day of 7th month, 1775, and was received. Henry Wilson, Jr. reportedly "continues to be active in the military preparations."

On 27th day of 4th month, 1776, a donation of 9 pounds, 5 shillings and 2 pence was made to Rachel Floyd "due to her necessity....and purchased a horse and corn for her" the following month. John Mason presented a certificate from New Garden Monthly Meeting in Chester County, Pennsylvania, dated 6th day of 4th month, 1776, and was received. Jesse Trump requested a certificate to Buckingham Monthly Meeting. David Brown requested a certificate for himself and wife Elizabeth Brown to Pipe Creek Monthly Meeting.

On 25th day of 5th month, 1776, Mary Choake was charged with "misconduct." Gittings Wilson "still persists in the practice of acting in the militia." Elizabeth Galloway (formerly Bowen) "hath so far erred as to consummate her marriage contrary to the rules of our discipline."

On 29th day of 6th month, 1776, Henry Wilson, Jr. continued "being concerned and active in military imployments" and was disowned "until he comes to reform for his outgoing." Johnkid Wilson "hath been and continues to join and practice in the military operations." David Moore reportedly gone out in marriage to a woman of our society.

On 27th day of 7th month, 1776, Gittings Wilson "hath fallen in with the practice of the times in bearing arms and learning war contrary to out disciplines" was disowned "until he condemns his misconduct to our satisfaction." Rachel Nailor presented a certificate from Gwyned Monthly Meeting in Pennsylvania, dated 28th day of 5th month, 1776, and was received into membership. David Wilson presented a certificate from Hopewell Monthly Meeting in Virginia, dated 3rd day of 6th month, 1776, and was received into membership. Isaiah Ratcliff presented a certificate from Abington Monthly Meeting in Pennsylvania, dated 27th day of 5th month, 1776, and was received into membership. James Parr had been under the oversight and care of Little Falls Preparative Meeting and was taken into membership at Gunpowder Monthly Meeting. James Spicer requested a certificate for his son Yeaman Spicer (a minor) to be directed to Middle Town Monthly Meeting in Pennsylvania. William Amos, Jr. was appointed overseer in stead of Henry Wilson, Jr. William Davis had been under the care of Patapsco Preparative Meeting with his two children, Joseph and William, and they were received into membership at Gunpowder Monthly Meeting.

On 31st day of 8th month, 1776, John Mason and Ann Howard declared their intention to marry. David Moore (son of William) reportedly "married by a priest to a woman of our religious society." John Ward "hath joined in learning the art of war and neglects the attendance of our religious meetings." Joseph Burgess requested a certificate for himself, wife and children to Deer Creek Monthly Meeting. Abraham Hough "hath joined himself in learning the art of war." John Green requested to be separated from Friends, and was subsequently disowned. Jesse Lancaster reportedly "hath gone out in marriage with a woman not in membership with Friends." Charles Pierpoint, Jr. "hath enlisted as a soldier."

On 28th day of 9th month, 1776, Elisha Tyson and Mary Amos declared their intention to marry. John Wells and Rachel Gassaway declared their intention to marry. Joseph Lancaster was charged with "attending a marriage consummated contrary to our discipline." Edward Connard "hath paid his fine for not mustering." Nathan Bond "hath some time been active in warlike preparations and is now enlisted in the Army." Rachel Floyd and her daughter Ana Floyd "hath gone out in marriage with men not of our society." Enoch Williams presented a certificate from Gwyned Monthly Meeting, dated 17th of 9th month, 1776, and was received into membership.

On 26th day of 10th month, 1776, Thomas Stockdale and Mary Patrick declared their intention to marry. Rachel Ward (wife of John Ward) "hath taken the oath."

On 30th day of 11th month 1776, Thomas Stockdale produced his mother's consent to marry, and a certificate from Abington Monthly Meeting. Job Spencer "hath enlisted in the military." Hannah Perine reportedly "hath gone out in marriage with a man of our society." Gerrard Hopkins (son of Samuel) charged with "fornication and being married by a priest."

On 28th day of 12th month, 1776, Benkid Wilson "offered a paper to this meeting to condemn his passing a fine for not bearing arms." Rachel Gash (late Floyd) and Ann Johnson (formerly Floyd) "hath gone out in marriage to men not of our society." Philip Hopkins manumitted his negro woman named Grace, William Parrish manumitted his negro man named Richard, and Mary Bowen manumitted her negro man named Simon. Hannah Stewart (formerly Perine) found "guilty of marrying outside the order." Amelia Moore (formerly Bond) "hath gone out in marriage with a man not of our society."

On 25th day of 1st month, 1777, Amos Ball "hath joined the military preparations." George Matthews was appointed an overseer for the Patapsco Meeting. Received "manumissions for 3 negro men, 5 negro women, and one mulatto woman, 5 boys and 6 girls under age to be free when lawful age, and 13 manumissions by Benjamin Howard, and 7 manunmitted by William Amos, Jr."

On 22nd day of 2nd month, 1777, Gerard Hopkins (son of Richard) reportedly "employed in diverse warlike preparations."

On 29th day of 3rd month, 1777, Richard Hooker and his children charged with "neglecting the attendance of our religious meetings and many or all of his children's conduct are in many instances not agreeable to Friends." Received "manumissions from Samuel Price for 4 negro men and one negro woman, Anthony, John, Thomas, Corsey, and Hannah, with one boy named Abraham when he arrives at the years of 21, and a girl named Hannah when she at the age of 18."

On 25th day of 4th month, 1777, David Lacey found guilty of "passing money bills altered from a small sum to a larger in order to defraud the publick," and was disowned. Received certificates from Warrington Monthly Meeting for Catherine Rissett, wife of Nicholas Rissitt, dated 7th day of 12th month, 1776, and one dated 9th day of 11th month, 1776, for her daughter Rachel Rissitt. Robert Merrick and wife Ruth and their children, Anne, James, Elizabeth, Robert and George, presented a certificate from Bush River Monthly Meeting in South Carolina, dated 31st day of 8th month, 1776, and were received into membership. Received manumission of Rachel Matthews for her negro woman Rachel. Robert Smith requested a certificate for himself and wife and four children to go to Buckingham Monthly Meeting in Pennsylvania. John Wilson requested to be excused from being an Elder, and it was granted. The following Friends were deemed to be suffering and were granted monies: Gabriel Vanhorn, Joseph Scott, Jacob Read, John Pierpoint, William Hayward, Joshua Smith, Aquila Thompson, Daniel Malsby, John Wilson, James Hicks, William Amos, Jr., Thomas Stockdale, James Parr, Benjamin Howard, John Hair, David Penington, and William Brown.

On 31st day of 5th month, 1777, John Ward was charged with "having joined in the military preparations, and his wife Rachel having taken the oath in open court." Francis Matthews attended this meeting with a certificate from Pipe Creek Monthly Meeting, dated 17th day of 4th month, 1777, and was received. Robert Cornthwait attended with a certificate from Nottingham Monthly Meeting for himself and his wife Grace, dated 26th day of 4th month, 1777. Jane Cates (formerly Nailor) "hath gone out in marriage to a man not of our society." Sarah Hopkins requested a certificate for her two sons, William and James, to Philadelphia Monthly Meeting. Samuel Hopkins and wife "hath resided within the verge of this meeting for some time past....and hath approved Samuel Hopkins' ministry."

On 28th day of 6th month, 1777, Aquila Hooker (son of Richard) has "joined in learning war." Elizabeth Cornthwait presented a certificate from Nottingham Monthly Meeting, dated 26th day of 4th month, 1777, and was received.

On 26th day of 7th month, 1777, Job Spencer condemned his own actions whereby he "enlisted as a soldier in the present time of commotion." Daniel Penington requested to be excused as overseer and Samuel Price (son of Mordecai) was appointed in his stead. John Malsby and wife Lydia and children, Susanna, Ann, William and Sarah, presented a certificate from Warrington Monthly Meeting, dated 10th day of 5th month, 1777, and were received. Ann Weeks presented a certificate from Deer Creek Monthly Meeting, dated 3rd day of 7th month, 1777, and was received. On 30th day of 8th month, 1777, James Mason presented a certificate from New Garden Monthly Meeting, dated 5th day of 7th month, 1777, and was received. Mordecai Price (son of Mordecai Price) manumitted 8 slaves. Stephen Roberts charged with being "guilty of playing cards."

On 27th day of 9th month, 1777, Francis Matthews and Mary Carr declared their intention to marry. Sarah Ryon condemned her own actions when she "consummated her marriage with one not of our society before an hireling minister." Sarah Bond and her children, William Bond, Sarah Bond and John Churchman Bond, presented a certificate from the Southern District of

Phildelphia, dated 25th day of 6th month, 1777, and were received. Abigail Connard presented a certificate from Abington Monthly Meeting, dated 26th day of 5th month, 1777, and was received.

On 25th day of 10th month, 1777, George Matthews and Sarah Nailor declared their intention to marry. Thomas Hughs requested "a few lines by way of a certificate to Fairfax Monthly Meeting in Virginia." Thomas Lacy and Elizabeth Hayhurst declared their intention to marry. George Matthews stated "he has a desire to travel through some parts of North Carolina and Virginia in order to see some of his relations and Friends in those parts, and desires a few lines from Friends of this meeting." Rachel Naylor presented a certificate from Nottingham Monthly Meeting, dated 11th day of 10th month, 1777.

On 27th day of 12th month, 1777, Charles Peirpoint "manumitted 8 slaves: Samuel, Boson Clark, with Priscilla and two children now born, also 3 minors, Esther, Samuel and Phebe, to be free when at the age of 18 years old the females and the boy at 21 years of age." Amos Ball reportedly "gone out in marriage with a woman not of our society." Isaiah Ratcliff charged with "the practice of horse racing and laying wages." Jacob Scott and Joseph Scott, and their wives and children, requested certificates to Fairfax Monthly Meeting.

On 31st day of 1st month, 1778, Leven Hill Hopkins presented a certificate from Deer Creek Monthly Meeting, dated 4th day of 12th month, 1777, and was received. Judith Ellicot and her children, David, Ann, Joseph, Latitia, Rachel, Benjamin and Mary, presented a certificate from Buckingham Monthly Meeting, dated 1st day of 9th month, 1777, and were received.

On 28th day of 2nd month, 1778, a certificate for Joseph Scott and his wife Ann and six children, and for Jacob Scott and his wife Elizabeth and their six children, was produced to go to Fairfax Monthly Meeting in Virginia. A certificate was produced for friend Ann Moore to visit some meetings in Pennsylvania and New York. Reported that William Slade and Henry Wilson, Sr. "hath taken a test which contains principles inconsistent with our peaceable religious profession." David Malsby requested a certificate to Deer Creek Monthly Meeting "in order to join in membership therewith."

On 28th day of 3rd month, 1778, Samuel Naylor had reportedly "fallen into the practice of laying wages on horse races, and foot races, and also paying a fine for not bearing arms." Daniel Matthews presented a certificate from Fairfax Monthly Meeting, dated 24th day of 5th month, 1777, and was received. Reported that John Paul and Benkid Wilson "hath taken a test which contains principles inconsistent with our religious peaceable profession."

On 25th day of 4th month, 1778, Daniel Treadway "hath taken a test containing principles inconsistent with our religious peaceable profession." John Mason appointed overseer in room of Henry Wilson, Sr. Richard Hopkins, Jr. and wife presented a certificate from Philadelphia Monthly Meeting, dated 31st day of 10th month, 1777, and were received.

On 30th day of 5th month, 1778, our Friend John Lloyd attended this meeting with a few lines from Gwynede Monthly Meeting. Enos Rogers and wife Margaret and children, John, Mordecai, Enos, Lewis, Sarah and Rachel, presented a certificate from Warrington Monthly Meeting, dated 11th day of 4th month, 1778, and were received. Reported that Rebecca Belt (now Tipton) had gone out in marriage with a person not of our society. David Lee requested to be joined in membership and was received. Johns Hopkins, Jr. "hath sold or disposed of two negroes, a girl and a boy, the girl till she is 24 years of age and the boy until 30 years of age, and also at the same time requested a certificate to West River Monthly Meeting." Received "manumissions for five slaves, Jacob, and Tamer, Margaret, John and Fanney, minors, when the girls arrive at 18 years of age and the boys at 21 years of age."

On 27th day of 6th month, 1778, Margaret Hunt charged with outgoing in marriage. Gerrard Hopkins (son of Samuel) requested to be reinstated into membership.

On 25th day of 7th month, 1778, Rebeckah Tipton (before marriage Belt) was "condemned for having her marriage solemnized by a priest." Ann Wicks [Weeks?] requested that her children (all minors), John Lancaster, Rachel, Matthew, Lydia and Benjamin, be received into membership, and they were. Moses Dillon also requested membership. Leven Hill Hopkins requested to join Deer Creek Monthly Meeting. Jane Berry and four of ther children presented a certificate to this meeting, but "some of her children having taken undue liberties, the matter will first be looked into by writing to the Haverford Monthly Meeting." Eleven slaves were reported manumitted. Jane Naylor asked to be released from being an Elder, and it was granted.

On --[?] day of 5th month, 1779, Richard Hopkins, Jr. requested a certificate for himself, wife and child to Philadelphia Monthly Meeting.

On 25th day of 6th month, 1779, P---[?] Moore attended this meeting with a certificate from Rights Town Monthly Meeting, dated 1st day of 3rd month, 1779. Robert Dutton charged with "having an unlawful child." On --[?] day of 9th month, 1779, a certificate for Rachel Shaw and her children, George, David, Samuel, and Ann, was produced. Sarah Bond requested to be joined in membership with Friends.

On 3rd day of 10th month, 1779, John Peirpoint (son of Charles) was charged "guilty of fighting, drinking to excess, using profain language, and neglecting to attend our religious meetings."

On 25th day of 12th month, William Pillar presented a certificate from ----[?] Monthly Meeting held near Charlesmont in the Kingdom of Ireland, and was received.

On 29th day of 1st month, 1780, James Mason and Rachel Scott declared their intention to marry. Cassandra Stump (formerly Wilson) charged with misconduct. John Price, Sr. and Joseph Burgess were charged with neglecting attendance at religious meetings. Our esteemed Friend Samuel Emlin visited from the Northern District of Philadelphia with a certificate dated 23rd day of 11th month, 1779.

On 29th day of 4th month, 1780, James Mason requested a certificate to New Garden Monthly Meeting.

On --[?] day of 6th month 1780, a certificate was produced "for Elias Ellicot, dated 6th day of 3rd month, 1780, at Buckingham, who hath settled within the verge of Elk Ridge Meeting, we therefore appoint David Brown to forward it to Indian Spring Monthly Meeting." Job Spencer requested a certificate to Abington Monthly Meeting.

On 29th day of 7th month, 1780, Joseph Hopkins (son of Samuel) charged with marrying a woman not of our society. Elenor Evans presented a certificate from Warrington Monthly Meeting, dated 13th day of 5th month, 1752[?]. George Hussey presented a certificate from Warrington Monthly Meeting, dated 8th day of 4th month, 1780.

On --[?] day of 8th month, 1780, Elizabeth Griffith was charged with "having lately married out from among us by a priest."

On 25th day of 11th month, 1780, a certificate was produced for Robert Merrick and his children, Anna, Jason and Robert, "having found nothing to hinder his having it." Thomas West produced a certificate for himself, his wife and children, Enos and Stacey, dated at Wrights Town Monthly Meeting in Bucks County, Pennsylvania, on 15th day of 11th month, 1780. George Jewel produced the same for his wife, Mary, and children, Alice and Mary. On 31st day of 12th month, 1780, John Ellicott was charged with "bearing of warlike weapons for the defense of himself and his property, and likewise he hath taken the test, and been married by a priest." William James charged with being "married by a priest to a woman not of our society." Certificate produced for Tue[?] Deaver and her children, Misael, Jonah and Margaret, from Fairfax Monthly Meeting, dated 27th day of 7th month, 1781[sic]. Misael Deaver reportedly "married from amongst us." Clerk forwarded the names of Bazel Deaver, Tue[?] Deaver, Jonah Deaver, and Margaret Deaver, to join Indian Spring Monthly Meeting. Friends of Patapsco have requested leave to remove their meeting to their new meeting house in Baltimore Town. Isaac Daws accused of having "detained part of the property of John Rees in an unfriendly manner."

On 27th day of 1st month, 1781, Jacob Tyson "hath gone so far astray as to have a child laid to his charge which he doth not deny." Mary Jones (formerly Burgess) charged with "marrying a man not in membership, and by a priest." David Galloway requested to be joined in membership, having for a long time been under the care of Little Falls Preparative Meeting. Susannah Galloway presented a certificate from Pipe Creek Monthly Meeting, dated 18th day of 1st month, 1781. Abel Spencer and wife Rebeckah and child Elizabeth presented a certificate from Abington Monthly Meeting, dated 31st day of 7th month, 1780. "A few lines by way of certificate was forwarded to this meeting for Abigail Moor to Friends of Pipe Creek Monthly Meeting," which were forwarded to them by William Parrish.

On 24th day of 2nd month, 1781, George Hussey found "guilty of committing fornication with Rachel Hayward, unto whom he is since married by a priest." Misael Deaver admitted he "had enlisted as a soldier in the present commotion attending this country, and had his marriage accomplished by a priest." Mary Hayhurst presented a certificate from Deer Creek Monthly Meeting, dated 1st day of 2nd month, 1781. William Scolfield reported to have "commenced suits at law against a Friend contrary to the good order, and hath likewise taken the test, and joined in war." Mary Patrick requested a certificate to Hopewell Monthly Meeting in Virginia.

On 28th day of 4th month, 1781, William Wood and Mary Smith intend to marry. Joseph Griffith presented a certificate from Fairfax Monthly Meeting, dated 24th day of 2nd month, 1781, and was received. Benjamin Lancaster was charged with "the misconduct of dancing."

On 30th day of 6th month, 1781, Samuel Gray presented a certificate from Wilmington Monthly Meeting, dated 11th day of 4th month, 1781, and was received. Catharine Hopkins asked to be joined in membership with Friends. Sarah Ryan was charged with "dancing and likewise hath committed adultery."

On 29th day of 9th month, 1781, Rachel Hopkins presented a certificate from Indian Spring, dated 19th day of 5th month, 1780, and was received. William Scholfield found guilty of "having taken a test...and enrolling and hiring a substitute in order to maintain war." A few lines in the case of Evan Griffith's children were directed to Sadsbury Monthly Meeting and forwarded by John Smith. Issachar Scholfield presented a certificate from Indian Spring Monthly Meeting, dated 17th day of 8th month, 1781, and was received.

On 27th day of 10th month, 1781, Elizabeth Wilson was charged with holding negroes in slavery. Rebeckah Naylor presented a certificate from Nottingham Monthly Meeting, dayed 6th day of 10th month, 1781, and was received.

On 24th day of 11th month, 1781, our Friend William Brown produced a certificate for himself and his wife Susannah, dated at the Southern District Monthly Meeting in Philadelphia the 24th day of 10th month, 1781, recommending him as a Minister and his wife as an Elder. John Scoggin requested a certificate to Pipe Creek Monthly Meeting.

On 29th day of 12th month, 1781, Thomas Carr was charged with "drinking spiritous liquors to excess and using unsavory language." Benjamin Wilson and Robert Dutton were charged with "continuing to hold their fellow men in slavery." Reported that Amoss Lacy, William Sharp, and Sarah Hayhurst "hath gone out in marriage."

On 28th day of 1st month, 1782, Sarah Hayhurst is now Sarah Newborough.

On 23rd day of 2nd month, 1782, Ruth Hayhurst, Mary Brown and William Wilson "hath gone out in marriage." George Matthews "hath been guilty of drinking spiritous liquors and fighting."

On 30th day of 3rd month, 1782, Edward Cunnard charged with "having absented himself from home during the present commotion and thereby given occasion for unfavorable suspicion respecting him." David Brown released from being Clerk at his own request, and John Wilson was appointed in his stead. James Mason, James Spicer and John Smith, Jr. "hath been guilty of horse racing and laying wagers."

On 25th day of 5th month, 1782, Ruth Hanaway (formerly Hayhurst) "hath gone out in marriage from amongst us."

On 29th day of 6th month, 1782, Hannah Scott presented a certificate from Fairfax Monthly Meeting, dated 25th day of 11th month, 1781, and was received. Some lines were produced for Elizabeth Polton and forwarded to Buckingham Monthly Meeting by Abraham Scott. Nehemiah Underwood and his wife Rachel and children, Benjamin, Sarah, and Willing [sic], presented a certificate from Warrington Monthly Meeting, dated 11th day of 8th month, 1782[sic], and were received. John Sharp requested a certificate to Deer Creek Monthly Meeting.

On 27th day of 7th month, 1782, Mary Davis (formerly Brown) "hath gone out in marriage from amongst us." Benjamin Lancaster and Nathan Lancaster found "guilty of dancing and frequenting places of diversion."

On 28th day of 9th month, 1782, William Lee presented a certificate from Wrights Town Monthly Meeting in Bucks County, Pennsylvania, dated 2nd day of 7th month, 1782, for himself and wife Ellener and children, Mary, Sebile, David and Elener. Mordecai Rogers "hath been guilty of dancing." Frances Malsby and Angelina Malsby requested to be received in membership.

On 26th day of 10th month, 1782, Edward Cunnard "hath been guilty of carrying warlike weapons and neglecting attendance at our religious meetings."

On 30th day of 11th month, 1782, Joseph Townsend presented some lines by way of a certificate for himself and wife Hannah from Concord Monthly Meeting in Chester County, Pennsylvania, dated 9th day of 10th month, 1782. William Jeffereis also presented the same from the same place. Catharine Bowen[?] presented a certificate from Fairfax Monthly Meeting in Virginia, dated 28th day of 9th month, 1782. Susanna Wilson joined in with the Methodists and chose to be discontinued from among Friends. Elizabeth Proser (formerly Colegate), "hath gone out in marriage to a man not in membership with us." Henry Cunnard was charged with "neglecting attendance at our religious meetings, frequenting places of diversion, and making too free use of spiritous liquors."

On 28th day of 12th month, 1782, Robert Woodcock and his wife Deborah presented a certificate from Wilmington, dated 10th day of 7th month, 1782, and were received. John Griffith and James Griffith (sons of Isaac Griffith) presented a certificate from Fairfax Monthly Meeting in Virginia, dated 23rd day of 11th month, 1782, and were received. John Maulsby requested to be released from being overseer and it was granted. John E. Rees reported as being "concerned in gaming."

On 25th day of 1st month, 1783, Hester Dyer "hath married contrary to the good order used among Friends by the help of a hireling minister and to a man not of our society." Francis Matthews requested a certificate for himself and his wife to Pipe Creek Monthly Meeting. James Carr "hath been guilty of differing and fighting." John Rogers and Susanna Hicks intend to marry. Tabitha Blagdon requested to be received in membership. James Brown and Joseph Floyd "hath fot married contrary to the good order by the help of an hireling minister to women not members of our society."

On 22nd day of 2nd month, 1783, Daniel Matthews (son of Oliver) "has an unlawful child laid to his charge by an unmarried woman and has left the parts."

On 29th day of 3rd month, 1783, Esther Henderson (formerly Dyer) "gave way so far as to accomplish her marriage by the assistance of a priest to one not of our society." Tabitha Blagdon and her daughter Ann Blagdon were received into membership. Joseph Rea and Benjamin Rea presented a certificate from Abington Monthly Meeting, dated 24th day of 6th month, 1782, and were received. John Malsby presented a certificate from Pipe Creek Monthly Meeting, dated 15th day of 2nd day, 1783, for himself, his wife Mary and their daughter, and were received. Isaac Griffith "having come to live within the verge of this meeting hath returned the certificate we gave him to Fairfax Monthly Meeting in Virginia, dated 24th day of 11th month, 1782." Samuel Lee requested a certificate for himself, his wife Mary and children, John, Mary and Rachel, to Wrights Town Monthly Meeting. Kettutah Parrish requested to be released from being an Elder due to being aged and infirm, and it was granted.

On 26th day of 4th month, 1783, Mary Fredd presented a certificate from Fairfax Monthly Meeting in Virginia, dated 28th day of 12th month, 1782. James Trimble presented a certificate from East Nottingham Monthly Meeting, dated 27th day of 7th month, 1782. Samuel Coale presented a certificate for himself, his wife Lidia and children, Mary, William, Skipwith and Joshua, from Pipe Creek Monthly Meeting, dated 13th day of 3rd month, 1783. Joshua Husband presented a certificate from Deer Creek Monthly Meeting, dated 27th day of 2nd month, 1783.

Om 31st day of 5th month, 1783, Enoch Spencer requested to be released from being an overseer and it was granted. Judith Cunnard requested a certificate to Fairfax Monthly Meeting for herself and four children, Sarah, Ann, Edward and Pamela. Certificate presented by Ganer[?] Lungan[?], formerly De---[?], from Abington Monthly Meeting, dated 31st day of 7th month, 1780[?]. Patience McClaskey presented a certificate from Concord Monthly Meeting in Pennsylvania, dated 5th day of 3rd month, 1783.

On 26th day of 7th month, 1783, Joseph Rhea reportedly married outside the society. Certificate presented by Alice Lukens, wife of Benjamin Lukens, for herself and several children, from Abington Monthly Meeting in Pennsylvania, dated 28th day of 11th month, 1774[?].

On 30th day of 8th month, 1783, Cadwallader Evans requested a certificate for his daughter Elenor Evans (a minor) to Warrington Monthly Meeting in Pennsylvania.

On --th[?] day of 9th month, 1783, Thomas Bull charged with having been married outside the society by a hireling minister. Isaac Williams and Rebecca Hayward intend to marry. Jesse and Dorothy Tyson presented a certificate from Horsham Monthly Meeting in Pennsylvania, dated 30th day of 7th month, 1783. George Mattews presented a certificate from Darby Monthly Meeting in Pennsylvania, dated 3rd day of 7th month, 1783.

On 25th day of 10th month, 1783, at Gunpowder, John Hair and William Parrish represented Gunpowder, Joseph Townsend and Thomas Stockdale represented Little Falls, and William Davis and David Wilson represented Baltimore Monthly Meetings. William Matthews (son of George) charged with "attending places of diversion and using language unbecoming a Christian people."

On 27th of 12th month, 1783, at Gunpowder, Mordecai Matthews and William Matthews represented Gunpowder, Moses Dillon and Jesse Tyson represented Little Falls, and Isaac Williams and Elisha Tyson represented Baltimore Monthly Meetings.

On --[?] day of 1st month, 1784, Martha Tudor was charged with misconduct. William Dilworth's certificate from Abington Monthly Meeting in Pennsylvania, dated in 6th month, 1773 [sic], was being returned as he reportedly may have gone out in marriage. William[?] Wilson presented a certificate from Hopewell Monthly Meeting in Virginia, dated 1st day of 12th month, 1783.

On 24th day of 4th month, 1784, John Price (son of Mordecai) was disowned for "bearing arms against the Indians."

On 29th day of 5th month, 1784, Joshua Price was disowned for being "married by a hireling priest." Certificates produced by: Jonathan[?] Thomas from Warrington Monthly Meeting, dated 8th day of 4th month, 1784; Ann Rice from Goshen[?] Monthly Meeting, dated 7th day of 5th month, 1784, for herself and children, Sarah, Joseph, Ann and George; William Dilworth from Abington Monthly Meeting in Pennsylvania, dated 28th day of 6th month, 1783; and, Francis Hopkins from Third Haven Monthly Meeting, dated 29th day of 1st month, 1784. All were received, but since William Dilworth had his marriage performed contrary to Friends, it will be looked into.

On 29th day of 1st month, 1785, the representatives to the monthly meeting were: Daniel Price and Nehemiah Underwood for Gunpowder; Jesse Tyson and Thomas Wilson for Little Falls; and, William Davis and Thomas Matthews for Baltimore. Dorothy Matthews produced a certificate from Bradford Monthly Meeting in Pennsylvania, dated 12th day of 11th month, 1784, and Ruth Hussey produced one from Warrington Monthly Meeting, dated 11th day of 12th month, 1784.

On 26th day of 2nd month, 1785, William Davis was charged with "attending horse races." Joseph Davis was charged with "marriage by the assistance of a priest." James Miller produced a certificate for himself and children, Thomas, Rachel and Israel, from Warrington Monthly Meeting, dated 8th day of 5th month, 1784, and Grace Mason produced one from Wilmington Monthly Meeting, dated 15th day of 12th month, 1784.

On 26th day of 3rd month, 1785, Thomas Buckingham produced a certificate from Kennett Monthly Meeting in Pennsylvania, dated 13th day of 7th month, 1769, which was received "but from the long time it has been delayed" it will be looked into. Rebecca Naylor requested a certificate to Nottingham Monthly Meeting. Catharine Rees produced a certificate for herself and son Daniel Rees from Warrington Monthly Meeting, dated 7th day of 8th month, 1784.

On 30th day of 4th month, 1785, Elizabeth Dare apologized for "marrying to a man not of this society by a priest." Richard Walsh requested to be received into membership. George Matthews charged with "drinking spiritous liquors to excess and gaming." James Mosely requested a certificate to Black Water Monthly Meeting in Surry County, Virginia. Ennion Williams and Hannah Hayward intend to marry. Friend Ann Moore reported deceased. Enoch Underwood and Morgan Jones produced a certificate from Warrington Monthly Meeting, dated 12th day of 3rd month, 1785, and William Scott produced one from Fairfax Monthly Meeting in Virginia, dated 26th day of 2nd month, 1785.

On 28th day of 5th month, 1785, Ann Burgess condemned for outoing in marriage. Mary Hannah (formerly Tucker) and Mareb Johnson (formerly Dawes) were likewise condemned. Elizabeth Dare requested a certificate to Indian Spring Monthly Meeting, and John Smith requested one for his two children Susanna and Lydia to New Garden Monthly Meeting, and one for his daughter Elizabeth to Kennett Monthly Meeting, both in Pennsylvania. Rebecca Moore produced a certificate from Pipe Creek Monthly Meeting for herself and children Hannah, Frances, William and Keturah.

On 25th day of 6th month, 1785, certificates were received from Charles Horseman and wife, John Horseman, and Mary Horsemn from Warrington Monthly Meeting, "but they having removed within the verge of Center Monthly Meeting in Virginia" the certificates were forwarded to them.

On 30th day of 7th month, 1785, a certificate was produced by Lewis Jordan from Pipe Creek Monthly Meeting, dated 15th day of 5th month, 1785, "but it appearing that he hath lately left these parts in a reproachful and clandestine manner," it will be looked into.

On 27th day of 8th month, 1785, John Evan Rees condemned of "fornication with Ann Lacey, a member of Little Falls Preparative Meeting, and likewise accomplishing his marriage with her by the assistance of a hireling." Mahlon Scholfield produced a certificate from Indian Spring Monthly Meeting, dated 19th day of this month.

On 24th day of 9th month, 1785, William Davis was charged that "soon after the decease of his wife he was married by the assistance of a priest to a woman whose former husband we have sufficient reason to believe was at that time living." Susanna Morris charged with "attending public dancings and being superfluous in her dress." Reuben Scooly and Esther Lacey intend to marry. John Dickinson produced a certificate from a Monthly Meeting held at New York, dated 8th day of 6th month, 1785.

On 29th day of 10th month, 1785, Rachel Hooker (formerly Belt) charged with having "her marriage accomplished by a hireling priest to a man not in unity with us." Susanna Bosley (formerly Price) charged with being "married contrary to the good order." Jesse Matthews requested a certificate to Warrington Monthly Meeting. William Pillar requested a certificate to Grange Six Weeks Meeting near Charlemount in the Kingdom of Ireland, snf Francis Hopkins requested one to Third Haven Monthly Meeting. Richard Floyd found guilty of "attending places of aversion and dancing thereat, and quarrelling and fighting." William Wood produced a certificate for himself and wife Mary and son Joel from Pipe Creek Monthly Meeting, dated 15th day of 9th month, 1785. George Yarnall produced a certificate for himself and wife Lydia and children, Sarah, Thomas, Susanna, George, Mary, Aaron, and Amoss, from Goshen Monthly Meeting in Pennsylvania, dated 11th day of 6th month, 1784, with an endorsement thereon by Pipe Creek Monthly Meeting held at Bush Creek the 18th day of 6th month, 1784.

On 26th day of 11th month, 1785, Anne Bussey (formerly Burgess) charged with "attending a marriage consummated contrary to the good order." John Belt (son of Richard) charged with "accompanying his sister to her marriage and neglecting attendance at our religious meetings." Joshua Husband, by way of Baltimore Preparative Meeting, requested a certificate to Deer Creek Monthly Meeting. John Mitchel produced a certificate for himself and wife Tacy and their daughter Mary, from Wilmington Monthly Meeting, dated 12th day of 10th month, 1785, and Susanna Harlan produced one from New Garden Monthly Meeting in Pennsylvania, dated 3rd day of 9th month, 1785.

On 31st day of 12th month, 1785, James Carey, of Baltimore Preparative Meeting, requested to be received into membership.

On 28th day of 1st month, 1786, Margaret Cook produced a certificate from New Garden Monthly Meeting in Pennsylvania, dated 5th day of 11th month, 1785, with the concurrence of the Quarterly Meeting held at London Grove.

On 25th day of 2nd month, 1786, Joseph Rees and Mary Rea[?] were disowned for being "married by a hireling minister." Friends produced a certificate for Judith Elicott[?] [Hiccott?] and her children, David, Joseph, Rachel, Benjamin and Mary. Elizabeth Cox (formerly Hopkins) charged with being married to a member by a priest. Benjamin Rhea charged with marrying contrary to rules. Baltimore Preparative Meeting reported the death of our Friends John Malsby, a minister, who died on 10th day of 9th month, 1785, aged near 32 years, and Hannah Scott, a minister, who died on 4th day of 12th month, 1785, in the 77th year of her age. Ephraim Lacey requested a certificate to Fairfax Monthly Meeting in Virginia, and James Miller requested one for himself and children, Thomas, Rachel, Israel, and Emilie, to Monallin Monthly Meeting in Pennsylvania.

On 29th day of 4th month, 1786, Abraham Clark requested to be received in membership. Jane Barry "hath for several years been recommended to this meeting by certificate from Haverford Monthly Meeting in Pennsylvania."

On 27th day of 5th month, 1786, Robert Cornthwait produced a certificate for himself and wife Grace and children, Elizabeth, Deborah, Thomas, Mary, and William, from Indian Spring Monthly Meeting, dated 21st day of 4th month, 1786. Joseph Engle produced a certificate from Chester Monthly Meeting in Pennsylvania, dated 23rd day of 9th month, 1786, and endorsed at Bradford Monthly Meeting.

24th day of 6th month, 1786, John Malsby requested a certificate for himself and wife Lydia and children, Susanna, Ann, William, Sarah, Elenor, John and Lydia, to Hopewell Monthly Meeting in Virginia. Abigail Cunnard requested a certificate to Fairfax Monthly Meeting in Virginia. James Carey requested a certificate to Indian Spring Monthly Meeting in order to marry a member thereof. William Webster produced a certificate from Deer Creek Monthly Meeting, dated 1st day of 6th month, 1786.

On 29th day of 7th month, 1786, Aquila Carr was charged with marrying contrary to the good order. Joseph Griffith and Catharine (before marriage Burson) condemned for marrying outside the good order. Margaret Dukehart requested that her children, Margaret, Elizabeth, John, Catharine and Volerisus, be taken under care of Friends. Lavalin Barry, Jr. charged with "using unbecoming language and swearing."

On 26th day of 8th month, 1786, Mordecai Rogers was condemned for being married by a hireling minister. Enoch Underwood requested a certificate to York Monthly Meeting, and Morgan Jones requested one to Warrington Monthly Meeting. David Lee "with the approbation of his wife" requested that his children, Hannah, Rebecca, Mary and Ralph, be taken under care of Friends. Mary Lancster requested to be received into membership.

Samuel Coale was released from being overseer at his request and David Brown was appointed in his stead. Elias Ellicott produced a certificate for himself and wife Mary from Indian Spring Monthly Meeting, dated 21st day of last month, and William Hawley produced one from Bradford Monthly Meeting in Pennsylvania, dated 14th day of last month.

On 30th day of 9th month, 1786, Catharine Hopkins was found guilty of "leaving her husband in an unreconciled manner without previously advising with her friends thereon and removing a considerable distance from amongst the society without a certificate of removal." Mary Lancaster, wife of Jesse, and her children, Mary, Isaiah, John and Benjamin, were received into membership. Henry Wilson reportedly had not settled within the verge of this meeting and requested a certificate to Deer Creek Monthly Meeting. Nehemiah Underwood requested to be released from being overseer and Abraham Scott was appointed in his stead. John Griffith charged with "uncleanness and leaving these parts in a clandestine manner to the injury and disadvantage of his master."

On 28th day of 10th month, 1786, Joseph Rice and Standish Barry were condemned for "deviating from our principles in their dress and address." Catharine Ball was condemned for "having a child in an unmarried state and afterwards accomplished her marriage contrary to the good order." Aaron Dyer and wife Elizabeth charged with attending a marriage accomplished contrary to the rules. Thomas Floyd charged with "drinking spiritous liquors and lately removing a considerable distance from these parts without ac- quainting his Friends thereof." Certificate produced by David Houlton from Exeter Monthly Meeting held at Maiden Creek in Pennsylvania, dated 31st day of 5th month, 1786.

On 25th day of 11th month, 1786, Catharine Randall (formerly Ball) condemned for outgoing in marriage. John Dickinson and John Bond were likewise charged. Samuel and Hannah England requested a certificate to Westland Monthly Meeting in Pennsylvania, and Mary Dawes, wife of Isaac, requested one to Indian Spring Monthly Meeting. Rachel and Sarah Hopkins, daughters of Richard, charged with "keeping slaves and neglecting the attending of our religious meeting."

On 30th day of 12th month, 1786, Thomas Lacey and wife Esther and son Ralph requested a certificate to Fairfax Monthly Meeting in Virginia. Thomas Lacey, Jr. charged with marrying contrary to the good order. William Amos, Jr. requested to be released as overseer and Enoch Spencer was appointed in his stead. William Trimble produced a certificate from Nottingham Monthly Meeting, dated 5th day of last month.

On 27th day of 1st month, 1787, John and Ann Rees apologized for marrying contrary to the order of Friends.

On 24th day of 2nd month, 1787, Josias Bowen condemned for "continuing to hold his fellow mortals ina state of abject slavery." Ebenezer Maule produced a certificate from Nottingham Monthly Meeting, dated 30th day of 12th month, 1786, but "returned to the meeting it came from as he is a bout to remove within the verge thereof." Mary Matthews, wife of Francis, produced a certificate from Pipe Creek Monthly Meeting, dated 14th day of 9th month, 1786.

On 31st day of 3rd month, 1787, Jane Erwin requested a certificate to Fairfax Monthly Meeting in Virginia.

On 28th day of 4th month, 1787, Mary Stevenson produced a certificate from Pipe Creek Monthly Meeting, dated 15th day of 3rd month, 1787.

On 26th day of 5th month, 1787, David Hayhurst charged with marrying contrary to the good order. Issacher Scholfield requested a certificate to Indian Spring Monthly Meeting. Mary Byrnes (formerly Erwin) found "guilty of unchastity and having her marriage accomplished from amongst Friends."

On 30th day of 6th month, 1787, Margaret Sanderson (formerly Hopkins) charged with marrying contrary to the good order.

On 28th day of 7th month, 1787, Ruth Hussey requested a certificate to Warrington Monthly Meeting. Isaac Morriss produced a certificate for himself and his wife Martha and children, Susanna, Benjamin, Ann and Mary, from Warrington Monthly Meeting [date illegible].

On 29th day of 9th month, 1787, Ruth Wood produced a certificate from New Garden Monthly Meeting in Pennsylvania, dated 4th day of 8th month, 1787.

On 27th day of 10th month, 1787, Samuel Coale requested a certificate for himself and wife Lydia and children, Mary, William, Skipwith, Joshua and Margaret, to Deer Creek Monthly Meeting.

On 29th day of 12th month, 1787, Daniel Matthews (son of Thomas) requested a certificate to marry Susanna Bartlett of Third Haven Monthly Meeting. William Scott charged with being married by a hireling minister.

On 26th day of 1st month, 1788, Nehemiah Underwood and Mary Price intend to marry.

On 23rd day of 2nd month, 1788, Sarah Green (formerly Pennington) condemned for going out in marriage. Elizabeth Cornthwait produced a certificate from Indian Spring Monthly Meeting, as did Thomas Brown for himself and wife Mary and daughter Mary, both dated 21st day of 12th month, 1787, and one for William Allibone from the same place, dated the 18th day. Grace McDermot produced a certificate from the Monthly Meeting held for the Northern District of Philadelphia, dated 25th day of 12th month, 1787. David Coulson produced a certificate from Nottingham Monthly Meeting, dated 28th day of 7th month, 1787. Certificate produced for the children of Lawrence Cox, viz. Jonah, Jane, Robert, John and Thomas, from Warrington Monthly Meeting, dated 8th day of 12th month, 1787. Thomas Byrnes produced a certificate from Wilmington Monthly Meeting, dated 13th day of 6th month, 1787.

On 29th day of 3rd month, 1788, Abraham Clark requested a certificate for himself and wife Mary and children, Sarah, Ann, Joseph, Mary and Elizabeth, to Sadsbury Monthly Meeting in Pennsylvania. Evan Rogers and Levi Rogers reported to have joined another society. Ruth Wood requested a certificate to New Garden Monthly Meeting. Rose Malsby produced a certificate for herself and her son Benjamin from Warrington Monthly Meeting in Pennsylvania, dated 12th day of 1st month, 1788. "Our Ancient Friend" Susanna Brown also produced one from Nottingham Monthly Meeting, dated 23rd day of last month.

On 26th day of 4th month, 1788, Rachel Barnaby, formerly Riffitt [or Rissett?], charged with marrying outside the order. John Dyer requested a certificate to Goose Creek Monthly Meeting in Virginia. Phebe Carr (formerly Dyer) charged with marrying outside the order. Dinah Young (formerly Cox) charged with marrying outside the order.

On 31st day of 5th month, 1788, William Riley and wife Sarah requested to be received into membership. Tacy Burgess produced a certificate from Deer Creek Monthly Meeting.

On 28th day of 6th month, 1788, Rebecca Scott, wife of Jesse, produced a certificate from Horsham Monthly Meeting in Pennsylvania, dated 30th day of 1st month, 1788.

On 30th day of 8th month, 1788, David Rees was charged with "having a child in an unmarried state."

On 27th day of 9th month, 1788, Elizabeth Laverly (formerly Moore) was charged with marrying outside the good order.

On 25th day of 10th month, 1788, Abraham Griffith requested a certificate to marry Rachel Taylor, a member of Fairfax Monthly Meeting in Virginia. Mordecai Matthews requested one in like manner to marry Ruth Hussey, a member of Warrington Monthly Meeting in Pennsylvania. Henry Wilson (son of Benkid) charged with "attending places of diversion, deviating from principles of dress and address, and holding his fellow men in a state of slavery." William Williams charged with committing fornication. William Brown proposed to serve in station of an Elder. Ann Carr charged with going out in marriage. Rachel Wells requested a certificate to Indian Spring Monthly Meeting for herself and children, Margaret and Ann. George Harris produced a certificate from Warrington Monthly Meeting in Pennsylvania, dated 12th day of 7th month, 1788.

On 29th day of 11th month, 1788, Thomas Maule produced a certificate for himself and wife Margaret from Nottingham Monthly Meeting, dated 24th day of 11th month, 1787. Elizabeth Williams, daughter of Isaac, produced a certificate from Richland Monthly Meeting in Pennsylvania, dated 6th day of 12th month, 1787.

On 27th day of 12th month, 1788, Ann Randall (formerly Carr) guilty of going out in marriage, as were Alice McClaskey (formerly Jewell) and Abigail Stevenson (formerly Moore). Aquila Jones produced a certificate from Deer Creek Monthly Meeting, dated 9th day of 10th month, 1788, as did Henry Worthington from the same place on the same date. Samuel Jones produced a certificate from York Monthly Meeting in Pennsylvania, dated 15th day of 10th month, 1788.

On 28th day of 2nd month, 1789, James Orr and Angeline Malsby intend to marry. Rossiter Scott requested a certificate to Gwynnedd Monthly Meeting in Pennsylvania "in order to marry Edith Lukens, a member thereof." Hannah Spencer charged with marrying outside the order.

On 28th day of 3rd month, 1789, Susanna Barton (formerly Sharp) charged with marrying outside the society. Mary Scott produced a certificate from Fairfax Monthly Meeting, dated 25th day of 10th month, 1788.

On 25th day of 4th month, 1789, Ruth Matthews produced a certificate from Warrington Monthly Meeting, dated 7th day of 3rd month, 1788. Ann Moore produced certificate from Buckingham Monthly Meeting in Pennsylvania, dated 5th day of 1st month, 1789. Thomas and Walter Pierpoint (minors) produced a certificate from Indian Spring Monthly Meeting, dated 20th day of 2nd month, 1789.

On 30th day of 5th month, 1789, William Lee charged with marrying outside the good order. George Harris and Susanna Rogers intend to marry. David Tucker condemned for neglecting religious meetings and marrying outside the good order.

On 27th day of 6th month, 1789, Aquila Parrish charged with "quarrelling, fighting, drinking to excess, and attending a marriage contrary to the good order." Hannah Barnett (formerly Spencer) condemned for marrying outside the good order. James Orr and wife Angelina requested a certificate to Deer Creek Monthly Meeting. Rachel Griffith, wife of Abraham, produced a certificate from Fairfax Monthly Meeting in Virginia, dated 23rd day of last month.

On 25th day of 7th month, 1789, Jonathan Cates [Coates?] produced a certificate for himself and his wife Jane and children, Grace, Jane, Elizabeth [and one name illegible], from Kennett Monthly Meeting in Pennsylvania. Mary Bond produced a certificate from the Mens and Womens Meeting held at Charlemount in the Kingdom of Ireland, dated 7th day of 6th month, 1787.

On 29th day of 8th month, 1789, Friends produced a certificate for Sarah Rogers and Margrett Rodgers and her two daughters, and "forwarded as directed."

On 26th day of 9th month, 1789, William Wood requested a certificate for himself and wife Mary and children Joel and Elizabeth and also a child named Cylas Smith who lives with them, to Pipe Creek Monthly Meeting. Sarah Scott produced a certificate from Wrights Town Monthly Meeting in Pennsylvania, dated in 5th month, 1789.

On 31st day of 10th month, 1789, Richard Webb (of Deer Creek Monthly Meeting) and Mary Maulsby intend to marry.

On 29th day of 11th month, 1789, Thomas Beale and wife Alice were condemned for "unnecessarily retailing spiritous liquors, being tavern keepers, and frequent disorders have appeared in their house reproachful to our society." Rachel Nailor requested a certificate to East Nottingham Monthly Meeting.

On 26th day of 12th month, 1789, our Friend Sarah Harrison and her companion Margarett Elliott some time ago produced a certificate from Philadelphia Monthly Meeting to visit Friends within the verge of this Monthly Meeting. Elizabeth Williams disowned for being married by a hireling.

On --[?] day of 1st month, 1790, Thomas Byrnes requested a certificate of removal to Wilmington Monthly Meeting. Jonathan Devenport and Margaret Dukehart intend to marry.

On 27th day of 2nd month, 1790, Mary Scott reportedly removed within the verge of Fairfax Monthly Meeting.

On 27th day of 3rd month, 1790, Jane Quinlan (formerly Cox) condemned for being married by a hireling and deviating in dress and address." Abner Parsons and Rachel Dyer intend to marry. Certificate produced some time ago from Jonathan Scott from Fairfax Monthly Meeting was now produced with an endorsement thereon. Mary Hayhurst, wife of James, requested a certificate for herself and children, Sarah, Rachel, Job, Ely, and Hannah, to Westland Monthly Meeting in Pennsylvania. Meriam Thysey[?] produced a certificate from Warrington Monthly Meeting. Nehemiah Underwood requested a certificate for himself and wife and children, Sarah, Benjamin, Willin[?], Rachel and Mary, to Deer Creek Monthly Meeting.

On 24th day of 4th month, 1790, Thomas Ely produced a certificate for himself and wife Hannah and children, George, Elizabeth, Mary, Hugh, and Amoss, from Deer Creek Monthly Meeting, dated 3rd day of 9th month, 1789. Grace Mason "hath gone out in marriage." John Dutton "had his marriage accomplished by a hireling."

On 29th day of 5th month, 1790, Ann Coats produced a certificate from Bradford Monthly Meeting in Pennsylvania, dated 14th day of 5th month, 1790, and Kezia Coats produced one from Kennet Monthly Meeting in Pennsylvania, dated 15th dy of 4th month, 1790. Mordecai Parish found "guilty of striking a man and dancing and drinking to excess." John Burgess requested his son John (a minor) be taken into membership.

On 26th day of 6th month, 1790, Ann Griffith reportedly "gone out in marriage." Certificate produced for Phebe Moore and daughter Ann Moore.

On 31st day of 7th month, 1790, Hannah Burk (formerly Hayhurst) condemned for going out in marriage.

On 26th day of 8th month, 1790, William Husband produced a certificate from Deer Creek Monthly Meeting, dated 3rd day of 2nd month, 1790. John Marsh produced a certificate for himself and wife Hannah from Warrington Monthly Meeting, dated 7th day of 8th month, 1790. Grace Corkin (formerly Mason) condemned for going out in marriage. Charles Hardesty requested to be received into membership. Joseph Townsend requested to be released from being overseer and John Brown was appointed in his stead.

On 25th day of 9th month, 1790, James Amos (of William) and Hannah Lee intend to marry. John Lee (of Samuel) and Sebellah Lee intend to marry. John Parson, Jr. and wife Susannah and children, Rebecca and John, requested to be taken into membership.

On 30th day of 10th month, 1790, Mary Tucker requested a certificate to Fairfax Monthly Meeting in Virginia. Elizabeth Dukehart charged with going out in marriage. Roberta[?] Mason produced a certificate from York Monthly Meeting for herself and he daughter Elizabeth, dated 4th day of 8th month, 1790. Mary Hayward produced a certificate from Deer Creek Monthly Meeting, dated 23rd day of 9th month, 1790. Ann Trimble produced a certificate from Hopewell Monthly Meeting in Virginia, dated 15th day of 7th month, 1790. Margaret Tyson produced a certificate from Indian Spring Monthly Meeting, dated 8th day of 7th month, 1790. Phebe Coates produced a certificate from Euchland[?] Monthly Meeting, dated 8th day of 7th month, 1790. John Matthews and Leah Price intend to marry. John Bond (son of Samuel) charged with "playing cards and neglecting attendance of meetings."

On 27th day of 11th month, 1790, Elizabeth Ball (formerly Dukehart) condemned for going out in marriage. Certificate for James Miller and his four children from this meeting to Monallen Monthly Meeting, dated 29th day of 4th month, 1786[?], "now returned, it appears that he has settled within the verge of another monthly meeting." Priscilla Carr requested to be received in membership. William Harris and David Hicks reportedly joined the Methodist Society.

On 25th day of 12th month, 1790, Aquilla Jones and Elizabeth Dillon intend to marry. Frances Martin requested to be received in membership.

On 29th day of 1st month, 1791, "request was made for a certificate for William Moore (son of John a minor) to York Monthly Meeting in Pennsylvania." Amos Pennington charged with going out in marriage. Abraham Scott requested to be released from being overseer and Mordecai Matthews was appointed in his stead. Mary Belt charged with "attending places of diversion and attending to dance." Rachel Mason requested that her daughter Rachel (a minor) be taken into membership. Little Falls Meeting reported that William Bull, an Elder, had died on 6th day of 11th month, 1790, in his 56th year. A memorial for Susanna Brown will also be prepared. Ruth Gilbert (formerly Fisher) charged with going out in marriage.

On 26th day of 2nd month, 1791, William Morgan and Sarah Price intend to marry.

On 26th day of 3rd month, 1791, David Holton requested a certificate to Philadelphia Monthly Meeting. Abel Spencer requested a certificate for himself and wife Rebeccah and children, Elizabeth, William, Sarah, Rebeccah, Abel and Reuben, to Deer Creek Monthly Meeting. Thomas Sharp, Jr. "hath a child laid to his charge in an unmarried state." Elizabeth Jones, wife of William, requested to be taken into membership. Hannah Nailor requested a certificate to Nottingham Monthly Meeting. Jesse Brown and Dorothy Matthews intend to marry. Elizabeth Devenport and Elizabeth Devenport, Jr. produced certificates for themselves from Ceacil Monthly Meeting, dated 12th day of 2nd month, 1791.

On 30th day of 4th month, 1791, our Friend John McKim "has now returned the certificate we gave him in the 11th month last with an endorsement thereon from Center Quarterly Meeeting in Guilford County, North Carolina, which is to us satisfactory." Jane Morrison requested to be taken into membership. John Bull "hath been in the practice of collecting such taxes as Friends have consciencious scruples against paying, and hath been guilty of fighting." William Hayward and Keziah Coates intend to marry.

On 28th day of 5th month, 1791, Abraham Dawes was received into membership. Amos James and Mary Lee intend to marry. Mary Kelso produced a certificate from Darby Monthly Meeting, dated 28th day of 10th month, 1790. Rachel Wells, "having returned with her husband to reside in Baltimore," produced a certificate from Indian Spring Monthly Meeting, dated 29th day of 11th month, 1788. Sarah Morgan requested a certificate to Fairfax Monthly Meeting in Virginia. John Ellicott requested a certificate for himself and wife Cassandra to Indian Spring Monthly Meeting.

On 24th day of 7th month, 1791, William Carr and Sarah Harbert intend to marry. Ann Perine requested to be taken into membership. Jehu Moore presented a certificate from Pipe Creek Monthly Meeting, dated 14th day of 5th month, 1791. Jemima Sulivan (formerly Hair) "has gone out in marriage with a man not in membership," as has Sarah Bigger (formerly Rice).

On 30th day of 7th month, 1791, Thomas Poultney produced a certificate from Fairfax Monthly Meeting, dated 25th day of 6th month, 1791, and Ann Poultney, his wife, produced one from Indian Spring Monthly Meeting, dated 18th day of 2nd month, 1791.

Om 27th day of 8th month, 1791, John Stockdale produced a certificate from Wrights Town Monthly Meeting in Pennsylvania, dated 3rd day of 5th month, 1791. Catharine Hooker who has been under the care of Gunpowder Preparative Meeting, requested to be taken into membership. Mary Helms (formerly Houstman) had gone out in marriage.

On 24th day of 9th month, 1791, Samuel Gilpin produced a certificate from Concord Monthly Meeting in Pennsylvania, dated 8th day of 6th month, 1791. William James requested a certificate for himself and Thomas Lacey, minor child of Thomas Lacey, Jr., deceased, to Fairfax Monthly Meeting in Virginia.

On 27th day of 10th month, 1791, Mary Tucker returned to live in Baltimore from Fairfax Monthly Meeting in Virginia.

On 26th day of 11th month, 1791, Joseph Dyer charged "with neglect in paying a just debt." Ann Scott, wife of Joseph, produced a certificate for her children, Rachel, Isaac, Jacob, Sarah and Anna, from Indian Spring Monthly Meeting, dated 21st day of 10th month, 1791, and also one for Hannah Hughes from New Garden Monthly Meeting in Pennsylvania, dated 6th day of 8th month, 1791.

On 31st day of 12th month, 1791, Benajah Brown[?] produced a certificate from New Garden Monthly Meeting in Chester County, Pennsylvania, dated 6th day of 8th month, 1791, "he having settled at Baltimore." Also, one from Edward Marshall, dated 14th day of 9th month, 1791, "he is settled at Little Falls Meeting." Likewise, William Thompson from Northern Monthly Meeting in Philadelphia, dated 22nd day of 9th month, 1791, "settled at Baltimore" and Isaac Hollingsworth from Kennett Monthly Meeting, dated 13th day of 10th month, 1791, "settled at Little Falls." Also, one for Thomas Fisher, a minor, from the Southern District Monthly Meeting in Philadelphia, dated 23rd day of 11th month, 1791. Our Friends Abel Thomas and Amos Lee attended from Maiden Creek Monthly Meeting in Pennsylvania. Joseph Engle requested a certificate to Chester Monthly Meeting held at Providence in Pennsylvania."

On 28th day of 1st month, 1792, representatives to the Monthly Meetings were: Mordecai Matthews and Daniel Price for Gunpowder; Samuel McConnel and David Harry for Little Falls; and, William Trimble and John McKim for Baltimore. Joshua Gibson produced a certificate from Kennet Monthly Meeting, dated 17th day of 11th month, 1791, for himself and wife Lydia and children, Hannah, John, Lydia, Deborah, Susannah, Eliza and Mary. John Davis produced a certificate from Chester Monthly Meeting in Pennsylvania, dated 28th day of 11th month, 1791.

On 26th day of 2nd month, 1792, Abraham Clark requested a certificate for himself and wife Mary and children, Sarah, Ann, Joseph, Mary, Elizabeth and Hannah, to Wrights Town Monthly Meeting in Bucks County, Pennsylvania. Sarah Hopkins (daughter of John) and Elizabeth Bowen (formerly Humphrey) reportedly "had their marriages accomplished by a hireling minister."

On 31st day of 3rd month, 1792, Samuel Thomas (a minor) presented a certificate from Indian Spring Monthly Meeting, dated 17th day of 2nd month, 1792. Mary Merryman (formerly Comley) had her "marriage accomplished by a hireling minister." Priscilla Jefferis requested a certificate for herself and her two children, Gravenor and Samuel, for Goshen Monthly Meeting in Pennsylvania. Charles Harding requested a certificate to Philadelphia Monthly Meeting.

On 28th day of 4th month, 1792, Thomas Sharp, Jr. "hath erred so far as to have a child laid to his charge while in an unmarried state."

On 28th day of 7th month, 1792, Ebenezer Maule requested a certificate to White Oak Swamp Monthly Meeting in Virginia. William Wilson (of John) charged with "not paying a just debt." William Wilson (of Henry) charged with "deviating from dress and address, and for sending a challenge to fight a duel."

On 25th day of 8th month, 1792, John Spicer and Rachel Spicer (formerly Lee) disowned for marrying outside the good order. Lawrence Buckley disowned for "marrying with the assistance of a hireling minister." Elinor

Maulsby condemned for "marrying outside the good order to a man not in membership and having a child born too soon after marriage." Samuel Wilson (son of Henry) charged with "deviating from dress and address, and neglecting meetings." William Thompson requested a certificate to the Northern District Monthly Meeting in Philadelphia.

On 29th day of 9th month, 1792, Martha Burges produced a certificate from Deer Creek Monthly Meeting, dated 26th day of 7th month, 1792. Susannah Jackson also produced one from New Garden Monthly Meeting in Pennsylvania, dated 4th day of 8th month, 1792. Joseph Jackson and Thomas Jackson (minors) produced a certificate from Wilmington Monthly Meeting, dated 15th day of 2nd month, 1792. Warrick Price and Susannah Coates intend to marry. William Carr requested a certificate for himself and wife Sarah and son Jesse to Westland Monthly Meeting in Pennsylvania, and James Carr also requested one for himself and his wife Elizabeth and children, Ann and Samuel, to the same meeting, as did Ann Harbert and Priscilla Carr. George Jewel reportedly "hath been concerned in purchasing lottery tickets."

On 27th day of 10th month, 1792, James Benson produced a certificate from Pipe Creek Monthly Meeting, dated 19th day of 5th month, 1792. Mary Parish reportedly "hath attended a place of diversion and been active in dancing."

On 24th day of 11th month, 1792, Hannah Nailor produced a certificate from Nottingham Monthly Meeting, dated 6th day of 10th month, 1792.

On 29th day of 12th month, 1792, certificate was produced for Joseph, John, Mary, Jane, James and Isaac Trimble (children of Isaac Trimble) from Deer Creek Monthly Meeting, dated 24th day of 5th month, 1792. Esther Scott condemned for "going out in marriage."

On 26th day of 1st month, 1793, Thomas Scott and Elizabeth Matthews intend to marry.

On 23rd day of 2nd month, 1793, Elizabeth Hanway produced a certificate from Kennett Monthly Meeting in Pennsylvania, dated 11th day of 10th month, 1792.

On 30th day of 3rd month, 1793, William Wilson (son of John) requested a certificate to Deer Creek Monthly Meeting. Hannah Moore condemned for being "married by a hireling."

On 27th day of 4th month, 1793, Benjamin Pearson produced a certificate from Exeter Monthly Meeting in Pennsylvania, dated 30th day of 1st month, 1793.

On 25th day of 5th month, 1793, Nicholas Parrish charged with "going out in marriage with a woman not of our society." Jacob Tyson requested to be released from being overseer and Thomas West was appointed in his stead.

On 29th day of 6th month, 1793, Ann Matthews requested a certificate for herself and her children, Elizabeth, Thomas, Hannah and Joshua, to Baltimore Monthly Meeting. Mary Belt charged with "outgoing in marriage." Samuel Robinson presented a certificate from Deer Creek Monthly Meeting, dated 25th day of 4th month, 1793.

On 27th day of 7th month, 1793, Moses Lukins produced a certificate for himself and wife Sarah and daughter Lydia (a minor) and Ezekiel Jones (a minor also living with him) from Deer Creek Monthly Meeting, dated 23rd day of 5th month, 1793. Thomas Stockdale requested a certificate for his minor children, William and Thomas, to Abington Monthly Meeting in Montgomery County, and son John to Redstone Monthly Meeting, both in Pennsylvania.

On 31st day of 8th month, 1793, Thomas Moore "hath a child laid to his charge in an unmarried state."

On 28th day of 9th month, 1793, Hannah Heddinton (formerly Moore) condemned for being married by a hireling minister. Mary Peddicaot (formerly Belt) condemned for "marrying by a hireling minister to a man not of the society." Elizabeth Prosser, Daniel Pennington, and several children had removed to Juniata in Pennsylvania without certificates. James Sharp (son of Thomas) condemned for being "married by a hireling minister."

On 26th day of 10th month, 1793, William Matthews and Elizabeth Hanway intend to marry. Jacob Tyson requested a certificate to Baltimore Monthly Meeting in order to marry Ann Prion [Perine?].

On 30th day of 11th month, 1793, Isaac Dawes requested a certificate to Indian Spring Monthly Meeting. Mary Nailor requested that her two younger children, William and Abraham, be taken into membership. John Price requested that his granddaughter, Rebecca Pits, be taken into membership.

On 28th day of 12th month, 1793, Jesse Matthews and Milkah Belt intend to marry. John Lancaster requested a certificate to Wright Borough Monthly

Meeting in Georgia. Thomas West requested a certificate for his son Jas.[?], a minor, to Baltimore Monthly Meeting.

On 22nd day of 2nd month, 1794, Joseph Belt condemned for being "married by a hireling minister."

On 29th day of 3rd month, 1794, Elizabeth Alibone produced a certificate from Indian Spring Monthly Meeting, dated 10th day of 5th month, 1792. James Benson and Elizabeth Price intend to marry. Edward Marshall requested a certificate to Providence Monthly Meeting in Rhode Island. Dorothy Tyson (now Webster) found "guilty of fornication and her marriage accomplished by a hireling to a man in profession with us."

On 28th day of 4th month, 1794, George Yarnal requested a certificate for seven of his children to Westland Monthly Meeting, viz. George, Mary, Aron, Amos, Ely, Mordecai and Susanna. Application made by Sadsbury Monthly Meeting for certificates for Sarah and Mary Griffith, daughters of Evan and Rebecca Griffith.

On 26th day of 7th month, 1794, John Matthews requested a certificate to Third Haven Monthly Meeting in order to marry Martha Yarnal, a member of said meeting. Certificate produced at this meeting for Hepzibah Brown from Woodbury Monthly Meeting, dated 9th day of 10th month, 1793, was endorsed to Baltimore Monthly Meeting. Moses Luking requested a certificate for Ezekiel Jones (a minor) to Deer Creek Monthly Meeting.

On 30th day of 8th month, 1794, Jesse Tyson requested a certificate to Baltimore Monthly Meeting for himself and wife Margaret and children, Elizabeth, Isaac and Thomas. Mary Hussey presented a certificate from Pipe Creek Monthly Meeting, dated 18th day of 5th month, 1793. Benjamin Pearson requested a certificate to Pipe Creek Monthly Meeting.

On 29th day of 9th month, 1794, Sarah McComas (formerly Howard) condemned for "being married by a hireling teacher to a man not of our society."

On 29th day of 11th month, 1794, Elizabeth Lowdon requested a certificate to Indian Spring Monthly Meeting. Samuel Price and Frances Moore intend to marry.

On 27th day of 12th month, 1794, Luke Amos reportedly "hath been active in the military orders, and likewise gone out in marriage with a woman not of our society." Martha Matthews, wife of John, produced a certificate for herself and daughter, Elizabeth Yarnal, from Third Haven Monthly Meeting, dated 13th day of 11th month, 1794. Lydia Weeks "hath had a child in an unmarried state."

On 31st day of 1st month, 1795, Samuel Nailor "hath had his marriage accomplished by the assistance of a hireling to a woman not of our society."

On 28th day of 2nd month, 1795, Ann Tyson (wife of Jacob) and Elizabeth Nailor attended this meeting with certificates from Baltimore Monthly Meeting. George Tyson "hath been guilty of card playing." Joshua Gibson requested a certificate to Redstone Monthly Meeting for himself and wife Lydia and children, Hannah, John, Lydia, Susannah, Eliza and Mary. Hannah Matthews requested a certificate to Baltimore Monthly Meeting.

On 28th day of 3rd month, 1795, Benjamin Weeks, an apprentice, "hath absconded, collected and taken a sum of his master's money." Jacob Lukins attended this meeting with a certificate from Deer Creek Monthly Meeting, dated 29th day of 1st month, 1795. Mary Howard "attended her sister's marriage which was accomplished contrary to our discipline." William Amos, Jr. requested a certificate for his son Benjamin to Baltimore Monthly Meeting. James Amos (of William) requested a certificate for himself and wife Hannah and children, Mary and David[?], to Baltimore Monthly Meeting. David Lee requested to be released from being and overseer and David Harry was appointed in his stead.

On 25th day of 4th month, 1795, Esther Tyson requested a certificate to Baltimore Monthly Meeting. Priscilla Jefferis presented a certificate for herself and children, Gravener and Samuel, from Gishen Monthly Meeting, dated 7th day of 11th month, 1794. Eleoner Griffith requested to be taken into membership. Sarah McComas "hath her marriage accomplished by the assistance of a hireling with a man not of our society." Mordecai Parrish "hath long neglected the attendance of meetings and attended a marriage accomplished contrary to the rules of our society." Esther Tyson, "being removed from this meeting, was released from the station of an Elder." David Dickenson "hath his marriage accomplished by the assistance of a hireling to a woman not of our society." Thomas Matthews "hath been guilty of fornication and had his marriage accomplished by the assistance of a hireling to a woman not of our society." Abraham Daws "hath been guilty of fighting and making too free use of spiritous liquors so as to be intoxicated thereby." Samiel Wilson requested a certificate to Baltimore Monthly Meeting. John Mason "hath made too free use of spiritous liquors."

Om 25th day of 7th month, 1795, Mordecai Price (of Mordecai) and Charity Comely "hath been guilty of fornication and since had their marriage accomplished by a hireling." Elizabeth Norris "guilty of slaveholding and has also suffered a marriage with the assistance of a hireling." Isaac Morris requested a certificate for himself and wife Martha and children, Susannah, Benjamin, Amos[?], Mary, Isaac, Enoch and Nehemiah, to Deer Creek Monthly Meeting.

On 29th day of 8th month, 1795, Thomas Morgan and Sarah Amos intend to marry. Sarah Right (formerly Dickinson) disowned for "having her marriage accomplished by a hireling." William Matthews requested a certificate for himself and wife Elizabeth to Indian Spring Monthly Meeting.

On 26th day of 9th month, 1795, Billingsley Bull "hath joined with and been active in the military duties." John Hair requested to be released from being an overseer and Samuel Matthews was appointed in his stead.

On 31st day of 10th month, 1795, Samuel Reed requested to be taken into membership, as also did Margaret Ann Lee (wife of William).

On 28th day of 11th month, 1795, Margaret Sanderson "produced an offering to this meeting to condemn her outgoing which is recommended to Baltimore Monthly Meeting to extend the necessary care." Mary Matthews (daughter of William) requested a certificate to Baltimore Monthly Meeting.

On 26th day of 12th month, 1795, Thomas Wilson requested a certificate for himself and wife Jane and children, David, Martha, Catharine, Samuel and Mary, to Hopewell Monthly Meeting in Virginia, and was later released from the station of an Elder due to his removal.

On 27th day of 2nd month, 1796, Elizabeth Naylor requested a certificate to Baltimore Monthly Meeting. Elizabeth Wheeler (formerly Jones) "had her marriage accomplished by the assistance of a hireling to a man not of our society." Sarah Morgan requested a certificate to Baltimore Monthly Meeting. Ann Shepherd (formerly Amoss) "hath gone out in marriage with a man in profession with us." David Harry requested to be released from being an overseer and Samuel McConnell was appointed in his stead.

On 26th day of 3rd month, 1796, Chalkly Albertsum attended this meeting an produced a certificate from Suttons Creek Monthly Meeting held near Suttons Creek, Perquimous [sic] County, North Carolina, dated 14th day of 11th month, 1795. Nathan Morris also produced a certificate from a Monthly Meeting held near Simmons Creek in Pasqatank [sic] County, North Carolina, dated 20th day of 2nd month, 1796. William Bond (of Samuel) "hath accomplished his marriage contrary to the good order." Thomas Lee "hath removed from amongst us to a distant part without a certificate."

On 30th day of 4th month, 1796, Martha Tuder requested her children, John, Joshua, Ann, Isaac, Elizabeth, and William, be taken into membership with Friends. Daniel Reese "hath had his marriage accomplished contrary to good order used amongst us and joined the Methodist society." Mary Tipton "hath attended a marriage accomplished by a hireling and has been active in dancing."

On 25th day of 6th month, 1796, William Amos requested a certificate for his son William Amos to Baltimore Monthly Meeting. Micajah Tipton "guilty of attending a marriage and dancing thereat." Reuben Griffith "guilty of attending places of diversion and dancing thereat."

On 30th day of 7th month, 1796, Jane Catts produced an offering to condemn her outgoing in marriage, and also requested a certificate to Nottingham Monthly Meeting. Benjamin Amos "hath been guilty of fighting and swearing and neglected the attendance of our religious meetings." William Maulsby "hath had his marriage accomplished contrary to the good order." Nathan Letter produced a certificate from Hopewell Monthly Meeting in Virginia, dated 4th day of 5th month, 1796.

On 27th day of 8th month, 1796, John Dickinson "sent in an acknowledgement to condemn his outgoing."

On 24th day of 9th month, 1796, Mary Hussey produced a certificate from Warrington Monthly Meeting, dated 13th day of 8th month, 1796. A certificate was produced for Rebeckah Moore and daughter Kitturah Moore. Ann Taylor produced an offering to condemn her outgoing, and later on the Fairfax Monthly Meeting was written to in this matter.

On 26th day of 11th month, 1796, Daniel Penington requested a certificate "for himself and wife Martha and their children, Elizabeth, John, Josiah and Levi, and his son Paul and his daughter Mary Hastings [Hestings?]." Mordecai Price and wife produced an offering to condemn their misconduct of "fornicating and being married by a hireling teacher." Elizabeth Wheeler produced an offering to condemn her misconduct for "outgoing in marriage."

GUNPOWDER MONTHLY MEETING CERTIFICATES OF REMOVAL, 1794-1800

On 28th day of 6th month, 1794, the following certificates were given: Edward Marshal to Providence Monthly Meeting in Rhode Island; Charles Harding to Northern District in Philadelphia; George Yarnal to Westland Monthly Meeting in Pennsylvania, with his children, Susannah, George, Mary, Aaron, Amos, Ely and Mordecai; and, Evan Griffith to Sadsbury Monthly Meeting in Pennsylvania, with his wife Rebecca and children, Sarah and Mary.

On 30th day of 8th month, 1794, Ezekiel Jones was given a certificate to Deer Creek Monthly Meeting.

On 27th day of 9th month, 1794, Benjamin Parsons was given a certificate to Pipe Creek Monthly Meeting.

On 25th day of 10th month 1794, Jesse Tyson was given a certificate to Baltimore Monthly Meeting, with his wife Margaret and children, Elizabeth, Isaac and Thomas.

On 31st day of 1st month, 1795, Elijah Lowdon was given a certificate to Indian Spring Monthly Meeting.

On 28th day of 3rd month, 1795, Hannah Matthews was given a certificate to Baltimore Monthly Meeting.

On 25th day of 4th month, 1795, the following certificates were given: Benjamin Amoss, son of William, to Baltimore Monthly Meeting; James Amoss, son of William, to Baltimore Monthly Meeting; and, Joshua Gibson to Redstone Monthly Meeting in Pennsylvania, with wife Lydia and children, Hannah, John, Lydia, Susannah, Eliza and Mary.

On 27th day of 6th month, 1795, the following certificates were given: Esther Tyson to Baltimore Monthly Meeting; and, Richard Price, son of Samuel, to Baltimore Monthly Meeting "and placed as an apprentice with his brother Warwick."

On 25th day of 7th month, 1795, Samuel Wilson was given a certificate to Baltimore Monthly Meeting.

On 25th day of 9th month, 1795, William Matthews was given a certificate to Indian Spring Monthly Meeting, with wife Elizabeth and children, Oliver, Ann, Elizabeth, Rebeckah, Meriam, Sarah, and Samuel Hanway.

On 31st day of 10th month, 1795, the following certificates were given: Isaac Morris to Deer Creek Monthly Meeting, with wife Martha and children, Susanna, Benjamin, Ann, Mary, Isaac, Enoch, Nehemiah, and John; and, Isaac Williams to Baltimore Monthly Meeting.

On 26th day of 12th month, 1795, Mary Matthews was given a certificate to Baltimore Monthly Meeting.

On 26th day of 3rd month, 1796, Sarah Morgan and her husband [no name given], and Elizabeth Nailor, were given certificates to Baltimore Monthly Meeting.

On 30th day of 4th month, 1796, Moses Lukins was given a certificate to Deer Creek Monthly Meeting, with wife Sarah and children, Lydia, Benjamin, and Rachel.

On 27th day of 6th month, 1796, Jane Cats was given a certificate to Nottingham Monthly Meeting.

On 30th day of 7th month, 1796, the following certificates were given: Thomas Maule to New Garden Monthly Meeting in Pennsylvania, with wife Margarett and children, Elizabeth and Caleb; Deborah Wilson to Baltimore Monthly Meeting, with children, Cathrine, Grace, William, John, Anna, Thomas, and David (all minors except Cathrine); William Amos, son of William Amos, Jr., to Baltimore Monthly Meeting; and, Margarett Sanderson to Baltimore Monthly Meeting. Nathan Litler was received by certificate from Hopewell Monthly Meeting in Virginia.

On 27th day of 8th month, 1796, Thomas Wilson was given a certificate to Hopewell Monthly Meeting in Virginia, with wife Jane and children, David, Martha, Cathrine, Samuel, Mary, and Thomas.

On 24th day of 9th month, 1796, Thomas Lee was given a certificate to Redstone Monthly Meeting in Pennsylvania.

On 29th day of 10th month, 1796, Rebecca Moore and daughter Kitturah Moore were given a certificate to Baltimore Monthly Meeting.

On 31st day of 12th month, 1796, the following certificates were given: Daniel Pennington to Warrington Monthly Meeting, with wife Martha and children, Elizabeth, John, Isaiah, and Levy; Paul Pennington to Warrington Monthly Meeting; and, Mary Heston to Warrington Monthly Meeting, noting that "she was young when she left our parts."

On 25th day of 2nd month, 1797, the following certificates were given: Mary Jewel, daughter of George and Mary Jewel, to Philadelphia Monthly Meeting; and, John Dickenson to New Cornwell Monthly Meeting in New York.

On 25th day of 3rd month, 1797, the following certificates were given: Jane Morrison to Redstone Monthly Meeting in Pennsylvania; William Matthews to Indian Spring Monthly Meeting; and, Isaiah Lancaster, minor son of Jesse, to Baltimore Monthly Meeting "as apprentice to John Wilson."

On 29th day of 4th month, 1797, Rachel Weeks was given a certificate to Baltimore Monthly Meeting.

On 24th day of 6th month, 1797, the following certificates were given: Ann Taylor to Fairfax Monthly Meeting in Virginia; and, Amos West, son of Thomas, to Baltimore Monthly Meeting "as apprentice to Israel Price."

On 29th day of 7th month, 1797, Rachel Scott was given a certificate to York Monthly Meeting in Pennsylvania.

On 25th day of 11th month, 1797, John Cornthwait was given a certificate to Baltimore Monthly Meeting.

On 28th day of 4th month, 1798, Anne Price was given a certificate to Baltimore Monthly Meeting.

On 26th day of 5th month, 1798, the following certificates were given: William Walton to Deer Creek Monthly Meeting, with wife Sarah and children, Lukens, Elizabeth, Alice, and Ann; John Wilson to Baltimore Monthly Meeting; and, Samuel Matthews to Baltimore Monthly Meeting, with wife Ann and children, Elizabeth, Sophia, Mary, and Samuel.

On 30th day of 6th month, 1798, the following certificates were given: Ruth Dickenson to Baltimore Monthly Meeting; and, Rachel Kinsey to Indian Spring Monthly Meeting.

On 28th day of 7th month, 1798, the following certificates were given: Catherine Hooker to Baltimore Monthly Meeting; John Burgess and Joseph Burgess, minor sons of Ann Burgess, to Deer Creek Monthly Meeting "as apprentices;" and, Mary Hussey to Baltimore Monthly Meeting.

On 24th day of 11th month, 1798, Dorithy Webster was given a certificate to Deer Creek Monthly Meeting.

On 29th day of 12th month, 1798, the following certificates were given: Samuel Reed to Baltimore Monthly Meeting, with wife Elizabeth and infant daughter Matilda; and Israel Pennington to Warrington Monthly Meeting in Pennsylvania.

On 26th day of 1st month, 1799, Fielder Richardson and wife Miriam were given a certificate to Fairfax Monthly Meeting in Virginia.

On 23rd day of 2nd month, 1799, Mary Perine was given a certificate to Baltimore Monthly Meeting.

On 27th day of 4th month, 1799, Samuel Naylor and wife Rebecca were given a certificate to Baltimore Monthly Meeting.

On 25th day of 5th month, 1799, Oliver Matthews and wife Phebe were given a certificate to Baltimore Monthly Meeting.

On 27th day of 7th month, 1799, John Dillon and Thomas Brown were given certificates to Baltimore Monthly Meeting.

On 26th day of 10th month, 1799, Keturah Parrish was given a certificate to Pipe Creek Monthly Meeting, and Jarrett Price was given one to Baltimore Monthly Meeting.

On 30th day of 11th month, 1799, George Jewell and wife Mary were given a certificate to Baltimore Monthly Meeting.

On 28th day of 12th month, 1799, Ann Shepherd, Phebe Carr and James Naylor were given certificates to Baltimore Monthly Meeting.

On 29th day of 3rd month, 1800, the following certificates were given: Sarah Ryon to Middletown Monthly Meeting in Pennsylvania; Gravener Jefferys to Baltimore Monthly Meeting "as apprentice to John Morgan"; and, Samuel Jefferys to Baltimore Monthly Meeting "as apprentice to Amos James."

On 31st day of 5th month, 1800, the following certificates were given: Ann Marsh to Baltimore Monthly Meeting; and, Joshua Stapleton to Baltimore Monthly Meeting, with wife Susanna and children, Samuel and Susanna.

On 26th day of 7th month, 1800, Robert Cornthwait and Priscilla Morgan were given certificates to Baltimore Monthly Meeting.

On 29th day of 11th month, 1800, Rachel Naylor was given a certificate to Baltimore Monthly Meeting.

On 27th day of 12th month, 1800, Mary Hussey was given a certificate to Warrington Monthly Meeting in Pennsylvania.

DEER CREEK MONTHLY MEETING, BIRTHS AND DEATHS, 1742-1800

John Coale, first son of William and Sarah, b. 15th day of 3rd month, 1762, and d. 8th day of 5th month, 1763, and bur. in Friends Burying Ground at Deer Creek on the 9th.

Isaac Coale, second son of William and Sarah, b. 29th day of 4th month, 1764.

Rigbie Coale, third son of above William and his second wife Elizabeth, b. 8th day of 10th month, 1771, and d. 177- [sic], and bur. in Friends Burying Ground at Deer Creek.

Christopher Wilson, first son of John (of Christopher) and Massanna, b. 12th day of 12th month, 1766.

Isaac Wilson, second son of John (of Christopher) and Massanna, b. 11th day of 10th month, 1768.

Children of Issac Webster (of Bush River) and wife Sarah: Isaac Webster, Jr., eldest son, b. 2nd day of 11th month, 1761; Joseph Webster, second son, b. 18th day of 1st month, 1764; Margaret Webster, first dau., b. 4th day of 3rd month, 1766; William Webster, third son, b. 24th day of 11th month, 1767; John Lee Webster, fourth son, b. 23rd day of 12th month, 1770; James Webster, fifth son, b. 6[?] day of 12th month, 1772; and, Robert and Samuel Webster, sixth and seventh sons, b. 8th day of 1st month, 1775.

Children of Jacob Giles and wife Johannah: Elizabeth Giles, b. 8th day of 6th month, 1747; James Giles, b. 2nd day of 12th month, 1749; Johannah Giles, b. 29th day of 5th month, 1751; Jacob Giles, b. 15th day of 3rd month, 1753 "New Stile;" Thomas Giles, b. 25th day of 12th month, 1754; Aquilla Giles, b. 29th day of 8th month, 1757; Edward Giles, b. 24th day of 4th month, 1759.

Mary Talbott, dau. of John (of Bush River) and Margaret, b. 11th day of 8th month, 1765.

Children of John Wilson (of the Barrens) and wife Anne: Joseph Wilson, b. 27th day of 3rd month, 1756; William Wilson, second son, b. 19th day of 2nd month, 1758; Frances Wilson, first dau., b. 7th day of 3rd month, 1760; Hannah Wilson, second dau., b. 16th day of 5th month, 1762; Martha Wilson, third dau., b. 8th day of 6th month, 1764; Anne Wilson, fourth dau., b. 7th day of 5th month, 1766; and, Grace Wilson, fifth dau., b. 10th day of 11th month, 1768.

Children of James Rigbie and wife Elizabeth: Nathan Rigbie, b. 5th day of 11th month, 1742; Sarah Rigbie, first dau., b. 22nd day of 6th month, 1744; Cassandra Rigbie, second dau., b. 15th day of 1st month, 1746; Elizabeth Rigbie, third dau., b. 11th day of 7th month, 1751; and, James Rigbie, second son, b. 27th day of 12th month, 1756.

Elizabeth Rigbie, wife of James, d. 22nd day of 7th month, 1759, and bur. at Deer Creek Meeeting Burying Ground.

Children of James Rigbie and wife Sarah: Massey Rigbie, first dau., b. 7th day of 7th month, 1762; Anna Rigbie, second dau., b. 12th day of 2nd month, 1764; and, Mercy Rigbie, third dau., b. 17th day of 3rd month, 1770.

Isaac Massey, son of Aquila and Sarah, b. 25th day of 9th month, 1756.

Nathan Rigbie, son of James and Elizabeth, d. in the 3rd month called March, 1767, and bur. in Friends Burying Ground at Deer Creek.

Massey Rigbie, dau. of James and Sarah, d. in the 3rd month, 1767, and bur. in Friends Burying Ground at Deer Creek.

Children of Daniel Robertson and wife Elizabeth: Elizabeth Robertson, first dau., b. 20th day of 2nd month, 1771; Margaret Robertson, second dau., b. 11th day of 2nd month, 1773; Mary Robertson, third dau., b. 9th day of 5th month, 1774; Hannah Robertson, fourth dau., b. 20th day of 6th month, 1776; Samuel Robertson, first son, b. 24th day of 7th month, 1778; and, Isaac Robertson, second son, b. 20th day of 10th month, 1780.

Ann Brown, dau. of [illegible] Brown and wife Sarah, b. 14th day of 10th month, 1772 [?].

Children of Henry Cowgill and wife Ruth: James Cowgill, first son, b. 26th day of 4th month, 1761 [Note: Record mistakenly shows year as 1771]; Mary Cowgill, first dau., b. 4th day of 7th month, 1764; Ruth Cowgill, second dau., b. 22nd dy of 10th month, 1766; Henry Cowgill, second son, b. 20th day of 1st month, 1769; and, Rachel Cowgill, third dau., b. 11th day of 4th month, 1771.

Children of Philip Coale (of Deer Creek) and wife Ann: Cassandra Coale, first dau., b. 6th day of 12th month, 1766; Frances Coale, second dau., b. 19th day of 9th month, 1768; Sarah Coale, third dau., b. 17th day of 8th month, 1770; Richard Coale, first son, b. 10th day of 7th month, 1772; Ann Coale, fourth dau., b. 16th day of 9th month, 1774; Elizabeth Coale, fifth dau., b. 25th day of 2nd month, 1777; William Coale, second son, b. 2nd day of 4th month, 1779; and, Philip Coale, third son, b. 16[?] day of 11th month, 1781.

Children of Samuel Willets and wife Ann: Sarah Willets, first dau., b. 16th day of 9th month, 1770; and, Cassandra Willets, second dau., b. 6th day of 5th month, 1774.

Children of Samuel Harris and wife Margarett: Joseph Harris, first son, b. 12th day of 1st month, 1754; Ann Harris, first dau., b. 29th day of 3rd month, 1755; Samuel Harris, second son, b. 22nd day of 9th month, 1756; Mary Harris, second dau., b. 12th day of 3rd month, 1758; John Harris, third son, b. 20th day of 11th month, 1759; Elizabeth Harris, third dau., b. 20th day of 11th month, 1761; George Harris, fourth son, b. 30th day of 11th month, 1763, and d. 15th day of 9th month, 1764, and bur. in Friends Burying Ground at Deer Creek; George Harris the 2nd, and fifth son, b. 12th day of 6th month, 1765; William Harris, sixth son, b. 25th day of 8th month, 1767; Benjamin Harris, seventh son, b. 16th day of 2nd month, 1769; Sarah Harris, fourth dau., b. 31st day of 8th month, 1771; Thomas Harris, eighth son, b. 24th day of 10th month, 1773, and d. 8th day of 11th month following, and bur. in Friends Burying Ground at Deer Creek; and, Thomas Harris the 2nd, and ninth son, b. ---- [blank].

Children of John Worthington and wife Priscilla: Sarah Worthington, first dau., b. 16th[?] day of 3rd month, 1770; Priscilla Worthington, second dau., b. 12th day of 3rd month, 1772; Henry Worthington, first son, b. 12th day of 7th month, 1773; John Worthington, second son, b. 22nd day of 12th month, 1774; Rachel Worthington, third dau., b. 21st day of 11th month, 1776; Charles Worthington, third son, b. 21st day of 10th month, 1778; Elizabeth Worthington, fourth dau., b. 14th day of 6th month, 1780; William Worthington, fourth son, b. 15th day of 3rd month, 1782; Cassandra Worthington, fifth dau., b. 26th day of 12th month, 1784, and d. 4th day of 9th month, 1785, and bur. in Friends Burying Ground at Deer Creek; Samuel Worthington, fifth son, b. 27th day of 4th month, 1786; and, Thomas Worthington, sixth son, b. ---- [blank].

Elizabeth Giles, first dau. of Jacob Giles, Jr. and wife Anna, b. 24th day of 9th month, 1774.

Children of Gerard Hopkins and wife Sarah: John Hopkins, first son, b. 7th day of 12th month, 1775; Leven Hopkins, second son, b. 20th day of 12th month, 1777; Frances Hopkins, first dau., b. 8th day of 8th month, 1779;

Susannah Hopkins, second dau., b. 26th day of 8th month, 1781; William Hopkins, third son, b. 10th day of 3rd month, 1783; Grace Jacob Hopkins, third dau., b. 15th day of 2nd month, 1785; and, Amelia Hopkins, fourth dau., b. 9th day of 12th month, 1787.

Children of Isaiah Balderston and wife Martha: Sarah Balderston, first dau., b. 30th day of 11th month, 1773; Ely Balderston, first son, b. 9th day of 5th month, 1786; Perthenia Balderston, second dau., b. 8th day of 3rd month, 1778; Jacob Balderston, second son, b. 27th day of 1st month, 1780, and d. 24th day of 12th month, 1781, and bur. in Friends Burying Ground at Deer Creek; Hugh Balderston, third son, b. 22nd day of 12th month, 1782; and, Jonathan Balderston, fourth son, b. 10th day of 6th month, 1785.

Children of Joshua Bennett and wife Mary: Rebeckah Bennett, first dau., b. 4th day of 1st month, 1785, and d. 29th day of 8th month, 1789, and bur. in Friends Burying Ground at Deer Creek; Mary Bennett, second dau., b. 1st day of 1st month, 1787, and d. 21st day of 8th month, 1789, and bur. in Friends Burying Ground at Deer Creek; Hannah Bennett, third dau., b. 14th day of 1st month, 1789; Joshua Bennett, first son, b. 17th day of 8th month, 1790; Mary Bennett, fourth dau. [Note: Record mistakenly shows her as third daughter], b. 17th day of 6th month, 1792; and, Sarah Bennett, fifth dau. [Note: Record mistakenly shows her as fourth daughter], b. 19th day of 3rd month, 1796.

Children of Joseph Husband and wife Mary: Joshua Husband, first son, b. 28th day of 12th month, 1764; Mary Husband, first dau., b. 5th day of 11th month, 1767; Sarah Husband, second dau., b. 18th day of 2nd month, 1770; Hannah Husband, third dau., b. 16th day of 10th month, 1772, and d. in the 4th month, 1786; William Husband, second son, b. 23rd day of 5th month, 1774; Joseph Husband, third son, b. 21st day of 3rd month, 1776; Elizabeth Husband, fourth dau., b. 2nd day of 2nd month, 1778; Lydia Husband, fifth dau., b. 18th day of 10th month, 1779; Samuel Husband, fourth son, b. 8th day of 1st month, 1782; and, Susanna Husband, sixth dau., b. 29th day of 9th month, 1783.

Joseph Husband, the father, d. 6th day of 5th month, 1786.

Children of Abel Spencer and wife Rebeckah: Elizabeth Spencer, first dau., b. 21st day of 4th month, 1780; William Spencer, first son, b. 4th day of 1st month, 1782; Sarah Spencer, second dau., b. 16th day of 5th month, 1783; Rebekah Spencer, third dau., b. 15th day of 12th month, 1785; Abel Spencer, second son, b. 11th day of 3rd month, 1788; Reuben Spencer, third son, b. 14th day of 12th month, 1790; and, Joseph Spencer, fourth son, b. 12th day of 6th month, 1793.

Children of Richard Webb and wife Elizabeth: Moses Webb, first son, b. 8th day of 6th month, 1777; James Webb, second son, b. 8th day of 12th month, 1778; Mercy Webb, first dau., b. 30th day of 4th month, 1780; Joseph Webb, third son, b. 3rd day of 9th month, 1781; Mary Webb, second dau., b. 2nd day of 10th month, 1784; John Webb, fourth son, b. 10th day of 5th month, 1786; and, Jesse Webb, sixth son, b. 20th day of 6th month, 1787.

Elizabeth Webb, wife of above Richard, d. 25th day of 7th month, 1787.

Richard Webb, sixth son of above Richard, by his wife Mary, b. 25th day of 8th month, 1791.

Children of Gideon Prevale and wife Mary: Ann Prevale, second dau., b. 22nd day of 7th month, 1777; Margret Prevale, third dau., b. 15th day of 12th month, 1778; Samuel Prevale, first son, b. 29th day of 9th month, 1780; John Prevale, second son, b. 14th day of 8th month, 1784; and, Elizabeth Prevale, "fith daughter of Gideon, the others deceased and not recorded," b. 14th day of 3rd month, 1788.

Children of Aquila Massey and wife Anna: James R. Massey, first son, b. 7th day of 7th month, 1794; Jonathan Massey, b. 25th day of 7th month, 1796; Sarah Bolton Massey, b. 17th day of 8th month, 1798, and d. 6th day of 9th month, 1801; Isaac Massey, b. 9th day of 10th month, 1801; Aquila Bolton Massey, b. 11th day of 2nd month, 1804; Rigbie Massey, b. 15th day of 2nd month, 1807; and, William Massey, b. 27th day of 4th month, 1809.

Children of Samuel Coale and wife Lydia: Mary Coale, first dau., b. 8th day of 8th month, 1777; William Coale, first son, b. 13th day of 1st month, 1779; Skipwith Coale, second son, b. 25th day of 9th month, 1780; Joshua Coale, third son, b. 16th day of 11th month, 1782, and d. 12th day of 7th month, 1802; Samuel Coale, fourth son, b. 15th day of 10th month, 1783, and d. 31st day of 8th month, 1804; Margarett Coale, second dau., b. 11th day of 2nd month, 1787; Joseph Coale, fifth son, b. 17th day of 1st month, 1790; Samuel Coale, sixth son, b. 17th day of 10th month, 1791; Lewis Coale, seventh son, b. 27th day of 11th month, 1793; Lydia Coale, third dau., b. 8th day of 11th month, 1798; and, Ellis P. Coale, eighth son, b. 1st day of 5th month, 1802.

Children of Joshua Husband and wife Margaret: Mary Husband, first dau., b. 29th day of 11th month, 1793; Joseph Husband, first son, b. 28th day of

6th month, 1796; Anna Husband, second dau., b. 23rd day of 1st month, 1798; Herman Husband, second son, b. 12th dy of 5th month, 1800; John Jewett Husband, third son, b. 10th day of 3rd month, 1803; Joshua Husband, fourth son, b. 16th day of 11th month, 1807; and, Margaret Husband, third dau., b. 12th day of 7th month, 1810.

Children of Isaac Jones and wife Elizabeth: Thomas Jones, first son, b. 26th day of 1st month, 1794; Asa Jones, second son, b. 23rd day of 4th month, 1795; and, John Jones and Mary Jones, third son and first dau., b. 2nd day of 11th month, 1796.

Children of Samuel Hopkins and wife Rachel: John Hopkins, first son, b. 4th day of 4th month, 1799; Priscilla Hopkins, first dau., b. 9th day of 7th month, 1801; Joseph Hopkins, second son, b. 18th day of 1st month, 1803, and d. 17th day of 8th month, 1803; Joseph Hopkins, third son, b. 13th day of 11th month, 1804; Henry Hopkins, fourth son, b. 4th day of 2nd month, 1807; Eliza Hopkins, second dau., b. 15th day of 4th month, 1809; Elenor Hopkins, third dau., b. 21st day of 9th month, 1811; and, Samuel Hopkins, fifth son, b. 24th day of 4th month, 1814.

DEER CREEK MONTHLY MEETING MARRIAGE CERTIFICATES, 1761-1800

James Rigbie, son of Nathan Rigbie, deceased, of Baltimore County, m. Sarah Massey, dau. of Isaac Boulton of Bucks County, Pa., and widow of Aquila Massey, late of Baltimore County, on 5th day of 2nd month, 1761, at Deer Creek. Witnesses: Joseph Hopkins, Ann Hopkins, Hosier Johns, Margaret Coale, Sarah Coale, Margaret Harris, Elizabeth Lee, Ann Rigbie, Sarah Rigbie, Jonathan Massey, Natt Rigbie, Jr., Sarah Rigbie, Cassandra Rigbie, N. Rigbie, Joseph Bolton, Philip Rigbie, Cassandra Rigbie, William Cox, Skipwith Coale, Joseph Hopkins, Jr., Joseph Hayward, Joh Forwood, Grace Wallis, Hannah Johns, Nathan Johns, Philip Coale, Cassandra Coale, Ann Johns, Joseph Jones, Samuel Harris.

William Coale, son of Skipwith Coale, deceased, m. Sarah Webster, dau. of Isaac Webster, deceased, both of Baltimore County, on 11th day of 4th month, 1761, near Bush River. Witnesses: Margaret Coale, Margaret Webster, Hannah Richardson, Margaret Talbot, John Talbot, Elizabeth Lee, Sary Worthington, Ann Hopkins, John Wallis, Sary Hammond, John Worthington, William Cox, Samuel Harris, Thomas Pycraft, Isaac Webster,

Cassandra Webster, James Webster, Elizabeth Webster, Cassandra Coale, Ann Webster, Hannah Johns, Samuel Webster, Richard Johns, Samuel Gover, Margaret Harris, Sary Coale, Cassandra Lee, Rachel Wilson, Joseph Wilson, Jr.

John Wallis, son of Samuel Wallis, deceased, m. Cassandra Coale, dau. of Skipwith Coale, deceased, both of Baltimore County, on 3rd day of 12th month, 1761, at Deer Creek. Witnesses: Margaret Coale, Grace Wallis, Edward Wallis, William Coale, Jr., Susannah Coale, Sarah Wallis, Francis Dallam, Richard Dallam, William Coale, Francis Wallis, Sarah Coale, Sarah W. Coale, James Rigbie, Sarah Rigbie, N. Rigbie, Sarah Rigbie, Anna Rigbie, Richard Johns, Philip Coale, Sarah Coale, Hosier Johns, Nathan Johns, Mary Johns, Sarah Rigbie, Jr., Ann Johns, Elizabeth Dallam, Sarah Worthington, Mary Worthington, Joseph Hopkins, Joseph Howard, Mary Hopkins, Pricila Gover, Charles Worthington.

Joseph Scott, son of Jacob and Hannah Scott, m. Ann Haward [Note: Record shows name spelled four different ways: Haward, Hawood, Howard and Hayward], both of Baltimore County, on 29th day of 4th month, 1762, at Deer Creek. Witnesses: Jacob Scott, Hannah Scott, Joseph Haward, Rebecah Haward, Betty Haward, Mary Scott, Betsy Gover, Joseph Jones, James Rigbie, Sarah Rigbie, Anne Hopkins, N. Rigbie, Joseph Hopkins, Grace Wallis, Peggy Harriss, Ann Rigbie, Sarah Coale, Cassy Rigbie, Mary Hopkins, Sarah Rigbie, Jr., Naomi Greenland, Cassy Gover, Mary Gover, Sarah Greenland, Skipwith Coale, Jos. Bruce, Samuel Richardson, Joseph Hopkins, Jr., Gerrard Hopkins, Jr., William Hopkins, Joseph Wilson, Ephraim Gover, Henry Coalson.

Jonathan Massey, son of Aquila Massey, deceased, m. Cassandra Webster, dau. of Isaac Webster, deceased, both of Baltimore County, on 6th day of 7th month, 1763, near the head of Bush River. Witnesses: Margaret Webster, Hannah Richardson, Margaret Talbot, John Talbot, Elizabeth Webster, Sary W. Coale, Alasanna Webster, Ann Webster, James Rigbie, Sary Rigby, N. Ribgy, Samuel Webster, Margaret Hill, William Coale, Jr., Anna Rigbie, William Cox, Mary Cox, Grace Wallice, Elizabeth Lee, Margaret Coale, Mary Webster, Rachel Lee, Mary Lee, Cassandra Rigbie, George Stuart, Sary Rigbie, Jr., Richard Wilmott, Joseph Wolsey.

Joseph Hurford, son of John and Hannah Hurford, of New Garden Monthly Meeting, Pennsylvania, m. Naomy Greenland, dau. of Flour Greenland, deceased, of Deer Creek, Baltimore County, Maryland, on 20th day of 10th month, 1763, at Deer Creek. Witnesses: John Hurford, Ann Greenland, Samuel Hurford, Isaac Hurford, Elisabeth Hurford, Richard Greenland, Sary Greenland, Mary Dixon, William Dixon, Richard Thomas, Grace Thomas, William Cox, John Cox, Sary Cox, James Rigbie, Sarah Rigbie, Joseph Hopkins, Ann Hopkins, Joseph Jones, Sarah Rigbie, Grace Wallace, Timothy Keen, Richard Johns, Sary W. Coale, Anne Rigbie, Sary Rigbie, Jr., Sary Coale, Samuel Richardson, Cassandra Wilson, Rachel Wilson, Cassandra Rigbie, Susannah Hopkins.

John Wilson, son of Christopher Wilson, of Cumberland County, Old England, deceased, and his wife Sarah, m. Alasanna Webster, dau. of Isaac Webster, of Baltimore County, deceased, and his wife Margret, on 14th day of 11th month, 1764, near the head of Bush River. Witnesses: Alasana Bond, Margaret Pleasants, Sary Rigby, Sary W. Coale, Elizabeth Webster, Ann Webster, Robert Pleasants, Samuel Webster, Margaret Webster, Hannah Richardson, Isaac Webster, Mary Tredway, Margaret Hill, Cassandra Lee, Rachel Lee, Cassandra Wilson, Rachel Wilson, Alasanna Bond, John Talbott, Margaret Richardson, Nathaniel Giles, Elisabeth Giles, Jno. Bond, N. Rigbie, Daniel Robertson, James Christie, Robert Key, Robert Christie, Daniel Richardson, Sophia Hall, Ann Fell, J. Thomas, Jr., William Wilson, Mary Cox, Hannah Day, Thomas Pycraft, William Cox.

William Coale, son of Skipwith Coale, deceased, m. Elizabeth Rigbie, dau. of James Rigbie, both of Baltimore County, on 18th day of 5th month, 1769, at Deer Creek. Witnesses: Grace Wallis, William Hopkins, Rachel Hopkins, Jane Allen, Joseph Husbands, Mary Husbands, Margret Gover, Sary Cox, Rachel Gover, Sarah Coale, Samuel Coale. N. Rigbie, Ann Willets, Amelia Coale, Sarah Rigbie, Samuel Willets, James Rigbie, Isaac Massey, Hannah Rigbie, James Rigbie, Sarah Rigbie, Margret Coale, Skipwith Coale, Philip Coale, Cassandra Coale, Susan Coale, Sarah Rigbie, Susan Rigbie, Cassandra Coale.

Joseph Hopkins, son of Joseph....[rest of page is blank].

Samuel Hopkins, son of Phillip Hopkins, deceased, of Anne Arundel County, and his wife Elizabeth, m. Mary Gover, dau. of Ephraim Gover, of Baltimore County, and his wife Elizabeth, on 8th day of 6th month, 1769, at Deer Creek. Witnesses: Elizabeth Hill, Susanna Hopkins, Margret Harris, Frances Dallam, Elizabeth Wilmott, James Lee, Joseph Hopkins, Jr., William Hopkins, Elizabeth Lee, Cassandry Wilson, Ann Hopkins, Skipwith Coale, Rachel Hopkins, Sarah Coale, Gerrard Hopkins (son of Richard?),

Cassandry Gover, Margret Gover, Joseph Hopkins, Gerrard Hopkins, Nicholas Hopkins, John Worthington, Joseph Wilson, Jr., James Rigbie, Sarah Rigbie, Grace Wallis, Cassandry Wilson, Rachel Wilson, Samuel Wilson, John Wilson.

George Pusey, son of John Pusey, late of Chester County, Pennsylvania, deceased, and his wife Catherine, m. Sarah Cox, dau. of William and Mary Cox, of Baltimore County, om 7th day of 9th month, 1769, at Deer Creek. Witnesses: N. Rigbie, G. Mason, James Rigbie, T. Woodward, Sarah Rigbie, Grace Wallis, Joseph Hopkins, William Hopkins, Sarah Coal, Elisabeth Hopkins, James Webb, Rachel Hopkins, John Wilson, Skipworth Coal, John Brice, William Cox, Mary Cox, John Pusey, John Cox, William Cox, [Jr.?], Elisabeth Cox, Joseph Husband, Mary Husband, Ann Stedman, Rachel Wilson, Casandry Sheridine, Hannah Rigbie, Joseh Prichard, Sarah Rigbie, John Worthington, John Stedman.

John Hopkins, son of Samuel Hopkins, deceased, and his wife Sarah, of Patapsco, Baltimore County, m. Elizabeth Chew, dau. of Joseph Chew, deceased, and his wife Sarah, of Deer Creek, on 24th day of 11th month, 1768, at Deer Creek. Witnesses: William Coale, Grace Wallis, James Rigbie, Joseph Jones, John Talbott, Frances Dallam, Susanna Coale, Skipwith Coale, Susanna Hopkins, Margret Harris, Sarah Coale, Mary Worthington, Joseph Hopkins, Jr., Samuel Harris, Joseph Hopkins, William Hopkins, Sarah Yeates, Samuel Hopkins, Margaret Hopkins, Thomas Chew, Elizabeth Hopkins, Ann Hopkins, Rachel Hopkins, Samuel Hopkins, John Wilson, Samuel Willetts, Ephraim Gover, Sarah Rigbie, Jr., William Webb, Gerrard Hopkins, Cassandra Rigbie.

Winston Smith Dallam, son of Richard Dallam, deceased, and his wife Frances, m. Margret Gover, dau. of Ephraim Gover, deceased, and Elizabeth his wife, both of Deer Creek, Baltimore County, on 9th day of 1st month, 1772. Witnesses: Margret Harris, Joseph Wilson, Jr., Susanna Dallam, Sarah Wallis, J. Patrick, Priscilla Gover, Elizabeth Lee, Ann Webster, Elizabeth Willmot, Mary Willmot, Sarah Coale, Philip Gover, Mary Lee, Rachel Wilson, Joseph Hopkins, Jr., Alisana Wilson, Ann Harris, Philip Coale, William Hopkins, John Worthington, Mary Cox, William Cox, John Bruce, Elizabeth Coale, John Wilson, Susanna Hopkins, Gerrard Hopkins, John Hopkins, Leven Hopkins, William Coale, Jr., William Husband, Skipwith Coale, Grace Wallis, Samuel Harris, Frances Dallam, Ann Coale, Richard Dallam, Sr., Elizabeth Hopkins, Cassandra Gover, Rachel Gover,

John Dallam, Joseph Husband, Mary Husband, Sarah Rigbie, James Rigbie, Ann Hopkins, Joseph Hopkins, Samuel Gover.

William Cox, son of William and Mary Cox, m. Rachel Gover, dau. of Ephraim Gover, deceased, and his wife Elisabeth, both of Deer Creek, Harford County, on 19th day of 5th month, 1774, at Deer Creek. Witnesses: Jos. Wilson, Samuel Wilson, Gittings Wilson, Winston Dallam, Samuel Harris, Samuel Wilson, Sr., W. Webb, Joseph Wilson, Jr., Samuel Worthington, John Smith, Solomon Reess [Reese], William Wise, Hollis Hanson, Leven Hopkins, William Ellis, Gittings Gover, Prissila Gover, Samuel Hopkins, Timothy Keen, Joseph Dove, Ephraim Read, Willm.[?] Morgan, Ann Harris, Joseph Hopkins, Sr., Skipwith Coale, William Hopkins, William Wilson, Richard Jones, Rachel Hopkins, Grace Wallis, Hannah Forwood, John Wilson, Thomas Ruckman, Sary Ruckman, Nathan Jones, John Forwood, Philip Coale, Joseph Husband, Mary Husband, Elisabeth Coale, William Coale, Jr., John Bruce, Sary Rigbie, Jr., Hannah Rigbie, William Wilson, Jr., Joseph Harris, John Kid Wilson, Mary Cox, John Cox, Elizabeth Hopkins, Cassandry Gover, Mary Banes Cox, Philiph Gover, Samuel Gover, Mary Hopkins, Margret Dallam, Elizabeth Cox, Elizabeth Lee, Sary Cox, Mary Wilmott, Prissila Gover, Sr., Ann Hopkins, Francis Dallam, Joseph Hopkins, Jr., John Worthington, Francis Wallis.

Cuthbert Warner, of Deer Creek Lower Hundred in Baltimore County, m. Rachel Hill, dau. of William Hill, of said hundred, on 18th day of 11th month, 1773, at Deer Creek. Witnesses: Joseph Hopkins, William Coale, Sr., Joseph Husband, Mary Husband, Grace Wallis, Hannah Rigbie, James Harris, Sr., Isaac Money[?], John Bond, Samuel Worthington, Sary Rigbie, Jr., Sary Rigbie, N. Rigbie, Hugh Ely, Sary Balderston, James Rigbie, James Rigbie, Jr., William Cox, Jr., Joseph Warner, Ruth Warner, Mary Hill, Benjamin Warner, Thomas Ely, Hannah Warner, Mary Warner, Thomas Ely, Mahlon Ely, Joseph Warner, Jr., Joseph Ely, Mary Warner, Joseph Warner, Rachel Ely.

Joseph Hopkins, Jr., son of Joseph and Ann Hopkins, m. Elizabeth Gover, dau. of Ephraim and Elizabeth Gover, both of Deer Creek, Baltimore County, on 9th day of 2nd month, 1769, at Deer Creek. Witnesses: Ann Hopkins, Elizabeth Hill, Margret Harris, Mary Gover, Margret Gover, Priscilla Wilson, Rachel Hopkins, Joseph Hopkins, Sr., Ephraim Gover, Casandrew Wilson, Rachel Wilson, Casandry Lee, Prissilla Wilson, Elizabeth Giles, Charlot Andrews, Casandrew Ward, Joseph Husband,

Elisabeth Wilson, Mary Wilson, John Worthington, Garrard Hopkins, John Wilson, Jr., Henry Wilson, Jr., Samuel Harris, Mary Husband, Philiph Gover, Priss. Gover, Elisabeth Lee, Samuel Lee, Jo. Jos. [sic] Wallis, Mary Worthington, Grace Wallis, Sary Wallis, John Dallam, Sary Coale, Mary Cox, Casandrew Wallis, Samuel Wilson, Samuel Hopkins, Skipworth Coale, Charles Worthington, Samuel Gover, Joseph Harris, Richard Downing, Joseph Wilson, [Jr.?], Josey[?] Lee, J. Patrick, James Lee, [Jr.?], W. Webb, John Wilson, Henry Parepont, Richard Rows, Edward Ward, Elizabeth Morgan, Samuel McWilliams.

Benjamin Sharpless, of the City of Philadelphia, son of Benjamin and Edith Sharpless, m. Sarah Rigbie, dau. of James and Elizabeth Rigbie, of Deer Creek, Baltimore County, on 4th day of 11th month, 1774, at Deer Creek. Witnesses: James Rigbie, Sarah Rigbie, Isaac Sharpless, Rebecky Sharpless, Elizabeth Coale, James Rigbie, Sr., Casandry Pearse, Sarah Rigbie, Casandry Sheridine, Skipworth Coale, William Cox, Sr., Rachel Cox, Sr., Sarah Coale, Ann Harris, Philiph Coale, Joseph Hopkins, Jr., John Worthington, Mary Husband, Ziba Faris, Mary Cox, Elisabeth Hopkins, William Coale, Jr., Sarah Coale, Isaac Massey, Margret Harris, Hannah Rigbie, Ann Rigbie, Ann Coale, Isack Coale, Susan Coale, Joseph Warner, Soffy Jay, Mary Hill.

Thomas Ely, Jr., of Harford County, m. Hannah Warner, dau. of Crosedale Warner, of said county, on 24th day of 1st month, 1776, at Deer Creek. Witnesses: James Rigbie, Sarah Rigbie, Joseph Warner, John Bruce, Cuthbert Warner, Mary Balderston, Aseph Warner, Mary Warner, Ruth Warner, Shem Hill, Martha Warner, Thomas Stapleton, Joseph Warner, Jr., Hezekiah Warner, Thomas Ely, Croasdel Warner, Mary Warner, Hugh Ely, Isaiah Balderston, Sarah Balderston, Martha Balderston, Rachel Ely, Ruth Ely, Mahlon Ely, Joseph Ely.

Stephen Norton m. Sophia Jay, both of Harford County, on 11th day of 4th month usually called April, 1776, at Deer Creek. Witnesses: N. Rigbie, Ann Hopkins, Elizabeth Hopkins, Skipwith Coale, Martha Wilson, Frances Wallis, Grace Wallis, Samuel Harris, William Scotten, Margret Harris, Charles Hopkins, Elizabeth Coale, Stephen Jay, Hannah Jay, Ann Coale, Susannah Coale, Elizabeth Jay, Hannah Jay, Hannah Johns, Philip Coale, Hannah Giles, Sarah Rigbie.

Samuel Coale, son of Skipwith Coale, deceased, and his wife Margret, of Harford County, m. Lydia Pusey, dau. of Joshua Pusey, deceased, and his wife Mary, of Chester County, Pennsylvania, on 17th day of 10th month, 1776, at Deer Creek. Witnesses: James Rigbie, Margret Harris, John Bruce, Philip Coale, Joseph Hopkins, Sr., William Hopkins, John Forwood, Grace Wallis, Susanna Hopkins, Frances Wallis, Hannah Moore Hopkins, Elizabeth Husband, Elizabeth Smith, Skipwith Coale, Mary Husband, Hannah Harvey, Lewis Pusey, Amos Harvey, Joseph Husband, Elizabeth Coale.

Richard Webb, son of James and Mary Webb, of Fawn Township, York County, Pennsylvania, m. Elizabeth Burgess, dau. of Joseph and Deborah Burgess, of said township, on 12th day of 2nd month called February, 1777, at Deer Creek in Harford County. Witnesses: Hugh McFadden, Margret Cooper, Ann Wilson, William McConnell, Priscilla West, Rachel West, Jesse Burgess, Joseph Tucker, Abraham Tucker, Elizabeth Tucker, Thomas Wilson, Jonathan West, John Wilson, John Wilson, John Cousins [Couzens?], William Wilson, Sally Wilson, Frances Young Wilson, Hannah Wilson, Elizabeth Morgan, Sarah Cousins, Rachel Pane, Mary Pane, William Cooper, James Webb, Mary Webb, Joseph Burgess, Deborah Burgess, Tacey Burgess, Sarah Webb, John Webb, George West, Sally Tucker.

George Mason, son of George Mason of Kennet Township, Chester County, Pennsylvania, m. Susanna Hopkins, dau. of William and Rachel Hopkins, of Harford County, Maryland, on 4th day of 12th month, 1778, at Deer Creek. Witnesses: Hannah Giles, Elizabeth Husband, Elizabeth Husband, Jr., Rachel Husband, Polley Husband, Susanna Husband, Mary Rowls, Susanna Hall, Grace Jacob, Nancy Mason, Mary Cox, Mary Husband, Elizabeth Wallis, Priscilla Gover, Hannah Hopkins, Thomas Andrews, Hannah Moore Hopkins, Elizabeth Wallis, Thomas Chew, James Lindley, Elihu Hall, Jr., John Worthington, Ann Harris, Thomas Andrews, Levi Woodson, Mary Cox, Joseph Hopkins, Richard Dallam, John Harris, Robert Gover, Samuel Hopkins, Cassandra Gover, James Rigbie, Sarah Rigbie, Hannah Richardson, John Forwood, John Bruce, Joseph Wilson, Jr., Samuel Gover, Joseph Miller, Samuel Hopkins, William Morgan, John Hopkins, Mary Worthington, Martha Wilson, Grace Mason, Elizabeth Hopkins, Sarah Hopkins, Mary Wilson, Susanna Chew, Frances Young Wilson, Monica Wheeler, Mary Ann Wheeler, Priscilla Gover, William Hopkins, Jane Mason, Benjamin Mason, John Mason, Gerrard Hopkins, Catherine Hall, James Mason, Joseph Hopkins, Margret Harris, Elizabeth Hopkins, Charles Hopkins, Joseph Hopkins, Jr., Levin Hill Hopkins, Joseph Husband,

Hezekiah Rolls, Grace Wallis, John Wilson (of Christopher), Jos. Wallis, Samuel Wilson, Samuel Harris, Jr., William Ellis.

Leven Hill Hopkins, son of William and Rachel Hopkins, m. Frances Wallis, dau. of Samuel Wallis, deceased, and his wife Grace, both of Harford County, on 18th day of 5th month, 1780, at Deer Creek. Witnesses: Samuel Hopkins, Joseph Wilson, Jr., Gittings Gover, Christopher Wilson, Isaac Wilson, Samuel Wallis, Richard Dallam, William Ellis, William Coale, Grace Coale, Isaac Massey, Ann Coale, Sarah Hopkins, Alexander McCaskey, Hannah McCaskey, Elizabeth Hopkins, Sarah Coale, Sarah Fisher, Hannah Moore Hopkins, Skipwith Coale, John Dun, Joseph Warner, Aseph Warner, William Cox, Sarah Rigbie, Anna Rigbie, Joseph Husband, Mary Husband, Mary Cox, Philip Coale, Ann Coale, John Wilson, John Bruce, Anna Bruce, Isaac Coale, Mary Ann McCaskey, Ann Harris, Mary Cox, Rachel Husband, J. Hall (Practitioner of Physick), Mary Husband, Elizabeth Harris, Robert Gover, Grace Wallis, William Hopkins, Rachel Hopkins, Gerrard Hopkins, Hannah Hopkins, Elizabeth Husband, Elizabeth Wallis, Cassandra Jacob, Margret Harris, Richard Johns, William Coale, Jr., Elizabeth Coale, Sarah Coale, William McCaskey, Charles Hopkins, John Harris, Margret Dallam.

James Hayhurst and Mary Warner, both of Harford County, m. 9th day of 11th month, 1780, at Deer Creek. Witnesses: Philip Coale, Elizabeth Coale, Priscilla Worthington, Ann Harris, Mary Cox, Hannah Forwood, Ann Willits, Joseph Stokes, Hannah Stokes, Joseph Kennard, Levi Kennard, Jacob Balderston, Mary Balderston, Sarah Balderston, Mahlon Ely, Mary Ely, Isaiah Balderston, Martha Balderston, Anne Warner, William Ely, Aaron Warner, Hannah Litton, William Murphey, Stephen Morford, Hezekiah Warner, Jonathan Richard [Prichard?], Ruth Hayhurst, Joseph Husband, William Ellis, William Coale, Benjamin Warner, Sarah Warner, James Hayhurst, John Hayhurst, Thomas Loney, Elizabeth Loney, Abel Spencer, Joseph Ely, Rachel Ely, Mary Warner, Thomas Ely, Jr., Joshua Smith, Martha Warner, John Smith, Jr., Hugh Ely, Sarah Ely.

Samuel Wallis, son of Samuel and Elizabeth Wallis, of Kent County, Maryland, m. Sarah Sharpless, widow of Benjamin Sharpless and dau. of James and Elizabeth Rigbie, of Harford County, on 11th day of 4th month called April, 1782, at Deer Creek. Witnesses: Rachel Cox, Jr., Ann Hopkins, Samuel Harris, Isaac Coale, Joshua Husband, William Hopkins, Samuel Harris, Jr., Sarah Ely, John Harris, Puree Lamb, J. Hall, Jr., Ann Coale,

Samuel Willits, Skipwith Coale, Joseph Hopkins, Jr., Skipwith Johns, Nathan Johns, Mary Cox, Margarett Harris, Elizabeth Wallis, Margarett Dallam, James Rigbie, Susannah Rigbie, Isaac Massey, William Coale, Jr., Elizabeth Coale, Cassandra Pearce, Ann Willits, Mary Rigbie, Skipwith Coale.

Richard Snowden, son of Samuel and Elizabeth Snowden, of Prince George's County, Maryland, m. Hannah Moore Hopkins, dau. of William and Rachel Hopkins, of Harford County, on 2nd day of 8th month, 1782, at Deer Creek. Witnesses: Richard Snow Thomas, Joseph Wheeler, John Smith, John Orrick[?], Charles Worthington, Mary Willmott, Priscilla Worthington, Mary Ann McCaskey, Elizabeth Harris, Hannah McCaskey, Hannah McCaskey, Ann Hopkins, Samuel Hopkins, Joseph Miller, William Coale, Elihu Hall, Richard Dallam, William Hopkins, Jr., Priscilla Gover, Elizabeth Coale, Margarett Dallam, John Bruce, Elizabeth Gover, John Wilson, Joseph Husband, J. Worthington, Mary Husband, John Harris, Joseph Harris, William Ellis, Alissanna Wilson, Samuel Harris, Jr., Samuel Gover, Gittings Gover, Samuel Gover, Joseph Wilson, Jr., William McCaskey, Daniel Richardson, William Wilson, Rodger Matthews, John Clark Jenkins, Robert Gover, John Chew Thomas, William Osborn, Philip Gover, John Dallam, Ralph Smith, Samuel Snowden, William Hopkins, Elizabeth Husband, Mary Snowden, Gerrard Hopkins, Leven Hill Hopkins, Charles Hopkins, Samuel Hopkins, Jr., Rachel Husband, Mary Husband (the younger), Susanna Husband, Elizabeth Husband (the younger), Mary Hopkins, Grace Mason, Elizabeth Hopkins, Mary Worthington, Ann Harris, Joseph Hopkins, Jr., Samuel Harris, John Hopkins, Sarah Worthington, Cassandra Gover, Hannah Jay.

Joseph Brinton, son of Moses Brinton, of Leacock Township, Lancaster County, Pennsylvania, m. Susannah Rigbie, dau. of James Rigbie, of Harford County, Maryland, on 8th day of 10th month, 1784, at Deer Creek. Witnesses: Mary Husband, Sarah Coale, Sarah Bolton, Sarah Corse, Priscilla Worthington, Henry Wilson, Susannah Rogers, Margaret Harris, Philip Coale, Mary Cox, Isaac Coale, Anna Coale, Ann Coale, Jr., Joseph Husband, Mary Moore, Elinor Brinton, Cassandra Webster, Ann Willits, William Coale, Ann Harris, John Corse, Isaac Webster, Moses Brinton, Elinor Brinton, Moses Brinton, Jr., James Rigby, Jr., Cassandra Corse, Elizabeth Coale, Anna Rigbie, Robert Moore, Massey Rigbie, James Rigbie, Sarah

Wallis, Sarah Wallis, Isaac Massey, Elizabeth Harris, Sarah Morgan, Cassandra Coale, John Hopkins, Sarah Burgess, Samuel Wallis.

William Ellis, son of Benjamin and Ann Ellis, deceased, of Chester County, Pennsylvania, m. Mercy Cox, dau. of William Cox, deceased, and his wife Mary, of Harford County, on 10th day of 2nd month, 1785. Witnesses: John Forwood, Mordecai Warner, Joshua Husband, Sarah Husband, Mary Ann McCaskey, Hannah McCaskey, Thomas Rodgers, Gerrard Hopkins, Samuel Hopkins, Joseph Harris, Jesse Morgan, Isaac Coale, John Harris, Sarah Worthington, Elizabeth Hopkins, Ann Coale, Freeborn Brown, Joseph Hopkins, Micajah Churchman, Frances Young Wilson, Sarah Day, Joseph Husband, Mary Husband, Elizabeth Hopkins, John WIlson, Alissannah Wilson, Ann Willits, William Hopkins, Anna Rigbie, Sarah Coale, Margret Dallam, Ruth Carter, Philip Coale, Cassandra Coale, Sarah Morgan, William Ellis, Mercy Ellis, Mary Cox, John Cox, Rachel Cox, Jr., Israel Cox, Mary Cox, Jr., Sarah Richardson, Margret Harris, Elizabeth Coale, Margret Churchman, Robert Gover.

Samuel Harris, son of Samuel and Margret Harris, m. Cassandra Gover, dau. of Ephraim Gover, deceased, and his wife Elizabeth, on 10th day of 3rd month, 1785. Witnesses: John Dallam, Thomas Wallis, John WIlson, William Cox, Samuel Gover, Skipwith Coale, Jacob Hall, Nicholas Eckson, John Smith, William Morgan, George England, Thomas Fisher, Mary Hall, Joseph Miller, Joseph Hopkins, William Coale, Jr., Rachel Cox, Jr., Elizabeth Gover, Sarah Staner[?], Charles Worthington, Henry Worthington, Joseph Husband, Mary Husband, John Worthington, Samuel Willits, Gerrard Hopkins, Charles Hopkins, Alasanna Wilson, George Harris, Benjamin Harris, Gideon Pervail, Israel Cox, Henry Stump, Jr., Philip Coale, Mary Ann McCaskey, Anna Rigbie, Ann Massey, Margaret Rodgers, Nancy Hopkins, Mary Skinner, Samuel Harris, Jr., Margaret Harris, Elizabeth Hopkins, Ann Harris, Margaret Dallam, Rachel Cox, Joseph Harris, Samuel Gover, Elizabeth Harris, John Harris, Gittings Gover, Robert Gover, Mary Pervail.

Isaac Coale, son of William and Sarah Coale, m. Rachel Cox, dau. of William Cox, deceased, and his wife Mary, on 7th day of 9th month, 1786. Witnesses: Frances Coale, John Forwood, Jacob Balderston, Cassandra Coale, Mary Ann McCaskey, Mary Husband, Sarah Coale, Ruth Wallace, Sarah Warner, James Wilson, Samuel Hopkins, Mary Husband, Jr., Micajah Churchman, Isaac Massey, Joshua Husband, Gainer[?] Churchman, Margret Dallam,

Mordecai Churchman, Dotty Smith, Hannah Wilson, Martha Wilson, Ann Benfield Wilson, Sally Smith, Sarah Day, Mary Balderston, Margret Coale, Sarah Richardson, John Wilson, Anna Rigbie, Peggy Webster, Elizabeth Pleasants, Alisanna Wilson, Hannah Richardson, Philip Coale, Mercy Rigbie, William Coale, Mary Cox, Elizabeth Coale, John Cox, William Cox, Skipwith Coale, Mary Cox, Jr., Christopher Wilson.

Joseph Jones, son of Isaac and Ann Jones, of Fawn Township, York County, Pennsylvania, m. Phebe Lukens, dau. of Benjamin and Alice Lukens, of Upper Deer Creek Hundred, Harford County, Maryland, on 18th day of 4th month, 1787, at Fawn Township Meeting. Witnesses: Tacey Burgess, Martha Balderston, Moses Dillon, William Amos, Jr., Richard Webb, Thomas Colley, John Elliott, Jr., John Cox, Susannah Mason, Samuel Hopkins, Mary Cox, Isaiah Balderston, Mary Lukens, John Webb, Jacob Lukens, Mary Balderston, George West, Hannah West, Moses Lukens, Jeremiah Heaton, Jr., William Heaton, Ezekiel Jones, Sarah Warner, Sarah Lukens, Magdalen Lukens, Isaac Jones, Anna Jones, Benjamin Lukens, Alice Lukens, Ann Jones, Jr., Aaron Warner, Charles Lukens, Isaac Jones, Jr., Anthony Jones.

Thomas Wilson, son of Peter Wilson of Cumberland County, Old England, deceased, and his wife Ann, m. Sarah Richardson, dau. of Nathan Richardson, of Harford County, deceased, and his wife Hannah, on 7th day of 2nd month, 1788, at Deer Creek. Witnesses: Joseph Miller, John Worthington, Mary Balderston, Joshua Husband, Jacob Balderston, Susannah Rogers, Philip Coale, Elizabeth Coale, William Coale, Rachel Coale, Margret Coale, Samuel Carter, William Stump, Samuel Coale, Samuel Hopkins, Mary Husband, Cassandra Stump, Skipwith Coale, Anna Rigbie, Joseph Harris, Gerrard Hopkins, Joseph Hopkins, Christopher Wilson, Isaac Massey, Isaac Coale, John Wilson, Ann Willets, Lee Webster, John Skinner Webster, Mary Cox, Charles Worthington, John Stump, Hannah Richardson, John Wilson, Margret Hill Bradford, Peter Wilson, Alesanna Wilson, Ann Jewett, Peggy Webster, Sarah Wilson.

Isaac Massey, son of Aquila Massey and wife Sarah, deceased, m. Margret Webster, dau. of Isaac and Sarah Webster, the latter deceased, all of Harford County, on 10th day of 6th month, 1788, near the head of Bush River. Witnesses: Sarah Wilson, Daniel Sheredine, Herman Stump, Elizabeth Robertson, Ann Jewett, Jos.[?] Rumsey, Daniel Robertson, Aquila Massey, Isaac Bolton, Sarah Bolton, Samuel Wallis, Philip Coale, Samuel Coale, Randel Wallis, Isaiah Balderston, Sarah Webster, James

Webster, Margret Jewett, Samuel Webster, Robert Webster, Thomas Webster, Cassandra Webster, Elizabeth Robertson, Hannah Richardson, Alisanna Wilson, James Rigbie, Jr., Cassandra Woodland, Isaac Webster, Cassandra Webster, Anna Rigbie, Joseph Webster, Wm.[?] Webster, Lee Webster, Samuel Webster, James Webster, Christopher Wilson, Elizabeth Johns.

John Tomkins, yeoman, of Fawn Township, York County, Pennsylvania, son of Benjamin and Mary Tomkins, m. Sarah Burges, dau. of Joseph and Deborough Burges, of Harford County, Maryland, on 20th day of 5th month, 1789, at Fawn Township. Witnesses: Susannah Rogers, Richard Webb, George West, Jacob Balderston, William Ely, Priscilla Kennard, Rachel Eaton, John Cox, Joseph Kennard, Jeremiah Heaton, Jr., Ann Ely, Joseph Ely, Ezekiel Jones, Isaac Jones, Jr., Priscilla West, Mary Balderston, Benjamin Lukens, Ellin Manifold, Mary Bennet, Joshua Bennet, Thomas Burges, Daniel Burges, Martha Burges, John Burges, Grace Burges, Letishe Burges, Martha Balderston, Rachel Ely, Ann Jones, Isaiah Balderston, Isaac Jones, Benjamin Tomkins, Joseph Burges, Mary Jenkins, Deborah Burges, Elizabeth Walton, Rachel Tomkins, Sarah Jenkins, Tacey Burgess, Elisha Walton.

Christopher Wilson, son of John and Alasannah Wilson, m. Margaret Coale, dau. of Skipwith and Sarah Coale, all of Harford County, on 10th day of 8th month, 1789, at Deer Creek. Witnesses: Jesse Hoops, William L. Coale, Nancy Woodland, Elizabeth Hopkins, Margaret Coale, Margaret Dallam, Mary Cox, Susannah Coale, Margaret Dallam, Lydia Coale, Peggy Robertson, John Jewett, Isaac Webster, Mary Husband, Martha Balderston, Sarah Ely, Isaiah Balderston, Mary Wilson, Isaac Starr, Jr., Cassandra Stump, Priscilla Worthington, James Robertson, Mary Balderston, Elizabeth Robertson, Catherine Hall, Samuel Robertson, Joseph Hopkins, Jr., Hosea Johns, Samuel Coale, Mary Perveil, Peter Wilson, Sarah Hopkins, Anna Rigbie, Sarah Day, Frances Hopkins, Gerrard Hopkins, Frances Coale, Sarah Coale, Ann Ely, Tracey Wiggins, Samuel Hopkins, Henry Wilson, Prisey Worthington, Mary Ann McCaskey, Frances Dallam, Sarah Husband, James Wilson, Joseph Harris, John Hopkins, Aquilla Massey, Gideon Perveil, John Dallam, Samuel Wallis, Jr., Enoch Story, Isaac Coale, John Lee Webster, Jr., Elizabeth Robertson, Cassandra Woodland, Ann Jewett, Cassandra Durbin, Joseph Wilson, Samuel Dallam, Thomas Wilson, Charles Hopkins, Anna Hopkins, Sarah Worthington, Sarah Chew, Margaret Massey, Sarah Webster, John Wilson, Alasannah Wilson, Skipwith Coale, Sarah Coale, Sarah Coale, Sarah Wilson, Isaac Wilson, John W. Wilson, Susanna Wilson, Margaret Wilson, Hannah Richardson, Nixon Wilson, William Coale, John Lee Webster, Elizabeth Webster, Daniel Robertson, Joseph Hopkins, Samuel Coale, Thomas Wilson, Joseph Worthington, Joshua Husband.

Daniel Mifflin, of Accomack County, Virginia, m. Mary Husband, the Elder, of Deer Creek in Harford County, Maryland, on 6th day of 11th month, 1789, at Deer Creek. Witnesses: Thomas Wilson, Joshua Bennet, Sarah Wilson, Mary Bennet, Margaret Massey, John Dallam, Martha Wilson, Mary Dallam, Sarah Cook, Tracey Wiggins, Hugh Ely, Joseph Warner, Margaret Wilson, Mary Cox, Isaiah Balderston, Hannah Wilson, Martha Wilson, Mary Wilson, William Hayward, Peter Wilson, Hannah Richardson, John Cox, Henry Wilson, Anna Rigbie, Ann Willits, Elizabeth Johns, Sillah [Fillah?] Brown, Jacob Balderston, Sarah Wilson, Christopher Wilson, Mary Husband, William Coale, Mary Coale, Rebekah Chambers, Ann Coale, Sarah Coale, Jr., Sarah Ely, John Wilson, Alisanna Wilson, Sarah Coale, Isaac Coale, Samuel Hopkins, Cassandra Stump, Ann Coale, Sr., Martha Balderston, Mary Balderston, Susannah Coale, Philip Coale, William Coale, Ellis Pusey, Joshua Pusey, Lydia Coale, Samuel Coale, Mary Husband, Hannah Pusey, Elizabeth Husband, Joshua Husband, William Husband, Joseph Husband, Sarah Husband, Elizabeth Pusey, Herman Stump, Rachel Husband.

William Hayward, of Baltimore Town, son of Joseph Hayward and wife Rebecca, of Baltimore Town, the former deceased, m. Mary Husband, dau. of Joseph Husband and wife Mary, late of Deer Creek in Harford County, the former likewise deceased, on 13th day of 5th month, 1790, at Deer Creek. Witnesses: William Coale, Isaac Coale, David E. Price, Ebenezer Maule, Christopher Wilson, Ann Coale, Frances Hopkins, Elizabeth Hawkins, William Jenkins, Sally Wilson, Martha Wilson, Jonathan Coates, Jr., Mary Cox, Hugh Ely, Sarah Ely, John Wilson (of Joseph), Sarah Coale, Philip Coale, Margaret Wilson, Frances Coale, Mary Husband, Mary Wilson, Mary Coale, John W. Wilson, Elizabeth Hopkins, Ruth Carter, Anna Rigbie, Margarett Massey, Hannah Richardson, Rachel Hopkins, Sarah Wallis, Mary Brown, Samuel Hopkins, Elizabeth Husband, William Wilson, Scott Hughes, Cassandra Coale, Mary Mifflin, Joshua Husband, Enion Williams, Sarah Husband, Hannah Williams, Sarah Hayward, Samuel Coale, Lydia

Coale, Margery Gilpin, Cassandra Stump, William Husband, John Stump, Jr., Herman Stump, John Wilson (of Christopher), William Coale, Skipwith Coale, Joseph Husband, Alasanna Wilson.

Moses Lukins, son of Benjamin and Alice Lukins, of Deer Creek Upper Hundred, Harford County, Maryland, m. Sarah Tomkins, dau. of Benjamin and Mary Tomkins, of Fawn Township, York County, Pennsylvania, on 28th day of 4th month, 1790, at Fawn Township Meeting. Witnesses: Richard Webb, Joshua Bennet, George West, Rebekah Mantle, Mary Webb, Sarah Tomkins, Gaynor Lukens, John McGough, Thomas Doran, Elizabeth Freeland, James Walton, Hannah Walton, John Tomkins, Isaac Strawbridge, Benjamin Lukens, Alice Lukins, Benjamin Tomkins, Mary Tomkins, Rachel Tomkins, Joel Evans, Phebe Jones, Mary Bennet, Charles Lukens, Ann Tomkins, Joseph Jones, Sarah Lukens, Mahdalen Lukens, Mary Lukens.

Aaron Warner, son of Crosdale and Mary Warner, m. Achsah Morgan, dau. of John Morgan, deceased, and his wife Mary, both of Harford County, on 4th day of 11th month, 1790, at Deer Creek. Witnesses: Cassa Bayles, Gerrard Hopkins, Sarah Hopkins, Frances Hopkins, Joseph Ely, Joseph Wiggins, Cassandra Coale, Ann Ely, Gideon Pervail, Silas Warner, Hugh Morgan, Drusilla Morgan, John Burges, George Harris, Elizabeth Johns, Ruth Carter, Anna Hopkins, Tracey Wiggins, Peter Wilson, Samuel Hopkins, Isaac Massey, Christopher Wilson, Croasdel Warner, Ann Bruce, Mary Warner, Agness Warner, Sarah Morgan, Hannah Ely, Joseph Warner, Ruth Warner.

Samuel Hopkins, son of William Hopkins, deceased, and his wife Rachel, m. Sarah Husband, dau. of Joseph Husband, deceased, and his wife Mary, both of Harford County, on 2nd day of 12th month, 1790, at Deer Creek. Witnesses: Frances Coale, Joel Morgan, Ruth Carter, Skipwith Coale, David E. Price, Isaac Coale, William Coale, Elizabeth Johns, Elizabeth Coale, Randal Wallis, Mary Gover, Aseph Warner, Martha Wilson, Cassandra Coale, Mary Wilson, Sarah Wilson, Rachel Hopkins, Lydia Coale, Joshua Husband, Gerrard Hopkins, Sarah Hopkins, Charles Hopkins, Frances Hopkins, Elizabeth Husband, Samuel Coale, John Hopkins, Philip Coale, Ann Coale, Anna Hopkins.

Nicholas Cooper, son of Nicholas and Sarah Cooper, of York County, Pennsylvania, m. Sarah Balderston, dau. of Isaiah and Martha Balderston, of Harford County, Maryland, on 3rd day of 11th month, 1791, at Deer

Creek. Witnesses: Hugh Ely, Alisanna Wilson, Joshua Brown, Samuel Coale, Sarah Hopkins, Francis Hopkins, Elizabeth Hopkins, Anna Rigbie, Joseph Hopkins, Slipwith Coale, Hannah Richardson, Elizabeth Johns, Rachel Hopkins, Thomas Wilson, Peter Wilson, Elizabeth Hawkins, Nathan Johns, Ann Coale, Mary Cooper, Joshua Husband, Alban Gilpin, Israel Cox, Alice Cooper, Stephen Cooper, Hugh Cooper, John Gill Barclay, James Barclay, John Ollemore[?] or Oshmore[?], William Chapman, William Cooper, Thomas Ely, John Wilson, Nicholas Cooper, Isaiah Balderston, Martha Balderston, Sarah Ely, John Barclay, Ecey[?] Cooper, Hannah Cooper, Ann Ely, Duckett Cooper, Sarah Barclay, Mary Cooper, Jacob Balderston, Mary Balderston.

Samuel Gover, son of Philip Gover and his wife Mary, deceased, m. Ann Hopkins, dau. of Joseph and Elizabeth Hopkins, both of Harford County, on 3rd day of 11th month, 1791, at Deer Creek. Witnesses: Ruth Warner, Sarah Wilson, Joshua Husband, Sarah Hopkins, Isaiah Balderston, Peter Wilson, Samuel Coale, Jacob Balderston, Eliza Hopkins, Francis Dallam, Eliza Husbands, Margaret Wilson, Cassandra Dallam, Elizabeth Hopkins, Rachel Husband, Margaret Wilson, Elizabeth Barr, Joseph Worthington, Mary Ann Gibson, Mary Cox, Mary Ann McCaskey, Joseph Wilson, Joseph Harris, James Jonston[?], James Robinet, John Lee Gibson, George Harris, Robert Randall, Christopher Wilson, John Smith, John Worthington, Samuel Hopkins, Thomas Wilson, Mas[?] Chew, Cartt[?] Thomas, Edward Prall, John Stump, Martha Wilson, Mary Husband, Sally Wilson, John W. Wilson, Joshua Brown, Ann Coale, Elizabeth Johns, Margaret Massey, Marth Balderston, Sarah Jonson, Elizabeth Dallam, Francis Hopkins, Richard S. Thomas, Skipwith Coale, Charles Hopkins, Samuel Gover, Robert Gover, William Cox, Nathaniel Gover, Ephraim Gover, Ephraim Gover, John Wilson, Alisanna Wilson, Cassandra Stump, Joseph Hopkins, Elizabeth Hopkins, Elizabeth Gover, Elizabeth Hopkins, Prissala Gover, Philip Gover, Robert Gover, John Hopkins, Gerrard Gover, Joseph Hopkins, Jr., Hannah Richardson, Ann Rigbie.

Joshua Husband, son of Joseph Husband, deceased, and his wife Mary, m. Margaret Jewet, dau. of Thadeus and Ann Jewet, both of Harford County, on 27th day of 2nd month, 1793, at Bush River. Witnesses: Mary Ruff, Joseph Warner, Jacob Balderston, Isaac Coale, Betey Richardson, Sarah Wilson, James Webster, Jr., Daniel Turner, Joseph Burges, Thomas [Turner, Jr.?], Hannah Richardson, James Orr, Richard Ruff, Henry Ruff, Isaac Webster,

Jr., Richard Bull, Thomas Webster, Elizabeth Johns, Isaac Robertson, Nancy Bull, William Wilson, John Lee Webster, John S. Webster, Susan Webster, Polly Webster, Ann Jewet, Lydia Coale, Elizabeth Husband, Elizabeth Robertson, Samuel Webster, Joseph Husband, Samuel Coale, John Jewet, Thomas Jewet, Samuel Hopkins, Daniel Robertson, Peggy Robertson, Samuel Webster, Jr., Herman Stump.

Charles Lukens, son of Benjamin and Alice Lukens, of Deer Creek Upper Hundred, Harford County, m. Sarah Coale, dau. of Philip Coale, deceased, and his wife Ann, of Deer Creek Lower Hundred, Harford County, on 4th day of 4th month, 1793, at Deer Creek. Witnesses: William Morgan[?], Hugh Morgan, Ezekiel Jones, Mary Balderston, James Webster, Margaret Dallam, Ann Coale, Lydia Coale, Mary Dallam, Silas Warner, Ruth Warner, Aseph Warner, Samuel Hopkins, John Wilson, Ann Rigbie, William Coale, Susannah Rodgers, Margaret Husband, Samuel Coale, Sarah Hopkins, Sarah Ely, Elizabeth Johns, Jr., Sarah Wilson, Jacob Balderston, Sarah Lukens, Skipwith Coale, Joseph Warner, Benjamin Lukens, Alice Lukens, Ann Coale, Cassandra Coale, Frances Coale, Richard Coale, Ann Coale, Elizabeth Coale, Richard Johns, Sally Wilson, Alice Lukens, Jr., Moses Lukens, Elizabeth Johns.

Aquilla Massey, son of Jonathan Massey and his wife Cassandra, deceased, m. Anna Rigbie, dau. of James Rigbie and his wife Sarah, deceased, all formerly of Harford County, on 3rd day of 10th month, 1793, at Deer Creek. Witnesses: William Wilson, Joseph Ford, Lydia Coale, Hugh Ely, Samuel Coale, Samuel Gover, Sarah Wilson, Ann Pervail, Samuel Hopkins, Ann Wilson, James Webster, Sarah Ely, John Lee Webster, Elizabeth Hopkins, Susannah Coale, Joseph Harrishall[?] or Joseph Harris Hall[?], Christopher Hall, Margaret Massey, Henry Wilson, Jacob Balderston, Christopher Wilson, Randal Wallis, Samuel Wallis, Samuel Hopkins, William Woodland, Elizabeth Coale, Cassandra Dallam, Drucilla Wilson, Mary Husband, Elizabeth Hopkins, Ruth Warner, William Cox, Isaac Massey, Anne Bull, Sarah Wallis, John Massey, Cassandra Willits, Cassandra Woodland, John Wilson, Isaac Coale, Richard Bull, Daniel Robertson, Jonathan Woodland, Ann Gover.

Joseph Ford, son of William and Rosanna Ford, m. Frances Coale, dau. of Philip and Ann Coale, deceased, both of Harford County, on 10th day of 4th month, 1794, at Deer Creek. Witnesses: Susanna Dallam, Susanna Hopkins, Elizabeth Johns, Sarah Coale, Samuel Coale, Lydia Coale, Susanna Hopkins, Jr., Sarah W. Hopkins, Sarah Hopkins, John Dallam, Skipwith Coale, Joseph Wilson Dallam, John Wilson (of Henry), Joel Hopkins, William Hopkins, John Ford, Richard Coale, Cassandra Coale, Sarah Lukins, Ann Coale, Philip Coale, William Coale, Elizabeth Hopkins, Polley Webster, Susan Webster, Peggy Webster, Elizabeth Coale, Susanna Coale.

William Ely, son of Thomas Ely and his wife Sarah, deceased, of Harford County, m. Martha Preston, dau. of Henry Preston and his wife Rachel, deceased, of York County, on 30th day of 4th month, 1794, at Fawn Township Meeting. Witnesses: Rachel Tomkins, Martha Bond, Mary Webb, Elizabeth Walton, Elizabeth Kennard, John Cox, Joshua Bennett, Mary Bennett, Elinor Manifold, Ann Tomkins, Joseph Kennard, Benjamin Tomkins, Mary Tomkins, Joseph Warner, Thomas Kennard, Sarah Tomkins, Priscilla Kennard, John Tomkins, Abel Spencer, Jacob Balderston, Hugh Ely, Joseph Ely, Levi Kennard, Ann Kennard, Rachel Ely, Ann Ely, Sarah Ely, William Chapman, Mary Chapman.

Aaron Boram, son of John and Ann Boram, both deceased, m. Elizabeth Johns, dau. of Nathan and Elizabeth Johns, both of Harford County, on 3rd day of 7th month, 1794, at Deer Creek. Witnesses: Benjamin Wilson, Samuel Hopkins (of W.), Mary Coale, William Cox, John Forwood, Joshua Husband, Peter Wilson, Samuel Coale, Jacob Balderston, Sarah Wilson, Elizabeth Dallam, Ann Worthington, Sarah Hopkins, Polly Churchman, Mordica Crawford, Ruth Crawford, Isaac Coale, Richard Coale, Rachel Coale, Susannah Stapleton, Nathan Johns, William Cox, Frances Crawford, Cassandra Bayles, Margaret Wilson, Elizabeth Coale, Henry Wilson, William Coale, Frances Hopkins, Mary Cox, Elizabeth Hopkins.

Jesse Hoops, son of David and Esther Hoops, of Kent County, Maryland, m. Sarah Wilson, dau. of John and Alisanna Wilson, of Harford County, on 26th day of 9th month, 1794, at Deer Creek. Witnesses: Peter Wilson, Rachel Coale, Frances Hopkins, Thomas Wilson, Margaret Shumaker, Susanna Hopkins, Skipwith Coale, William Coale, John Stump, Elizabeth Coale, Hugh Morgan, Isaac Vanbiber, Nixon Wilson, Nancy Wilson, Thomas Wilson, Isaac Coale, John L. Webster, James[?] Brown, Daniel Robertson, Isaac Webster, Elizabeth Robertson, Polley Webster, Ann Jewett, Peggy Webster, Sarah Wilson, Susanna Webster, Margaret Massey, Ann Pervail, David Hoops, John Wilson, Alasanna Wilson, Esther Hoopes, Joseph Hoopes, Lydia Hoopes, Thomas Hoopes, Susanna Wilson, Christopher

Wilson, Isaac Wilson, Margaret Wilson, Margaret Wilson, James Wilson, John W. Wilson.

Richard Johns, son of Nathan and Elizabeth Johns, m. Sarah Wilson, dau. of Benjamin and Elizabeth Wilson, both of Harford County, on 30th day of 10th month, 1794, at Deer Creek. Witnesses: Sarah Wilson, Samuel Bayles, Mary Pervail, John Forwood, Samuel Hopkins, Samuel Coale, Mary Wilson, Hannah Wilson, Elizabeth Jay, Gerrard Hopkins, Jacob Balderston, Sarah Wallis, Ann Pervail, William Worthington, Joseph Dallam, Philip Coale, Elizabeth Coale, Joseph Brinton, Ann Massey, William Cox, Jr., Skipwith Coale, Lydia Stapleton, Nathan Johns, Benjamin Wilson, Elizabeth Johns, Margaret Wilson, Sarah Wilson, John Wilson, Frances Crawford, Cassandra Bayles, Nathan Johns, Sarah W. Hopkins, Lydia Coale, Cassandra Coale, Peter Wilson, Margaret Dallam.

Richard Coale, son of Philip Coale, late of Harford County, and his wife Ann, both deceased, m. Alesanna Wilson, dau. of Thomas Wilson, of said county, and his wife Ann, the latter deceased, on 1st day of 1st month, 1795, at Deer Creek. Witnesses: Susanna Coale, Elizabeth Hopkins, Jacob Balderston, Mary Balderston, Joshua Husband, Margaret Husband, Samuel Hopkins [of J.?], Margaret Massey, James Wilson, David Clendinin, Reuben Stump, Frances Hopkins, Martha Wilson, Joseph Wilson, Sarah Wilson, Sarah Wilson, Mary Dallam, Peter Wilson, John Dallam, Adam Clendinin, Susannah Webster, Peggy Webster, John Wilson, Sarah W. Hopkins, Susannah Rogers, Margaret Dallam, Peggy Wilson, William Coale (of Wm.), Pricilla Wilson.

John Burges, of Fawn Township, York County, Pennsylvania, son of Joseph and Deborah Burges, of Cambel County, Virginia, m. Drusilla Morgan, dau. of John Morgan, of Harford County, Maryland, deceased, and his wife Ann, on 28th day of 10th month, 1795, at Deer Creek. Witnesses: Martha Tomkins, Rachel Tomkins, John Tomkins, Sarah Wilson, Susanna Stapleton, Armfield Morgan, Hugh Ely, Rachel Ely, Ruth Warner, William Ely, William Coale, Joshua Stapleton, Croasdel Warner, Jr., Asa Warner, Aquilla Massey, George Harris, Martha Ely, Agness Warner, Ann Warner, Anna Bruce, Hugh Morgan, Sarah Nicar, Tacey Burges, Daniel Burges, Martha Burges, Sarah Tomkins, Elizabeth Coale, Sarah Warner, Silas Warner, Croasdel Warner, Robert Bruce, John Bruce, Sarah Ely,

John Sharp, son of Thomas and Susannah Sharp (the latter deceased) of Harford County, m. Elizabeth Walton, widow of William Walton, and dau.

of Anthony and Elizabeth Kennard, of York County, Pennsylvania (the former deceased), on 3rd day of 6th month, 1795, at Fawn Township Meeting. Witnesses: Mary Underwood, Benjamin Bond, Martha Bond, John Cox, Sarah Underwood, Elizabeth Heaton, Charlotte Sharp, Elizabeth McClery, Richard Webb, Mary Webb, Joshua Bennet, Mary Bennet, Benjamin Tomkins, Mary Tomkins, Abel Spencer, Elizabeth Kennard, Joseph Walton, Thomas Sharp, Susanna Barton, Levi Kennard, Jacob Balderston, Mary Balderston, Ann Kennard, Thomas Kennard, Anthony Kennard.

Amos Evans, of Fawn Township, York County, Pennsylvania, son of Griffith Evans, of said county, and his wife Jane, deceased, m. Rachel Tomkins, dau. of Benjamin and Mary Tomkins, of said county, on 28th day of 9th month, 1796, at Fawn Township Meeting. Witnesses: Joseph Walton, William Mantle, Mathew Clark, James Walton, Hannah Walton, Rachel Eaton, Elisha Walton, Elizabeth Walton, Martha Ely, Sarah Underwood, Abraham Strawbridge, Rebeccah Strawbridge, Elizabeth Spencer, Moses Lukens, Sarah Lukens, Mary Webb, Joshua Bennett, Mary Bennett, Mary Bond, David Eaton, Sarah Pinnix, Robert Allen, Abel Spencer, Massa Webb, Martha Burges, James Doves, Rachel Doves, Griffith Evans, Benjamin Tomkins, Mary Tomkins, Ann Tomkins, Joel Evans, Sarah Tomkins, John Tomkins, Isaac Jones, Thomas McMillen, Jane McMillen, Bilinder Manyfold, Phebe Jones, Alice Murphy, Richard Webb, Alice Lukens, Benjamin Lukens.

Thomas Jay, of Harford County, son of Stephen and Hannah Jay, both deceased, m. Sarah Wilson, dau. of Thomas and Ann Wilson, both deceased, on 2nd day of 3rd month, 1797, at Deer Creek. Witnesses: Benjamin Wilson, Samuel Coale, Ann Coale, Nathaniel Harply, Robt.[?] Archer, Philip Gover, William Coale, John Worthington, Margaret Massey, Prissilla Worthington, Sarah Coale, Isaac Coale, Hannah Wilson, Susanna Dallam, Thomas Wilson, Isaac Massey, Francis Caslang[?], William Coale, Jacob Balderston, Richard Ward, Samuel Hopkins (of W.), William McCoy, Sarah Hopkins, Sarah W. Hopkins, Stephen Norton, John Wilson, Peter Wilson, Hannah Thompson, Sarah Wilson, Elizabeth Jay, Martha Jay, Peggy Wilson, James Thompson, Christopher Wilson, Peter Wilson (of Thomas), Thomas Wilson (of D.), Isaac Wilson, Joseph Wilson, John Dallam, A. Clendinin, Martha Wilson, Mary Dallam, Sarah Wilson [of W.?].

Samuel Hopkins, son of Joseph and Elizabeth Hopkins (the former deceased), m. Rachel Worthington, dau. of John and Priscilla Worthtington, both of Harford County, on 3rd day of 5th month, 1798, at Deer Creek. Witnesses: Samuel Worthington, William Worthington, Thomas Worthington, William Watson, John Prevale, Joseph Miller, Samuel Coale, Nathaniel Gover, Edward Morgain, Martha Jay, Alesanna Wilson, Sarah Ely, Lydia Coale, Margaret Miller, Eliza Worthington, John Hopkins, Ephraim Hopkins, Elizabeth Hopkins, Priscilla Worthington, Joseph Hopkins, Priscilla Miller, Eliza Hopkins, John Worthington, Jr., Eliza Coale, William Coale, Joseph Wilson, Peter Wilson, Hugh Morgan, D. Labar, John Lee, Joseph Worthington, Isaac Coale.

John Carter, son of John and Hannah Carter, of Pennsylvania (the former deceased), m. Rebecca Harland, dau. of David and Alice Harland (the former deceased), on 14th day of 6th month, 1798, at Deer Creek. Witnesses: Samuel Carter, Elizabeth Coale, William Coale, Lewis Harland, Jeremiah Harland, Joel Carter, John Carter, Jr., Amelia Hopkins, Samuel Coale, Nicholas Cooper, Isaac Coale, Gerrard Hopkins, Mary Churchman, Susanna Hopkins, Easther Stump, Lydia Hoopes, Sarah Wilson, John Forsythe, Alice Harland, Ann Carter, Alisanna Wilson, Susanna Duttan [Dallam?], Sarah Warner, John Worthington, Peter Wilson, Isaac Wilson, Henry Stump, Jr., Thomas Wilson, Samuel Hopkins (of Wm.), Joshua Husbands, David E. Price, James Wells, Hannah Harland, Susanna Wilson.

Joseph Wiggins m. Ann Bruce, relict of John Bruce, both of Harford County, on 3rd day of 1st month, 1799, at Deer Creek. Witnesses: Isaac Massey, Sarah Trago, Joseph Warner, Gerard Hopkins, Sarah W. Hopkins, Mary Warner, Sarah Warner, Amos Warner, Asa Warner, John Warner, Agness Crosdale Warner, Ann Warner, Sarah Ely, Harriet Swaney, Peter Wilson, Samuel Coale, Joseph Ely, Nicholas Cooper, Jr., Isaac Wilson, Stephen Norton, Ann Massey, Samuel Hopkins (of J.?), Richard Ward, Jacob Balderston, Joshua Husbands, John Wilson, Susanna Wilson, Bezleel Wiggins, Sarah Nigar, Hugh Morgain, Margret Wiggins, Sarah Wiggins, Elizabeth Wiggins, John Wiggins, Hugh Ely, Aran Warner, Amelia Warner.

ABSTRACTS OF DEER CREEK MONTHLY MEETING MINUTES, 1759-1800

On 30th day of 12th month, 1760, James Rigbie, son of Nathan Rigbie, deceased, intends to marry Sarah Massey, daughter of Isaac Bolton of Bucks

County, Pennsylvania, and widow of Aquila Massey, deceased. Also reported that Ann Johns (widow) has since deceased. Thomas Bishop requested to be taken into membership.

On 3rd day of 2nd month, 1761, Martha Pain denied granting permission for her son John Pain to marry outside the society. Certificate of removal was given to Sarah Hawkins and her son Benjamin to Hopewell Monthly Meeting in Virginia. William Cox was appointed clerk.

On 3rd day of 3rd month, 1761, William Coale, son of Skipwith Coale, deceased, intends to marry Sarah Webster, daughter of Isaac Webster, deceased. Thomas Saunders, son of Edward, "hath by keeping unprofitable company, been induced to dance." Certificate from New Garden Monthly Meeting received from James Webb and wife, with their children, Richard, Hannah, John and Sarah, by way of Nottingham Meeting.

On 28th day of 5th month, 1761, Elizabeth Hayward requested a certificate to Sadsbury Monthly Meeting.

On 30th day of 6th month, 1761, Philip Gover and Mary Hopkins intend to marry. Certificate requested for Joseph Jacob Wallis to Philadelphia Monthly Meeting since he is apprentice to Charles Jervis, a friend of that city. Certificate received from Bradford Monthly Meeting in Pennsylvania for Gideon Pearson.

On 29th day of 9th month, 1761, certificate from Buckingham Monthly Meeting in Pennsylvania received from Jane Murray, wife of Alexander Murray. Certificate from West River Monthly Meeting received from Samuel Hopkins, son of Philip Hopkins, deceased. Elizabeth Williams, wife of George, requested to be taken into membership.

On 3rd day of 11th month, 1761, certificate from [illegible] Monthly Meeting received from Gerrard Hopkins and wife Agnes. George Robinson requested a certificate to West River Monthly Meeting. John Wallis, son of Samuel Wallis, deceased, intends to marry Cassandra Coale, daughter of Skipwith Coale, deceased.

On 29th day of 12th month, 1761, Skipwith Coale charged with misconduct, and he subsequently asked forgiveness.

On [?] day of 2nd month, 1762, Margaret Bishop, wife of Thomas, was received into membership.

On 3rd day of 3rd month, 1762, Joseph Husband requested a certificate to New Garden Monthly Meeting to marry Mary Pusey, daughter of Joshua and Mary Pusey, deceased. Certificate from Sadsbury Monthly Meeting received from Samuel Richardson.

On 30th day of 3rd month, 1762, Joseph Scot, son of Jacob and Hannah Scot, intends to marry Ann Hayward.

On 27th day of 4th month, 1762, reported that Ann Johns, daughter of Richard Johns, deceased, was "lately married by a priest and her sister Mary Johns was in attendance." Certificate from Pardshaw Hall in Cumberland County, Old England, received from John Wilson, son of Christopher Wilson, lately deceased. Ann Rigbie, daughter of Nathan and Cassandra Rigbie, requested to be taken into membership.

On 5th day of 6th month, 1762, Hannah Johns (wife of Aquila Johns) and Ann Scot (wife of Joseph Scot) requested a certificate to Gunpowder Monthly Meeting.

On 29th day of 6th month, certificate from East Nottingham Monthly Meeting received from Henry Cowgil, Jr. and wife Ruth. Certificate of removal requested by Joseph Husband to East Nottingham Monthly Meeting. Certificate from Philadelphia Monthly Meeting received from Edward Watters. Certificate from Pardshaw Hall Monthly Meeting in Old England received from Jonathan Hudson, now residing at Joppa.

On 3rd day of 8th month, 1762, charges brought against Ann Crockett (formerly Ann Johns). Certificate from New Garden Monthly Meeting at London Grove received from John Smith, wife Elizabeth, and children, Joshua, John, and Mary. Certificate from Philadelphia Monthly Meeting received from Edward Wallis. Moses Hill "hath been guilty of gross and scandalous language, and other disorderly conduct."

On 31st day of 8th month, 1762, Hannah Wilson reported "lately married to a man not of this society." James Rigbie charged with "detaining some moneys due to John Hunt." Certificate requested for Gideon Pearson who lately removed to Bradford Monthly Meeting.

On 5th day of 10th month, 1762, Hannah Jay (formerly Wilson) charged with marrying outside the society.

On 2nd day of 11th month, 1762, Nathan Johns condemned his actions for outgoing in marriage. Frances Dallam, wife of Richard Dallam, produced a certificate from Herring Creek Monthly Meeting. Anna Rigbie, daughter of Nathan Rigbie, deceased, was joined in membership.

On 3rd day of 2nd month, 1763, certificate from Colchester Monthly Meeting, Old England, received from Baines Cox.

On 3rd day of 3rd month, 1763, James Crawford was joined in membership.

On 5th day of 5th month, 1763, Jonathan Massey, son of Aquila Massey, deceased, intends to marry Cassandra Webster, daughter of Isaac Webster, deceased.

On 30th day of 6th month, 1763, Daniel Robertson presented a certificate from Gunpowder Monthly Meeting.

On 4th day of 8th month, 1763, Baines Cox stated he intended to embark for Europe shortly, and requested a certificate to Colchester Monthly Meeting in Old England.

On 1st day of 9th month, 1763, Joseph Hurford, son of John and Hannah Hurford, of New Garden Monthly Meeting in Pennsylvania, intends to marry Naomi Greenland, daughter of Flower Greenland, deceased. Certificate produced for Jonathan Hudson to Pardshaw Monthly Meeting in Old England.

On 1st day of 12th month, 1763, certificate from West River Monthly Meeting received from Sarah Webster, wife of Isaac.

On 2nd day of 2nd month, 1764, certificate from Parshaw Hall Monthly Meeting, Old England, received from John Wilson.

On 5th day of 5th month, 1764, a certificate was requested for John Smith and wife and children who had removed within the verge of Wilmington Monthly Meeting.

On 29th day of 5th month, 1764, certificate from East Nottingham Monthly Meeting received from Phebe Moobrey, wife of Robert Moobrey, and Margaret Brown, a daughter by a former husband, and four small children, William, Ann, Phebe, and Mary.

On 5th day of 6th month, 1764, Philip Johns charged with outgoing in marriage.

On 2nd day of 10th month, 1764, John Wilson, son of our late friend Christopher Wilson, of Old England, deceased, and Sarah his wife, intends to marry Alisanna Webb, daughter of Isaac Webster, deceased, and Margaret his wife. Mary Durbin (late Johns) and Elizabeth Husband (late Hopkins) expressed sorrow for their misconduct.

On 1st day of 11th month, 1764, certificate from East Nottingham Monthly Meeting received from John Cousins, his wife Sarah, and daughter Susanna.

On 1st day of 1st month, 1765, William Hopkins requested a certificate for his son William who is lately bound as an apprentice to a friend in Philadelphia.

On 31st day of 1st month, 1765, Gerrard Hopkins, son of William, was "accused of disorderly conduct in a late voyage to the West India Islands and likewise since his return had been guilty of fighting."

On 4th day of 4th month, 1765, certificate was requested for Samuel Webster, son of Isaac, deceased, to Philadephia Monthly Meeting where he is bound as an apprentice to a friend in that city.

On 1st day of 8th month, 1765, James Crawford "condemned his misconduct in depriving Baines Cox of his bargain." Mary Worthington (late Hopkins) condemned for outgoing in marriage. John Lee Webster and Jonathan Massey charged with purchasing negroes. Certificate requested for Ann Crockett, wife of Samuel, now living within the verge of East Nottingham Monthly Meeting.

On 5th day of 9th month, 1765, reported that "a difference has long subsisted between William Hopkins and Joseph Wilson, the former conceiving Joseph to detain part of his land." Philip Coale, son of William, was lately married by a priest to a woman not of our society.

On 3rd day of 10th month, 1765, James Rigbie requested "a few lines as he intends to visit some meetings in the lower part of Virginia."

On 5th day of 12th month, membership found that it would be "expedient to visit our friend Joseph Jones and his family whose circumstances require the care of friends."

On 2nd day of 1st month, 1766, certificate requested for Samuel Wallis "who has lived a considerable time in Philadelphia."

On 5th day of 4th month, 1766, Isaac Lee, son of James, "had lately been married to a woman not of our society by a priest."

On 30th day of 4th month, 1767, Rachel Vancleave charged with misconduct. Certificate from Gunpowder to Concord Monthly Meeting for George Briggs who had removed to Philadelphia.

On 4th day of 6th month, 1767, certificate from Wrights Town Monthly Meeting in Bucks County, received from Agnes Vance who now resides with her husband near Bush River Meeting. Certificate from East Nottingham Monthly Meeting received from Ephraim Johnson, son of Benjamin, who now resides with his father within the verge of this meeting, and also one from Ann Johnson, daughter of Benjamin, and Mary Johnson. Mary Worthington (formerly Hopkins) condemned her misconduct. Lydia and Ellen Cowgill, daughters of Henry Cowgill, requested membership from East Nottingham, but since they had both married men not of this society, the matter will be looked into first. Friends requested their meeting be moved from the school house to a house of Jacob Giles' near Bayside. Cassandra Rigbie, daughter of Nathan and Sarah, "has gone out in marriage."

On 2nd day of 7th month, 1767, certificate from East Nottingham received from Alice Cowgill for herself and her two minor children, John and Alice. Grace Wallis requested a certificate for her son Thomas, a minor, to Philadelphia Monthly Meeting.

On 3rd day of 9th month, 1767 reported that "John Lee Webster has had a quarrel and a battle with Dr. James Spavold."

On 1st day of 10th month, 1767, friend Comfort Hoeg and her companion Sarah Barney attended this meeting with a certificate from the monthly meeting at Hamton in New Hampshire and the quarterly meeting at Salem, and also one from the monthly meeting at Nantucket. Cassandra Sheredine charged with misconduct.

On 3rd day of 12th month, 1767, Ellen and Lydia Manyfold (formerly Cowgill) continued [see 4th of 6th month, 1767]. Skipwith Johns charged for drinking to excess. Jacob Giles requested a certificate for his five sons, James, Jacob, Thomas, Aquilla, and Edward, the first bound as an apprentice to a friend in Philadephia, and the others placed in school in that city.

On 3rd day of 3rd month, 1768, Edward Mitchell Ramsay, a young man who had served as an apprentice in East Nottingham, has lately come within the verge of this meeting and requested membership. Reported that "meetings at Deer Creek and Bay Side have been pretty well attended since last account, [with] Bush River rather thin, partly occassioned by indisposition, [and] from York County no account, but it appears their attendance [is] as usual."

On 2nd day of 6th month, 1768, certificate from Exeter Monthly Meeting in Pennsylvania received from Samuel Willits.

On 4th day of 8th month, 1768, certificate from Sadsbury Monthly Meeting received from Joseph Husband and wife and children, Joshua and Mary.

On 1st day of 9th month, 1768, certificate from Wilmington Monthly Meeting received from Hannah Robinson, wife of George, who now resides near Ashmead's Mill.

On 29th day of 9th month, 1768, John Hopkins, son of Samuel, late of Patapsco Meeting and wife Sarah, intends to marry Elizabeth Chew, daughter of Joseph Chew, late of Deer Creek, and wife Sarah. Reported that Daniel Robertson and Elizabeth Webster were married by a priest. [Note: His name is also given as Daniel "Robinson" in the minutes].

On 3rd day of 11th month, 1768, Samuel Willits, son of Henry and Sarah Willits, late of Exeter Monthly Meeting in Bucks County, Pennsylvania, deceased, intends to marry Ann Rigbie, daughter of Nathan and Cassandra Rigbie, late of Deer Creek, deceased. Certificate from East Nottingham Monthly Meeting received from Sarah Cox, wife of John. Certificate from Philadephia Monthly Meeting received from Samuel Hopkins.

On 5th day of 1st month, 1769, Joseph Hopkins, son of Joseph and Ann Hopkins, intends to marry Elizabeth Gover, daughter of Ephraim and Elizabeth Gover.

On 2nd day of 3rd month, 1769, certificate from New Garden Monthly Meeting received from Mary Miller, wife of William, both now residing within the verge of our meeting.

On 29th day of 3rd month, 1769, William Coale, son of Skipwith Coale, deceased, intends to marry Elizabeth Rigbie, daughter of James Rigbie.

On 4th day of 5th month, 1769, Samuel Hopkins, son of Philip Hopkins, deceased, and wife Elizabeth, intends to marry Mary Gover, daughter of Ephraim and Elizabeth Gover.

On 1st day of 6th month, 1769, certificate from Wilmington Monthly Meeting received from David Schofield and wife Rachel and their three minor children, Samuel, John and Enoch. Reported that Sarah Rigbie, wife of James Rigbie, has removed to New Garden Monthly Meeting.

On 3rd day of 8th month, 1769, George Pusey, late of New Garden Monthly Meeting, son of John Pusey, deceased, and Catherine his wife, intends to marry Sarah Cox, daughter of William and Mary Cox. Deborah Low requested to come under the care of friends.

On 31st day of 8th month, 1769, certificate requested by John Worthington to go to Gunpowder Monthly Meeting and marry Priscilla Wilson, daughter of Henry Wilson. Certificate requested by Elizabeth Hopkins to Gunpowder Monthly Meeting. Ann Lancaster, daughter of Benjamin Lancaster, "guilty of fornication and having a bastard child." [Note: Subsequent minutes show that her mother knew of the young man in "the liberty of her house," and also that her father Benjamin had "taken to strong drink"]. Reported that Cassandra Wallace, widow of John Wallace, had been married by a priest.

On 1st day of 3rd month, 1770, Mary Worthington, wife of Charles Worthington, Jr., requested her minor son Joseph be taken under care of friends.

On 5th day of 7th month, 1770, certificate from Buckingham Monthly Meeting in Bucks County, Pennsylvania, received from Thomas Ruckman and wife Sarah who removed with the verge of this meeting. James Giles, son of Jacob, some time ago removed to Philadelphia Monthly Meeting as an apprentice, has returned to Maryland and reportedly has been married by a priest to woman not of our society. Rachel Lancaster requested a certificate for herself and her four children to Gunpowder Monthly Meeting.

On 30th day of 8th month, 1770, certificate from New Garden Monthly Meeting received from Lydia Pusey.

On 4th day of 10th month, 1770, certificate received from Gunpowder Monthly Meeting for Priscilla Worthington.

On 1st day of 10th month, 1770, John Course, of Kent County in Maryland, intends to marry Cassandra Rigbie, daughter of James Rigbie, who was present and gave his consent.

On 3rd day of 1st month, 1771, certificate from Taller[?] Monthly Meeting received from Joseph Stokes. Ann Stuart (late Johnson), daughter of Benjamin Johnson, "is married to a man not of our society."

On 31st day of 1st month, 1771, Cassandra Morgan (late Lee) "is married to a man not of our society."

On 30th day of 5th month, 1771, certificate from Wrights Town Monthly Meeting, in Bucks County, received from Ruth Warner, wife of Joseph Warner.

On 1st day of 7th month, 1771, certificate from Wright Town Monthly Meeting, in Bucks County, received from Sarah Wiggins, wife of Joseph Wiggins.

On 31st day of 10th month, 1771, Winstant Smith Dallam, son of Richard and Frances Dallam, intends to marry Margarett Gover, daughter of Ephraim and Elizabeth Gover.

On 2nd day of 6th month, 1772, certificates from Buckingham Monthly Meeting received from: Benjamin Warner and wife Sarah; Mary McCoy and her five children; and, Jacob Balderson, his wife Mary, and Hannah Kennard, a minor.

On 30th day of 7th month, 1772, certificate from Nottingham Monthly Meeting received from Jane White.

On 3rd day of 9th month, 1772, Cassandra Massey "has gone out in marriage to a man not of our society."

On 3rd day of 11th month, 1772, certificate from Philadelphia Monthly Meeting received for Mary Williams' three children [no names given].

On 31st day of 12th month, 1772, Eleanor Manyfold produced a paper condemning her misconduct for outgoing in marriage.

On 3rd day of 6th month, 1773, certificate from East Nottingham Monthly Meeting received from Catherine Cogal. Ann Dewit [Jewit?] to be "visited about outgoing in marriage and also Margaret Webster and Margaret Talbott, her mother and sister, on that account."

On 1st day of 7th month, 1773, certificate from Gunpowder Monthly Meeting received from Croasdel Warner, his wife Mary, and thei seven children [no names given]. Jane Murrey requested her children, except Mary who is of age, be taken under care of friends.

On 5th day of 8th month, 1773, certificate from Buckingham Monthly Meeting received from Ruth Ely, and also from Sarah Ely and her husband.

On 30th day of 9th month, 1773, certificate Warrington Monthly Meeting received from Mary Chandler and her husband. Cuthbert Warner, son of Joseph and Ruth Warner, intends to marry Rachel Hill, daughter of William and Mary Hill.

On 4th day of 11th month, 1773, certificate from Nottingham Monthly Meeting received from Mary McCaskey.

On 3rd day of 5th month, 1774, certificate received from Henry Cogal and wife and children [no names given], and also his sister Alice Cogal.

On 31st day of 3rd month, 1774, Hannah Webb, daughter of James Webb, guilty of fornicating and outgoing in marriage. Mary Worthington requested that two of her children, Charles and Ann, be taken into membership.

On 5th day of 5th month, 1774, Gerrard Hopkins, son of William and Rachel Hopkins, intends to marry Sarah Wallis, daughter of Samuel Wallis, deceased, and wife Grace.

On 2nd day of 6th month, 1774, certificate from Philadelphia Monthly Meeting received from Anna Giles and her husband, and also one from Old England for Sarah Wilson, daughter of Christopher Wilson.

On 30th day of 6th month, 1774, certificate from Kennet Monthly Meeting received from Elizabeth Barker.

On 6th day of 10th month, 1774, Benjamin Sharpless, son of Benjamin Sharpless, of Pennsylvania, intends to marry Sarah Rigbie, daughter of James Rigbie, of Harford County.

On 3rd day of 11th month, 1774, Hester Giles asked to be taken under care of friends.

On 1st day of 12th month, 1774, certificate from Third Haven Monthly Meeting received from Rebecca Richardson. John Bruce intends to marry Ann Morgan.

On 5th day of 1st month, 1775, Sarah Sharpless requested a certificate to Philadelphia Monthly Meeting.

On 2nd day of 2nd month, 1775, Gideon Purveal intends to marry Mary Harris, daughter of Samuel and Margaret Harris.

On 1st day of 6th month, 1775, Hannah Rigbie "has gone out in marriage to a man not of our society and by a priest."

On 31st day of 8th month, 1775, Sophia Jay "having for some considerable time been unde our care, now requests to be joined in membership."

On 2nd day of 11th month, 1775, Thomas Ely, son of Thomas Ely, intends to marry Hannah Warner, daughter of Croasdel Warner. Mary Wilson (late Lee) "has gone out in marriage with her first cousin and was married by a priest."

On 1st day of 2nd month, 1776, Elizabeth Lee was questioned "about the clearness of her daughter's [Mary] marriage."

On 29th day of 2nd month, 1776, Stephen Norton intends to marry Sophia Jay, daughter of Thomas Jay, deceased.

On 5th day of 9th month, 1776, Samuel Coale, son of Skipwith Coale, deceased, and wife Margaret, intends to marry Lydia Pusey, daughter of Joshua and Mary Pusey, of New Garden Monthly Meeting, deceased.

On 31st day of 10th month, 1776, Mary Webb, daughter of James and Mary Webb, "has married to a man not of our society by a priest."

On 2nd day of 1st month, 1777, certificate from Gunpowder Monthly Meeting received from Joseph and Deborah Burgess and their children, Elizabeth, Jonathan, Tacey, Jesse, Thomas, Sarah, Nathan, John, Daniel, Leticia, Joseph [and one name illegible].

On 5th day of 6th month, 1777, John Forwood freed these slaves: Negro Ralph, born 15th day of 10th month, 1769, to be free on 15th day of 10th month, 1790; Negro ---- [name unclear], age about 25 years, her freedom and her offspring forever, and her son Bennett, born in 1772, to be free at 21 years of age. Joseph Husbands freed Negro man named Jess[?] and Negro boy named Jack to be free at 21 years of age; and, Samuel Coale freed Negro girl named Belinda to be free at 18 years of age. John Wilson freed six Negroes: Fortune, age 40, and Hannah his wife, age about 21, and their children: Melinda, a girl aged 3 years; Jack[?], son aged about 2 years; Sophia, a daughter, about 1 year old, and Comfort, a daughter, about 6 weeks old. James Crawford freed his Negroes: Sam[?] and Hester his wife, and their children: Perinah, Jacob, and Charity; and a Negro woman named Jane. John Wilson, son of Joseph, requested his children be received into membership.

On 3rd day of 7th month, 1777, Ann Weeks (formerly Lancaster) requested a certificate to Gunpowder Monthly Meeting.

On --[?] day of 8th month, 1777, certificate from Southern District of Philadelphia received from Sarah Hill, wife of James. Reported that Sarah Hopkins, wife of Gerrard, and Hannah Jay, wife of John, had paid the fines imposed on their husbands in lieu of service in the militia.

On 2nd day of 10th month, 1777, George Payne and wife Rachel and their children, Rachel, Martha, Sarah, Alice and George, all in their minority, requested a certificate to Hopewell Monthly Meeting in Virginia. Mary Baines Brown (late Cox) charged with outgoing in marriage.

On 30th day of 10th month, 1777, Leavin Hopkins requested a certificate of removal to Gunpowder Monthly Meeting. Joseph Wiggins paid a fine in lieu of service in the militia.

On 4th day of 12th month, 1777, certificate requested for Peter Wilson to Pardshaw Monthly Meeting in Old England, "he being gone to reside there." Reported that Henry Johns had joined the society of people called Methodists.

On 1st day of 1st month, 1778, Robert Gover "deviated so far from society principles as to join the militia."

On 5th day of 3rd month, 1778, William Coale, Jr. "visited Margaret Webster and her daughter Ann Jewett and her husband and advised them as directed on the releasement of some Negroes in the possession of Dr. Jewett and wife." Reported that John Worthington and Skipwith Coale "had lately taken a test prescribed by the present powers [and] contrary to Friends' principles." Henry Johns, who joined the Methodists, was disowned and further charged with "being an assistant in stealing away Nathan Rigbie's daughter for marriage with his brother Skipwith." Joseph Warner charged with paying a fine in lieu of service in the militia. Jacob Giles, Jr. charged with "supplying the militia troops with provisions and other warlike appearances, and that he struck one of his neighbors who acknowledged it."

On 30th day of 4th month, 1778, Margaret Hill Richardson, daughter of Nathan Richardson, deceased, and wife Hannah, "had let out her affections to a man not of our society and was married to him by a priest." [Next meeting shows her name as Margaret Hill Bradford, late Richardson]. Robert Morgan, son of Lydia, deviated so far as to join the militia.

On 2nd day of 7th month, 1778, Richard Proctor requested to be accepted into membership. Joseph and Ann Hopkins, William Hopkins, Isaac Webster, and David Robertson charged with the "practice of holding their fellow men in a state of slavery." Ann Mooberry, daughter of Robert and Phebe, charged with misconduct. Certificate requested for Robert McCoy and his brother William McCoy to Chester Monthly Meeting in Pennsylvania.

On 30th day of 7th month, 1778, Joseph Hopkins charged with having taken the test. Certificate produced by John Talbot "for the enlargement of the following Negroes: Murrier and her children then born, vizt. Mary, Hester, Hagar, Robert, Hannah, James and Hercules, and Negro Wapping now set free, and Negro William."

On 4th day of 10th month, 1778, certificate requested for Shem Hill, son of William and Mary Hill, to Wilmington Monthly Meeting.

On 5th day of 11th month, 1778, George Mason, of New Garden Monthly Meeting, son of George Mason, later of same meeting, deceased, and Jane his wife, intends to marry Susannah Hopkins, daughter of William Hopkins, a member of Deer Creek Monthly Meeting. Certificate of manumission presented by Hannah Richardson for the freedom of a Negro man named Harry, aged about 30 years, and her Negro woman named Nelly, aged about 20 years, and a Negro boy named Cato to be free when he arrives at age 21 on 1st day of 11th month, 1784.

On 4th day of 2nd month, 1779, certificate produced for David Maulsby to Gunpowder Monthly Meeting.

On 4th day of 3rd month, 1779, reported that Samuel Harris and William Ellis "had been out in the back woods near Shamokin and had there taken a test, the tenour[?] of which was inconsistent with our Christian principles." Certificate requested for Susannah Mason, wife of George, for New Garden Monthly Meeting.

On 1st day of 4th month, 1779, certificate from Buckingham Monthly Meeting in Pennsylvania received from Sarah Scarborough, wife of John Scarborough, to this meeting [and] "whose paper of acknowledgement for her outgoing in marriage was accepted by that meeting."

On 29th day of 4th month, 1779, certificate from Buckingham Monthly Meeting in Pennsylvania received from Isaiah Balderson and wife Martha.

On --[?] day of 1st month, 1780, certificate of removal requested for Eleazor Brown, wife [Sarah] and children [Thomas, Ann, Margaret and Joseph; recorded 5th month].

On 2nd day of 3rd month, 1780, certificate of removal requested for Martha Warner, "now infirm, she is likely to return to this neighborhood." Certificate of removal also requested for Aseph Warner to Wrights Town Monthly Meeting in Pennsylvania. Levin Hill Hopkins, son of William and Rachel Hopkins, intends to marry Frances Wallis, daughter of Samuel Wallis, deceased, and his wife Grace.

On 4th day of 5th month, 1780, certificate of removal requested for Jos. Tucker to Hopewell Monthly Meeting in Virginia.

On 3rd day of 8th month, 1780, Mary Dallam (late Wilson) condemned for outgoing in marriage, for which she then "appeared sensible of her breach of a rule of our discipline and expressed sorrow." John Wilson, son of Joseph Wilson, "found averse to fulfilling his engagement for the releasement of his Negroes, and that he is also charged with petitioning the assembly for liberty to take the test, which he did not deny."

On 31st day of 8th month, 1780, certificate requested for five of Thomas Bishop's children "who were with their parents some years ago removed to Redstone Settlement, to recommend them to Hopewell Monthly Meeting in Virginia, but as they were all in their minority when they left these parts and some are now grown pretty near of age, this meeting thinks it may be proper to make inquiries [on] how these children have conducted [themselves] in those parts since their removal." A few lines received from John Cousins condemning "his imprudent conduct in removing from his settlement in Fawn Township without the consent or advice of his friends." James Hayhurst, son of James and Ann Hayhurst, of Gunpowder Monthly Meeting, intends to marry Mary Warner, daughter of Benjamin and Sarah Warner, of Deer Creek Monthly Meeting.

On 2nd day of 11th month, 1780, Phebe Moobrey, daughter of Robert Moobrey, "has been guilty of fornication and had a child in an unmarried state."

On 30th day of 11th month, 1780, Richard Johns produced a certificate to free the Negroes in his possession. [Minutes in 3rd month, 1781, indicate he is deceased].

On 4th day of 1st month, 1781, certificate from Exeter Monthly Meeting received from Ann Willits, wife of Samuel Willits, and minor daughter Cassandra. Mary Hayhurst lately removed with her husband James Hayhurst to Gunpowder Monthly Meeting and requested a certificate of removal.

On 1st day of 2nd month, 1781, Richard Proctor charged "by persuasion or weakness, or both, had taken strong drink, so as he appeared to others to be somewhat intoxicated." William Cox produced a certificate to free his Negroes: Negro woman Phebe and her daughter Esther, freed some years past; Negro Robin set free on 1st day of 8th month last, at the time he was age 21; and Negro Jacob, Negro Sam, and Mulatto Ned Wall [?] free when each are age 21.

On 1st day of 3rd month, 1781, Levin Hill Hopkins freed his Negro John, age 43 years. Certificate from Philadelphia Monthly Meeting received from Elizabeth Wallis, wife of Joseph Jacob Wallis, and their minor children, John Lukens Wallis, Grace Wallis and Sarah Wallis. Samuel Harris produced a certificate to free his Negroes: Negro Tower, Negro Dinah and Negro Timber[?] already freed; and, Negro Marish, age 11; Negro Lydia, age 8; Negro Polley, age 6; Negro Beckah, age 9; all free at age 18.

On 5th day of 7th month, 1781, reported that Martha Warner, daughter of Benjamin Warner, had gone out in marriage to a man not of out society and was married to Jacob Forwood, son of Samuel Forwood.

On 2nd day of 8th month, 1781, William Cox, Jr. produced a certificate to free his Negroes: Negro James, age 10; Negro Hester, age 8; Negro Sarah, age 5; Negro Dinah, age 2 1/2; the boys free when age 21 and the girls when 18.

On 1st day of 11th month, Gideon Purveal produced a certificate to free his Negro girl Rachel when she arrives at age 18 around the 1st day of 11th month, 1785. Skipwith Coale "through weakness or fear of suffering had paid some money demanded of him as substitute and muster fine."

On 29th day of 11th month, 1781, certificate from Bradford Monthly Meeting received from Samuel Carter.

On 28th day of 2nd month, 1782, Samuel Wallis, of Kent County, Maryland, son of Samuel and Elizabeth, late of said county, deceased, intends to marry Sarah Sharpless, daughter of James Rigbie and widow of Benjamin Sharpless. John Murra [Murray] has been "guilty of quarrelling with a young man which proceeded to blows, and paying money to redeem property taken for a muster fine, and having gone out in marriage to a young woman not of our society and was married by a Baptist Preacher." Mary Wilson (late Talbott) charged with outgoing in marriage.

On 30th day of 5th month, 1782, Elizabeth Lee signed a manumission to free her negroes. Richard Snowden, of Prince George's County, son of Samuel and Elizabeth Snowden, intends to marry Hannah Moore Hopkins, daughter of William and Rachel Hopkins, of Harford County, and the parents of the young woman appeared and gave consent. Sarah Wallace, wife of Samuel, requested a certificate to Cical [Cecil] Monthly Meeting.

On 5th day of 9th month, 1782, Hannah Moore Snowden reqeusted a certificate to Indian Spring Monthly Meeting.

On 30th day of 1st month, 1783, Sarah Rigbie (late Brown) charged with misconduct.

On 5th day of 4th month, 1783, certificate produced for Mary Warner which was approved [no destination indicated].

On 5th day of 7th month, 1783, certificate from Cecil Monthly Meeting in Kent County received from Martha Parsons.

On 1st day of 4th month, 1784, Elizabeth Wallis, wife of Joseph Jacob Wallis, requested in behalf of her minor children, Thomas Wallis and Gainor Lukins Wallis, to be taken into membership.

On 5th day of 6th month, 1784, Sarah Morgan, daughter of Lydia Morgan, "accomplised her marriage by the assistance of Baptist Teacher to a man not of our society."

On 1st day of 7th month, 1784, reported that the case of Margaret Talbot (now Bradford) will be looked into. Certificate from Horsham Monthly Meeting received from Ann Jones and husband and their seven minor children, Joseph, Ezekiel, Ann, Isaac, Anthony, Rebeckah, and Jonathan. Certificate from Abington Monthly Meeting, dated in 1774, and directed to Gunpowder Monthly Meeting, was endorsed from said meeting to this meeting, for Alice Lukins and seven children, Jacob, Moses, Charles, Phebe, Sarah, Magdalen, and Mary, "the aforesaid certificate being dated so many years ago past" the matter was looked into and Alice Lukins appeared "on behalf of her three youngest children, Gainer, Alice, and Ann, and requested that they be received into membership, which was granted."

On 5th day of 9th month, 1784, Joseph Brinton, son of Moses and Eliner Brinton, of Lancaster County, Pennsylvania, intends to marry Susanna Rigbie, daughter of James and Elizabeth Rigbie, the latter deceased. At the next meeting, his parents appeared in person, and her father sent a letter, all consenting to the marriage. Joseph also produced a few lines from Sadsbury Monthly Meeting.

On 7th day of 11th month, 1784, Susanna Brinton requested a certificate to Sadsbury Monthly Meeting.

On 30th day of 12th month, 1784, William Ellis, son of Benjamin and Ann Ellis, deceased, intends to marry Mary Cox, daughter of William and Mary Cox, the former deceased.

On 5th day of 2nd month, 1785, Samuel Harris, son of Samuel and Margaret Harris, intends to marry Cassandra Gover, daughter of Ephriam and Elizabeth Gover, the former deceased.

On 2nd day of 6th month, 1785, Margaret Wallis guilty of "retaining a negro in a state of slavery, attending a place of diversion such as musick and dancing, and her dress and address are painful to friends."

On 30th day of 6th month, 1785, Elizabeth Webb, wife of Richard Webb, produced a paper condemning her past misconduct. Hannah West, wife of George West, requested to come under the care of friends.

On 4th day of 8th month, 1785, Mary Husband was released from acting as an assistant to the clerk of the woman's meeting and Ruth Carter was appointed in her place.

On 1st day of 9th month, 1785, Elizabeth Trimble, wife of Isaac Trimble, produced a certificate from New Garden Monthly Meeting for herself and her husband and their five children, Joseph, John, Mary, Jane, and James. Ruth Warner, wife of Aseph Warner, produced a certificate from Buckingham Monthly Meeting for herself and her husband and their son Aseph Warner.

On 3rd day of 11th month, 1785, Frances Miller (late Wilson) "has married a man not of our society and accomplished same before a Baptist Teacher."

On 3rd day of 3rd month, 1786, certificate from Ceisel [Cecil] Monthly Meeting in Kent County, received from Sarah Wallis and her husband and their children, Ann and Samuel.

On 29th day of 6th month, 1786, certificate from Kennet Monthly Meeting received from Priscilla McCoy, wife of William McCoy.

On 3rd day of 8th month, 1786, Isaac Coale, son of William and Sarah Coale, the latter deceased, intends to marry Rachel Cox, daughter of William and Mary Cox, the former deceased.

On 5th day of 10th month, 1786, Sarah Worthington "has gone out in marriage and accomplished same by the assistance of a Baptist Teacher, and also attended a dancing school."

On 2nd day of 11th month, 1786, certificate requested for Benjamin Warner, wife and children, Joseph,, Benjamin, and Rachel, in their minority, to Maidenbrook Monthly Meeting. Certificate requested for Samuel Harris and wife Margaret and their children, Ann and Elizabeth, of age, and William, Benjamin, Sarah, and Thomas, in their minority, and also for Samuel Harris, Jr. and wife Cassandra, and for William Ellis and wife Mercy and their young daughter Mary, all to Maidenbrook Monthly Meeting. Anna Massey (now Bull) "has married a man not of our society and accomplished same before a Baptist Teacher."

On 4th day of 1st month, 1787, certificate from Gunpowder Monthly Meeting received from Henry Wilson. Sarah Worthington and Ann Hopkins "have so far taken undue libertys as to attend at a dancing school, and at a marriage consumated contrary to our discipline."

On 1st day of 2nd month, 1787, reported that Ann Wilson, daughter of John Wilson (son of Joseph), "had been married by the assistance of a Presbyterian Minister."

On 31st day of 5th month, 1787, Ann Jewet (formerly Webster) produced a paper condemning her outgoing in marriage.

On 5th day of 7th month, 1787, certificate requested for Elizabeth Wallis, wife of Thomas, and minor children, Joseph, Mary, and Samuel, to Exeter Monthly Meeting. Elizabeth Heaton requested "such of her children that is in their minority be taken under care of friends." [Later minutes give their names as Joseph, Abner, Levan, and Elizabeth; and the eldest son Isaiah will be considered also]. Susannah Rodgers produced a paper condemning her outgoing in marriage some years back.

On 2nd day of 8th month, 1787, Ann Jewet requested her three minor children, Margret, John, and Thomas, be taken into membership. Thomas Wilson requested his minor daughters Alisanna and Sarah be taken into membership. Daniel and Elizabeth Robertson, who sometime ago were disowned for holding Negroes in a state of slavery, sent a manumission in and they were then reinstated into membership.

On 4th day of 10th month, 1787, Richard Proctor was disowned for "having divers times taken to strong drink to excess." Isaac Webster produced a paper of condemnation for "not taking the advice of manumitting the Black People which he then held as slaves."

On 1st day of 11th month, 1787, Aquila Massey charged with "deviating from the principles as to be concerned with horse racing."

On 29th day of 11th month, 1787, certificate from New Garden Monthly Meeting received from John Wilson (son of John).

On 3rd day of 1st month, 1788, Isaac Webster produced a paper of condemnation for "some years back being disowned for holding Negroes in slavery, since which it has been my lot to be marry'd by the assistance of a hireling priest." Thomas Wilson, son of Peter Wilson, decease, and his wife Ann, of Old England, intends to marry Sarah Richardson, daughter of Nathan Richardson, deceased, and wife Hannah.

On 28th day of 2nd month, 1788, reported that Sarah Wilson, daughter of Joseph, had been married to a man not of our society and with the assistance of a Methodist Preacher.

On 3rd day of 4th month, 1788, certificate requested for Cuthbert Wiggins, a minor son of Joseph, who has moved to Wrights Town Monthly Meeting under the care of his grandfather. Certificates from Horshem Monthly Meeting at Bybery received from Benjamin Tomkins [sic], wife Mary, and their minor children, Rachel and Ann, and from Elizabeth Tompkins [sic], daughter of the above friends, all of which live within the verge (now) of this meeting.

On 1st day of 5th month, 1788, certificate produced for Tacey Burgess. Isaac Massey, son of Aquila Massey and Sarah his wife, deceased, intends to marry Margaret Webster, daughter of Isaac and Sarah Webster, the latter deceased, all formerly of this county.

On 5th day of 6th month, 1788, Elizabeth Robinson [also spelled Robertson in the minutes] produced a paper of condemnation, with her husband, "for holding my fellow creatures in a state of bondage."

On 3rd day of 7th month, 1788, certificate from Banbery Monthly Meeting in Oxford County, Old England, received from James Tasker, his mother Mercy Tasker, and sister Mercy Raker, now Byfield, removed to this meeting. Hannah Jay [now Thompson], daughter of Stephen Jay, "has gone out in marriage with a man not of our society and was married to him by the assistance of a priest."

On 31st day of 7th month, 1788, Ann Crawford (formerly Wilson) was sometime ago disowned for being married by a hireling minister, and lately returned from Redstone, now requests reinstatement.

On 4th day of 9th month, 1788, certificates from Horshem Monthly Meeting at Bybery received at Deer Creek Monthly Meeting from John Tompkins and Elisha Walton, two young men who now reside within the compass of Fawn Particular Meeting.

On 2nd day of 10th month, 1788, certificate produced for Ann Crawford to Westland Monthly Meeting, and for Aquila Jones and Henry Worthington, both to Gunpowder Monthly Meeting.

On 1st day of 1st month, 1789, Mary Cox, Jr. found guilty of fornication by her having a child in an unmarried state. Mary Worthington requested her two minor children, Mary and Elizabeth, be taken into membership.

On 5th day of 2nd month, 1789, Elisha Walton and Elizabeth Tompkins "found guilty of fornication with each other since which they have been married by the assistance of a magistrate." William McCoy released at his own request from being an overseer, and Samuel Coale appointed in his place. Certificate from Sadsbury Monthly Meeting received from Sarah Morgan. Mary Cox informed the meeting that she "had a prospect of residing the chief of the ensuing summer at her son-in-law's, William Ellis, within the verge of Exeter Monthly Meeting and that per adventure she might attend that monthly meeting and its branches with our concurrence."

On 2nd day of 4th month, 1789, certificate from Abington Monthly Meeting in Pennsylvania received from Benjamin Lukens.

On 30th day of 4th month, 1789, John Tompkins and Sarah Burgess intend to marry, and Mary Tompkins being present gave her consent, and Joseph Burgess sent in a few lines giving his consent.

On 4th day of 6th month, 1789, certificate from Philadelphia Monthly Meeting, for the Northern District, received from Elizabeth Pusey. Sarah Day, wife of John Day, "has for sometime been under the care of the Preparative Meeting and now desires to join us [Deer Creek Monthly Meeting]." John Cox appointed clerk to succeed John Wilson.

On 2nd day of 7th month, 1789, Joseph Ely and Ann (late Jones) his wife, were married by a Baptist Teacher. Mary Hill guilty of having "gone out in an unbecoming manner and has also been guilty of fornication."

On 30th day of 7th month, 1789, Christopher Wilson, son of John and Alasanna Wilson, intends to marry Margaret Coale, daughter of Skipwith and Sarah Coale. Certificate requested by Nathan Johns for himself and wife and minor children, Elizabeth, Nathan, Ann, and Mary, to Westland

Monthly Meeting, and Thomas Ely requested one for himself and wife and children, George, Elizabeth, Mary, Hugh, and Amoss, to Gunpowder Monthly Meeting. Joseph Worthington "has been guilty of using prophane language and quarreling."

On 3rd day of 9th month, 1789, Richard Johns requested a certificate to Westland Monthly Meeting.

On 8th day of 10th month, 1789, Joseph Jones produced a paper of condemnation for assisting Joseph Ely in his outgoing in marriage. Richard Webb requested a certificate to Gunpowder Monthly Meeting in order for marriage. Certificate from Horsham Monthly Meeting received from Benjamin Bond and wife Mary and their children, Martha, Elizabeth, Silas, and Ruth. Certificate from Gunpowder Monthly Meeting received from James Orr and wife Angelina. Daniel Mifflin, of Accomack County, Virginia, intends to marry Mary Husband, relict of Joseph Husband, deceased.

On 5th day of 11th month, 1789, Nathan Johns and family, and Richard Johns, report "they had dropt the thoughts of moving for the present." Joseph Worthington charged with misconduct regarding "his appearance in dress and address." Certificate "read here from Abington Monthly Meeting for Sarah Tompkins and she received a member of Fawn Meeting." Frances Crawford and Cassandra Bayley (both late Johns) "have accomplished their marriages by the assistance of a Baptist Teacher." Margaret Bradford (formerly Talbot) produced a paper condemning her outgoing in marriage.

On 3rd day of 12th month, 1789, certificate produced for Joel Carter, a minor, from Concord Monthly Meeting.

On 31st day of 12th month, 1789, certificate requested for James Wilson, a minor, to Goshen Monthly Meeting, and one for William Husband, a minor, to Gunpowder Monthly Meeting. Certificate produced for Mary Mifflin and her four minor children, Elizabeth, Lydia, Samuel, and Susanna Husband, to Motherkiln Monthly Meeting, "she having removed to reside with her husband within the verge thereof." Mary Hill, having a child in an unmarried state, "has gone off to Buckingham Monthly Meeting in an unbecoming manner," and the matter will be looked into.

On 3rd day of 2nd month, 1790, John Tomkins and Sarah his wife "charged of being guilty of fornication with each other before marriage which appears by their having a child too early after marriage." Sarah Worthington (now

Johnson) "has let out her affections to a man not of our society and was married to him by the assistance of a Baptist Teacher."

On 4th day of 3rd month, 1790, certificate from Gunpowder Monthly Meeting received from Mary Webb with her two minor children, David and Mary Malsby.

On 25th day of 3rd month, 1790, certificate from Horsham Monthly Meeting in Pennsylvania received from James Walton and wife Hannah and their three minor children, Joseph, Benjamin, and Elizabeth. Joshua Bennet appointed one of the overseers of Fawn Meeting. William Hayward, son of Joseph Hayward, deceased, and wife Rebecka, intends to marry Mary Husband, daughter of Joseph Husband, deceased, and wife Mary. Moses Lukens, son of Benjamin and Alice Lukens (the parents being present), intends to marry Sarah Tompkins, daughter of Benjamin and Mary Tompkins.

On 27th day of 5th month, 1790, John Carter charged with "having been married to a woman not of our society by the assistance of a man formerly a Methodist Teacher."

On 29th day of 7th month, 1790, reported that the certificate obtained by George West from this meeting sometime ago is now returned, and it is reported that he has gone out in marriage to a woman not of our society and by the assistance of a Magistrate.

On 26th day of 8th month, 1790, Mary Hayward requested a certificate to Gunpowder Monthly Meeting, "she being moved to live with her husband within the verge thereof."

On 23rd day of 9th month, 1790, Aaron Warner, son of Crosdal Warner and wife Mary, intends to marry Achsah Morgan, daughter of John Morgan, deceased, and wife Ann.

On 28th day of 10th month, 1790, certificate produced at Deer Creek Monthly Meeting from Gunpowder Monthly Meeting for Joseph Burgess and wife Ann and their son John, a minor, which was received and they became members of the Bush River Particular Meeting. Reported that "our late worthy friend Mary Cox in her last illness dropt some weighty sentences both to friends and others, some of which we are informed are committed to writing, the collecting and preserving of which it is thought might be profitable to survivors," so the parts will be collected and forwarded [to the Quarterly Meeting]. Samuel Hopkins, son of William Hopkins, deceased, and wife Rachel, intends to marry Sarah Husband, daughter of Joseph Husband, deceased, and his wife Mary.

On 23rd day of 12th month, 1790, certificate requested for Jessee Vore and wife and two children, Hannan and Thomas, to Wilmington Monthly Meeting, and one for Sarah Lukens to New Garden Monthly Meeting.

On 24th day of 2nd month, 1791, Elizabeth Jay found "guilty of attending a place of diversion and took part in dancing." Certificate from Gunpowder Monthly Meeting received from Nehemiah Underwood and wife Mary and their six children, Sarah, Benjamin, Willing, Rachel, Mary, and Enoch.

On 24th day of 3rd month, 1791, Nehemiah Underwood requested a certificate for his daughter Sarah to Warrington Monthly Meeting.

On 28th day of 4th month, 1791, reported that Grace Wilson "has joined the Methodist Society."

On 23rd day of 6th month, 1791, Archibald Murray "has been guilty of quarreling and fighting." Joseph Jones "has lately attended at a muster field and has been guilty of quarreling and holding vain sports dancing at his house." Certificate from Buckingham Monthly Meeting received from Anthony Kinnard and wife Elizabeth. Certificate from Haddenfield Monthly Meeting, in the Jerseys, received from Isaac Massey. Certificate from Warrington Monthly Meeting received from Caleb Bailey, "dated in first month last, but be being removed within the verge of Kennet Monthly Meeting."

On 28th day of 7th month, 1791, Croasdal Warner, Jr. "has gone out in marriage to a woman not of our society, and accomplished same by the assistance of a Baptist Teacher." Reported that Phebe Jones, wife of Joseph Jones, "has lately behaved in a very unbecoming manner, she being charged with privately keeping company with a young man, that her and her husband had separated from each other, and that she also had pertook in dancing." Sarah Wilson, daughter of Benjamin and Catherine Shaw, requested to be taken into membership. Certificate from Buckingham Monthly Meeting received from Elizabeth Walton and her minor son Joseph Walton. Certificate from Gunpowder Monthly Meeting received from Abel Spencer and wife, with their six minor children, William, Sarah, Rebecah, Elizabeth, Abel, and Reuben.

On 25th day of 8th month, 1791, John Wilson (of Joseph) produced "a manumission for divers Negroes in his possession." Elizabeth Wilson produced a paper condemning her outgoing in marriage. Rebecah Spencer, wife of Abel, "appeared here [Deer Creek Monthly Meeting] for whom a certificate was produced to last meeting, and she was received into Fawn Particular Meeting."

On 22nd day of 9th month, 1791, Samuel Gover, son of Philip and Mary Gover, deceased, intends to marry Ann Hopkins, daughter of Joseph and Elizabeth Hopkins, who were present, "but as they are in a degree between first and second cousins, friends at the preparative meeting advised against it" and the matter will be looked into further. Nicholas Cooper, son of Nicholas and Sarah Cooper, intends to marry Sarah Balderson, daughter of Isaiah and Martha Balderson, who were present.

On 27th day of 10th month, 1791, Joseph Warner was released from overseer and Samuel Hopkins succeeded him. Certificate received for Martha Preston from the Monthly Meeting for the Northern District of Philadelphia and she was received into the Fawn Particular Meeting.

On 24th day of 11th month, 1791, certificate from Wilmington Monthly Meeting received from Isaac Wilson and his wife Susannah with their minor daughter Alasanna Wilson.

On 29th day of 3rd month, 1792, Elizabeth Wilson produced a paper condemning her actions, stating "I suffered my affections to be let out to my first cousin, a person not of our society, to whom I was married by the assistance of a Baptist Teacher." [Written 22nd day of 9th month, 1791]. Prissilla Worthington, Frances Dallam, and Martha Wilson, Jr. "have all let out their affections to men not of our society and have accomplished their marriage contrary to the good order." [Later minutes give Prissilla's married name as Robinett, and her mother's name was Prissilla Worthington; and, Frances' married name was Smith and her mother's name was Margaret Dallam, and the marriage was performed at her house with her mother's consent]. Reported that Lydia Manifold had joined the Methodists. Isaac Trimble requested a certificate for himself and six children, Joseph, John, Mary, Jane, James, and Isaac, in their minority, to Gunpowder Monthly Meeting. Isaac Jones was released as overseer and Abel Spencer succeeded him.

On 26th day of 4th month, 1792, Aaron Boram was accepted into membership. John Sharp found guilty of fornication.

On 24th day of 5th month, 1792, Elizabeth Jay found "guilty of attending a place of diversion and dancing." Certificate from Bradford Monthly Meeting in Chester County received from Samuel Taylor and he became a member of Deer Creek Particular Meeting.

On 28th day of 6th month, 1792, reported that Joseph Webster had his marriage accomplished by a hireling teacher. James Hill requested a certificate to Nottingham Monthly Meeting, Martha Burgess requested one for Gunpowder Monthly Meeting, and Tacey Wiggins requested one for Wrights Town Monthly Meeting. Certificate from East Nottingham Monthly Meeting received from Elizabeth Hugo and she became a member of Deer Creek Particular Meeting.

On 26th day of 7th month, 1792, Elizabeth Gover, daughter of Philip Gover, was disowned for "holding her fellow creatures in a state of bondage."

On 23rd day of 8th month, 1792, certificates were requested for Joseph Burgess and his wife and two daughters, Letitia and Grace, and also for Thomas Burgess, John Burgess, and Daniel Burgess, all to South River Monthly Meeting in Virginia.

On 27th day of 9th month, 1792, Richard Webb reported by Fawn Meeting to have "so far given way to passion as to strike a man, which he does not deny." Samuel Jay reported by Deer Creek Meeting to have "attended a dancing school with an intent to learn to dance, and that he has also been concerned in purchasing and dispensing of lottery tickets, and that he has widely deviated in dress and address." Certificates received from Concord Monthly Meeting for John Carter, a minor, and from Nottingham Monthly Meeting for James Wilson, both of whom became members of Deer Creek Particular Meeting, and also one from Gwined Monthly Meeting for Amoss Evans, who became a member of Fawn Meeting.

On 25th day of 10th month, 1792, reported that Elizabeth Pusey, "who sometime ago produced to this meeting a certificate, is now removed and settled in Philadephia." Isaiah Balderson requested a certificate for himself and his wife and children, Ely, Parthenia, Hugh and Jonathan, all in their minority, to Gunpowder Monthly Meeting.

On 22nd day of 11th month, 1792, Mary Dallam produced a paper condemning her marriage several years ago contrary to the good order. Certificates requested by Elizabeth Hugo, and William and Jesse Morgan, to Baltimore Monthly Meeting.

On 27th day of 12th month, 1792, Sarah Day and Catherine Shaw requested certificates to Baltimore Monthly Meeting. Certificate from Nottingham Monthly Meeting received from Lydia Quarell.

On 24th day of 1st month, 1793, Margaret Dallam was disowned "for allowing her daughter's marriage in her own house to a man not of our society." Joshua Husbands, son of Joseph Husbands, deceased, and his wife Mary, intends to marry Margaret Jewit, daughter of Thadeus and Ann Jewit. Certificates requested for John Warner, a minor, to Wrights Town Monthly Meeting, and one for John Wallas Hopkins, a minor, to York Monthly Meeting.

On 21st day of 2nd month, 1793, Samuel Jay found guilty of "buying and selling lottery tickets, frequently attending places of diversion and dancing, departing so far from our plain way as to follow the vain fashions of the world in dress and address, and wholly declining attendance of our religious meetings." Charles Lukins, son of Benjamin and Alice Lukins, intends to marry Sarah Coale, daughter of Philip Coale, deceased, and his wife Ann. Sarah Morgan (now Sarah Nigar) found "guilty of marrying a man not of our society by the assistance of a hireling teacher."

On 28th day of 3rd month, 1793, testimony produced against Mary Dungan (late Lukins) for her marriage outside the society by a Baptist Teacher. Certificate received from Goshen Monthly Meeting in Pennsylvania for James Wilson, son of John Wilson, who has returned to live within the compass of Deer Creek Monthly Meeting. Certificate requested for John Webster Wilson to Cecill Monthly Meeting in Kent County, and one for Samuel Robertson, a minor, to Gunpowder Monthly Meeting.

On 24th day of 4th month, 1793, Isaac Jones charged with having "sometime ago taken a woman to keep his house and that he had made purposal of marriage to her too early after the decease of his wife, that he flighted the advice and tender labour of his friends, and has accomplished his marriage with her by the assistance of a Baptist Teacher." John Tomkins and wife requested their minor son Joseph Tomkins be received into membership. Certificates requested for Moses Lukins and wife Sarah and their minor daughter Lydea, and for Ezekiel Jones, minor son of Joseph Jones, both to Gunpowder Monthly Meeting.

On 25th day of 5th month, 1793, Abner Heaton found guilty of "stripping to fight and using bad language, and also attending a place of diversion and dancing." [Later minutes show he had resided for sometime at Baltimore].

On 27th day of 6th month, 1793, Aquilla Massey produced a paper condemning himself "for not attending to principles by undertaking the office of a collector, taking an oath, and also attending a horse race." On 25th day of 7th month, 1793, Benjamin Wilson requested his six minor children, Joseph, Hannah, William, Henry, Benjamin, and Martha, be taken into membership.

On 29th day of 8th month, 1793, Aquila Massey, son of Jonathan and Cassandra Massey, deceased, intends to marry Anna Rigbie, daughter of James and Sarah Rigbie, deceased.

On 26th day of 9th month, 1793, John Massey charged with "wantonly injuring another man's property, which he acknowledges, and on another occasion stripping of his clothes in order to fight and made use of unbecoming language." John Dallam and Joseph Ford requested to be taken into membership. William Wilson produced a certificate from Gunpowder Monthly Meeting and he was received as a member of Bush River Particular Meeting.

On 24th day of 10th month, 1793, John Cox, Jr. charged with marrying a woman not of the society with the assistance of a Baptist Teacher. Bazeleel Wiggins found guilty in "wantonly injuring the property of another man, using unbecoming language, and deviating much from plainness in dress." Letter received from Horsham Monthly Meeting concerning Elizabeth Jones (late Walton) setting forth that she had before her marriage with Isaac Jones applied for their certificate. Certificate forwarded to Baltimore Monthly Meeting for Isaac Trimble. Certificate requested for John Worthington, Jr., a minor, to Baltimore Monthly Meeting. Certificate from Warrington Monthly Meeting received from Sarah Underwood and she was received a member of Fawn Particular Meeting. William Wilson requested his two minor children, Isaac and James Wilson, be taken into membership, and they were received.

On 28th day of 11th month, 1793, certificate requested for Amoss Evans and one for William Walton, his wife Sarah and minor child Lukins Evans, all to Baltimore Monthly Meeting.

On 23rd day of 1st month, 1794, Martha Hill requested a certificate to Baltimore Monthly Meeting.

On 20th day of 2nd month, 1794, Richard Coale produced a paper condemning his misconduct by "fighting and using profane language." Samuel Webster found "guilty of fornication and marrying a woman contrary to the good order established amongst us." Joseph Ford, son of William and Rosanna Ford, intends to marry Frances Coale, daughter of Philip and Ann Coale, deceased.

On 27th day of 3rd month, 1794, William Ely, son of Thomas and Sarah Ely, deceased, intends to marry Martha Preston, daughter of Henry and Rachel Preston, both deceased. Certificate requested for Benjamin Underwood and Moses Webb, both minors, to York Monthly Meeting. Margaret Reese (late Morgan) found "guilty of fornication and marrying a man not in membership with us" and with the assistance of a Baptist Teacher.

On 24th day of 4th month, 1794, certificates requested for Charles Worthington, son of Charles, and John Lee Webster, Jr., both to Baltimore Monthly Meeting; one for Thomas Webster, a minor, who is placed to a friend within the compass of Indian Spring Monthly Meeting; and one for Samuel Carter for himself and wife Rith and their eight minor children, Joel, Agner, Hannah, Sarah, Samuel, Rachel, Jeremiah, and Ann, to Nottingham Monthly Meeting. John Massey disowned for fornication, wantonly injuring a man's property, and using profane language. Aaron Boram, son of John and Ann Boram, both deceased, intends to marry Elizabeth Johns, daughter of Nathan and Elizabeth Johns. William Chapman charged with "marrying a woman not in membership with us by the assistance of a hireling teacher."

On 24th day of 7th month, 1794, Joseph Preston requested a certificate to Baltimore Monthly Meeting.

On 28th day of 8th month, 1794, Jesse Hoops, son of David and Esther Hoops, intends to marry Sarah Wilson, daughter of John and Alisanna Wilson. Richard Johns, son of Nathan and Elizabeth Johns, intends to marry Elizabeth Wilson, daughter of Benjamin and Elizabeth Wilson. Jacob Lukins requested a certificate to Gunpowder Monthly Meeting.

On 23rd day of 10th month, 1794, Frances Crawford [Crafford] produced a paper condemning herself for marrying outside the society by the assistance of a hireling teacher.

On 27th day of 11th month, 1794, Samuel Webster (son of Isaac) charged with fornication and marrying by the assistance of a hireling teacher. Samuel Coale, son of Philip and Ann Coale, both deceased, intends to marry

Alasanna Wilson, daughter of Thomas and Ann Wilson, the latter deceased. Certificates requested for Sarah Hoops to Cecil Monthly Meeting, and for Levan Hopkins, a minor, to York Monthly Meeting. Certificate received from South River Monthly Meeting recommending John Burgess as a member.

On 25th day of 12th month, 1794, Randal Wallis charged with misconduct by being "concerned in a lottery and hath much neglected the attendance of our religious meetings." Certificate from Warrington Monthly Meeting received from Jehu Thomas and Sarah his wife, with their seven children, Sarah, Benjamin, Jehu, Susanna, Rachel, Mordecai, and Isaac. Robert Webster charged with taking strong drink to excess.

On 29th day of 1st month, 1795, Ezekiel Jones charged with marrying to a woman not in membership and by a Baptist Teacher.

On 26th day of 2nd month, 1795, Mary Forwood (late Murray) has gone out in her marriage to a man not of our society. Ephraim Gover Hopkins has "attended at a muster field and also has consummated his marriage with a woman not of our society." Joseph Heaton has been "guilty of quarreling, fighting, and making use of unbecoming language." Elizabeth Heaton, Jr. has "attended a marriage not of our society and so far partook of their mirth as to join them in dancing." On 26th day of 3rd month, 1795, Archibald Murray has accomplished his marriage contrary to the good order.

On 23rd day of 4th month, 1795, certificate requested for William Coale (of Samuel), a minor, to Kennett Monthly Meeting in Pennsylvania. Bazaleel Wiggans reportedly accomplished his marriage with a woman not of our society by the assistance of a Baptist Teacher. Certificate requested for James Webb, a minor, to York Monthly Meeting in Pennsylvania. John Sharp, son of Thomas and Susanna Sharp, the latter deceased, intends to marry Elizabeth Walton, relict of William Walton.

On 28th day of 5th month, 1795, certificate requested for William Coale (of Philip) to New Garden Monthly Meeting. Certificate from Baltimore Monthly Meeting received from Amos Evans who was received into Fawn Particular Meeting. Certificate requested for Joseph Ford and his wife Frances and their minor son Philip, to Baltimore Monthly Meeting.

On 25th day of 6th month, 1795, Ann Wallis (late Worthington) "has gone out in her marriage to a man not in membership and with assistance of a

Baptist Teacher." Certificate from Warrington Monthly Meeting received from Thomas McMillan and his wife Jane, with their minor child Edith.

On 25th day of 7th month, 1795, William Hill, a minor and son of James Hill, deceased, "is desirous of being put out as an apprentice, and Samuel Hopkins and Silas Warner are appointed to assist him in the choice of a master and to inquire into his school education."

On 27th day of 8th month, 1795, John Burgess, son of Joseph and Deborah Burgess, intends to marry Drusilla Morgan, daughter of John Morgan, deceased, and his wife Ann.

On 24th day of 9th month, 1795, certificate from Warrington Monthly Meeting received from Febe [Phebe] Jones who was received a member of Fawn Particular Meeting.

On 26th day of 11th month, 1795, Charles Worthington (of John) charged with "being active in publicly exhibiting a play." Cassandra Dallam charged with "attending a place of diversion where a play was exhibited and in her dress and address had deviated from that simplicity and plainness that truth requires." Elizabeth Dallam later charged with this same "misconduct."

On 24th day of 12th month, 1795, certificate from Gunpowder Monthly Meeting received from Isaac Morris and his wife Martha, and their eight minor children, Susanna, Benjamin, Ann, Mary, Isaac, Enoch, Nehemiah, and John. Certificate requested for John Burgess and his wife Drusilla to South River Monthly Meeting in Virginia.

On 28th day of 1st month, 1796, certificate requested for Philip Coale (son of Philip), a minor, to New Garden Monthly Meeting. Joshua Bennett released from being an overseer and Benjamin Tomkins succeeded him.

On 25th day of 2nd month, 1796, Thomas Wilson found "guilty of taking strong drink to excess." On 28th day of 4th month, 1796, certificate requested for Mahlon Ely to Baltimore Monthly Meeting. Silas Warner submitted a report on behalf of the Trustees of the School for Black Children.

On 24th day of 5th month, 1796, Ann Burgess was released from station of an Elder since she had removed within the verge of another monthly meeting. Jacob Balderston was released from being an overseer and Silas Warner succeeded him. Certificates requested for Andrew McCoy and Joseph McCoy to Baltimore Monthly Meeting. Certificate from Gunpowder Monthly Meeting received from Moses Lukins and his wife Sarah, with their three minor children, Lydia, Benjamin, and Rachel.

On 28th day of 7th month, 1796, certificate from Nottingham Monthly Meeting received from Alice Harlan, Sr. and her daughter Rebecca Harlan, and they were received into Deer Creek Particular Meeting on 25th day of 8th month, 1796.

On 25th day of 8th month, 1796, certificate requested for James Wilson (son of John) to Cedar Creek Monthly Meeting in Virginia. Amos Evans, son of Griffith Evans, intends to marry Rachel Tomkins, daughter of Benjamin and Mary Tomkins.

On 22nd day of 9th month, 1796, Sarah Hill requested a certificate to Nottingham Monthly Meeting. Reported that Sarah Paris (late Thomas) had gone out in marriage with the assistance of a hireling minister.

On 27th day of 10th month, 1796, certificate requested for William Hill, a minor, to Nottingham Monthly Meeting.

On 24th day of 11th month, 1796, certificate requested for Joseph Burgess and wife Ann, with their minor son John, to Gunpowder Monthly Meeting. Reported that John Lukins Wallace, Grace Wallace, and Sarah Wallace, children of Joseph and Elizabeth Wallace, moved with their parents several years back when in their minority to within the compass of Exeter Monthly Meeting, and they have a right of membership.

On 26th day of 1st month, 1797, Thomas Jay, son of Stephen and Hannah Jay, both deceased, intends to marry Sarah Wilson, daughter of Thomas and Ann Wilson, both deceased.

On 23rd day of 3rd month, 1797, Skipwith Coale found guilty of marrying a woman not in membership by the assistance of a hireling teacher. Cassandra Coale also found guilty of marrying a man not in membership by the assistance of a Methodist Teacher.

On 27th day of 4th month, 1797, Rachel Eaton requested to be taken in membership and was received into Fawn Particular Meeting. William Wilson found guilty of accomplishing his marriage with the assistance of a Baptist Teacher.

On 22nd day of 6th month, 1797, Elizabeth Hopkins (the younger) charged with "attending a marriage where there was music and dancing and partook in part." Frances Hopkins mentioned that she "has a prospect of removing with her family to reside in Baltimore Town."

On 27th day of 7th month, 1797, certificate requested for Joshua Stapleton and wife Susanna, with their three minor children, Robert, Samuel, and Susanna, to Gunpowder Monthly Meeting. Certificate from South River Monthly Meeting in Virginia received from Thomas Burgess, who is removed from thence to within the verge of this meeting [Deer Creek]. Sarah Davis produced a paper condemning her misconduct in marrying a man outside the society. Certificate from Gunpowder Monthly Meeting received from Isaac Morris and his wife Martha, with their eight minor children, Susanna, Benjamin, Ann, Mary, Isaac, Enoch, Nehemiah, and John, and they were received as members of Fawn Particular Meeting. Reported that Elizabeth Richardson (late Heaton) has gone out in marriage to a man not of our society.

On 24th day of 8th month, 1797, certificate requested for George West to Westland Monthly Meeting. Certificate requested for Frances Hopkins and her two minor children, Elizabeth and Joel, to Baltimore Monthly Meeting.

On 28th day of 9th month, 1797, certificate requested for Ann Pervail to Calawissey[?] Monthly Meeting. Anne Frinal requested membership in Fawn Preparative Meeting.

On 26th day of 10th month, 1797, certificate from Richland Monthly Meeting in Pennsylvania received from Eli Kennard and his three minor children, William, Thomas, and Joseph, who were received into Fawn Particular Meeting. Gideon Pervail, Recorder of Certificates of Removal, being deceased, Isaac Massey is appointed for that service.

On 23rd day of 11th month, 1797, Cassandra McCoy produced a paper condemning herself for marrying to a man not of the society with the assistance of a Methodist Teacher. Rebeckah Jones requested a certificate to Abington Monthly Meeting, and Joseph Husbands to Baltimore Monthly Meeting.

On 29th day of 3rd month, 1798, Samuel Hopkins, son of Joseph Hopkins, deceased, and his wife Elizabeth, intends to marry Rachel Worthington, daughter of John and Pricilla Worthington. Certificates requested by Charles Lukins and wife Sarah to Baltimore Monthly Meeting, one for Thomas Burgess to South River Monthly Meeting in Virginia, and one for Abel Spencer and his wife Rebeccah, with their seven minor children, Elizabeth, William, Sarah, Rebeccah, Abel, Rubin, and Joseph. Hugh Ely requested to be released from recording marriage certificates and births and burials, and Aquila Massey was appointed for that service.

On 26th day of 4th month, 1798, John Carter intends to marry Rebeccah Harlan. Reported that Gainer Parsons (late Lukins) accomplished her marriage by the assistance of a Baptist Teacher. Martha Bond requested a certificate to Horsham Monthly Meeting.

On 24th day of 5th month, 1798, John Juit [Jewet] requested a certificate to Baltimore Monthly Meeting.

On 28th day of 6th month, 1798, Philip Hopkins charged with "going out in marriage to a woman not of our soceity by the assistance of a Baptist Teacher." Certificate requested for Nixon Wilson to Baltimore Monthly Meeting.

On 26th day of 7th month, 1798, John Hopkins charged with "going out in marriage to a woman not of our society by the assistance of a hireling teacher."

On 23rd day of 8th month, 1798, certificate from Gunpowder Monthly Meeting received from Ann Burgess, her son Joh Burgess, and Joseph Gallion, an apprentice, and they were received as members of Bush Particular Meeting. Abel Spencer released from overseer and Moses Lukins succeeded him.

On 27th day of 9th month, 1798, Asa Warner reported to have "gone out in marriage to a woman not of our society." John Wiggins "found guilty of fighting and has also joined a company who are learning the art of war."

On 25th day of 10th month, 1798, Hannah Stump (late Wilson) "had gone out in marriage to a man not of our society." Certificate requested for Skipwith Coale, a minor, son of Samuel Coale, to Baltimore Monthly Meeting.

On 22nd day of 11th month, 1798, certificate from York Monthly Meeting received from Mary Webb. Certificate requested for Phebe Jones to Warrington Monthly Meeting.

On 24th day of 12th month, 1798, Joseph Wiggins and Ann Bruce intend to marry. Gaynor Parsons produced a paper condemning her going out in marriage.

On 21st day of 2nd month, 1799, certificate received from John Webster Wilson [no place named] and he was received into Bush Particular Meeting.

Certificate received from Gunpowder Monthly Meeting for Dorithy Webster and forwarded to Baltimore Monthly Meeting as she has removed within their verge. Isaac Webster requested a certificate to Baltimore Monthly Meeting to accomplish his marriage with a member of that meeting.

On 28th day of 3rd month, 1799, informed by Deer Creek Preparative Meeting that Margaret Webster, wife of Samuel, requested their five minor children, William, Cassandra, John, Elizabeth, and Lee, be received into membership. Informed by Fawn Preparative Meeting that a certificate was requested for Thomas McMillen, his wife Jane, and their two minor children, Edith and Deberough, to Baltimore Monthly Meeting.

On 4th day of 5th month, 1799, certificate from Philadelphia Monthly Meeting received from Alice Harlan. Informed by Fawn Preparative Meeting that a certificate was requested for James Walton's two minor sons, Joseph and Benjamin, to be placed as apprentices in Philadelphia Monthly Meeting.

On 27th day of 6th month, 1799, our esteemed friend Henry Hull attended this meeting with a certificate from Creek Monthly Meeting held at Nine Partners in the State of New York. Certificate from Harsham Monthly Meeting in Pennsylvania received from Elizabeth Jones. Reported that Joseph Hopkins has gone out in marriage to a woman not of this society and by assistance of a hireling teacher. Informed by Fawn Preparative Meeting that Isaac and Elizabeth Jones requested their four minor children, Thomas, Asa, John, and Mary, be received into membership. Massey Webb requested a certificate to Baltimore Monthly Meeting.

On 25th day of 7th month, 1799, informed by Fawn Preparative Meeting that Nehemiah Underwood requested a certificate for his minor son William to Baltimore Monthly Meeting.

On 29th day of 8th month, 1799, certificate requested by Richard Johns and wife Sarah to Westland Monthly Meeting, and to the same place for Benjamin Wilson and his three minor children, Henry, Benjamin Kid, and Martha. Nehemiah Underwood requested a certificate for his daughter Mary Underwood to Warrington Monthly Meeting.

On 26th day of 9th month, 1799, informed by Fawn Preparative Meeting that "Mary Webb, Jr. has been guilty of fornication, which appears by her having an illegitimate child, which she says is to a man then in a married state."

On 24th day of 10th month, 1799, Daniel Robertson [name also spelled Robinson here in the record] released from station of overseer at his request and James Oarr [Orr] succeeded him. Reported that Hugh Ely, our clerk, is deceased. Sarah Allen (late Underwood) found "guilty of outgoing in marriage by assistance of a hireling minister."

On 26th day of 12th month, 1799, Sarah Janney (late Wilson) found "guilty of outoing in marriage by assistance of a Baptist Teacher." Certificate requested for Ann Coale, the younger, to Baltimore Monthly Meeting. Inquiry received from Buckingham Monthly Meeting regarding Priscilla West and Joseph Kennard who were formerly disowned for outgoing in marriage.

On 23rd day of 1st month, 1800, certificate from Kennet Monthly Meeting received from William Coale, who has removed to reside within the compass of our meeting. Isaac Coale appointed clerk due to death of Hugh Ely. Fawn Meeting proposed Ely Kinnard to succeed Benjamin Tomkins, deceased, in the station of overseer. Bill received, and paid, for the education of John Prevail.

On 23rd day of 2nd month, 1800, Benjamin Underwood charged with misconduct regarding his master and spiritous liquors and he also has moved within the verge of this meeting.

On 27th day of 3rd month, 1800, certificate from Richland Monthly Meeting received from Hannah Kennard. Certificate requested by John W. Wilson to Baltimore Monthly Meeting in order for marriage with Lucrecia Tyson. Certificate requested by Thomas Juitt for Baltimore Monthly Meeting.

On 27th day of 5th month, 1800, Alice Lukins charged with attending a place of diversion and joining in a dance. Ann Steward [also spelled Stewart and Stuart later in the record], late Morris [Norris?], found "guilty of fornication which appears by her having a child too soon after marriage, and the accomplishing of her marriage to a man not of our society."

On 26th day of 6th month, 1800, Jane Scotten requested to be taken into membership. Margaret Webster returned her certificate given in 12th month of 1799, as she has returned to reside within the verge of this meeting. William Cox was charged with detaining a Negro woman in servitude after she attained her full age, so he honored his former manumission and declared her free. William Cox, the younger, charged with "attending places of diversion and made a party in a dance." Antony [sic] Jones "guilty of marrying a woman not in membership with us, by the assistance of a Baptist Teacher."

On 24th day of 7th month, 1800, Alice Harlan requested a certificate to Philadelphia Monthly Meeting.

On 28th day of 8th month, 1800, the committtee appointed by the Quarterly Meeting to take into consideration the proposal of making some alterations in the Monthly Meeting quotes [quotas?] consisted of John Cox, Jacob Balderston, Moses Dillon, John Mitchell, George Ellicott, and Caleb Bentley. Ann Plummer (late Wallice) "has gone out in marriage to a man not of our society with the assistance of a hireling teacher." Certificate requested for Thomas Norton, a minor, to Baltimore Monthly Meeting. Certificate requested by Aaron Boram, his wife Elizabeth, and their daughter Ann, to Westland Monthly Meeting near the settlement of Redstone.

On 27th day of 11th month, 1800, Joseph Husband, son of Joseph Husband, deceased, and wife Mary, intends to marry Sarah Brown, daughter of Freeborn and Mary Brown. Certificate requested by Isaac Wilson, his wife Susannah, and their three minor children, Alesanna, David, and John, and one for John Wilson, one for Nargarett Wilson, and one for Ann Wilson [name is given as Anna later in record], to Baltimore Monthly Meeting. Certificate requested by Nicholas Cooper, his wife Sarah, and their four minor children, Parthenia, Isaiah, Elizabeth, and Martha, to Baltimore Monthly Meeting. Informed by Fawm Preparative Meeting that Leven Heaton "has been guilty of fighting, drinking to excess, and using bad language." Moses Webb "has accomplished his marriage with a woman not of our soceity by the assistance of a Baptist Teacher."

On 25th day of 12th month, 1800, certificate from Horsham Monthly Meeting received from Mary Bond. David Stokes "has gone out in his marriage with a woman not of our society and by the assistance of a Baptist Teacher." Susannah Hopkins (late Dallam) "has consummated her marriage by the assistance of a Baptist Teacher." Joshua Brown, son of Joshua and Hannah Brown, both deceased, intends to marry Sarah Ely, relict of Hugh Ely.

DECEASED MEMBERS OF BALTIMORE MONTHLY MEETING, 1674-1800

Phebe Albion, d. 3rd day of 6th month 1796.

Elias Albion, d. in 1800.

Benjamin Amos, son of Joseph and Rachel Amos, b. 6th day of 3rd month, 1794; d. 3rd day of 8th month, 1800.

Mary Atkinson, dau. of Joseph and Rachel Atkinson, b. 6th day of 3rd month, 1797, d. 17th day of 8th month, 1800; bur. at Elk Ridge.

William Brown, b. 1653; came to America from England in 1696; m. (1) Dorothea ----, died at sea [no date]; (2) Ann Mercer; (3) Catharine Williams; d. 23rd day of 6th month, 1746.

Mercer Brown, son of William Brown and Ann Mercer, b. 27th day of 12th month, 1686 [sic]; m. (1) Jane Richards; (2) Dianna Churchman; d. in 1733.

Dianna Brown, widow of Mercer Brown, and dau. of John and Hannah Churchman, b. 7th day of 6th month, 1699, and d. 1st day of 1st month, 1766; m. (2) Mordecai James [?].

David Brown, son of Mercer Brown and Dianna Churchman, b. 1731; m. (1) Sarah B. Brown; (2) Elizabeth ----; d. in 1781; bur. at Patapsco B. G.

Sarah B. Brown, dau. of Joshua Brown and Hannah Gatchel (from West Nottingham), b. 6th day of 11th month, 1740; m. David Brown; d. 1st day of 1st month, 1759; bur. at Patapsco.

David Brown, son of David and Elizabeth Brown, b. 18th day of 12th month, 1758; d. 1793 [?]; bur. at Little Britain.

Joshua R. Brown, d. 2nd day of 3rd month, 1794.

Mary Burgess, d. 29th day of 3rd month, 1794.

Samuel Beal, son of Thomas, d. 27th day of 8th month, 1794.

Joseph Beal, son of Thomas, d. 21st day of 9th month, 1794.

Grace Beal, dau. of Thomas, d. 1st day of 10th month, 1794.

Ruthy Brown, dau. of Jesse Brown and Dorothy Matthews, b. 7th day of 2nd month, 1794; d. 8th day of 3rd month, 1797.

William Coale, Sr., d. 30th day of 10th month, 1678; m. (1) Hester ----; (2) Hannah ----; (3) Elizabeth ----.

William Coale, son of William and Hester, d. ----, 1700.

William Coale, son of William and Hannah, d. 6th month, 1715.

Hannah Cornthwait, dau. of John Cornthwait and Mary Mathews, b. 26th day of 5th month, 1775; d. 10th day of 10th month, 1778; bur. in City Grounds.

Mary M. Cornthwait, dau. of Oliver Mathews and Hannah Johns, m. Robert Cornthwait; d. 6th day of 2nd month, 1781; bur. in City Grounds.

Gerard Cowman, third son of Joseph Cowman and Sarah Hall, b. 6th day of 5th month, 1762; d. 31st day of 12th month, 1789.

Jonathan Coats, son of Jonathan and Jane, b. 28th day of 5th month, 1764; d. 1st day of 10th month, 1793; bur. in City Grounds.

Robert Cox, b. 3rd day of 11th month, 1735; d. 21st day of 1st month, 1795; bur. in City Grounds.

Jane Coates, b. 23rd day of 11th month, 1735; m. Jonathan Coates; d. 16th day of 5th month, 1795; bur. in City Grounds.

Robert Cornthwait, son of Robert Cornthwait and Aliceanna Wilson, b. 9th day of 8th month, 1789; d. 14th day of 12th month, 1789.

Joseph Canby, son of Samuel and Elizabeth, b. 25th day of 1st month, 1799, and came with his parents to Baltimore from Darby Monthly Meeting on 4th day of 8th month, 1800; d. 25th day of 1st[sic] month, 1800; bur. in City Grounds.

Robert Caddy, d. 20th day of 8th month, 1800; bur. in City Grounds; came to Baltimore from New York Monthly Meeting on 14th day of 6th month, 1798.

Isaac Granton Cornthwait, b. 30th day of 10th month, 1790; d. 20th day of 8th month, 1800; bur. in City Grounds.

Robert Cornthwait, b. 6th day of 7th month, 1749; d. 30th day of 8th month, 1800.

Elizabeth Davenport, dau. of ---- Davenport and Margaret Dukehart, d. 20th day of 2nd month, 1794; bur. in City Grounds.

Jonathan Davenport, b. 24th day of 5th month, 1759; d. 13th day of 8th month, 1797; bur. in City Grounds.

Gideon Dare, Jr., son of Gideon Dare and Elizabeth Wilson, m. (1) ----, and (2) Lydia M. Hibberd; d. 8th day of 8th month, 1800; bur. in City Grounds.

Elias Ellicott, son of Andrew Ellicott and Elizabeth Brown, b. 27th day of 12th month, 1757, and died young.

Joseph Ellicott, son of Andrew Ellicott and Ann Bye, b. 8th day of 10th month, 1732; m. Judith Bleaker in 1753; d. 15th day of 7th month, 1780; bur. at Ellicott Mills.

Nathaniel Ellicott, son of Jonathan Ellicott and Sarah Harvey, b. 1782; d. 1786; bur. at Ellicott Mills.

Frances Ellicott, dau. of Jonathan Ellicott and Sarah Harvey, b. 5th day of 12th month, 1785 (twin to Eliźabeth) and d. in 1790; bur. at Ellicott Mills.

Evan Thomas Ellicott, son of Elias Ellicott and Mary Thomas, b. 17th day of 9th month, 1788; d. 10th day of 8th month, 1791; bur. at Sandy Spring.

Ann Ellicott, dau. of Elias Ellicott and Mary Thomas, b. 24th day of 8th month, 1798; d. 15th day of 1st month, 1799; bur. in City Grounds.

John Ellicott, son of Andrew Ellicott and Ann Bye (from Buckingham Monthly Meeting, Pennsylvania), b. 28th day of 12th month, 1739; m. (1) Leah Brown in 1771, and (2) Cassandra Hopkins; d. 1795; bur. at Ellicott Mills.

Philip Ford, son of Joseph and Frances, b. 9th day of 1st month, 1795; d. 5th day of 9th month, 1795.

Edward Ford, son of Joseph and Frances, b. 17th day of 11th month, 1796; d. 12th day of 9th month, 1797.

Mary Fisher, b. 28th day of 1st month, 1725; d. 2nd day of 12th month, 1795.

Gerard Hopkins, m. Margaret Johns in 1700; d. in 1743.

Margaret Hopkins, dau. of Richard Johns and Elizabeth (Kinsey) Sparrow; m. Gerard Hopkins; d. in 1749.

Gerard Hopkins, son of Gerard Hopkins and Margaret Johns, b. 17th day of 3rd month, 1709; m,. Mary Hall; d. 3rd day of 7th month, 1777.

Elenn Humphrey, dau. of David Humphrey and Elizabeth Roberts (from Montgomery County, Pennsylvania, in 1761), b. 14th day of 3rd month, 1747; unmarried; d. 9th day of 1st month, 1793; bur. in City Grounds.

John Hussey, son of George and Rachel, b. 8th day of 9th month, 1782; d. 27th day of 4th month, 1783.

Rachel Hussey, son of George and Rachel, b. 19th day of 10th month, 1785; 7th day of 11th month, 1785.

Elenn Humphrey, dau. of David Humphrey and Elizabeth Roberts (from Montgomery County, Pennsylvania, in 1761), b. 14th day of 3rd month, 1747; unmarried; d. 9th day of 1st month, 1793; bur. in City Grounds.

John Hussey, son of George and Rachel, b. 8th day of 9th month, 1782; d. 27th day of 4th month, 1783.

Rachel Hussey, son of George and Rachel, b. 19th day of 10th month, 1785; 7th day of 11th month, 1785.

Samuel Hayward, son of William and Mary, b. 12th day of 5th month, 1792; 14th day of 8th month, 1793; bur. at Patapsco B. G.

Sarah Hopkins, dau. of John Giles and Cassandra Smith, b. 26th day of 12th month, 1723; m. Samuel Hopkins on 2nd day of 9th month, 1740; d. 17th day of 5th month, 1795; bur. in City Grounds.

Joshua Hayward, son of William and Mary, b. 21st day of 11th month, 1796; d. 16th day of 7th month, 1797; bur. in City Grounds.

Thomas Hopkins, son of Johns Hopkins and Elizabeth Harris, b. 19th day of 12th month, 1774; d. 16th day of 7th month, 1798.

Rachel Hussey, b. 19th day of 9th month, 1758; m. George Hussey; d. 3rd day of 3rd month, 1799.

Mary Hill, b. 20th day of 12th month, 1724; d. 12th day of 3rd month, 1800.

Edward Hopkins, son of Gerard T. Hopkins and Dorothy Brooke, b. 9th day of 12th month, 1798; d. 9th day of 3rd month, 1800; bur. in City Grounds.

Gerard Hopkins, son of Samuel Hopkins and Sarah S. Giles, b. 26th day of 4th month, 1742; m. (1) ---- Dawes, and (2) Rachel Wilson, dau. of Henry Wilson, and widow of Samuel Harris; b. 18th day of 4th month, 1800.

Margaret Jackson, b. 9th day of 5th month, 1750; m. Isaac Jackson; d. 11th day of 3rd month, 1795.

Joseph Jackson, b. 25th day of 3rd month, 1779; d. 13th day of 7th month, 1797.

Samuel Jackson (from New Garden Monthly Meeting on 11th day of 7th month, 1799), died at sea [no date given].

Nathan Johns, Jr., son of Nathan and Elizabeth (from Deer Creek Monthly Meeting on 12th day of 4th month, 1798), d. 14th day of 11th month, 1799; bur. in City Grounds.

Sarah Jackson, dau. of Isaac and Margaret, b. 21st day of 7th month, 1776; m. N--- [sic] Tyson; d. 8th day of 7th month, 1800; bur. in City Grounds.

Jacob Kinsey, son of Isaiah and Rachel (from Indian Spring Monthly Meeting on 12th day of 12th month, 1779), d, 27th day of 7th month, 1800.

Isaiah Kinsey, Jr., son of Isaiah and Rachel (from Indian Spring Monthly Meeting on 12th day of 12th month, 1779), d. 2nd day of 9th month, 1800.

Mary Lee, dau. of John and Isabella, b. 1st day of 3rd month, 1793; d. 8th day of 3rd month, 1793.

Jesse Thomas Lee, son of John and Isabella, b. 18th day of 5th month, 1794; d. 3rd day of 6th month, 1794.

Elenora Lee, dau. of John and Isabella, b. 28th day of 9th month, 1795; d. 11th day of 2nd month, 1800.

Ann Moore (from Gunpowder Monthly Meeting in 1780), b. 16th day of 9th month, 1710; d. 11th day of 11th month, 1783; bur. in Patapsco B. G.

John Malsby (member by request in 1773), b. 17th day of 9th month, 1753; m. Mary Starr; d. 10th day of 9th month, 1785; bur. in Patapsco B. G.

Marian Marsh, infant of John Marsh and Hannah Matthews, b. 6th day of 5th month, 1792; d. 29th day of 7th month, 1792; bur. in Patapsco B. G.

William Mason, son of George and Susanna (from New Garden Monthly Meeting, Pennsylvania, on 10th day of 12th month, 1795), d. 22nd day of 6th month, 1795[sic].

Susanna Mason, dau. of George and Susanna (from New Garden Monthly Meeting, Pennsylvania, on 10th day of 12th month, 1795), d. 26th day of 6th month, 1795[sic].

Emelia Matthews, dau. of William Matthews and Elizabeth Hanway, b. 1st day of 5th month, 1798; d. 17th day of 8th month, 1799.

Mary Marsh, dau. of William and Ann Marsh, b. 7th day of 6th month, 1800; d. 15th day of 10th month, 1800.

John Naylor, d. 14th day of 9th month, 1796.

Elizabeth Naylor, dau. of Samuel and Rebecca (from Gunpowder Monthly Meeting on 2nd day of 5th month, 1796), b. 8th day of 8th month, 1793; d. 9th day of 5th month, 1800; bur. in City Grounds.

Ann Price (from Indian Spring Monthly Meeting on 8th day of 3rd month, ----), d. 6th day of 7th month, 1792.

Samuel Price, son of Warrick and Susanna, b. 6th day of 8th month, 1793; d. 22nd day of 8th month, 1793.

Simon Perine, b. 16th day of 10th month, 1768; d. 8th day of 1st month, 1795.

Jane Price, dau. of Warrick and Susanna, b. 29th day of 10th month, 1794; d. 19th day of 3rd month, 1795.

Jonathan Price, dau. of Warrick and Susanna, b. 19th day of 12th month, 1795; d. 13th day of 7th month, 1796.

Simon Peter Perine, d. 25th day of 9th month, 1797.

Mauldin H. Perine, son of Peter Perine and Mary Howard, b. 17th day of 8th month, 1798; d. 18th day of 8th month, 1798.

Ann Price, dau. of Israel and Hannah, b. 4th day of 3rd month, 1798; d. 22nd day of 8th month, 1799.

John Evans Reese, son of John Reese and Catharine Evans, b. 3rd day of 8th month, 1758; m. Ann Lacy; d. 3rd day of 10th month, 1799.

Hannah Stump, dau. of John Stump and Cassandra Wilson, b. about 1780; unmarried; died about 1780[sic]; bur. in City Grounds.

Sarah Scott, dau. of Joseph and Ann, b. 27th day of 7th month, 1781; d. 13th day of 5th month, 1793.

Rachel Scott, dau. of Joseph and Ann, b. 7th day of 1st month, 1773; d. 17th day of 5th month, 1793.

Jacob Scott, son of Joseph and Ann, b. 19th day of 6th month, 1778; d. 20th day of 5th month, 1793.

Jesse Scott, son of Rossiter and Edith, b. 18th day of 12th month, 1791; d. 4th day of 7th month, 1793.

Ann Sheppard, b. 14th day of 11th month, 1772; d. 11th day of 8th month, 1796.

Abraham Scott, son of Rossiter and Edith, b. 21st day of 1st month, 1791; d. 22nd day of 8th month, 1796.

Joseph Scott (from Fairfax Monthly Meeting on 14th day of 7th month, 1796); m. Ann ----; d. 27th day of 7th month, 1799.

Sarah Sheppard, b. 2nd day of 8th month, 1733; 24th day of 12th month, 1799.

Rebecca Spencer, m. Abel Spencer; d. 7th day of 9th month, 1800.

Josiah Stewart, b. 1714; d. in 10th month, 1800.

Philip Thomas (from Bristol, England in 1651), b. about 1620; m. Sarah Harrison; d. in 1674.

Sarah Thomas (from Bristol, England in 1651), m. Philip Thomas; d. in 1687.

Philip Thomas, first child of Philip and Sarah (from Bristol, England in 1651), b. in 1649; d. in 1687.

Sarah Thomas, second child of Philip and Sarah (from Bristol, England in 1651), b. about 1650; m. John Mears in 1674; d. in 5th month, 1675.

Elizabeth Thomas, third child of Philip and Sarah (from Bristol, England in 1651), m. (1) William Coale, and (2) Edward Talbott; d. in 1726. [Note: There is a second entry in the record for this woman which contains the same information, except Edward's name is spelled "Talbot"].

Edward Talbot, son of Richard and Elizabeth, m. Elizabeth Thomas; d. in 1st month, 1692. [Note: There is a second entry in the record for this man which indicates that he was the second son of Richard and Elizabeth, and that he married Elizabeth Coale, nee Thomas].

Samuel Thomas, son of Philip and Sarah, b. 1655; m. Mary Hutchins; d. in 7th month, 1743.

Mary Thomas, dau. of Francis Hutchins [Huchins?] and wife Elizabeth, m. Samuel Thomas on 15th day of 5th month, 1688; d. in 7th month, 1751.

Martha Thomas, fourth [sic] child of Philip and Sarah, m. Richard Arnold; d. in 1687.

Mary C. Thomas, dau. of Richard Snowden and Eliza Coale, b. in 1712; m. Samuel Thomas; d. in 1755.

Samuel Thomas, fifth [sic] child of Philip and Sarah, m. Mary Coale.

Philip Thomas, eldest son of Samuel Thomas and Mary Hutchins [Huchins?], b. in 1694; m. (1) Frances Holland in 1712, and (2) Ann Chew in 1724; d. in 1st month, 1763.

Ann C. Thomas, dau. of Samuel Chew and wife Mary, m. Philip Thomas (his second wife); d. in 7th month, 1777.

Sarah Thomas, first child of Samuel Thomas and Mary Hutchins, b. in 1689; m. Joseph Richardson on 25th day of 10th month, 1705; no date of death given.

Elizabeth Thomas, second child of Samuel Thomas and Mary Hutchins, b. 19th day of 12th month 17--; m. Richard Snowden; d. 19th day of 12th month, 1717.

Esther Tyson, second child of Elisha Tyson and Mary Amos, b. 23rd day of 2nd month, 1779, and died in infancy; bur. in City Grounds.

Mary Tucker, b. 28th day of 1st month, 1725; d. in 2nd day of 12th month, 1795.

Isaac Tucker, second son of Matthias Tyson and Esther Shoemaker, d. ---- [not dates given; probably in 1796].

Esther Shoemaker Tucker, widow of Isaac Tyson, and daughter of Isaac Shoemaker, d. 8th day of 9th month, 1796.

John England Townsend, son of Joseph and Mary, b. 4th day of 1st month, 1797; d. 1st day of 2nd month, 1797; bur. in City Grounds.

Esther Tyson, fourth child of Isaac Tyson and Margaret Hopkins, b. 22nd day of 3rd month, 1796; d. 19th day of 8th month, 1797.

Mary Martha Townsend, dau. of Joseph and Mary, b. 4th day of 1st month, 1797; d. 18th day of 11th month, 1797; bur. in City Grounds.

Mary Townsend, second wife of Joseph Townsend, and daughter of George and Dorothy Matthews, b. 30th day of 4th month, 1764; d. 7th day of 3rd month, 1799; bur. in City Grounds.

James Pemberton Townsend, son of Joseph Townsend and Mary Matthews, b. 16th day of 12th month, 1798; d. 9th day of 3rd month, 1799; bur. in City Grounds.

Esther Tyson, dau. of Isaac Tyson and Esther Shoemaker, b. 22nd day of 5th month, 1796; died 19th day of 8th month, 1797; bur. in City Grounds.

Philip and Samuel Thomas, twin sons of Samuel Thomas and Mary Snowden, b. 12th day of 1st month, 1774; died in 1795. [Note: Unclear in record whether one or both died].

Ann Underwood, dau. of Enoch and Mary (from Warrington Monthly Meeting), b. 11th day of 4th month, 1799; d. 17th day of 8th month, 1800.

David Wilson, son of David and Jane, b. 26th day of 6th month, 1794; d. 15th day of 4th month, 1795; bur. in City Grounds.

Robert Webster (from Deer Creek Monthly Meeting), b. 11th day of 7th month, 1795; d. 19th day of 11th month, 1795; bur. in Amsterdam, Holland.

John Lee Webster, Jr. (from Deer Creek Monthly Meeting), b. 12th day of 3rd month, 1795; d. in 1797.

Isaac Williams (from Gunpowder Monthly Meeting), m. Rebecca ----; d. 2nd day of 7th month, 1795.

Charles Wilson, son of Stephen and Mary, b. 26th day of 4th month, 1798; d. 5th day of 7th month, 1798.

Jesse West, son of Joseph West and Susanna Wiley (from England - no date given), b. 13th day of 12th month, 1769; unmarried; d. 18th day of 12th month, 1799; bur. in City Grounds.

William Wilson, son of John and Deborah (from Gunpowder Monthly Meeting - no date given), b. 21st day of 8th month, ----; d. 21st day of 8th month, 1800.

Grace Wilson, dau. of John and Deborah (from Gunpowder Monthly Meeting - no date given), d. 3rd day of 9th month, 1800.

BALTIMORE MONTHLY MEETING CERTIFICATES OF REMOVAL 1796-1800

"This book after having been lost for many years was recovered in 1877 and re-bound, the first twenty pages are missing. Signed by Edwin Blackburn."

On 8th day of 9th month, 1796, certificate for William Carpenter and wife Rachel and children, Lydia, George, Hannah, John, and Joseph, to Bradford Monthly Meeting in Pennsylvania.

On 12th day of 3rd month, 1795, certificate given at Dublin Monthly Meeting for Barker Thacker, son of William, "to Philadelphia Monthly Meeting or elsewhere" was received in Baltimore in the 11th month, 1795, and forwarded to York Monthly Meeting on the 8th day of 12th month, 1796.

On 20th day of 10th month, 1796, certificate for Thomas Fisher, Jr. to the Southern District of Philadelphia.

On 11th day of 3rd month, 1796, certificate given at Brighthouse Monthly Meeting at Bradford for James Wilson, a young man, was received in Baltimore in the 6th month, 1796, and forwarded to White Oak Swamp, Virginia, on the 8th day of 12th month, 1796.

On 8th day of 12th month, 1796, certificate for James Amoss and wife Hannah and children, Mary and Lee, to Gunpowder Monthly Meeting.

On 12th day of 1st month, 1797, certificate for Lawrence and Ann Rice to Crooked Run Monthly Meeting in Virginia.

On 11th day of 5th month, 1797, certificate for Ezekiel Harlan to Nottingham Monthly Meeting, noting his good conduct in Baltimore during "his short stay amongst us."

On 8th day of 3rd month, 1798, certificate for Mary Matthews to Gunpowder Monthly Meeting.

On 8th day of 3rd month, 1798, certificate for George W. Field to Philadelphia Monthly Meeting.

On 12th day of 4th month, 1798, certificate for Isaac Johnson to Southland Monthly Meeting in Virginia, noting that "soon after expiration of his apprenticeship [in Baltimore] he removed from amongst us."

On 10th day of 5th month, 1798, certificate for Elizabeth Naylor to Nottingham Monthly Meeting.

On 8th day of 11th month, 1798, certificate for Rebecca Moore to Gunpowder Monthly Meeting, noting her good conduct in Baltimore during "her short stay amongst us."

On 10th day of 1st month, 1799, certificate for Jesse Medcalf to Hopewell Monthly Meeting in Virginia.

On 14th day of 2nd month, 1799, certificate for Henry Kendall to Westminster Monthly Meeting.

On 8th day of 8th month, 1799, certificate for Elizabeth Webster (of Isaac) to Deer Creek Monthly Meeting.

On 14th day of 11th month, 1799, certificates for Nathan Johns, Jr. and Joseph Wilson to Westland Monthly Meeting in Pennsylvania.

On 23rd day of 5th month, 1799, certificate from Deer Creek Monthly Meeting for Thomas McMillen and wife Jane and minor children, Edith and Deborah, was received in Baltimore in the 10th month, 1799, and forwarded to Warrington Monthly Meeting in Pennsylvania on 9th day of 1st month, 1800.

At the last meeting in 1799 in Baltimore, John Hall attended with a certificate dated in the 3rd month, 1799, from Pardshaw Monthly Meeting in South Britain, which was recorded in Baltimore on the 9th day of 1st month, 1800.

On 9th day of 1st month, 1800, certificate for Stephen Grelett [Gielett?], who visited in company with John Hall, to go [return] to New York Monthly Meeting.

On 13th day of 11th month, 1798, certificate from Motherkiln Monthly Meeting for Mary Stokeley, was received in Baltimore on 9th day of 1st month, 1800.

On 13th day of 2nd month, 1800, certificate for William Copeland to Western Branch Monthly Meeting in Isle of Wight County, Virginia.

On 13th day of 3rd month, 1800, certificate for Elizabeth Amos and husband [no name] to Gunpowder Monthly Meeting.

On 12th day of 6th month, 1800, certificate for Daniel Hanson to Blackwater Monthly Meeting in Virginia, noting "his short residence amongst us" in Baltimore.

On 10th day of 7th month, 1800, certificate for Robert Bartlett to Third Haven Monthly Meeting, noting he is "returning to you, apprenticeship completed."

On 10th day of 7th month, 1800, certificate for Catharine England and husband [no name] to Gunpowder Monthly Meeting.

Ob 12th day of 6th month, 1800, certificate for Oliver Matthews (of William) and wife Phebe to Gunpowder Monthly Meeting.

On 14th day of 8th month, 1800, certificate for Sarah Brelsford to Falls Monthly Meeting in Bucks County, Pennsylvania.

On 9th day of 10th month, 1800, certificates for Nathan Johns and wife Elizabeth and daughter Mary, and Ann Johns, to Westland Monthly Meeting in Pennsylvania.

On 2nd day of 7th month, 1800, certificate from Horsham Monthly Meeting in Pennsylvania, for Martha Bond, was received in Baltimore and then forwarded to Deer Creek Monthly Meeting on 13th day of 11th month, 1800.

On 11th day of 12th month, 1800, certificate for Martha Hill to Gunpowder Monthly Meeting.

ABSTRACTS OF BALTIMORE MONTHLY MEETNG
MEMORIALS, 1783-1800

Ann Moore, deceased, was born in Pennsylvania on the 16th day of 9th month, 1710, and her mother died when she was very young. Testimony given at Gunpowder Monthly Meeting stated she moved to Maryland in 1753 with her husband and family, and resided in Baltimore Town for the last three years. Ill five weeks, she died on 11th day of 11th month, 1783.

John Malsby, deceased, late of Baltimore Town, was born in Pennsylvania on the 17th day of 9th month, 1753, and his family moved to Maryland when he was young, settling near Gunpowder Monthly Meeting. He joined Friends in 1773 and moved to Pipe Creek Monthly Meeting in 1778. He married Mary Starr in 1783 and later moved with his family to Baltimore Town. He died on 10th day of 9th month, 1785.

Mary Cox, deceased, of Deer Creek Monthly Meeting, was born at Eghamhith in Great Britain and was educated in the profession of the Church of England. She married late Friend William Cox, deceased, and soon after moved to this country. She was called to the ministry of Friends in the 39th year of her age, and died on 15th day of 8th month, 1790, aged about 69 years.

James Rigbie, deceased, of Deer Creek Monthly Meeting, was a son of Nathan Rigbie who was by profession of the Episcopal Church. He became High Sheriff of the county around 1742 and joined Friends after hearing Edmund Peckner from Great Britain when he visited America. He became a Minister in 1749, and died on 6th day of 1st month, 1790, in the 70th year of his age.

Susanna Brown, of Gunpowder Monthly Meeting, widow of our esteemed Friend William Brown, deceased, was born in the 7th month, 1701 to John and Hannah Churchman of Nottingham in Pennsylvania. She married and lived in Philadelphia a long time, and became an Elder of Friends. She died on 25th day of 8th month, 1790, aged near 80 years, and was interred at Little Falls.

Philip Coale, of Deer Creek Monthly Meeting, was a son of William and Sarah Coale. He was educated in Friends and became an Elder. He married and had a family, and died on 8th day of 4th month, 1791, aged about 53 years.

Hannah Matthews, an Elder of Friends, and late wife of Oliver Matthews, died on 15th day of 11th month, 1791, in her 64th year.

[The following deaths are recorded in the Baltimore Monthly Meeting records for testimonials given at meetings held by Friends outside of northern Maryland from 1783 to 1795].

Joseph Berry, of Third Haven Monthly Meeting, Talbot County, Maryland, died on 22nd day of 10th month, 1783, age 52.

John Bartlett, of Third Haven Monthly Meeting, Talbot County, died on 26th day of 8th month, 1784, age 42.

James Berry, of Third Haven Monthly Meeting, Talbot County, died on 24th day of 1st month, 1785, age 56.

Elisha Kirk, of York Monthly Meeting, born in Pennsylvania, and died on 11th day of 4th month, 1790, age 33.

William Matthews, of York Monthly Meeting, born in Virginia, and died on 7th day of 5th month, 1792, age 60.

William Wilson, of Westland Monthly Meeting, Pennsylvania, born in Delaware, died on 15th day of 8th month, 1795, age 56.

William Underwood, of Warrington Monthly Meeting, Pennsylvania, born in Pennsylvania, and died on 18th day of 5th month, 1795, age 64.

Peter Cleaver, of Warrington Monthly Meeting, Pennsylvania, born in Pennsylvania, and died on 12th day of 8th month, 1795, age 64.

Martha Mendenhall, of Hopewell Monthly Meeting, Virginia, died on 28th day of 10th month, 1794, age 82.

BALTIMORE MONTHLY MEETING EASTERN DISTRICT---
BIRTHS, DEATHS, DISOWNMENTS AND REMOVALS
REGISTERED BETWEEN 1793 AND 1800

[Note: This register contains birth and deaths as early as 1717, and disownments and removals from 1793 on. Many other siginificant items have been entered as well, such as subsequent marriages and certificates of removal. For the purposes of this book, any and all entries occurring prior to 1800 have been abstracted, including a number of entries for which no dates were written in register--H. C. Peden].

John Brown, b. --th day of 9th month, 1747[?]; disowned [date illegible]; his wife Mary Brown, b. 16th day of 10th month, 1750; their son, James Brown, b. 26th day of 9th month, 1776; and, their dau. Frances Brown, b. 6th day of 11th month, 1785, m. Nicholas S. Jones and was disowned.

William Brown, b. 23rd day of 3th month, 1753; his wife, Elizabeth Brown, b. 3rd day of 9th month, 1753, and d. 22nd day of 12th month, 1800 (interred the next day); their dau. Esther Brown, b. 30th day of 12th month, 1775, m. Eli Balderston; their daughter Hannah Brown, b. 21st day of 9th month, 1777, m. Js.[?] Price, and removed by certificate [date illegible]; their son, Joseph Brown, b. 13th day of 7th month, 1779; their dau. Ann Brown, b. 30th day of 5th month, 1785, m. Samuel S. Smith, and removed by certificate [date illegible]; their dau. Elizabeth Brown, b. 17th day of 8th month, 1788; and, their dau. Mary Brown, b. 19th day of 5th month, 1792.

George Matthews, b. 19th day of 9th month, 1729, and d. in 1811; his wife, Sarah Matthews, b. 1st day of 6th month, 1743; their dau. Ann Matthews, b. 26th day of 9th month, 1778, m. S. Cole, and removed by certificate [date illegible].

Joseph Townsend, b. 26th day of 2nd month, 1756; his wife Mary Townsend, b. 30th day of 4th month, 1764, and d. 7th day of 3rd month, 1799; their dau. Hannah Painter Townsend, b. 3rd day of 2nd day, 1789, m. Samuel Jefferis, and removed to the western district; and, their son Nicholas Waln Townsend, b. 30th day of 10th month, 1792.

William Trimble, b. 10th day of 10th month, 1744; his wife, Hannah Trimble, b. 18th day of 1st month, 1745; his son, John Trimble, b. 27th day of 10th month, 1775, and disowned on 9th day of 8th month, 1798; his dau. Sarah Trimble, b. 9th day of 8th month, 1778, and d. 9th day of 7th month, 1794 (interred the next day); his son James Trimble, b. 20th day of 11th month, 1782; and, their son William Trimble, b. 13th day of 11th month, 1789.

David Brown, b. 13th day of 9th month, 1751; his wife Elizabeth Brown, b. 11th day of 3rd month, 1755; their dau. Elizabeth Brown, b. 15th day of 11th month, 1778, and m. John Trimble on 15th day of 3rd month, 1798; their son David Brown, b. 25th day of 10th month, 1782; their son George Brown, b. 25th day of 4th month, 1785; and, their son John Brown, b. 28th day of 3rd month, 1788.

Rebecca Williams, b. in 1737, and d. in 1810; her dau. Sarah Hayward, b. 1st day of 5th month, 1771, m. Isaac Brookes.

Gerrard Hopkins, b. 26th day of 4th month, 1742, d. 18th day of 4th month, 1800, and interred on the 20th; his wife, Rachel Hopkins, b. 9th day of 12th month, 1751; their son Henry Hopkins, b. 23rd day of 9th month, 1779; their dau. Priscilla Hopkins, b. 4th day of 12th month, 1780; their son Gerrard Hopkins, b. 27th day of 6th month, 1786; their son Richard Hopkins, b. 9th day of 12th month, 1791; and, their son Samuel Harris [sic], b. 17th day of 9th month, 1774 [sic].

William Riley, b. 25th day of 9th month, 1762; his wife Sarah Riley, b. 21st day of 9th month, 1767 (both removed to western district); their son Benjamin Riley, b. 22nd day of 9th month, 1785, and d. 4th day of 7th month, 1797 (interred same day); their dau. Ann Riley, b. 6th day of 8th month, 1787 (removed to western district); their son William Riley, b. 25th day of 7th month, 1789, and d. 6th day of 7th month, 1796 (interred next day); and, their son ---- Riley [page torn], b. 20th day of 5th month, 1801 (removed to western district).

----a [page torn] Tyson, b. 18th day of 2nd month, 1750; his wife, Mary Tyson, b. 10th day of 5th month, 1758; their son Isaac Tyson, b. 10th day of 10th month, 1777; their dau. Lucretia Tyson, b. 1st day of 9th month, 1780, and m. John W. Wilson; their dau. Mary Tyson, b. 4th day of 9th month, 1785; their son William Tyson, b. 2nd day of 10th month 1782; and, their son Nathan Tyson, b. 14th[?] day of 11th month, 1787 (all removed to western district).

Robert Cornthwait, b. 6th day of 7th month, 1749; his wife, Grace Cornthwait, b. 15th day of 12th month, 1749; their dau. Elizabeth Cornthwait, b. 7th day of 1st month, 1778, and m. Benjamin Amos; their dau. Deborah Cornthwait, b. 30th day of 7th month, 1779; their son Thomas Cornthwait, b. 30th day of 3rd month, 1781; their dau. Mary Cornthwait, b. 20th day of 12th month, 1782; their son William Cornthwait, b. 16th day of 10th month, 1784; their son John Cornthwait, b. 11th day of 10th month, 1786; their son Robert Cornthwait, b. 9th day of 8th month, 1789; and, their son ---- [page torn] Cornthwait, b. ---- [page torn], 1790[?].

---- [page torn] Harris, b. ---- [page torn] 1754; his wife, Susanna Harris, b. 22nd day of 2nd month, 1762; their dau. Mary Harris, b. 13th day of 8th month, 1790; and, their dau. Beulah Harris, b. 6th day of 8th month, 1792 (all removed to western district and then by certificate to Warrington Monthly Meeting on 29th day of 3rd month, 1793.)

James Carey, b. 22nd day of 12th month, 1757; his wife Martha Carey, b. 7th day of 11th month, 1761; their son John Ellicott Carey, b. 2nd day of 2nd month, 1789; and, their son Samuel Carey, b. 6th day of 3rd month, 1791.

Elias Ellicott, b. 4th day of 1st month, 1759; his wife Mary Ellicott, b. 14th day of 8th month, 1768; their dau. Elizabeth Ellicott, b. 17th day of 2nd month, 1787, and m. L. Wethered; and, their dau. Rachel Ellicott, b. 17th day of 2nd month, 1791 (all removed to the western district).

John Mitchel, b. 8th day of 8th month, 1756; his wife Tacy Mitchel, b. 20th day of 3rd month, 1752; their dau. Mary Mitchel, b. 2nd day of 9th month, 1783, and m. John Ellicott (all removed to the western district).

Amos James, b. 13th day of 10th month, 1763; his wife Mary James, b. 5th day of 7th month, 1769; their dau. Ann James, b. 2nd day of 9th month, 1792 (all removed to the western district).

Thomas Poultney, b. 29th day of 9th month, 1762; his wife Ann Poultney, b. 7th day of 8th month, 1771 (removed to western district).

John Evan Rees, b. 3rd day of 8th month, 1758, and d. 3rd day of 10th month, 1799 (interred next day); his wife Ann Rees, b. 24th day of 7th month, 1761 (m. James McCormick and was disowned in 1805); their son Thomas Rees, b. 3rd day of 7th month, 1789; their dau. Maria Rees, b. 21st day of 5th month, 1791 (removed to western district).

John Lee, b. 21st day of 3rd month, 1764; his wife, Sebella Lee, b. 9th day of 10th month, 1772; disowned on 14th day of 3rd month, 1799 (removed to western district).

John Marsh, b. 26th day of 5th month, 1762; his wife, Hannah Marsh, b. 31st day of 10th month, 1759 (removed to western district); their dau. Rebecca Marsh, b. 18th day of 11th month, 1790; their dau. Miriam Marsh, b. 6th day of 5th month, 1792, and d. 29th day of 12th month, 1792 (interred next day).

Aquila Jones, b. 1st day of 10th month, 1758; his wife Elizabeth Jones, b. 2nd day of 12th month, 1773; their daughter Susanna B. Jones, b. 24th day of 12th month, 1791 (removed to Red Stone Monthly Meeting, Pennsylvania, by certificate dated 29th day of 11th month, 1793).

Jonah Thomas, b. 8th day of 1st month, 1761 (disowned 10th day of 11th month, 1796); his wife Rebecca Thomas, b. 3rd day of 4th month, 1767; their son Benjamin Thomas, b. 12th day of 9th[?] month, 1790.

---- [page torn] Hicks, b. 2nd day of 2nd month, 1736; his wife Mary Hicks, b. 25th day of 9th month, 1746; their dau. Ann Hicks, b. 31st day of 12th month, 1763, and m. Joseph McCoy; their dau. Mary Hicks, 31st day of 3rd month, 1766, and disowned 29th day of 11th month, 1793; their dau. Jane Hicks, b. 15th day of 2nd month, 1771, and disowned 24th day of 4th month, 1794; their dau. Bathshe Hicks, b. 15th day of 4th month, 1777; their son Henry Hicks, b. 6th day of 5th month, 1779, and d. 4th day of 11th month, 1797 (interred same day); their dau. Tamer Hicks, b. 19th day of 6th month, 17781; their son James Hicks, b. 22nd day of 4th month, 1786.

Margaret Dukehart, b. 30th day of 10th month, 1743; her son John Dukehart, b. 8th day of 3rd month, 1775; her dau. Catharine Dukehart, b. 28th day of 9th month, 1779, and m. James Brown in 4th month, 1799; her son Valerius Dukehart, b. 11th day of 9th month, 1783.

Jonathan Davenport, b. 24th day of 5th month, 1759, and d. 13th day of 8th month, 1797 (interred same day); his wife Margaret Davenport, b. 29th day of 1st month, 1771; their son Joseph Davenport, b. 7th day of 8th month, 1791.

Rachel Wells, b. 15th day of 4th month, 1741; her dau. Margaret Wells, b. 6th day of 9th month, 1777, and disowned 11th day of 12th month, 1794; he dau. Ann Wells, b. 14th day of 2nd month, 1779, and disowned 10th day of 3rd month, 1796.

Jonathan Coates, b. 17th day of 11th month, 1728; his wife Jane Coates, b. 23rd day of 11th month, 1735, and d. 16th day of 5th month, 1795 (interred next day); their dau. Ann Coates, b. 12th day of 5th month, 1757, and removed by certificate 8th day of 1st month, 1795, to Fairfax Monthly Meeting; their dau. Hannah Coates, b. 5th day of 7th month, 1761; their son Jonathan Coates, b. 28th day of 5th month, 1764, and d. 1st day of 10th month, 1793 (interred on the 3rd following); their dau. Phebe Coates, b. 23rd day of 7th month, 1766; their dau. Grace Coates, b. 16th day of 7th month, 1771, m. ---- [blank] Knox, and removed to western district; their dau. Jane Coates, b. 28th day of 8th month, 1776; their dau. Elizabeth Coates, b. 8th day of 9th month, 1779, and m. Amos West.

Isaiah Jackson, b. 15th day of 3rd month, 1748, and disowned on 9th day of 2nd month, 1797; his wife Margaret Jackson, b. 9th day of 5th month, 1750, and d. 11th day of 3rd month, 1795 (interred next day); their dau. Ann Jackson, b. 9th day of 7th month, 1774, and disowned on 11th day of 12th month, 1794; their dau. Sarah Jackson, b. 21st day of 7th month, 1776, and

m. N. West on 8th day of 7th month, 1800; their son Thomas Lewis Jackson, b. 10th day of 10th month, 1778, and disowned on 11th day of 4th month, 1799; their dau. Mary Jackson, b. 10th day of 12th month, 1782, and recommended to Third Haven Monthly Meeting on 13th day of 6th month, 1799; their dau. Frances Jackson, b. 24th day of 6th month, 1785; their son John Jackson, b. 31st day of 5th month, 1788.

Elizabeth [?] Davenport [no birth date given], d. 20th day of 2nd month, 1794 (interred next day); her dau. Elizabeth Davenport, b. 6th day of 8th month, 1772, and disowned on 4th day of 5th month, 1795.

Mary Boyd, b. in 5th month, 1730.

Mary Helm [no birth date given], removed by certificate on 8th day of 1st month, 1795, to Fairfax Monthly Meeting, Virginia.

David Wilson, b. 4th day of 10th month, 1753; his wife Jane Wilson, b. 1st day of 2nd month, 1756; their dau. Elizabeth Wilson, b. 16th day of 3rd month, 1789, and m. John Cornthwait.

William Hayward, b. 8th day of 1st month, 1760; his wife Mary Hayward, b. 5th day of 11th month, 1767; their son Joseph Hayward, b. 19th day of 2nd month, 1791; their son Samuel Hayward, b. 12th day of 5th month, 1792, and d. 14th day of 8th month, 1793 (interred next day).

Jesse Brown, b. 1st day of 1st month, 1765; his wife Dorothy Brown, b. 19th day of 10th month, 1769.

Rossiter Scott, b. 8th day of 12th month, 1756; his wife Edith Scott, b. 28th day of 11th month, 1763; their son Abraham Scott, b. 21st day of 1st month, 1790, and d. 22nd day of 8th month, 1796; their son Jesse Scott, b. 18th day of 12th month, 1791, and d. and interred 4th day of 7th month, 1793.

Margaret Fisher, b. 4th day of 1st month, 1737; her son Samuel Fisher, b. 31st day of 7th month, 1765, removed to Trent Monthly Meeting, North Carolina, by certificate on 26th day of 7th month, 1793, returned and disowned on 30th day of 5th month, 1794; her dau. Eunice Fisher, b. 1st day of 7th month, 1769, and disowned 13th day of 2nd month, 1800; her son Josiah Fisher, b. 7th day of 7th month, 1772, and disowned 11th day of 9th month, 1794; her dau. Hannah Fisher, b. 9th day of 9th month, 1775, and disowned 25th day of 4th month, 1794.

Grace McDermot, b. 25th day of 11th month, 1759, and disowned 31st day of 3rd month, 1794.

George Hussey, b. 4th day of 3rd month, 1758, and disowned 4th day of 10th month, 1800; his wife Rachel Hussey, b. 19th day of 9th month, 1758, and d. 3rd day of 3rd month, 1799; their son Joseph Hussey, b. 15th day of 6th month, 1781; their son John Hussey, b. 8th day of 9th month, 1782, and d. 27th day of 4th month, 1783; their son George Hussey, b. 13th day of 2nd month, 1784; their dau. Rachel Hussey, b. 19th day of 10th month, 1785, and d. 1st day of 11th month, 1785; their dau. Rachel Hussey, b. 29th day of 10th month, 1786; their son William Hussey, b. 12th day of 9th month, 1788, and subsequently "released from membership having joined the Methodist Society"; their dau. Rebecca Hussey, b. 9th day of 9th month, 1790, and m. Robert Young; their son Ennion Hussey, b. 20th day of 5th month, 1792.

---- [page torn], b. 9th day of 9th month, 1741.

---- [page torn] Miller, b. 21st day of 10th month, 1754, and disowned 28th day of 7th month, 1793; his son Thomas Miller, b. 21st day of 1st month, 1778; his dau. Rachel Miller, b. 9th day of 12th month, 1779; his son Israel Miller, b. 23rd day of 11th month, 1781; his dau. Emelie Miller, b. 2nd day of 10th month, 1786 (and the children were recommended by certificate of removal to Maiden Creek Monthly Meeting, Pennsylvania, on 10th day of 9th month, 1795).

Ann Rice, b. 4th day of 8th month, 1731, and recommended to Crooked Run Monthly Meeting on 12th day of 1st month, 1797; her son George Rice, b. 27th day of 8th month, 1767, and disowned on 14th day of 5th month, 1795.

Sarah Hopkins, b. 26th day of 12th month, 1723, and d. 15th day of 5th month, 1795; her dau. Elizabeth Hopkins, b. 17th day of 8th month, 1751, and m. J. Webster; her son Johns Hopkins, b. 6th day of 6th month, 1764, and disowned on 13th day of 7th month, 1797.

Elizabeth Hopkins, wife of John Hopkins, b. 18th day of 7th month, 1747; her son Thomas Hopkins, b. 19th day of 12th month, 1774, and d. at sea on 16th day of 7th month, 1798.

Mary Stevenson [no birth date given] was recommended to New Hope Monthly Meeting in the Western Territory on 12th day of 11th month, 1795.

Sarah Shepherd, b. 2nd day of 8th month, 1733[?], and d. 24th day of 12th month, 1799; her son Thomas Shepherd, b. 1st day of 8th month, 1767, and disowned on 14th day of 7th month, 1796; her dau. Ann Shepherd, b. 14th day of 11th month, 1772, and disowned on 11th day of 8th month, 1796; her son Moses Shepherd, b. 16th day of 5th month, 1775 (removed to the western district).

Mary Jones, b. 24th day of 8th month, 1764.

Mary Kelso, b. 21st day of 2nd month, 1755.

Thomas Buckingham, b. 13th day of 2nd month, 1746, and disowned on 26th day of 7th month, 1793.

Warrick Price, b. 10th day of 6th month, 1769; his wife Susanna Price, b. 23rd day of 7th month, 1766.

John Naylor, b. 28th day of 2nd month, 1717, and d. 14th day of 9th month, 1796 (interred same day); his dau. Elizabeth Naylor, b. 18th day of 4th month, 1758, and removed by certificate to Gunpowder Monthly Meeting on 11th day of 12th month, 1794.

Elizabeth Dyer, wife of Aaron Dyer, b. in 4th month, 1757; their son Joseph Dyer, b. 16th day of 2nd month, 1780; their dau. Mary Dyer, b. 14th day of 8th month, 1781; their son, Aaron Dyer, b. 12th day of 3rd month, 1786; their son Josiah Dyer, b. 22nd day of 1st month, 1788; their son Benjamin Dyer, b. 14th day of 8th month, ---- [blank]. All were recommeded by certificate of removal to Indian Spring Monthly Meeting on 8th day of 10th month, 1795.

Hannah Hughes, b. 1st day of 1st month, 1747, and removed to the western district.

Jehu Moore, single man [no birth date given] removed to Pipe Creek Monthly Meeting on 24th day of 1st month, 1794.

Richard Walsh, single man [no birth date given] disowned on 8th day of 1st month, 1795.

Simon Perine, b. 16th day of 10th month, 1768, and disowned on 8th day of 1st month, 1795.

---- [page torn] Davis [illegible?], single man noted as deceased [no date given for birth or death].

---- [page torn], single man, "died on a voyage to sea, time not ascertained."

Joseph Pierpoint, single man, b. 4th day of 4th month, 1747, and disowned on 8th day of 10th month, 1795.

Thomas Pierpoint, single man, b. 12th day of 7th month, 1772, and disowned on 11th day of 12th month, 1794.

Malden Perine, single man, b. 9th day of 2nd month, 1771, and disowned on 21st day of 2nd month, 1794.

Robert Cox, single man, d. 21st day of 1st month, 1795.

Walter Pierpoint, single man, b. 6th day of 4th month, 1770, and removed by certificate [place not state] on 12th day of 3rd month, 1795.

William Floyd, single man, died in the State of Kentucky [no date given].

Mary Hill, single woman, b. 20th day of 12th month, 1724, and d. 12th day of 3rd month, 1800.

Mary Burgess, single woman, b. 14th day of 2nd month, 1749, and d. 29th day of 3rd month, 1794 (interred next day).

Mary Tucker, single woman, b. 28th day of 1st month, 1725, and d. 2nd day of 12th month, 1795 (interred next day).

Elenor Humphrey, single woman, b. 14th day of 3rd month, 1746, and d. 9th day of 1st month, 1793 (interred next day).

Susanna Harlan, single woman, b. 31st day of 8th month, 1750.

Tacy Burgess, single woman, b. 21st day of 6th month, 1761.

Martha Burgess, single woman, b. 6th day of 9th month, 1768, married Js.[?] Norbury and removed to western district.

Sarah Scott, single woman, b. 2nd day of 3rd month, 1744.

Ann Perine, single woman, b. 25th day of 10th month, 1762, and removed by certificate on 11th day of 9th month, 1794 [place not stated].

Miriam Hussey, single woman, b. 25th day of 12th month, 1770, and disowned on 25th day of 4th month, 1794.

Margaret Perine, single woman, b. 25th day of 2nd month, 1767 (removed to the western district).

Mary Barry, single woman, b. 20th day of 8th month, 1776.

Frances Martin, single woman, b. 20th day of 5th month, 1772, married Robert Hough [no date given].

Mary Floyd, single woman [no birth date given] was disowned on 13th day of 8th month, 1795.

Henry Worthington, apprentice lad, b. 22nd day of 12th month, 1774, and disowned on 14th day of 2nd month, 1799.

William Allibone, apprentice lad, b. 6th day of 7th month, 1772, and removed by certificate on 14th day of 8th month, 1794 [no place given].

Isaac Johnson, spprentice lad, b. 4th day of 6th month, 1776, and removed by certificate on 12th day of 4th month, 1798 [no place given].

Peter Perine, apprentice lad, b. 26th day of 5th month, 1773.

Israel Price, apprentice lad, b. 30th day of 5th month, 1772.

Samuel Thomas, apprentice lad, b. 13th day of 11th month, 1776, and disowned on 9th day of 2nd month, 1797.

William Husband, apprentice lad, b. 23rd day of 5th month, 1774, and removed by certificate on 10th day of 3rd month, 1796 [no place given].

Thomas Fisher, apprentice lad, b. 21st day of 10th month, 1776.

John Cox, apprentice lad, b. 18th day of 8th month, 1775.

Thomas Cox, apprentice lad, b. in 4th month, 1778, and removed by certificate to Bush River Monthly Meeting in South Carolina on 26th day of 7th month, 1793.

Children of John Jackson: Rachel Jackson, b. 15th day of 9th month, 1769, and disowned on 27th day of 9th month, 1793; Susanna Jackson, b. 27th day of 7th month, 1775, and removed by certificate to Southern District of Philadelphia on 13th day of 8th month, 1795; Joseph Jackson, b. 25th day of 3rd month, 1779, and disowned on 13th day of 7th month, 1797.

Children of Thomas Beal: Joseph Beal, d. 27th day of 9th month, 1794; Ann Beal and Thomas Beal, removed by certificate to Fairfax Monthly Meeting on 11th day of 12th month, 1794; Grace Beal, d. 1st day of 10th month, 1794; Samuel Beal, d. 27th day of 9th month, 1794.

Lewis Hopkins, son of P. Hopkins, recommended by certificate to Crooked Run Monthly Meeting in Virginia on 26th day of 7th month, 1793.

William Mathews Townsend, son of Joseph and Mary Townsend, b. 27th day of 12th month, 1792.

Isaiah Balderston, b. 24th day of 2nd month, 1753; his wife Martha Balderston, b. 19th day of 12th month, 1739; their son Ely Balderston, b. 9th day of 5th month, 1776; their dau. Pathenia Balderston, b. 8th day of 3rd month, 1778, and m. John Dukehart; their son Hugh Balderston, b. 22nd day of 12th month, 1782 (removed to the western district); their son Jonathan Balderston, b. 10th day of 6th month, 1785 (removed to the western district).

All were received by certificate from Deer Creek Monthly Meeting on 28th day of 12th month, 1792.

Sarah Mendenhall (widow), received by certificate from Philadelphia Monthly Meeting on 25th day of 1st month, 1793, and removed to Indian Spring Monthly Meeting by certificate dated 24th day of 1st month, 1794.

Mary Love (widow), received by certificate from Monallin Monthly Meeting on 25th day of 1st month, 1793, and m. John McKim on 24th day of 9th month, 1795.

Thomas Mendenhall and wife Hannah, and their children Eleanor Mendenhall, Thomas Mendenhall, John Wilson Mendenhall, and Sarah Mendenhall, were received by certificate from Philadelphia Monthly Meeting on 25th day of 1st month, 1793, and removed to Indian Spring Monthly Meeting by certificate dated 24th day of 1st month, 1794.

Children of Isaac Trimble: Joseph Trimble, John Trimble, Mary Trimble, Jane Trimble, James Trimble, and Isaac Trimble, were received by certificate from Deer Creek Monthly Meeting on 25th day of 1st month, 1793. [Joseph, Jane, James and Isaac removed to the western district (no date given) and Mary was disowned on 9th day of 2nd month, 1797, noted as having married George Peters; no date given].

Caleb Floyd (a young man) was received by certificate from Fairfax Monthly Meeting on 22nd day of 2nd month, 1793, and was disowned on 26th day of 7th month, 1793.

Sarah Day (wife of John Day) and Catherine Shaw were received by certificate from Deer Creek Monthly Meeting on 22nd day of 2nd month, 1793.

Samuel Morthland (a minor) was received from Warrington Monthly Meeting on 22nd day of 2nd month, 1793, and removed to Warrington on 29th day of 11th month, 1793.

Joseph Scott (a young man) was received from Indian Spring Monthly Meeting on 29th day of 3rd month, 1793, and was disowned on 13th day of 8th month, 1795.

Ann Morgan (widow) was received from Nottingham Monthly Meeting on 29th day of 3rd month, 1793. Deceased [no date given].

Hannah Naylor (a young woman) was received from Nottingham Monthly Meeting on 29th day of 3rd month, 1793, and was disowned on 14th day of 9th month, 1797.

Elizabeth Hugo (wife of Thomas B. Hugo) was received from Deer Creek Monthly Meeting on 29th day of 3rd month, 1793, and recommended to Gunpowder Monthly Meeting on 13th day of 3rd month, 1800.

James Carey, son of James and Martha Carey, b. 10th day of 3rd month, 1793.

Sarah Tyson, dau. of Elisha and Mary Tyson, b. 11th day of 3rd month, 1793. Deceased [no date given].

Evan Thomas Ellicott, son of Elias and Mary Ellicott, b. 6th day of 12th month, 1792. Removed to the western district [no date given].

Elizabeth Poultney, dau. of Thomas and Ann Poultney, b. 2nd day of 12th month, 1792. Removed to the western district [no date given].

Ann Rees, dau. of John and Ann Rees, b. 1st day of 4th month, 1793, and d. 20th day of 7th month, 1793 (interred same day).

John Smith Riley, son of William and Sarah Riley, b. 7th day of 2nd month, 1793. Removed to the western district [no date given].

Mary Lee, dau. of John and Sebella Lee, b. 1st day of 3rd month, 1793, and d. 8th day of 3rd month, 1793.

Rebecca Thomas, dau. of Jonah [Josiah?] and Rebecca Thomas, b. 13th day of 1st month, 1793. Deceased [no date given].

Henry Wilson, son of Henry, Jr. and Margaret Wilson, his case recommended by Gunpowder Monthly Meeting, disowned on 26th day of 4th month, 1793.

Joseph Scott's family: his wife Ann Scott, b. 22nd day of 1st month, 1741 [removed to the western district; no date given]; their dau. Rachel Scott, b. 7th day of 1st month, 1773, and d. 17th day of 5th month, 1793 (interred next day); their son Isaac Scott, b. 4th day of 2nd month, 1775 [removed to the western district; no date given]; their son Jacob Scott, b. 19th day of 6th month, 1778, and d. 20th day of 5th month, 1793 (interred next day); their dau. Sarah Scott, b. 27th day of 7th month, 1781, and d. 13th day of 5th month, 1793 (interred next day); their dau. Ann Scott, b. 27th day of 3rd month, 1784 [removed to the western district; no date given].

Esther Pancoast was received by request on 27th day of 9th month, 1793, married R. Sinclair - disowned [no date given].

---- [page torn] Matthews (widow of Thomas Matthews) and children Elizabeth Matthews, Thomas Matthews, Hannah Matthews (married a Brown), and Joshua Matthews, were received by certificate from Gunpowder Monthly Meeting on 30th day of 8th month, 1793.

Isaac Trimble was received by certificate from Deer Creek Monthly Meeting on 29th day of 11th month, 1793, and removed to the western district [no date given].

Hannah Marsh, dau. of John and Hannah Marsh, b. 11th day of 12th month, 1793. [Removed to the western district; no date given]).

Mary Hayward, dau. of William and Mary Hayward, b. 30th day of 12th month, 1793.

Ruth Brown, dau. of Jesse and Dorothy Brown, b. 7th day of 2nd month, 1794, and d. 8th day of 3rd month, 1797 (interred next day).

Stacy West (a minor) was received from Deer Creek Monthly Meeting on 21st day of 2nd month, 1794.

Isaac Hussey, son of George and Rachel Hussey, b. 22nd day of 3rd month, 1794.

William Morgan and Jesse Morgan were received from Deer Creek Monthly Meeting on 28th day of 3rd month, 1794. Jesse Morgan was disowned on 14th day of 7th month, 1796.

William Walton and wife Sarah Walton, and their son Lukens Walton, were received by certificate from Deer Creek Monthly Meeting on 28th day of 3rd month, 1794, and recommended to Gunpowder Monthly Meeting [no date given].

Rebecca Midhiff (wife of Abraham Midhiff) and their children, Abraham Midhiff, David Midhiff, William Midhiff, Joshua Midhiff, Ann Buffington Midhiff, and Jesse Midhiff, were received by certificate from Nottingham Monthly Meeting on 28th day of 3rd month, 1794. David Midhiff is noted as being deceased [no date given] and Ann Buffington Midhiff married a Poteet [no date given].

Elizabeth Allibone (a young woman) was received by certificate from Indian Spring Monthly Meeting and endorsed by Gunpowder Monthly Meeting on

25th day of 4th month, 1794, and recommended by certificate on 13th day of 8th month, 1795, to Northern District of Philadelphia.

Esther Rees, dau. of John and Ann Rees, b. 25th day of 5th month, 1794. [Removed to the western district; no date].

Amos Evans (a young man) was received by certificate from Deer Creek Monthly Meeting on 30th day of 5th month, 1794, and removed by certificate to Deer Creek Monthly Meeting on 12th day of 3rd month, 1795.

Jesse Thomas Lee, son of John and Sebella Lee, b. 18th day of 5th month, 1794, and d. 3rd day of 6th month, 1794.

John Worthington (a minor) was received by certificate from Deer Creek Monthly Meeting on 30th day of 5th month, 1794.

William Waterhouse (single man) was received by certificate from Indian Spring Monthly Meeting on 30th day of 5th month, 1794. [Removed to the western district; no date given].

Samuel Price, son of Warrick and Susanna Price, b. 6th day of 8th month, 1793, and d. 22nd day of 8th month, 1793.

Martha Hill (young woman) was received by certificate from Deer Creek Monthly Meeting on 12th day of 6th month, 1794, and removed by certificate on 11th day of 12th month, 1800 [no place given].

William Carpenter and wife Rachel and their children, Lydia Carpenter, George Carpenter, Hannah Carpenter, and John Carpenter, were received by certificate from Bradford Monthly Meeting in Pennsylvania on 11th day of 9th month, 1794, and were "recommended to said meeting on 8th day of 9th month, 1796, with their 3rd son named Joseph."

Mary Stapleton (young woman) was received by certificate from Philadelphia Monthly Meeting on 11th day of 9th month, 1794, and disowned on 8th day of 12th month, 1796.

Miriam James, "daughter of Amos James (a minor), was received by request of her father on 11th day of 9th month, 1794, and born on 13th day of 5th month, 1787." [Removed to the western district; no date given].

Hephzibah Brown (now the wife of Malden Perine) was received by her certificate from Woodbury Monthly Meeting (at their request) on 9th day of 10th month, 1794, and was disowned on 8th day of 1st month, 1795.

Granville Sharp Townsend, son of Joseph and Mary Townsend, b. 30th day of 10th month, 1794.

Jacob Pugh (young man) was received by certificate from Nottingham Monthly Meeting on 13th day of 11th month, 1794.

Ann Trimble ("a young woman omitted from the original list") was recommended by certificate to Hopewell Monthly Meeting on 4th day of 9th month, 1795.

Elizabeth Davenport, dau. of Jonathan and Elizabeth Davenport, b. 8th day of 1st month, 1794.

David Wilson, son of David and Jane Wilson, b. 26th day of 6th month, 1794, and d. 15th day of 4th month, 1795.

William James, son of Amos and Mary James, b. 25th day of 7th month, 1794. [Removed to the western district; no date].

Jane Price, dau. of Warrick and Susanna Price, b. 29th day of 10th month, 1794, and d. 19th day of 3rd month, 1795.

Jesse Tyson and wife Margaret and their children, Elizabeth Tyson, Isaac Tyson and Thomas Tyson, were received by certificate from Gunpowder Monthly Meeting on 8th day of 1st month, 1795. [Removed to the western district; no date].

Philip Ford, son of Joseph and Frances Ford, b. 9th day of 1st month, 1795, and d. 5th day of 9th month, 1795.

Tacy Ellicott, dau. of Elias and Mary Ellicott, b. 14th day of 1st month, 1795. [Removed to western district; no date].

Benjamin Ellicott (a young man) was received by certificate from Indian Spring Monthly Meeting on 12th day of 2nd month, 1795. [Removed to the western district; no date given].

Isaac Brookes (a young man) was received by certificate from Indian Spring Monthly Meeting on 12th day of 2nd month, 1795.

William Delworth was received by certificate from Indian Spring Monthly Meeting on 12th day of 3rd month, 1795. Deceased [no date given].

James Love (a minor) was received from Monallin Monthly Meeting on 12th day of 3rd month, 1795.

John Lee Webster, Jr. was received from Deer Creek Monthly Meeting on 12th day of 3rd month, 1795, and died in 1797.

Evan Thomas Poultney, son of Thomas and Ann Poultney, b. 22nd day of 3rd month, 1795. [Removed to the western district; no date given].

Hannah Matthews (young woman) was received from Gunpowder Monthly Meeting on 9th day of 4th month, 1795, and married William Morgan [no date given].

Thomas Morgan was received by request on 9th day of 4th month, 1795.

Benjamin Amoss (minor) was received from Gunpowder Monthly Meeting on 14th day of 5th month, 1795, and died on 3rd day of 8th month, 1800.

Joseph Jay was received from Deer Creek Monthly Meeting on 14th day of 5th month, 1795, and disowned on 9th day of 2nd month, 1797.

Mary Underwood (wife of Enoch Underwood) was received by request on 11th day of 6th month, 1795, and recommended by certificate to Warrington Monthly Meeting on 13th day of 8th month, 1795.

Hannah Carey, dau. of James and Martha Carey, b. 7th day of 8th month, 1795.

Elizabeth Lee, dau. of John and Sebella Lee, b. 28th day of 6th month, 1795. [Removed to western district; no date].

James Amoss and wife Hannah and their children, Mary Amoss and David Amoss, were received from Gunpowder Monthly Meeting on 13th day of 8th month, 1795, and recommended to Gunpowder Monthly Meeting on 8th day of 12th month, 1796.

Samuel Wilson (young man) was received from Gunpowder Monthly Meeting on 13th day of 8th month, 1795.

Esther Tyson (widow) was received from Gunpowder Monthly Meeting on 13th day of 8th month, 1795, and died on 8th day of 9th month, 1796.

Richard Price (minor) was received from Gunpowder Monthly Meeting on 13th day of 8th month, 1795.

Joseph Ford and wife Frances and son Philip Ford were received from Deer Creek Monthly Meeting on 13th day of 8th month, 1795. Philip Ford died on 5th day of 9th month, 1795. [Removed to western district; no date given].

Hannah Toach (wife of Henry Toach) and her daughters Rachel Toach [who later married Samuel Coots], Mary Toach [who later married an Underwood], and Barbary Toach [who later married an Underwood], were received from Indian Spring Monthly Meeting on 13th day of 8th month, 1795.

Lydia Williams was received from Indian Spring Monthly Meeting on 10th day of 9th month, 1795.

Isaac Williams was received from Gunpowder Monthly Meeting on 12th day of 11th month, 1795, and died on 2nd day of 7th month, 1798.

George Mason and wife Susanna and their children, William Mason, George Mason, Rachel Mason and Susanna Mason, were received from New Garden Monthly Meeting on 10th day of 12th month, 1795. William died on 22nd day of 6th month, 1795, and Susanna (daughter) died on 26th day of 6th month, 1795. George removed to western district [no date].

Larkin Read (young man) was received from Indian Spring Monthly Meeting on 10th day of 12th month, 1795.

Barker Thacker was received from Dublin Monthly Meeting on 10th day of 12th month, 1795, and removed to the western district [no date given].

Jonathan Price, son of Warrick and Susanna Price, b. 19th day of 12th month, 1795, and d. 13th day of 7th month, 1796.

---- [page torn] Field (young man) was received from Philadelphia Monthly Meeting on 14th day of 1st month, 1796, and removed by certificate [place not given] on 8th day of 3rd month, 1798.

Philip Thomas (minor) was received from Indian Spring Monthly Meeting on 14th day of 1st month, 1796, and removed to the western district [no date given].

Amos Smith (minor) was received from Goose Creek Monthly Meeting on 14th day of 1st month, 1796.

Guli Hugo and Samuel Hugo, children of Eliz. Hugo, were received by their mother's request on 14th day of 1st month, 1796. Guli Hugo was disowned on 12th day of 9th month, 1799, and Samuel Hugo was recommended to Gunpowder Monthly Meeting on 13th day of 3rd month, 1800.

Elisha Tyson, son of Elisha and Mary Tyson, b. 28th day of 1st month, 1796. [Removed to western district; no date].

Robert Webster (young man) was received from Deer Creek Monthly Meeting on 11th day of 2nd month, 1796, and died at Amsterdam on 19th day of 11th month, 1795 [sic].

Sarah Morthland (young woman) was received from Warrington Monthly Meeting on 11th day of 2nd month, 1796.

Mary Matthews (young woman) was received from Gunpowder Monthly Meeting on 11th day of 2nd month, 1796, and recommended to Gunpowder Monthly Meeting on 8th day of 2nd month, 1798.

Samuel Wilson, son of David and Jane Wilson, b. 22nd day of 2nd month, 1796.

Joseph Hibbard (minor) was received from Pipe Creek Monthly Meeting on 10th day of 3rd month, 1796.

Esther Tyson, dau. of Jesse and Margaret Tyson, b. 22nd day of 3rd month, 1796, and d. 19th day of 8th month, 1797.

James Ellicott (young man) was received from Indian Spring Monthly Meeting on 2nd day of 5th month, 1796, and removed to the western district [no date given].

Sarah Morgan (wife of Thomas Morgan) was received from Gunpowder Monthly Meeting on 2nd day of 5th month, 1796.

Elizabeth Naylor was received from Gunpowder Monthly Meeting on 2nd day of 5th month, 1796, and recommended to Nottingham Monthly Meeting on 10th day of 5th month, 1798.

Ann Butler (widow) and son John Butler, b. 17th day of 3rd month, 1793, and son Joseph Butler, b. 8th day of 1st month, 1793 [sic], were received from Falls Monthly Meeting on 12th day of 5th month, 1796. [Ann Butler is noted as having married William Waterhouse and removed to the western district, but no date is given].

James Wilson (young man) was received from Brighouse Monthly Meeting in Great Britain on 9th day of 6th month, 1796, and was recommended to White Oak Swamp Monthly Meeting on 8th day of 12th month, 1796.

Joseph Scott was received from Fairfax Monthly Meeting on 14th day of 7th month, 1796, and died on 27th day of 7th month, 1799.

Joseph Thornburgh was received from Warrington Monthly Meeting on 14th day of 7th month, 1796.

Robert Hough (young man) was received from Indian Spring Monthly Meeting on 14th day of 7th month, 1796, and removed to the western district [no date given].

Robert Bartlett (minor) was received from Third Haven Monthly Meeting on 14th day of 7th month, 1796, and recommended to Third Haven Monthly Meeting on 10th day of 7th month, 1800.

Izak Procter (young man) was received from New York Monthly Meeting on 11th day of 8th month, 1796, and removed to the western district [no date given].

Henry Kendall (young man) was received from Hardshaw Monthly Meeting on 11th day of 8th month, 1796, and removed by certificate [place not given] on 14th day of 2nd month, 1799.

Martha McCoy (young woman) was received from Deer Creek Monthly Meeting on 11th day of 8th month, 1796, and recommended to Westminster Monthly Meeting in London on 14th day of 2nd month, 1799.

Gerrard T. Hopkins and wife Dorothy Hopkins were received from Indian Spring Monthly Meeting on 8th day of 9th month, 1796, and removed to western district [no date given].

Andrew McCoy and Joseph McCoy (brothers) were received from Deer Creek Monthly Meeting on 8th day of 9th month, 1796, and removed to the western district [no date given].

William Amoss (minor) was received from Gunpowder Monthly Meeting on 8th day of 9th month, 1796.

Phebe Allibone produced a certificate on 13th day of 10th month, 1796 [place not given], and died on 3rd day of 6th month, 1796 [sic].

Levis Janney and wife Mary and their children, Mary Janney, Israel Janney, George Fox Janney, Benjamin Say Janney, and Elizabeth Janney, were received from Abbington Monthly Meeting on 13th day of 10th month, 1796.

John Wallace Hopkins (young man) was received from York Monthly Meeting on 13th day of 10th month, 1796.

Deborah Wilson (wife of John Wilson) and their children, Catharine Wilson, Grace Wilson, William Wilson, John Wilson, Anna Wilson, and Thomas Wilson, were received from Gunpowder Monthly Meeting on 13th day of 10th month, 1796. Grace Wilson and William Wilson died on 21st day of 8th month, 1800, and John Wilson (son) died on 3rd day of 9th month, 1800. Anna Wilson married William Proctor (no date given). [Note: There may be one and possibly two other children, but the page is torn off at the bottom].

Edward Ford, son of Joseph and Frances Ford, b. 17th day of 10th month, 1796, and d. 12th day of 8th month, 1797.

Hannah Hussey, dau. of George and Rachel Hussey, b. 25th day of 10th month, 1796.

Margaret Sanderson (wife of Thomas Sanderson) was received from Gunpowder Monthly Meeting on 10th day of 11th month, 1796.

Benjamin Ellicott, son of Elias and Mary Ellicott, b. 13th day of 11th month, 1796. [Removed to the western district; no date given].

Sarah Brown, dau. of David and Elizabeth Brown, b. 19th day of 11th month, 1796.

Samuel Riley, son of William and Sarah Riley, b. 20th day of 11th month, 1796.

Joshua Hayward, son of William and Mary Hayward, b. 21st day of 11th month, 1796, and d. 16th day of 7th month, 1797.

John Morgan, Jr. was received by request on 10th day of 11th month, 1796.

Rebecca Moore and her daughter Keturah Moore were received from Gunpowder Monthly Meeting on 8th day of 12th month, 1796, and recommended to Gunpowder Monthly Meeting on 8th day of 11th month, 1798. [Keturah Moore is noted as being deceased, but no date is given].

Samuel G. Jones (young man) was received from Philadelphia Monthly Meeting on 12th day of 1st month, 1797, and disowned on 13th day of 3rd month, 1800.

Ezekiel Harlan was received from Nottingham Monthly Meeting on 12th day of 1st month, 1797, and recommended to Nottingham Monthly Meeting on 11th day of 5th month, 1797.

Daniel Byrnes was received from Wilmington Monthly Meeting on 12th day of 1st month, 1797.

Samuel Byrnes and wife Hannah and their daughter Ruth Byrnes (with Sarah Townsend, their apprentice) were received from Wilmington Monthly Meeting on 12th day of 1st month, 1797.

Caleb Byrnes, son of Samuel and Hannah Byrnes, b. 22nd day of 1st month, 1797.

Mary Matthews Townsend and Joseph England Townsend, daughter and son of Joseph and Mary, b. 4th day of 1st month, 1797. Joseph England

Townsend d. 1st day of 2nd month, 1797, and Mary Matthews Townsend d. 18th day of 11th month, 1797.

Mary James, dau. of Amos and Mary James, b. 29th day of 3rd month, 1797. Removed to western district [no date given].

Andrew Ellicott and wife Esther and son John Ellicott were received from Buckingham Monthly Meeting on 11th day of 5th month, 1797, and removed to western district [no date given].

William Procter (minor) was received from York Monthly Meeting in Great Britain on 11th day of 5th month, 1797.

Charles Worthington (minor) was received from Deer Creek Monthly Meeting on 11th day of 5th month, 1797, and was later disowned [no date given].

Philip Coale (minor) was received from Deer Creek Monthly Meeting on 11th day of 5th month, 1797.

Elizabeth Husband (young woman) was received from Motherkiln Monthly Meeting on 11th day of 5th month, 1797.

Rachel Weeks (young woman) was received from Gunpowder Monthly Meeting on 11th day of 5th month, 1797.

Children of Mary Jones: William Jones, b. 9th day of 4th month, 1786; Anne Jones, b. 9th day of 4th month, 1788, and married V. Dukehart [no date given]; Robinson Jones, b. 4th day of 3rd month, 1790; and, Deborah Jones, b. 6th day of 6th month, 1793. All were received by request on 11th day of 5th month, 1797.

Mahlon Ely was received from Deer Creek Monthly Meeting on 13th day of 7th month, 1797, and removed to the western district [no date given].

William Marsh was received from Warrington Monthly Meeting and Ann Marsh from Gunpowder Monthly Meeting on 13th day of 7th month, 1797. [Removed to western district; no date given].

Stephen Wilson and wife Mercy and their children, Benjamin Wilson, Oliver Wilson, Isaac Wilson, Betty Wilson, and Joseph Wilson, were received from Wilmington Monthly Meeting on 10th day of 8th month, 1797.

Margaret Marsh (young woman) was received from Warrington Monthly Meeting on 10th day of 8th month, 1797, and married James Naylor [no date given].

Amos West (minor) was received from Gunpowder Monthly Meeting on 10th day of 8th month, 1797.

Sarah Scott, dau. of Rossiter and Edith Scott, b. 20th day of 8th month, 1797.

Mary Hopkins, dau. of Gerrard T. and Dorothy Hopkins, b. 12th day of 8th month, 1797. [Removed to the western district; no date given].

Andrew Ellicott, Jr. was received from Indian Spring Monthly Meeting on 14th day of 9th month, 1797, and removed to the western district [no date given].

James W. Sloan (young man) was received from Northern District Philadelphia Monthly Meeting on 14th day of 9th month, 1797.

Jasper Cope (young man) and Israel Cope (young man) were received from Northern District Philadelphia Monthly Meeting on 14th day of 9th month, 1797.

Isaiah Lancaster (minor) was received from Gunpowder Monthly Meeting on 14th day of 9th month, 1797.

Mary Mifflin (widow) and her children, Lydia Husband, Samuel Husband, and Susanna Husband, were received from Motherkiln Monthly Meeting on 14th day of 9th month, 1797. Susanna Husband married a Plummer [no date given].

Martha Dukehart, dau. of John and Parthenia Dukehart, b. 2nd day of 9th month, 1797.

Elenor Lee, dau. of John and Sebella Lee, b. 28th day of 9th month, 1797, and d. 11th day of 2nd month, 1800.

Frances Hopkins (widow) and her children, Elizabeth Hopkins and Joel Hopkins, were received from Deer Creek Monthly Meeting on 12th day of 10th month, 1797.

Joseph Aborn [Abom?], a young man, was received from Salem Monthly Meeting in Massachusetts on 9th day of 11th month, 1797, and was disowned on 12th day of 6th month, 1800.

William Copeland (minor) was received from Western Branch Monthly Meeting on 9th day of 11th month, 1797, and "recommended back to W.B." on 13th day of 2nd month, 1800.

Elizabeth Marsh (young woman) was received from Warrington Monthly Meeting on 9th day of 11th month, 1797.

John Shoemaker Tyson, son of Jesse and Margaret Tyson, b. 7th day of 11th month, 1797. [Removed to the western district; no date given].

Margaret Carey, dau. of James and Martha Carey, b. 22nd day of 11th month, 1797.

John Cornthwait (young man) was received from Gunpowder Monthly Meeting on 11th day of 1st month, 1798.

Joseph Husband (young man) was received from Deer Creek Monthly Meeting on 11th day of 1st month, 1798.

Joseph Wilson (minor) was received from Deer Creek Monthly Meeting on 11th day of 1st month, 1798, and recommended to Westland Monthly Meeting on 14th day of 11th month, 1799.

Elizabeth Balderston, dau. of Ely and Esther Balderston, b. 8th day of 2nd month, 1798.

Hannah West (young woman) received from London Grove Monthly Meeting on 8th day of 2nd month, 1798.

Ann Price, dau. of Israel and Hannah Price, b. 4th day of 3rd month, 1798, and d. 22nd day of 8th month, 1799.

Deborah Tyson, dau. of Elisha and Mary Tyson, b. 12th day of 3rd month, 1798.

William Matthews and wife Elizabeth and his children, Ann Matthews, Elizabeth Matthews, Rebecca Matthews, Miriam Matthews, and Sarah Matthews, and their son and daughter Samuel Hanway Matthews and Lydia Matthews, were received from Indian Spring Monthly Meeting on 8th day of 3rd month, 1798.

Elizabeth Johns (wife of Nathan Johns) and their children, Nathan Johns, Ann Johns, and Mary Johns, were received from Deer Creek Monthly Meeting on 12th day of 4th month, 1798, and recommended to Westland Monthly Meeting on 14th day of 11th month, 1799, and 9th day of 10th month, 1800.

Charles Wilson, son of Stephen and Mercy Wilson, b. 26th day of 4th month, 1798, and d. 5th day of 7th month, 1798.

Emelie Matthews, dau. of William and Elizabeth Matthews, b. 1st day of 5th month, 1798, and d. 17th day of 8th month, 1798.

Robert Addy (young man) was received from New York Monthly Meeting on 14th day of 6th month, 1798, and died on 20th day of 8th month, 1800.

John Wilson was received from Gunpowder Monthly Meeting on 14th day of 6th month, 1798.

Samuel Matthews and wife Ann and their children, Elizabeth Matthews, Sophia Matthews, Mary Matthews, and Samuel Matthews, were received from Gunpowder Monthly Meeting on 14th day of 6th month, 1798. [Elizabeth Matthews is noted as marrying Jos. White; no date given].

Anne Price (young woman) was received from Gunpowder Monthly Meeting on 14th day of 6th month, 1798. Deceased [no date given].

Thomas McAteer, Jr. (minor) was received from Wilmington Monthly Meeting on 14th day of 6th month, 1798, and was disowned on 14th day of 8th month, 1800.

Susanna Martin (wife of Athenatius Martin) was received from Third Haven Monthly Meeting on 14th day of 6th month, 1798.

Charles Lukens and wife Sarah were received from Deer Creek Monthly Meeting on 14th day of 6th month, 1800.

Thomas Hayward, son of William and Mary Hayward, b. 29th day of 6th month, 1798.

James Wainright (young man) was received from Third Haven Monthly Meeting on 12th day of 7th month, 1798, and removed to the western district [no date given].

Harriott Ford, dau. of Joseph and Frances Ford, b. 4th day of 8th month, 1798. [Removed to western district; no date].

Malden Perine, son of Peter and Mary Perine, b. 7th day of 8th month, 1798, and d. 18th day fof 8th month, 1799.

John Jewett (young man) was received from Deer Creek Monthly Meeting on 9th day of 8th month, 1798.

Moses Janney (young man) was received from Fairfax Monthly Meeting on 9th day of 8th month, 1798.

Ruth Dickenson (widow) was received from Gunpowder Monthly Meeting on 9th day of 8th month, 1798.

Mary Hussey (young woman) was received from Gunpowder Monthly Meeting on 9th day of 8th month, 1798, and married Elisha Hunt [no date given].

Hannah Dutton (wife of Benjamin Dutton) was received from Philadelphia Monthly Meeting on 9th day of 8th month, 1798.

Abel Spencer and wife Rebecca and their children, Elizabeth Spencer, William Spencer, Sarah Spencer, Rebecca Spencer, Abel Spencer, Reuben Spencer, and Joseph Spencer, were received from Gunpowder Monthly Meeting on 9th day of 8th month, 1798. [Noted that Elizabeth Spencer married a Potter(?), and Sarah, Rebecca, Abel, Reuben and Abel (the father) removed to the western district; no date given].

Ann Ellicott, dau. of Elias and Mary Ellicott, b. 24th day of 8th month, 1798, and d. 15th day of 1st month, 1799.

William Husband (young man) was received from Motherkiln Monthly Meeting on 13th day of 9th month, 1798.

James Hill (young man) was received from Nottingham Monthly Meeting on 13th day of 9th month, 1798, and was disowned on 10th day of 7th month, 1800.

Aaron Packer (young man) was received from Warrington Monthly Meeting on 13th day of 9th month, 1798, and was disowned on 14th day of 8th month, 1800.

Jonathan Marsh (young man) was received from Warrington Monthly Meeting on 13th day of 9th month, 1798, and removed to the western district [no date given].

Nixon Wilson (young man) was received from Deer Creek Monthly Meeting on 13th day of 9th month, 1798.

Catharine Hooker (young man) was received from Gunpowder Monthly Meeting on 13th day of 9th month, 1798, and married George England [no date given]. Recommended to Gunpowder Monthly Meeting on 10th day of 7th month, 1800.

Winston Smith Dallam (young man) was received from Deer Creek Monthly Meeting on 11th day of 10th month, 1798, and was disowned on 13th day of 3rd month, 1800.

Samuel Harlan (young man) was received from Concord Monthly Meeting on 11th day of 10th month, 1798, and removed to the western district [no date given].

Oliver Fuller (young man) was receibed from Salem Monthly Meeting in Massachusetts on 8th vay of 11th month, 1798.

Jesse West (young man) was received from Chester Monthly Meeting on 8th day of 11th month, 1798. Deceased [no date given].

Elizabeth Naylor (young woman) was received from Nottingham Monthly Meeting on 8th day of 11th month, 1798.

Edward Hopkins, son of Gerrard T. and Dorothy Hopkins, b. 9th day of 12th month, 1798, and d. 9th day of 3rd month, 1800.

Ruth Byrnes (widow) was received from Wilmington Monthly Meeting on 13th day of 12th month, 1798, and removed to the western district [no date given].

Thomas Webster (young man) was received from Indian Spring Monthly Meeting on 13th day of 12th month, 1798.

Ennion Williams and wife Hannah were received from Indian Spring Monthly Meeting on 10th day of 1st month, 1799, and removed to the western district [no date given].

Isaac Vore and wife Rebecca and their children Sarah Vore, Rachel Vore (later married a Mills), Benjamin Vore, Jacob Vore and Isaac Vore, were received from Indian Spring Monthly Meeting on 10th day of 1st month, 1799. [Rebecca, Sarah. Benjamin, Jacob and Isaac removed to the western district; no date given].

Nathan Johns was received from Deer Creek Monthly Meeting on 10th day of 1st month, 1799, and was recommended to Westland Monthly Meeting on 14th day of 11th month, 1799.

Skipwith Coale (minor) was received from Deer Creek Monthly Meeting on 10th day of 1st month, 1799.

Lydia Green was received from Fairfax Monthly Meeting on 10th day of 1st month, 1799.

Catharine Daughdy, widow, was received by request on 10th day of 1st month, 1799.

Cassandria Thornburgh, wife of Jos. Thornburgh, was received from Indian Spring Monthly Meeting on 14th day of 2nd month, 1799.

Sarah Hopkins (young woman), Richard Carter (young man), and Elizabeth Tyson (wife of Isaac Tyson) were received from Indian Spring Monthly Meeting on 14th day of 2nd month, 1799. [Elizabeth removed to western district; no date given].

Samuel Reed and wife Elizabeth and their daughter Matilda Reed were received from Gunpowder Monthly Meeting on 14th day of 2nd month, 1799.

Isaac Evans (minor) was received from Greenwich Monthly Meeting on 14th day of 2nd month, 1799, and removed to the western district [no date given].

James Pemberton Townsend, son of Joseph and Mary Townsend, b. 16th day of 12th month, 1798, and d. 9th day of 3rd month, 1799.

John Brown, son of Jesse and Dorothy Brown, b. 5th day of 4th month, 1796, and George Brown, son of Jesse and Dorothy Brown, b. 26th day of 2nd month, 1799.

Mary Trimble, dau. of John and Elizabeth Trimble, b. 13th day of 3rd month, 1799. [Removed to western district; no date].

Eliza Marsh, dau. of John and Hannah Marsh, b. 8th day of 3rd month, 1799. [Removed to western district; no date].

Dorothy Webster was received from Gunpowder Monthly Meeting on 14th day of 3rd month, 1799.

Enoch Underwood and wife Mary and their children, James Underwood, Benjamin Underwood, and Ann Underwood, were received from Warrington Monthly Meeting on 11th day of 4th month, 1799. Ann died on 17th day of 8th month, 1800.

Vincent Bonsall and wife Sarah and their children, William Bonsall and Catharine Bonsall, were received from Wilmington Monthly Meeting on 9th day of 5th month, 1799.

James Carey Hough, son of Robert and Frances Hough, b. 3rd day of 6th month, 1799. [Removed to western district; no date].

Daniel Hanson (young man) received from Salem Monthly Meeting in Massachusetts on 13th day of 6th month, 1799, and recommended to Black Water Monthly Meeting on 12th day of 6th month, 1800.

John Ransome and wife Elizabeth and their daughter Elizabeth, were received from Amawalk Monthly Meeting on 13th day of 6th month, 1799.

Oliver Matthews and wife Phebe were received from Gunpowder Monthly Meeting on 13th day of 6th month, 1799, and were recommended to Gunpowder Monthly Meeting on 12th day of 6th month, 1800.

Samuel Naylor and wife Rebecca were received from Gunpowder Monthly Meeting on 13th day of 6th month, 1799.

Mary Perine (wife of Peter Perine) was received from Gunpowder Monthly Meeting on 11th day of 7th month, 1799.

James Neal (young man) and Thomas Sherwood (young man) were received from Third Haven Monthly Meeting on 11th day of 7th month, 1799.

George Harris and wife Susanna and their children, Mary Harris, Beulah Harris, Ann Harris, and George Harris, were received from Warrington Monthly Meeting on 11th day of 7th month, 1799, and removed to the western district [no date given].

Samuel Jackson (minor) was received from New Garden Monthly Meeting on 11th day of 7th month, 1799, and "deceast at sea, time unknown."

Philip Thomas Tyson, son of Isaac and Elizabeth Tyson, b. 23rd day of 6th month, 1799. [Removed to the western district; no date given].

Margaret Dukehart, dau. of John and Parthenia Dukehart, b. 12th day of 7th month, 1799.

Hannah Underwood (wife of Abraham Underwood) and their children, Jane Underwood and Elihu Underwood, were received from Warrington Monthly Meeting on 8th day of 8th month, 1799, and removed to western district; no date given].

Mercy Webb (young woman) was received from Deer Creek Monthly Meeting on 8th day of 8th month, 1799.

Benjamin Fell and wife Jane and their daughters Mary Fell and Leah Fell, were received from New Garden Monthly Meeting on 12th day of 9th month, 1799.

John Dillon (young man) and Thomas Brown were received from Gunpowder Monthly Meeting on 12th day of 9th month, 1799.

James Fisher (young man) was received from York Monthly Meeting on 12th day of 9th month, 1799.

Dennis Read was received from Indian Spring Monthly Meeting on 12th day of 9th month, 1799, and removed to the western district [no date given].

Granville Scott, son of Rossiter and Edith Scott, b. 17th day of 9th month, 1799.

John Harlan (young man) was received from Nottingham Monthly Meeting on 10th day of 10th month, 1799.

Rachel Reynolds (wife of Joshua Reynolds) was received from Nottingham Monthly Meeting on 10th day of 10th month, 1799.

William Hayward (of William) and wife Kezia and their children, Isaac Hayward, John Hayward, Elizabeth Hayward, Jonathan Hayward, and Mary Ann Hayward, were received from Indian Spring Monthly Meeting on 10th day of 10th month, 1799, and removed to the western district [no date given].

Thomas McMillan and wife Jane and their daughters Edith McMillan and Deborah McMillan, were received from Deer Creek Monthly Meeting on 10th day of 10th month, 1799, and returned by certificate on 9th day of 1st month, 1800.

Hannah Larabee, dau. of Daniel and Anna Larabee, b. 7th day of 11th month, 1799. [Removed to western district; no date].

Jarred Price (young man) was received from Gunpowder Monthly Meeting on 14th day of 11th month, 1799.

Stephen Cook, Jr. (young man) was received from London Grove Monthly Meeting on 14th day of 11th month, 1799.

Thomas Ellicott (young man) was received from Fairfax Monthly Meeting on 12th day of 12th month, 1799.

Isaac Kinsey and wife Rachel and his children Isaac Kinsey, Mary Kinsey, Hannah Kinsey, Jacob Kinsey, Joseph Kinsey, Oliver Kinsey, and their son Thomas Kinsey, were received from Indian Spring Monthly Meeting on 12th day of 12th month, 1799. Jacob Kinsey died 2nd day of 9th month, 1800.

"The following members constituting Elk Ridge Preparative Meeting were received from Indian Spring Monthly Meeting on the 12th day of the 12th month, 1799: William Hayward (later moved to western district; no date given) and wife Sidney and their children, John Hayward, Rachel Hayward (later married an Updegraff; no date given), and Rebecca Hayward; Priscilla Plummer (widow) and her sons Thomas Plummer and James Plummer (removed to the western district when it was established); Judith Ellicott (widow) and her sons Joseph Ellicott and Benjamin Ellicott (removed to the western district); John Pierpoint; and, Ann Pierpoint and her daughter Deborah Pierpoint."

Jonathan Ellicott, b. 9th day of 11th month, 1756; his wife, Sarah Ellicott, b. 20th day of 5th month, 1764; their son, Samuel Ellicott, b. 13th day of 12th month, 1783; their dau. Elizabeth Ellicott, b. 5th day of 12th month, 1785, and m. William Tyson [no date given]; their son Nathaniel Ellicott, b. 26th day of 4th month, 1791; their son William Ellicott, b. 15th day of 10th month, 1793; their dau. Sarah Ellicott, b. 27th day of 2nd month, 1796; and, their dau. Frances Ellicott, b. 24th day of 7th month, 1798. Removed to the western district [no date given].

George Ellicott, b. 28th day of 3rd month, 1760; his wife Elizabeth Ellicott, b. 26th day of 5th month, 1763; their son James Ellicott, b. 3rd day of 1st month, 1792; their dau. Elizabeth Ellicott, b. 5th day of 12th month, 1793; their dau. Martha Ellicott, b. 13th day of 9th month, 1795; and, their son George Ellicott, b. 16th day of 7th month, 1798. Removed to the western district [no date given].

Benjamin Rich, b. 12th day of 9th month, 1760; his wife Sarah Rich, b. 9th day of 3rd month, 1774; their dau. Ann Rich, b. 3rd day of 8th month, 1797; and, their son John Rich, b. 26th day of 1st month, 1799.

Samuel Smith and his wife Hannah [no births dates given]; their son Elias Smith, b. 8th day of 2nd month, 1796; their son George Smith, b. 15th day of 9th month, 1797; and, their dau. Esther Smith, b. 7th day of 10th month, 1799. Removed to the western district [no date given].

Joseph Heston and his wife Ann [no birth dates given]; his son Samuel Heston, b. 27th day of 8th month, 1781; his son Joseph Heston, b. 14th day of 1st month, 1783; his dau. Phebe Heston, b. 26th day of 5th month, 1786, and married a Wright; their dau. Letitia Heston, b. 1st day of 1st month, 1791; their son William Heston, b. 24th day of 3rd month, 1798. Removed to western district [no date given].

Joseph Atkinson, b. 8th day of 9th month, 1763; his wife Rachel Atkinson, b. 9th day of 2nd month, 1763; their dau. Sarah Atkinson, b. 12th day of 2nd month, 1789; their dau. Rachel Atkinson, b. 25th day of 9th month, 1790; their dau. Ruth Atkinson, b. 3rd day of 5th month, 1793; their son Isaac Atkinson, b. 1st day of 3rd month, 1795; their dau. Mary Atkinson, b. 6th day of 3rd month, 1797, and d. 17th day of 8th month, 1800; and, their son Joseph Atkinson, b. 6th day of 10th month, 1798. Removed to the western district [no date given].

James Gillingham and his wife Elizabeth [no birth dates given]; their son John Gillingham, b. 31st day of 10th month, 1787; their son William Gillingham, b. 30th day of 11th month, 1788; their son George Gillingham, b. 4th day of 10th month, 1790; their dau. Elizabeth Gillingham, b. 2nd day of 10th month, 1792; their son Ezra Gillingham, b. 21st day of 10th month, 1794; and, their dau. Mary Gillingham, b. 10th day of 5th month, 1801. Removed to the western district [no date given].

Ann Read (wife of Jacob Read) and her dau. Mary Brown, and their sons Charles Read and Joseph Read [no birth dates given]. Removed to the western district [no date given].

Hannah Pierpoint (widow) and her son Walter Pierpoint and her dau. Mary Pierpoint (married a Cosley) [no birth dates given]. Removed to the western district [no dates given].

Joseph Pierpoint, single man [no dates given].

Misael Pierpoint (single man), removed to western district.

Joshua Stewart (single man), b. in 1714; d. 10th month, 1800.

John Ellicott (single man), b. 16th day of 9th month, 1769; removed to the western district.

Elias Allibone (single man), died in 1800.

Amos Gillingham (single man), died in 1801.

Samuel Godfrey (single man), removed to western district.

Sarah Atkinson (single woman), removed to western district.

Abigail Atkinson (single woman), removed to western district.

Sarah Brelsford, single woman, was recommended and removed to Falls Monthly Meeting on 14th day of 8th month, 1800.

Joshua Riley, son of William and Sarah Riley, b. 16th day of 9th month, 1798, and d. 3rd day of 8th month, 1799.

Joshua Riley (2nd), son of William and Sarah Riley, b. 19th day of 1st month, 1800; removed to the western district [no date given].

Amos Brown (young man) was received from Dover Monthly Meeting in New Hampshire on 9th day of 1st month, 1800.

Ezekiel Harlan (young man) was received from Nottingham Monthly Meeting on 9th day of 1st month, 1800.

James Naylor (young man) was received from Gunpowder Monthly Meeting on 9th day of 1st month, 1800.

Amos Vickers (young man) was received from Buckingham Monthly Meeting on 9th day of 1st month, 1800. Deceased [no date given].

Mercey McAteer (wife of Thomas McAteer) was received from Philadelphia Southern District Monthly Meeting on 9th day of 1st month, 1800.

Mary Jewell (wife of George Jewell) and their son George Jewell, their son William Jewell, their son John Jewell, their dau. Sarah Jewell, and their son Joseph Jewell, were received from Gunpowder Monthly Meeting on 9th day of 1st month, 1800.

Elisha Talbot (minor) and Jacob Janney (minor) were received from Fairfax Monthly Meeting on 13th day of 2nd month, 1800.

Willing Underwood (minor) was received from Deer Creek Monthly Meeting on 13th day of 2nd month, 1800.

Hannah Brown (young woman) was received from Philadelphia Monthly Meeting on 13th day of 2nd month, 1800.

Ann Coale (young woman) was received from Deer Creek Monthly Meeting on 13th day of 2nd month, 1800.

Mary Brown, dau. of James and Catharine Brown, b. 23rd day of 2nd month, 1800, and John Brown, son of James and Catharine Brown, b. 30th day of 12th month, 1802.

Elizabeth Price, dau. of Israel and Susanna Price, b. 11th day of 2nd month, 1800.

Edward Wilson (young man) was received from Knaresborough[?] Monthly Meeting in Great Britain on 13th day of 2nd month, 1800.

Mary Morgan, dau. of John and Ann Morgan, b. 24th day of 12th month, 1799.

Elizabeth James, dau. of Amos and Mary James, b. 25th day of 12th month, 1799. Removed to western district [no date].

William Morgan, son of Thomas and Sarah Morgan, b. 10th day of 7th month, 1796, and Thomas Morgan, son of Thomas and Sarah Morgan, b. 7th day of 3rd month, 1800.

Joseph Hewes (young man) was received from Wilmington Monthly Meeting on 13th day of 3rd month, 1800.

Ann Sheppard (wife of Thomas Sheppard) was received from Gunpowder Monthly Meeting on 13th day of 3rd month, 1800. Removed to the western district [no date given].

William Reese, son of John and Ann Reese, b. 18th day of 3rd month, 1800. Removed to the western district [no date].

John Naylor, son of Samuel and Rebecca Naylor, b. 19th day of 3rd month, 1800.

Betsy Byrnes, dau. of Samuel and Hannah Byrnes, b. 8th day of 4th month, 1800.

Rebecca Procter (wife of Izak Procter) was received from Falls Monthly Meeting on 10th day of 4th month, 1800. Removed to the western district [no date given].

Eli Plummer and his wife Alice and their son James Plummer were received from New Garden Monthly meeting on 10th day of 4th month, 1800; their dau. Sinah Plummer, b. in 1804.

Jacob Norbary was received from York Monthly Meeting on 10th day of 4th month, 1800, and d. on 25th day of 3rd month, 1803, aged 75 years, 9 months, and 26 days.

Caleb Bonsall (young man) was received from London Grove Monthly Meeting on 10th day of 4th month, 1800.

John D, Sutton (young man) was received from Fairfax Monthly meeting on 10th day of 4th month, 1800. Removed to the western district [no date given].

Thomas Jewett (young man) was received from Deer Creek Monthly Meeting on 10th day of 4th month, 1800.

Israel French (young man) was received from Goose Creek Monthly Meeting on 10th day of 4th month, 1800.

Gravener Jefferis (minor) and Samuel Jefferis (minor) were received from Gunpowder Monthly Meeting on 8th day of 5th month, 1800. Removed to the western district [no date].

Phebe Carr was received from Gunpowder Monthly Meeting on 8th day of 5th month, 1800, and d. 16th day of 12th month, 1801.

David Houlton (a minor) was received from Philadelphia Northern District Monthly Meeting on 8th day of 5th month, 1800.

Mary Marsh, dau. of William and Ann Marsh, b. 7th day of 6th month, 1800, and d. 15th day of 10th month, 1800.

Jane Harris, dau. of George and Susanna Harris, b. 6th day of 7th month, 1800, and d. 7th day of 9th month, 1800.

Samuel Cookson and his wife Olive and their dau. Mary Cookson and their son Joseph Cookson were received from Nottingham Monthly Meeting on 12th day of 6th month, 1800. Removed to western district [no date given].

Evan Harry (young man) was received from Kennett Monthly Meeting on 12th day of 6th month, 1800.

Gideon Hughes (minor) was received by request on 12th day of 6th month, 1800 [and later removed to Middleton, Ohio].

Joshua Stapleton and his wife Susanna and their son Samuel Stapleton and their dau. Susanna Stapleton were received from Gunpowder Monthly Meeting on 10th day of 7th month, 1800.

Martha Balderston, dau. of Ely and Esther Balderston, b. 8th day of 8th month, 1800.

Harman Hayward, son of William and Mary Hayward, b. 10th day of 8th month, 1800. Deceased [no date given].

Samuel Canby and his wife Elizabeth and their son Joseph Canby (b. 25th day of 1st month, 1799) were received from Darby Monthly Meeting on 14th day of 8th month, 1800.

Joseph Hopkins (minor) was received from Indian Spring Monthly Meeting on 14th day of 8th month, 1800.

Robert Cornthwait (young man) was received from Gunpowder Monthly Meeting on 14th day of 8th month, 1800.

Mary Helms (widow) was received from Crooked Run Monthly Meeting on 14th day of 8th month, 1800, and d. 14th day of 12th month, 1801.

Priscilla Morgan (wife of John Morgan) was received from Gunpowder Monthly Meeting on 14th day of 8th month, 1800.

Mary Jackson (young woman) was received from Third Haven Monthly Meeting on 14th day of 8th month, 1800.

George Carey, son of James and Martha Carey, b. 9th day of 9th month, 1800.

William Matthews, son of William and Elizabeth Matthews, b. 17th day of 4th month, 1798.

Ann John (young woman) was received from Concord Monthly Meeting on 11th day of 9th month, 1800, and noted as marrying a Haines [no date given].

Peter Pollard and his wife Elizabeth and their dau. Eunice Pollard, their dau. Mary Pollard, their son David Pollard, and their dau. Sarah Pollard, were received from Nantucket Monthly Meeting on 13th day of 11th month, 1800.

Israel Pleasants and his wife Ann P. Pleasants and their son Samuel Pleasants, their son Thomas Franklin Pleasants, their dau. Sarah Pleasants, their dau. Mary Pleasants, their dau. Elizabeth Pleasants, their dau. Ann Pleasants, their dau. Hannah Pleasants, and their son Israel Pemberton Pleasants, were received from Philadelphia Monthly Meeting on 13th day of 11th month, 1800.

William Hambleton and his wife Mary and their son Benjamin Hambleton, their son James Hambleton, their dau. Rachel Hambleton, their son Joseph Hambleton, their dau. Mary Hambleton, and their son William Hambleton, were received from New Garden Monthly Meeting on 13th day of 11th month, 1800. [Mary Hambleton, the mother, is subsequently noted as deceased, but no date is given].

William Matthews, son of Samuel and Ann Matthews, b. 25th day of 10th month, 1800. Deceased [no date given].

Elizabeth Kinsey, dau. of Isaac and Rachel Kinsey, b. 29th day of 11th month, 1800.

Deborah Hopkins, dau. of Gerrard T. and Dorothy Hopkins, b. 27th day of 11th month, 1800.

James Hampton Wilson, son of Stephen and Mercy Wilson, b. 23rd day of 11th month, 1800. Deceased [no date given].

John Brooks, son of Isaac and Sarah Brooks, b. 7th day of 11th month, 1800.

Samuel Poultney [middle name missing due to torn page], son of Thomas and Ann Poultney, b. 16th day of 6th month, 1797; Philip Thomas, son of Thomas and Ann Poultney, b. 18th day of 5th month, 1799; and, Rachel

Thomas Poultney, dau. of Thomas and Ann Poultney, b. 14th day of 7th month, 1801. Removed to the western district [no date given].

William Price, son of Warrick and Susanna Price, b. 27th day of 9th month, 1797, and Ann Price, dau. of Warrick and Susanna Price, b. 7th day of 5th month, 1800.

Amos Alley (young man) was received from Fairfax Monthly Meeting on 11th day of 12th month, 1800.

Children of Mayerel[?] Sanderson: Sarah Sanderson, b. 26th day of 9th month, 1791; Rachel Sanderson, b. 20th day of 11th month, 1793; Catharine Sanderson, b. 10th day of 7th month, 1796; and, Ann Sanderson, b. 8th day of 8th month, 1799.

Children of Thomas and Sarah Morgan: William Morgan, b. 10th day of 7th month, 1796; Mary Morgan, b. 17th day of 4th month, 1798; Thomas Morgan, b. 3rd day of 7th month, 1800; and, Susanna Morgan, b. 15th day of 3rd month, 1803.

Children of Sanuel and Rebecca Naylor: Ann Naylor, b. 17th day of 2nd month, 1796; Elizabeth Naylor, b. 8th day of 8th month, 1798, and d. 9th day of 5th month, 1800; John Naylor, b. 19th day of 3rd month, 1800; Joseph Naylor, b. 3rd day of 10th month, 1802; and, Charles Naylor, b. 12th day of 9th month, 1804.

Children of Elias and Mary Ellicott: Thomas Ellicott, b. 11th day of 12th month, 1799; Andrew T. Ellicott, b. 23rd day of 12th month, 1801; James Ellicott, b. 3rd day of 1st month, 1804; John Ellicott, b. 18th day of 1st month, 1805; Samuel Ellicott, b. 11th day of 8th month, 1806.

Deborah, Elizabeth, Margaret, and Sarah Thornburgh (minors) received by request on 8th day of 2nd month, 1798.

Abigail Medcalf received by request on 13th day of 3rd month, 1800.

Daniel Larrabee and his wife Ann Larrabee were received from New York Monthly Meeting on 12th day of 12th month, 1799.

Nicholas Riley, son of William and Sarah Riley b. 9th day of 1st month, 1795.

John Hopkins (young man), son of John and Elizabeth Hopkins, "born 25th day of 3rd month, 1777, and removed with his parents from Gunpowder and joined Baltimore Monthly Meeting on its first establishment, and it being found that the record of his birth was omitted by the meeting, it is now entered on record by direction of the monthly meeting, verbally given to the recorder, John Trimble, on 11th day of 5th month, 1808."

Susanna Plummer, wife of Joseph Plummer, was born 29th day of 9th month, 1783.

Mary Wayble was born 10th day of 3rd month, 1782.

BALTIMORE MONTHLY MEETING, EASTERN DISTRICT, MARRIAGE CERTIFICATES, 1794-1800

Jacob Tyson, of Harford County, son of Isaac Tyson, deceased, and his wife Esther, of Baltimore County, m. Ann Perine, dau. of Peter Perine, deceased, and his wife Hannah Perine (now Stuart), of Baltimore County, on the 2nd day of the 1st month, 1794, in Baltimore Town. Witnesses: George Matthews, David Brown, William Brown, James P. Boyd, David Wilson, John Marsh, Jesse Brown, William Riley, John Mason, Isaiah Balderston, John Brown, Martha Balderston, Mary Brown, Ann Scott, Sarah Matthews, Elizabeth Patrick, Elisha Tyson, Nathan Tyson, Malden Perine, Moses Shepherd, Isaac Tyson, Peter Perine, William Norris, John Mitchel, Tacy Mitchel, Margaret Perine, Mary Mitchel, Heppy Perine, Lucretia Tyson, Grace Coates, Mary Boyd, Esther Pancoast, Susanna Price, Francis Martin.

John McKim, of Baltimore Town, m. Mary Love, widow of William Love of York County, Pa., deceased, on the 4th day of the 9th month, 1795, in Baltimore Town. Witnesses: Joseph Townsend, William Brown, Mary Brown, Hannah Marsh, Isaac Williams, John Brown, Thomas Fisher, Jr., John Hillen, John Hayes, John Dukehart, Susanna Mason, Margaret Tyson, Mary Shields, Susanna Morthland, Phebe Thornburgh, Deborah Thornburgh, John McKim, Jr., Samuel McKim, David Brown, Thomas Poultney, Elias Ellicott, William Trimble, William Riley, John Marsh, Thomas Thornburgh, Alexander McKim, Sarah Comly, Robert McKim, Joseph Thornburgh, Jane Shields, David Shields, James Love, Eliza McKim, Charine McKim, Margaret McKim, Isabella McKim.

John Dukehart, of Baltimore Town, son of Volerius Dukehart, deceased, and Margaret his wife, m. Parthenia Balderston, dau. of Isaiah Balderston, of Baltimore Town, and Martha his wife, on the 15th day of the 12th month, 1796, in Baltimore Town. Witnesses: Joseph Townsend, John McKim, Robert Cornthwait, Susanna Mason, Hannah Marsh, Margaret Tyson, Catharine Hooker, Hannah P. Townsend, Dorothy Brown, Grace Coates,

Susanna Martin, Rachel Martin, Susanna Price, Dorothy Hopkins, Ann Butler, Clementine Doney, Elizabeth VanWyck, Esther Brown, Lydia Harden, Mary McKim, Mary Brown, Samuel Wilson, William Riley, Gerrard Hopkins, Elisha Tyson, William Brown, John Brown, John Trimble (of William), Thomas Letter, Daniel Colvin, Thomas Morgan, Gerrard T. Hopkins, William Cole, Jesse Brown, Isaiah Balderston, Martha Balderston, Margaret Dukehart, David Wilson, Jane Wilson, Ann Matthews, Elizabeth Ball, Margaret Davenport, Volerius Dukehart, Catharine Dukehart, William Ball, Ely Balderston, William Wilson, Hannah Wilson.

Israel Price, of the City of Baltimore, son of Samuel Price, of Baltimore County, and Ann his wife (deceased), m. Hannah Brown, dau. of William Brown, of the City of Baltimore, and Elizabeth his wife, on the 18th day of the 5th month, 1797, in Baltimore City. Witnesses: Joseph Townsend, Daniel Price, Richard Price, Amos West, David Hulton, Jonathan Balderston, William Trimble, Elias Ellicott, John Hillen, William Riley, Benjamin Riley, Jonathan Davenport, David Wilson, Samuel Wilson, John Trimble (of Isaac), John Cornthwait (of Jno.), Isaiah Balderston, Martha Balderston, David Brown, John Wilson, Ann Matthews, Fanny Brown, Catharine Wilson, Mary Brown, Ann Matthews, Jane Wilson, Elizabeth Dukehart, Grace Wilson, Jane Trimble, Deborah Cornthwait, Martha Hill, Sarah Matthews, Margaret Davenport, Parthenia Dukehart, Samuel Price, William Brown, Elizabeth Brown, Mary Price, Esther Brown, Ann Reese, Samuel Price, Jr., Warrick Price, Mordecai Price, John E. Reese, Joseph Brown, Susanna Price, Ann Price, Ann Brown, Mary Matthews, Rebecca Medcalf, Mary Jones, Mary Hill.

Ely Balderston, of Baltimore City, son of Isaiah Balderston, of said city, and Martha his wife, m. Esther Brown, dau. of William Brown, of Baltimore City, and Elizabeth his wife, on the 16th day of the 11th month, 1797, in the City of Baltimore. Witnesses: John Jones, Joseph Townsend, Elisha Tyson, William Riley, John McKim, David Brown, Jesse Brown, Amos James, John Brown, David Wilson, John Wilson, Daniel Colvin, Volerius Dukehart, William Husband, John Trimble (of Isaac), John Cornthwait, John Dillon, Samuel Wilson, Jesse Medcalf, Mary Mifflin, Susanna Mason, Sarah Procter, Hannah Marsh, Deborah Cornthwait, Elizabeth Matthews, Elizabeth Cornthwait, Sarah Riley, Mary McKim, Eliza Torrence, Ann Torrence, Elizabeth Torrence, Grace Wilson, Elizabeth Hopkins, Elizabeth Husband, Jane Wilson, Isaiah Balderston, William Brown, Martha Balderston,

Elizabeth Brown, Mark Balderston, Parthenia Dukehart, John Dukehart, Hugh Balderston, Jonathan Balderston, Israel Price, Hannah Price, Joseph Brown, John E. Rees, Anne Brown, Fanny Brown, Catharine Dukehart, Ann Scott, Merab Johnson.

Robert Hough, of the City of Baltimore, son of Joseph Hough of Bucks County, Pa., and Mary his wife, m. Frances Martin, dau. of John Martin late of Baltimore, deceased, and Margaret his wife, on the 15th day of the 2nd month, 1798, in the City of Baltimore. Witnesses: Andrew Ellicott, Jr., Philip Thomas, Nathan Tyson, William Riley, James Ellicott, Gerrard T. Hopkins, Elias Ellicott, Jesse Brown, William Husband, John Brown, Joshua Matthews, Tacy Mitchel, Elizabeth Husband, Jane Wilson, Grace Coates, Ann Hicks, Mary Barry, Alice Evans, Lucretia Tyson, Mary Mitchel, Mary Ellicott, Eliza Ellicott, Rebecca Hough, Mary Randall, Margaret Randall, Jno. Randall, William Martin, Samuel Martin, John E. Carey, John Hough, James Carey, William Brown, John Norris.

John Trimble, of the City of Baltimore, son of Isaac Trimble, of the City of Baltimore, and Elizabeth his wife, deceased, m. Elizabeth Brown, dau. of David Brown, of the City of Baltimore, and Elizabeth his wife, on the 15th day of the 3rd month, 1798, in the City of Baltimore. Witnesses: George Matthews, Edmund Channel, Jesse Brown, John Brown, Jr., Joseph Hibberd, Ely Balderston, John Marsh, William Riley, John Dukehart, William Brown, Isaiah Balderston, Amos James, Gerrard T. Hopkins, John Cornthwait, Samuel Wilson, John McKim, William Matthews (of Oliver), Thomas Mecteer, Jr., Hannah P. Townsend, Hannah Marsh, Catharine Dukehart, Martha Davis, Frances Brown, Jane Trimble, Mary Brown, Mary Davis, Elizabeth Brown, Jr., Susanna Martin, Dorothy Hopkins, Mary Jones, Elizabeth Matthews, Sarah Riley, Parthenia Dukehart, Martha Balderston, Ann Matthews, Ann Yellott, Isaac Trimble, David Brown, Elizabeth Brown, James Brown, George Peters, Mary Peters, John Brown, David Brown, Sarah Matthews, James Trimble, George Brown, Isaac Trimble, Jr., Mary Mifflin, Elizabeth Johns, Elizabeth Husband, Sarah Hayward, Mary Townsend, Mary McKim, Frances Davis.

William Waterhouse, of the City of Baltimore, son of Joshua and Elizabeth Waterhouse, of New Jersey, m. Ann Butler, of the City of Baltimore, dau. of Joseph and Mary Mitchel, of Pennsylvania, on the 17th day of the 5th month, 1798, in the City of Baltimore. Witnesses: David Brown, William Riley, William Brown, John McKim, Jos. Way, John Ellicott, Daniel Byrnes,

Benjamin Ellicott, John Deur, John E. Reese, Andrew Ellicott, Jr., James Ellicott, Volerius Dukehart, William Husband, John Brown, Gerrard T. Hopkins, Moses Sheppard, Martha Carey, Susanna Mason, Mary Tyson, Grace Coates, Ann Hicks, Elizabeth Trippe, Hannah Byrnes, Ann Sheppard, Lucretia Tyson, Rachel Moore, Julia Hugo, Edith Scott, Jane Wilson, Hannah P. Townsend, Elizabeth Johns, Amos James, Thomas Sheppard, John Mitchel, Tacy Mitchel, Mary Mitchel, Hannah Dutton, Elias Ellicott, Mary Mifflin, Sarah Barney, Margaret Tyson, Sarah Tyson, Mary James, Catharine Dukehart, Lydia Husband, Susanna Martin, Ann Matthews, Margaret Dukehart, Martha Balderston, William Jones, Nathan Tyson, Thomas McIlsey.

John Morgan, of Baltimore City, son of John Morgan, of Baltimore City, and Mary his wife, deceased, m. Ann Matthews, dau. of William Matthews, of Baltimore City, and Ann his wife, deceased, on the 20th day of the 9th month, 1798, in Baltimore City. Witnesses: John McKim, William Brown, Jacob Pugh, David Wilson, Robert Cornthwait, Jno. Cornthwait, Oliver Matthews (of William), Samuel Wilson, John Dillon, Hosea Morgan, William Cornthwait, James Brown, Jesse Brown, Enos Alley, Samuel Lippincott, Israel Price, Isaac Trimble, Jr., Volerius Dukehart, Elizabeth Matthews, Elizabeth Pugh, Elizabeth Hugo, Rebecca Medcalf, Sarah Morgan, Grace Wilson, Elizabeth Cornthwait, Deborah Cornthwait, Grace Cornthwait, Elizabeth Matthews, Catharine Wilson, Mary Matthews, Mary Mifflin, Mary Hicks, Susan Norris, Sarah Stewart, Dorothy Brown, John Morgan, William Matthews, Thomas Morgan, Joel Morgan, William Morgan (of Jno.), Jesse Morgan, Jr., Jesse Morgan, Sarah Hopkins, Mary Mitchel, Elizabeth Husband, Catharine Dukehart, Hannah Price, Ann Riley, Margaret Randall, Mary Hussey, Hannah Matthews, Julia Hugo, Ann Matthews, Elizabeth Matthews, Mary Dillon.

Isaac Webster, of Harford County, m. Elizabeth Hopkins, dau. of Samuel Hopkins, of Baltimore County, and Sarah his wife, deceased, on the 12th day of the 4th month, 1799, in Baltimore City. Witnesses: Jos. Townsend, Andrew Ellicott, John Brown, William Riley, James Ellicott, John Dukehart, Gerrard Hopkins, Jr., John Jewett, F. Sanderson, William Harris, John S. Webster, Mary Brown, Sarah Hopkins, Elizabeth Hopkins, Dolly Webster, Cath. Daughdy, Francis Davis, William Norris, Jr., Andrew Ellicott, Jr., Nicholas Hopkins, Thomas Webster, Henry Hopkins, James Webster, Gerrard Hopkins, John Hopkins, Cassandra Thornburgh, Rachel Hopkins,

Thornburgh, Priscilla Hopkins, Sophia Carroll, P. Gough, Mary Boyd, M. Hesselius, M. W. Howard, Margaret Thornburgh, Sarah Thornburgh, Martha Balderston, Martha Davis.

James Brown, of the City of Baltimore, son of John Brown, of said city, and Mary his wife, m. Catharine Dukehart, dau. of Volerius Dukehart, of the same place, deceased, and Margaret his wife, on the 18th day of the 4th month, 1799, in Baltimore City. Witnesses: Andrew Ellicott, Jr., Isaac Tyson, Gerrard T. Hopkins, John McKim, David Wilson, William Ball, Jesse Brown, William Hayward, John Riley, Caleb Waller, John Cornthwait, John Ball, Hugh Balderston, George Brown, Matthias Maris, Joshua Matthews, John Brown, Jonathan Balderston, David Brown, Jr., John Dillon, Samuel Wilson, James Wainright, Jr., Mordecai Amoss, William Jones, Mary McKim, Elizabeth Matthews, Frances Brown, Heppy Perine, Mary Dillon, Catharine Wilson, Jane Trimble, Hannah Matthews, Ann Riley, Elizabeth Brown, Deborah Wilson, Rebecca Williams, Hannah P. Townsend, Elizabeth Wilson, Ann Matthews, Anna Jones, Catharine Daughdy, Mary Mitchel, Sarah Hopkins, Rachel Mason, Elizabeth Thomas, Mary Barry, Jane Wilson, Esther Balderston, John Brown, Mary Brown, Mary Hill, Margaret Dukehart, Ann Matthews, David Brown, Sr., Mary Davis, Sarah Riley, William Riley, Volerius Dukehart, John Dukehart, Martha Davis, Jos. Townsend, Martha Balderston, Isaiah Balderston, Margaret Randall, Ann Hicks, Mary Boyd, Mary Jones, William Brown, Richard Wallis.

William Amoss, Jr., of Harford County, son of William Amoss and Hannah his wife, the latter deceased, m. Elizabeth Hugo, of the City of Baltimore, dau. of William Morgan, deceased, and Ann his wife, on the 24th day of the 10th month, 1799, in the City of Baltimore. Witnesses: John Wilson, William Brown, Gerrard T. Hopkins, Robert Cornthwait, Elisha Tyson, John Norris, William Amoss, Gravener Jefferis, Samuel Jefferis, Hosea Morgan, Samuel B. Hugo, Nathan Tyson, William Medcalf, Isaac Tyson, Jane Jacob, Mary Tyson, Jehosheba Brown, Mary Mitchel, Elizabeth Norris, William Riley, William Waterhouse, Susanna Martin, Mary Hicks, Ann Matthews, Jane Wilson, Ann Riley, Hannah Williams, Elizabeth Morsell, Mary Mifflin, Mary McKim, Mary Brown, Elizabeth Johns, Tacy Mitchel, Sarah Morgan, Rebecca Medcalf, Abigail Medcalf, Lucretia Tyson, Susanna Norris, William Amoss, Ann Morgan, John Morgan, Benjamin Amoss, Jesse Morgan, Priscilla Morgan, Thomas Morgan, John Trimble (of William), William

Jacob, Joel Morgan, William Morgan (of Jno.), Elizabeth Morgan, Hannah Amoss, Ann Morgan, Hepzibah Perine, Rachel Bull.

George England, of Harford County, son of Joseph England, of said place, and Elizabeth his wife, both deceased, m. Catharine Hooker, dau. of Thomas Hooker, of Baltimore County, and Hannah his wife, on the 26th day of the 12th month, 1799, in the City of Baltimore. Witnesses: David Brown, John Wilson, William Riley, John Dukehart, John McKim, Volerius Dukehart, Ennion Williams, William Brown, Thomas Mecteer, Levis Janney, John Brown, John Brown, John Hillen, Robert Sinclair, Rachel Smith, Jane Coates, Sarah Procter, Mary Mifflin, Mary McKim, Margaret Dukehart, Hetty Sinclair, Rachel Stapleton, Margaret Hulton, Elizabeth Dukehart, Fanny Brown, Mercy Mecteer, Jane Wilson, Tacey Burgess, Mary Mitchel, Phebe Coates, Rachel Mason, Sarah Hopkins, Rebecca Procter, Elizabeth England, Thomas Hooker, Jr., Henry Stevenson, John Hargrove, Hannah Hargrove, Jos. Townsend, Granville S. Townsend, Hannah P. Townsend, Ann John, Isaiah Balderston, Martha Balderston, George Matthews, Sarah Matthews, Ann Matthews, Mercy Webb, Susanna Price, Rebecca Medcalf.

Isaac Brookes, of the City of Baltimore, son of Isaac Brookes, of Darby Township, Delaware County, Pa., and Hannah his wife, m. Sarah Hayward, dau. of Joseph Hayward, of Baltimore County, deceased, and Rebecca his wife, on the 26th day of the 12th month, 1799, in Baltimore City. Witnesses: David Brown, John Wilson, John Dukehart, Volerius Dukehart, John McKim, Levis Janney, John Cornthwait, William Riley, William Trimble, William Husband, Joseph Husband, Isaac Scott, Thomas Sherwood, James Brown, John Hillen, Josiah Brown, Jonathan Roberts, Evan McHinstry[?], Mary Mifflin, Mary McKim, Hannah Scott, Hannah Trimble, Margaret Dukehart, Lydia Wells, Jehosheba Brown, Elizabeth Husband, Lydia Husband, Susanna Husband, Rachel Reynolds, Catharine England, Mercy Mecteer, Ann John, Martha Balderston, Jane Wilson, Rebeckah Procter, Sarah Procter, Rebecca Williams, Sarah Scott, Ann Scott, John Brooks, Hannah Williams, William Hayward, Ennion Williams, Rachel Hussey, Stephen Cook, Jos. Townsend, Granville S. Townsend, Hannah P. Townsend, Elizabeth Johns, Thomas Mecteer, John Brown, Richard Price, Isaiah Balderston, John Jewett, Ann Matthews, Sarah Hopkins.

James Naylor, of the City of Baltimore, son of John Naylor, of Baltimore County, and Mary his wife, m. Margaret Marsh, dau. of John Marsh, of York County, Pa., and Margaret his wife, on the 16th day of the 1st month, 1800, in the City of Baltimore. Witnesses: John McKim, Volerius Dukehart, Richard Price, William Riley, William Brown, Joseph Hibberd, Jos. Thornburgh, John Mitchel, John Marsh, Mary McKim, Ann Matthews, Elizabeth Matthews, Jane Wilson, Mary Clark, Mary Hussey, Susanna Harlan, Mary Catts, Thomas Miles, John Naylor, Sr., Elizabeth Naylor, Cassandra Thornburgh, John Marsh, Ann Matthews, Hannah West, George Matthews, Hannah Marsh, Mary Mifflin, Mary Simmons, Mary Mitchel, Deborah Thornburgh, Lucretia Tyson, Sarah Morthland, Tacy Mitchel, Rachel Mason, Phebe Coates, Margaret Tyson.

John Webster Wilson, of Harford County, son of John Wilson, of same place, and Alisanna his wife, m. Lucretia Tyson, dau. of Elisha Tyson, of the City of Baltimore, and Mary his wife, on the 15th day of the 5th month, 1800, in the City of Baltimore. Witnesses: John Brown, Volerius Dukehart, Andrew Ellicott, Amos James, Jos. Thornburgh, Moses Sheppard, Joel Morgan, George Mason, Benjamin Ellicott, James Ellicott, Samuel Jefferis = Hardiville [sic], Henry Try = Bayreau [sic], William Husband, John Mitchel, Mary Mifflin, Jos. Townsend, P. E. Thomas, William Norris, Jasper Coope, Thomas Poultney, Jacob Hoffman, Thomas Ellicott, Isaac Scott, Jos. Scott, Jr., P. Thomas, Arnaud Cornell.[?], John Norris, Mary Brown, Elisha Tyson, Mary Tyson, Isaac Tyson, Mixon Wilson, William Tyson, Nathan Tyson, Mary Tyson, Thomas Wilson, Margaret Wilson, Nancy Wilson, John L. Webster, Cassandra Thornburgh, Elizabeth Webster, Martha Carey, Elizabeth George, Hannah Scott, Susanna Norris, Rachel Tyson.

Benjamin Amoss, of the City of Baltimore, son of William Amoss, Jr., of Harford County, and Susanna his wife (deceased), m. Elizabeth Cornthwait, dau. of Robert Cornthwait, of the City of Baltimore, and Grace his wife, on the 22nd day of the 5th month, 1800, in Baltimore City. Witnesses: Thomas Lyell, William Riley, Jesse Tyson, Gerrard T. Hopkins, John Norris, John Morgan, John Wilson, Amos James, Mary Mifflin, Elizabeth Johns, Rachel Kinsey, Dorothy Brown, Ann Hicks, Priscilla Morgan, Esther Balderston, Elizabeth Reed, William Amoss, Jr., Robert Cornthwait, Grace Cornthwait, Deborah Cornthwait, Thomas Cornthwait, Mary Cornthwait, William Cornthwait, Jno. Cornthwait, Jr., Martha Amoss, Robert Cornthwait, Jr., John Cornthwait.

ABSTRACT OF BALTIMORE MONTHLY MEETING MINUTES, 1792-1800

"A list of the names of the members constituting Baltimore Preparative Meeting, being accordingly produced [at the opening of the Monthly Meeting at Baltimore on 2nd day of 11th month, 1792] was examined, corrected and is as follows:

John Brown in the station of an Elder and Overseer, with his wife Mary and their two children James and Frances;

William Brown in the station of an Elder, with his wife Elizabeth and their six children, Esther, Hannah, Joseph, Ann, Elizabeth, and Mary;

Rebecca Williams in the station of an Elder, with her daughter Sarah Hayward;

William Trimble in the station of an Overseer, with his wife Hannah and their four children, John, Sarah, James, and William;

Joseph Townsend and his wife Mary and their two children, Hannah Painter Townsend and Nicholas Waln Townsend;

John McKim with his son William Duncan McKim;

George Matthews with his wife Sarah and their daughter Ann;

David Brown with his wife Elizabeth and their four children, Elizabeth, David, George, and John;

Gerrard Hopkins with his wife Rachel and their five children, Samuel, Henry, Priscilla, Gerrard, and Richard;

Elias Ellicott with his wife Mary and their two children, Elizabeth and Rachel;

Elisha Tyson with his wife Mary and their five children, Isaac, Lucretia, Mary, William, and Nathan;

Robert Cornthwait with his wife Grace and their seven children, Elizabeth, Deborah, Thomas, Mary, William, John, and Isaac Granthum;

George Harris with his wife Susanna and their two children, Mary and Beulah;

James Carey with his wife Martha and their two children, John Ellicott and Samuel;

John Mitchel with his wife Tacy and their daughter Mary;

Thomas Poultney and his wife Ann;

John Evan Rees with his wife Ann and their two children, Thomas and Maria;

Amos James with his wife Mary and their daughter Ann;

John Lee with his wife Sebella;

John Marsh with his wife Hannah and their two children, Rebecca and Miriam;

Aquila Jones with his wife Elizabeth and their daughter Susanna Buffington Jones;

Jonah Thomas with his wife Rebecca and their son Benjamin;

Margaret Dukehart (widow) and her three children, John, Catharine, and Volerius;

William Riley with his wife Sarah and their four children, Benjamin, Ann, William, and Volerius;

James Hicks with his wife Mary and their seven children, Ann, Mary, Jane, Bathsheba, Henry, Tamer, and James;

Jonathan Davenport with his wife Margaret and their son Joseph;

Elizabeth Davenport (wife of Joseph Davenport) and their daughter Elizabeth, Jr.;

Rachel Wells (wife of John Wells) and their two children, Margaret and Ann;

David Wilson with his wife Jane and their daughter Elizabeth;

Jonathan Coates with his wife Jane and their six children, Ann, Hannah, Phebe, Grace, Jane, and Elizabeth;

Isaiah Jackson with his wife Margaret and their six children, Ann, Sarah, Thomas Lewis, Mary, Frances, and John;

George Hussey with his wife Rachel and their six children, Joseph, George, Rachel, William, Rebecca, and Ennion;

Mary Boyd (wife of Andrew Boyd);

Mary Helm (wife of Leonard Helm);

Grace McDermott (wife of John McDermott);

William Hayward with his wife Mary and their two children, Joseph and Samuel;

Rossiter Scott with his wife Edith and their two children, Abraham and Jesse;

Jesse Brown with his wife Dorothy;

James Miller with his four children, Thomas, Rachel, Israel, and Emelie;

Ann Rice (wife of Lawrence Rice) and their son George;

Margaret Fisher (widow) and her four children, Samuel, Eunice, Josiah, and Hannah;

Sarah Hopkins (widow) and her two children, Elizabeth and Johns;

Mary Dawes (wife of Francis Dawes) and their daughter Eda;

Mary Stevenson (wife of Nicholas Stevenson);

Mary Jones (wife of Robinson Jones);

Mary Kelso (wife of John Kelso);

Sarah Sheppard (widow) and her three children, Thomas, Ann, and Moses;

Elizabeth Hopkins (wife of John Hopkins) and their son Thomas;

Warrick Price and his wife Susanna;

Thomas Buckingham;

John Naylor and his daughter Elizabeth;

Hannah Hughes (widow);

Elizabeth Dyer (wife of Aaron Dyer) and their five children, Joseph, Mary, Aaron, Josiah, and Benjamin;

Single Men: Jehu Moore, Richard Walsh, Simon Perine, John Davis, David Coulson; Joseph Pierpoint; Thomas Pierpoint; Malden Perine; Robert Cox; William Floyd; Walter Pierpoint; and, Jonathan Coates, Jr.;

Single Women: Mary Hill (widow), Mary Burgess (widow), Mary Tucker (widow), Elenor Humphrey, Susanna Harlan, Tacy Burgess, Martha Burgess, Sarah Scott, Ann Perine, Miriam Hussey, Mary Barry, Frances Martin, Mary Floyd, and Margaret Perine;

Children of Thomas Beal: Joseph, Ann, Thomas, Grace, and Samuel;

Children of John Jackson: Rachel, Susanna, and Joseph;

Lewis Hopkins, son of Philip Hopkins;

Apprentice Lads: Henry Worthington, William Allibone, Isaac Johnson, Peter Perine, Israel Price, Samuel Thomas, William Husband, Thomas Fisher, John Cox, and Thomas Cox.

This meeting being now separated from being a branch of Gunpowder Monthly Meeting, directs that the Preparative Meeting held in Baltimore report of the state thereof in future to this Monthly Meeting."

On 28th day of 12th month, 1792, Isaiah Balderston produced a certificate from Deer Creek Monthly Meeting for himself, his wife Martha, and their four children, Ely, Pathenia, Hugh, and Jonathan.

On 25th day of 1st month, 1793, the following certificates were produced: one for Thomas Mendenhall, his wife Hannah, and their four children, Eleanor, Thomas, John Wilson, and Sarah, from Philadelphia Monthly Meeting; and, one for the minor children of Isaac Trimble - Joseph, John, Mary, Jane, James and Isaac - from Deer Creek Monthly Meeting.

The following members not being recorded on our original list tho' residents amongst us at the time of our separation from Gunpowder Monthly Meeting: Ann Scott (wife of Joseph Scott) and their children Rachel, Isaac, Jacob, Sarah, and Ann; and, Ann Trimble (a young woman), daughter of John Trimble of Virginia.

On 22nd day of 2nd month, 1793, the following certificates were produced: one for Caleb Floyd from Fairfax Monthly Meeting; one for Samuel Morthland from Warrington Monthly Meeting; one for Sarah Day and one for Catharine Shaw from Deer Creek Monthly Meeting. George Harris requested a certificate for himself, his wife Susanna, and their two children, Mary and Beulah, to Warrington Monthly Meeting.

On 29th day of 3rd month, 1793, the following certificates were produced: one for Joseph Scott from Indian Spring Monthly Meeting; one for Hannah Naylor and one for Ann Morg--[torn page] from Nottingham Monthly Meeting; and, one for Elizabeth Hugo from Deer Creek Monthly Meeting.

On 28th day of 6th month, 1793, Esther Pancoast requested to come under care of Friends, and there were complaints that Thomas Buckingham and Caleb Floyd had "their marriages accomplished by the assistance of hirelings to women not of our society." Also, Thomas Cox had removed to reside at Charleston, South Carolina [Bush River Monthly Meeting], and Samuel Fisher and Josiah Fisher had settled at Newburn, North Carolina [Trent

Monthly Meeting], and Lewis Hopkins (son of Philip) had removed within the verge of Crooked Run Monthly Meeting in Virginia.

On 30th day of 8th month, 1793, Ann Matthews (widow) produced a certificate for herself and four children, Elizabeth, Thomas, Hannah, and Joshua, from Gunpowder Monthly Meeting. A complaint was made against Rachel Coates (formerly Jackson) for having her marriage accomplished by the assistance of a hireling.

On 27th day of 9th month, 1793, Aquila Jones requested a certificate for himself, his wife Elizabeth, and their two children, Susanna Buffington and Hannah, to Red Stone Monthly Meeting in Pennsylvania.

On 25th day of 10th month, 1793, Samuel Morthland requested a certificate to Warrington Monthly Meeting in Pennsylvania. A charge was made against Mary Underwood (formerly Hicks) for having her marriage accomplished by the assistance of a hireling with a member of our society. And friend Sarah Lundy visited from Kingwood Monthly Meeting in New Jersey.

On 29th day of 11th month, 1793, Isaac Trimble produced a certificate from Deer Creek Monthly Meeting. Thomas Morgan requested to come under the care of Friends. Jacob Tyson and Ann Perine declared their intention to marry. Our friends Deborah Darby and Rebecca Young attended and produced certificates from Shropshire Monthly Meeting.

On 27th day of 12th month, 1793, Jehu Moore requested a certificate of removal to Pipe Creek Monthly Meeting. Also, Thomas Mendenhall, his wife Hannah, and their four children, Eleanor, Thomas, John Wilson, and Sarah, to Indian Spring Monthly Meeting. A complaint was made against Jane Warner (formerly Hicks) for having her marriage accomplished by the assistance of a hireling to a man not of our society [record shows his name was James].

On 24th day of 1st month, 1794, Malden Perine charged with accomplishing his marriage by the assistance of a hireling.

On 21st day of 2nd month, 1794, Grace McDermott charged with adultery "as she has had a child in the absence of her husband, which she acknowledges is not his." Stacy West, son of Thomas (a minor) produced a certificate from Gunpowder Monthly Meeting.

On 28th day of 3rd month, 1794, a certificate was produced for William and Jesse Morgan from Deer Creek Monthly Meeting. A complaint was made against Miriam Hussey and Hannah Fisher, "each of them having had a child in an unmarried state." And the following certificates were produced: one from William Walton and Sarah his wife and their child named Lukens, from Deer Creek Monthly Meeting; one for Jesse Midhiff from Nottingham Monthly Meeting; and, one fro Rebecca Midhiff and her five children, Abraham, David, William, Joshua, and Ann Buffington, from Nottingham Monthly Meeting.

On 25th day of 4th month, 1794, Elizabeth Allibone produced a certificate from Indian Spring Monthly Meeting with an endorsement from Gunpowder Monthly Meeting. The certificate granted to Samuel Fisher to Trent Monthly Meeting in North Carolina was returned with the following information: "That he had never attended their meetings as they know of, and had also accomplished his marriage out of the society."

On 12th day of 6th month, 1794, Martha Hill produced a certificate from Deer Creek Monthly Meeting.

On 10th day of 7th month, 1794, William Allibone requested a certificate of removal to Northern District of Philadelphia.

On 14th day of 8th month, 1794, Ann Tyson (wife of Jacob) requested a certificate of removal to Gunpowder Monthly Meeting.

On 11th day of 9th month, 1794, Amos James requested that his daughter Miriam (a minor) be taken under care of Friends. William Carpenter produced a certificate for himself, his wife Rachel, and their four children, Lydia, George, Hannah, and John, from Bradford Monthly Meeting in Pennsylvania. Also, Mary Stapleton produced one from the monthly meeting at Philadelphia.

On 9th day of 10th month, 1794, Hepzibah Brown produced a certificate from Woodbury in New Jersey, and endorsed by Gunpowder Monthly Meeting.

On 13th day of 11th month, 1794, Jacob Pugh produced a certificate from Nottingham Monthly Meeting held at Little Britain. Joseph Beal requested a certificate for Thomas and Ann Beal (children of his brother Thomas Beal, deceased) to Fairfax Monthly Meeting in Virginia. A complaint was made against Thomas Pierpoint for having his marriage accomplished contrary to the good order, and the same complaint made against his wife Margaret [late Wells, as noted in later minutes in 1795]. Also a complaint against Ann Jamison (formerly Jackson) in like manner. Elizabeth Naylor requested a certificate of removal to Gunpowder Monthly Meeting.

On 11th day of 12th month, 1794, a complaint was made against Hepzibah Perine (formerly Brown) for having her marriage accomplished contrary to the good order. Ann Coates requested a certificate of removal to Fairfax Monthly Meeting in Virginia, and Mary Helm requested one to Crooked Run Monthly Meeting in Virginia.

On 8th day of 1st month, 1795, Amos Evans requested a certificate to Deer Creek Monthly Meeting. Jesse Tyson produced a certificate for himself, his wife Margaret, and their three children, Elizabeth, Isaac, and Thomas, from Gunpowder Monthly Meeting.

On 12th day of 2nd month, 1795, Benjamin Ellicott produced a certificate from Indian Spring Monthly Meeting, and Isaac Brookes produced one from Goshen Monthly Meeting in Pennsylvania, directed to Indian Spring Monthly Meeting. Walter Pierpoint requested a certificate to Indian Spring.

On1 2th day of 3rd month, 1795, the following certificates were produced: one for William Delworth from Indian Spring Monthly Meeting; one for James Love (a minor) from Monallin Monthly Meeting held at Huntington; and, one for John Lee Webster from Deer Creek Monthly Meeting. Richard Walsh was disowned for "not using suitable endeavors to discharge his just debts, and had been removed for some years past from amongst the society." Simon Perine was disowned for "being concerned in military services." Ann Trimble requested a certificate to Hopewell Monthly Meeting in Virginia.

On 9th day of 4th month, 1795, Hannah Matthews attended with a certificate from Gunpowder Monthly Meeting. Complaint made against Elizabeth Rice (formerly Davenport) "for having her marriage accomplished contrary to the good order to a man not of our society."

On 14th day of 5th month, 1795, Benjamin Amoss (a minor) produced a certificate from Gunpowder Monthly Meeting, and Joseph Jay produced one from Deer Creek Monthly Meeting. George Matthews was disowned for "contracting a debt in an unjustifiable manner and neglects to pay the same."

On 9th day of 7th month, 1795, George Rice was disowned for "attending public plays." Joseph Scott, Jr. charged with marrying contrary to the good order [to Mary Resskey? (formerly Floyd), as noted in later minutes]. Rachel Wells charged with "quarrelling with her sister-in-law." Susannah Jackson requested a certificate to Southern District of Philadelphia, and

Mary Underwood requested one to Warrington Monthly Meeting in Pennsylvania.

On 13th day of 8th month, 1795, the following certificates were produced: one for James Amoss, his wife Hannah, and their two children, Mary and David, from Gunpowder Monthly Meeting; one for Samuel Wilson from Gunpowder; one for Esther Tyson from same place; one for Richard Price (son of Samuel), a minor, from same place; one for Joseph Ford, his wife Frances, and their son Philip, from Deer Creek Monthly Meeting; one for Hannah Roach from Indian Spring for herself and three children, Rachel, Mary, and Barbary. John McKim and Mary Love declared their intention to marry. Thomas Morgan requested a certificate in order to marry Sarah Amoss, daughter of William Amoss, Jr., of Gunpowder Monthly Meeting. Certificate requested for Thomas, Rachel, Israel, and Emelie Miller, children of James Miller, to Maiden Creek Monthly Meeting in Pennsylvania.

On 10th day of 9th month, 1795, certificate requested for Elizabeth Dyer, wife of Aaron Dyer, who removed with her husband within the verge of Indian Spring Monthly Meeting with her five children, Joseph, Mary, Aaron, Josiah, and Benjamin.

On 8th day of 10th month, 1795, Mary Stevenson requested a certificate to New Hope Monthly Meeting in the Western Territory. Jonah Thomas charged with the "practice of retailing spiritous liquors."

On 12th day of 11th month, 1795, Isaac Williams produced a certificate from Gunpowder Monthly Meeting. William Trimble informed the meeting that "he has a prospect of accompanying our friend John Wigham from Europe in his religious visit to the Southerly Governments."

On 10th day of 12th month, 1795, George Mason produced a certificate for himself, his wife Susanna, and their four children, William, George, Rachel, and Susanna, from New Garden Monthly Meeting in Pennsylvania. Also one for Barker Thacker from the monthly meeting held in Dublin, and one for Larkin Read from Indian Spring Monthly Meeting.

On1 14th day of 1st month, 1796, the following certificates were produced: one for George Field from Philadelphia Monthly Meeting; one for Philip E. Thomas (a minor) from Indian Spring Monthly Meeting; and, one for Amos Smith (a minor) from Goose Creek Monthly Meeting in Virginia. Joseph Pierpoint was disowned for "a breach of trust." Ann Partridge (formerly

Wells) had "her marriage accomplished by the assistance of a hireling." Elizabeth Hugo applied for her two children, Gulie and Samuel, taken under care of friends.

On 11th day of 2nd month, 1796, Robert Webster produced a certificate from Deer Creek Monthly Meeting. William Husband requested a certificate to Motherkiln Monthly Meeting in Delaware. Ann Sheppard [now Allison, as noted in subsequent minutes] was charged with having "attended a marriage accomplished contrary to our discipline as also public plays."

On 10th day of 3rd month, 1796, the following certificates were produced: one for Sarah Morthland from Warrington Monthly Meeting; one for Mary Matthews (daughter of William) from Gunpowder Monthly Meeting; one for Joseph Hibberd (a minor) from Pipe Creek Monthly Meeting. John Morgan, Jr. requested to be taken under care of friends. Elias Ellicott to serve in station of an overseer in the room of John McKim who requested to be released.

On1 4th day of 4th month, 1796, Mary Bonsall (formerly Stapleton) charged with having her marriage accomplished contrary to the good order. James Ellicott produced a certificate from Indian Spring Monthly Meeting, and Sarah Morgan (wife of Thomas) and Elizabeth Naylor produced each one from Gunpowder Monthly Meeting.

On 12th day of 5th month, 1796, Jesse Morgan and Thomas Sheppard charged with marrying outside the good order. Ann Butler produced a certificate from a monthly meeting held at the Falls in Bucks County, Pennsylvania, for herself and her two children, John and Joseph (minors).

On 9th day of 6th month, 1796, Esther Sinclair (formerly Pancoast) charged with marrying outside the good order. James Wilson produced a certificate from Brighouse Monthly Meeting in Bradford, Great Britain.

On 14th day of 7th month, 1796, the following certificates were produced: one for Joseph Scott from Fairfax Monthly Meeting; one for Joseph Thornburgh from Warrington Monthly Meeting; one for Robert Hough from Indian Spring Monthly Meeting; and, one for Robert Bartlett (a minor) from Third Haven Monthly Meeting.

On 11th day of 8th month, 1796, the folllwing certificates were produced: one for Izak Procter from a monthly meeting held at New York; one for Henry Kendall from Hardshaw Monthly Meeting in Lancashire, Old England, and directed to New York Monthly Meeting; and, one for Martha

McCoy from Deer Creek Monthly Meeting. William Carpenter "has removed with his family within the verge of Bradford Monthly Meeting in Pennsylvania without a certificate. Mary Morgan (wife of John) requested to be taken into membership. "

On 8th day of 9th month, 1796, the following certificates were produced: one for Gerrard Hopkins (of Johns) and Dorothy his wife from Indian Spring Monthly Meeting; one for Andrew and Joseph McCoy [McCay?], from Deer Creek Monthly Meeting; one for William Amoss (son of William Amoss, Jr.), a minor, from Gunpowder Monthly Meeting. Certificate produced for Elias Allibone (son of Benjamin) from Redstone Monthly Meeting in Pennsylvania, but it appears his residence is within the verge of Indian Spring Monthly Meeting, it is therefore endorsed to said meeting. Certificate produced for William Carpenter, his wife Rachel, and their five children, Lydia, George, Hannah, John and Joseph. Thomas Fisher requested a certificate of removal to Southern District of Philadelphia.

On 13th day of 10th month, 1796, Robert Cornthwait produced a certificate for his sister Phebe Allibone from Redstone Monthly Meeting, "and gave information that she deceased soon after her arrival at this place." Levis Janney produced a certificate from Abington Monthly Meeting in Pennsylvania for himself, his wife Mary, and their four children, Elizabeth, Isarel, George Fox and Benjamin Say. John Wallace Hopkins produced a certificate from York Monthly Meeting, and Deborah Wilson (wife of John) also produced one from Gunpowder Monthly Meeting for herself and seven children, Catharine, Grace, William, John, Anna, Thomas, and David. James Wilson requested a certificate to White Oak Swamp Monthly Meeting in Virginia, and Barker Thacker requested one to New York Monthly Meeting. Samuel Thomas (of Samuel) has removed within the verge of Indian Spring Monthly Meeting without requesting a certificate. Isaiah Jackson, Larkin Read, and Joseph Jay charged with accomplishing their marriages contrary to the good order.

On 10th day of 11th month, 1796, Margaret Sanderson produced a certificate from Gunpowder Monthly Meeting. Rachel Wells apologized for "disagreeing with her sister-in-law Elenor Richmore." John Dukehart and Parthenia Balderston declared their intention to marry.

On 8th day of 12th month, 1796, Mary Peters (formerly Trimble) charged with marrying contrary to the good order. Ann Rice (wife of Lawrence) has removed with her husband within the verge of Crooked Run Monthly

Meeting in Virginia. Keturak Moore produced a certificate for herslf and her mother Rebecca Moore from Gunpowder Monthly Meeting.

On 12th day of 1st month, 1797, the following certificates were produced: one for Samuel G. Jones from Philadelphia Monthly Meeting; one for Ezekiel Harlan from Nottingham Monthly Meeting; one for Daniel Byrnes from Wilmington Monthly Meeting; one for Samuel Byrnes and his wife Hannah with their daughter Ruth Byrnes, and Sarah Townsend (an apprentice), both minors, from the same place. Elisha Tyson and William Hayward were appointed to collect money for the relief of the Indians. Jonah Thomas was disowned for "retailing spiritous liquors and holding a slave which he refuses to manumit."

On 9th day of 3rd month, 1797, Hannah Green (formerly Naylor) charged with marrying contrary to the good order, was disowned on 14th day of 9th month, 1797.

On 13th day of 4th month, 1797, Mary Peters (formerly Trimble) disowned for marrying with assistance of a hireling. Israel Price and Hannah Brown declared their intention to marry. Ezekiel Harlan requested a certificate to Nottingham Monthly Meeting. John McKim "laid before this meeting a transaction which had taken place some time back respecting his having procured a quantity of light gold (or half Johannes) supposed to be coined in this place, for the West India market, and that he had forwarded them thither in trade, but the circumstance having occasioned a painful exercise to his mind, produced an offering as his testimony against the practice."

On 11th day of 5th month, 1795, the following certificates were produced: one for Andrew Ellicott, his wife Esther, and their son John (a minor) from Buckingham Monthly Meeting in Pennsylvania; one for William Procter from York Monthly Meeting in Great Britain; one for Charles Worthington (a minor) from Deer Creek Monthly Meeting; one for Philip Cole (a minor) from the same place; one for Elizabeth Husband from Motherkiln Monthly Meeting in Delaware; and, one for Rachel Weeks from Gunpowder Monthly Meeting. Samuel Thomas disowned for attending public plays and having his marriage accomplished contrary to the good order. Mary Jones requested that her four children, William, Anne, Robinson, and Deborah, be taken under care of friends.

On 8th day of 6th month, 1797, Johns Hopkins charged with accomplishing his marriage contrary to the good order of friends, was disowned on 13th day of 7th month, 1797.

On 13th day of 7th month, 1797, certificates were produced for Mahlon Ely from Deer Creek Monthly Meeting and for William Marsh from Warrington Monthly Meeting.

On 10th day of 8th month, 1797, Joseph Jackson was "disowned for deviating from plainess in dress and address, and also attending public places of diversion." Also, the following certificates were produced: one for Stephen Wilson, his wife Mercy, and their five children, Benjamin, Oliver, Isaac, Betsey, and Joseph, from Wilmington Monthly Meeting; one for Margaret Marsh from Warrington Monthly Meeting in Pennsylvania; and, one for Amos West (a minor) from Gunpowder Monthly Meeting.

On 14th day of 9th month, 1797, the following certificates were produced: one for Andrew Ellicott, Jr. from Indian Spring Monthly Meeting held at Sandy Spring; one for James W. Sloan from the Northern District of Philadelphia; one for Jasper Cope from said meeting; one for Israel Cope from Philadelphia Monthly Meeting; one for Isaiah Lancaster (a minor) from Gunpowder Monthly Meeting; one for Mary Mifflin from Motherkiln Monthly Meeting in Delaware; and, one for Lydia, Samuel, and Susanna Husband (minors), children of our friend Mary Mifflin, from same place. Isaac Tyson requested a certificate to Indian Spring Monthly Meeting in order to marry Elizabeth Thomas, a member thereof. Hannah Morgan (formerly Matthews) was charged with marrying contrary to the good order.

On 12th day of 10th month, 1797, Larkin Read was disowned for marrying by assistance of a hireling minister. Ely Balderston and Esther Brown declared their intention to marry, and their parents being present gave their consent. Francis Hopkins produced a certificate for herself and two minor children, Elizabeth and Joel, from Deer Creek Monthly Meeting.

On 9th day of 11th month, 1797, the following certificates were produced: one for Joseph Aborn from Salem Monthly Meeting in Massachusetts; one for William Copeland (a minor) from a monthly meeting held at the western branch, Isle of Wight County, Virginia; and, one for Elizabeth Marsh.

On1 4th day of 12th month, 1797, Isaac Johnson requested a certificate of removal to Southland Monthly Meeting in Virginia.

On 11th day of 1st month, 1798, the following certificates were produced: one for John Cornthwait from Gunpowder Monthly Meeting; one for Joseph Husband from Deer Creek Monthly Meeting; and, one for Joseph Wilson (a minor) from Deer Creek Monthly Meeting. James Brown apologized for "making too free use of spiritous liquors, attending public plays, gaming, using unbecoming language, joining in with divers corrupt associations, whilst under the pernicious effects of strong drink, frequently conducted in an undutiful manner to my parents, for all which I am not sorry." Robert Hough and Frances Martin declared their intentions to marry. Mary Matthews, daughter of William, requested a certificate of removal to Gunpowder Monthly Meeting.

On 8th day of 2nd month, 1798, the certificate previously endorsed to New York Monthly Meeting for Barker Thacker was returned, noting that "no such person is to be found within the verge thereof." John Trimble and Elizabeth Brown declared their intention to marry. Joseph Thornburgh requested that his four children, Deborah, Elizabeth, Margaret, and Sarah, be taken under care of friends. George W. Field requested a certificte of removal to Philadelphia Monthly Meeting. George Mason was charged with "making too free use of spiritous liquors." John Trimble (of William) reportedly had his marriage accomplished contrary to the good order [and it was later reported on 14th day of 6th month, 1798, that "a short time previous to his outgoing in marriage he cohabitted with another woman at a tavern whilst in an unmarried state under the character of her being his wife."].

On 8th day of 3rd month, 1798, William Matthews produced a certificate from Indian Spring Monthly Meeting for himself, his wife Elizabeth, and their seven children, Ann, Elizabeth, Rebecca, Miriam, Sarah, Samuel, Hanway, and Lydia.

On12th day of 4th month, 1798, Elizabeth Johns produced a certificate from Deer Creek Monthly Meeting for herself and her three minor children, Nathan, Ann, and Mary, and recommending her as a minister. Elizabeth Naylor requested a certificate to East Nottingham Monthly Meeting. William Riley, Gerrard T. Hopkins, Frances Hopkins, and Mary McKim were appointed to serve in the station of Elders. William Waterhouse and Ann Butler declared their intention to marry.

On 14th day of 6th month, 1798, the following certificates were produced: one for Robert Oddy from New York Monthly Meeting; one for John Wilson from Gunpowder Monthly Meeting; one for Samuel Matthews, his wife Ann, and their four minor children, Elizabeth, Sophia, Mary, and Samuel; one for Ann Price from the same place; one for Thomas Mecteer, Jr. from Wilmington Monthly Meeting; one for Susanna Martin from Third Haven Monthly Meeting; and, one for Charles Lukens and his wife Sarah, from Deer Creek Monthly Meeting. William Trimble condemned his misconduct in "being concerned in a contract made with the City Commissioners for paving one of the streets in Fells Point and at the same time sat as a Commissioner for making the same." Peter Perine charged with having his marriage accomplished contrary to the good order.

On 9th day of 8th month, 1798, the following certificates were produced: one for John Jewitt from Deer Creek Monthly Meeting; one for Moses Janney (a minor) from Fairfax Monthly Meeting; one for Ruth Dickenson (who did not appear due to being in an infirm state) from Gunpowder Monthly Meeting; one for Mary Hussey from the same place; one for Hannah Dulton [Dutton?] from Phildelphia Monthly Meeting; and, one for Abel Spencer, his wife Rebecca, and their seven minor children, Elizabeth, William, Sarah, Rebecca, Abel, Reuben, and Joseph. Joseph Townsend reported he has received $35 in subscriptions towards reprinting the journal of George Fox. Jesse Madcalf [Medcalf] requested a certificate of removal to Hopewell Monthly Meeting in Virginia. John Morgan, Jr. and Ann Matthews (of William) declared their intention to marry.

On 13th day of 9th month, 1798, the following certificates were produced: one for William Husband from Motherkiln Monthly Meeting in Delaware; one for James Hill from Nottingham Monthly Meeting at Little Britain; one for Aaron Packer from Warrington Monthly Meeting; one for Jonathan Marsh from the same place; one for Nixon Wilson from Deer Creek Monthly Meeting; and, one for Catharine Hooker from Gunpowder Monthly Meeting.

On 11th day of 10th month, 1798, the following certificates were produced: one for Winston Smith Dallam (a minor) from Deer Creek Monthly Meeting; and, one for Samuel Harlan from Concord Monthly Meeting and directed to Pipe Creek Monthly Meeting. Marriage of John Morgan and Ann Matthews reported to have been orderly accomplished. Joseph Thornburgh requested a certificate to Indian Spring Monthly Meeting in order to marry Cassandria Ellicott, a member thereof. Reported that Henry Worthington "has joined himself as a volunteer in a military company to learn the art of war." Complaint made against Sarah Tyson (formerly Jackson) for marrying contrary to the good order. Rebecca Moore requested a certificate of removal to Gunpowder Monthly Meeting.

On 8th day of 11th month, 1798, the following certificates were produced: one for Oliver Fuller from Salem Monthly Meeting in Massachusetts; one for Jesse West from Chester Monthly Meeting at Providence, Pennsylvania; and, one for Elizabeth Naylor from Nottingham Monthly Meeting. Catharine Daughdy requested to be joined in membership. Complaint made against John Lee for "taking an oath to admit him into the office of Constable and for administering the same in the execution thereof."

On 13th day of 12th month, 1798, our ancient friend Ruth Byrnes produced a certificate from Wilmington Monthly Meeting, and Thomas Webster produced one from Indian Spring Monthly Meeting. Joshua Reynolds requested to be taken into membership.

On 10th day of 1st month, 1799, the following certificates were produced: one for Ennion Williams and his wife Hannah from Indian Spring Monthly Meeting; one for Isaac Vore, his wife Rebecca, and their five minor children, Sarah, Rachel, Benjamin, Jacob, and Isaac; one for Nathan Johns from Deer Creek Monthly Meeting; and, one for Lydia Green from Fairfax Monthly Meeting. Henry Kendall, "having lately embarked for Europe, informed this meeting in writing that he requested a certificate of removal to Westminster Monthly Meeting." Martha Norbury (formerly Burgess) and Julia Trimble (formerly Hugo) reportedly had their marriages accomplished contrary to the good order.

On 14th day of 2nd month, 1799, the following certificates were produced: one for Cassandra Thornburgh, wife of Joseph Thornburgh, one for Sarah Hopkins, one for Richard Carter, and one for Elizabeth Tyson, wife of Isaac Tyson, all from Indian Spring Monthly Meeting; one for Samuel Reed and his wife Elizabeth and their infant daughter Matilda, from Gunpowder Monthly Meeting; and, one for Isaac Evans (a minor) from Greenwich Monthly Meeting in New Jersey. Jacob Pugh reportedly had his marriage accomplished contrary to the good order. Thomas Jackson charged with "neglecting the attendance of our religious meetings, associating himself with unprofitable company and had clandestinely taken the property of another and felloniously applied it to his own use."

On 14th day of 3rd month, 1799, John E. Rees apologized "for bringing an action of law for the recovery of a just debt against a person under dealings at the time but retaining a right of membership amongst Friends." Isaac Webster, of Deer Creek Monthly Meeting, and Elizabeth Hopkins, of this meeting, declared their intention to marry. James Brown and Catharine Dukehart declared their intention to marry. Dorothy Webster produced a certificate from Gunpowder Monthly Meeting, last directed to Deer Creek Monthly Meeting, and endorsed by that meeting to this meeting.

On 11th day of 4th month, 1799, Enoch Underwood and his wife Mary produced a certificate for themselves and their three children, James, Benjamin, and Ann, from Warrington Monthly Meeting in Pennsylvania; also one for Elizabeth Lowden from Indian Spring Monthly Meeting. Reported that Thomas Jackson had left these parts, so there was no opportunity to talk to him about his misconduct. Isaac Webster produced a certificate from Deer Creek Monthly Meeting informing of his clearness for marriage.

On 9th day of 5th month, 1799, the marriages of Isaac Webster to Elizabeth Hopkins and James Brown to Catharine Dukehart were reported to have been orderly accomplished. Mary Jackson (daughter of Isaiah) requested a certificate of removal to Third Haven Monthly Meeting. Vincent Bonsall and his wife Sarah produced a certificate for themselves and their two minor children, William and Catharine, from Wilmington Monthly Meeting.

On 13th day of 6th month, 1799, the following certificates were produced: one for Daniel Hanson from Salem Monthly Meeting in Massachusetts; one for John Ransome and his wife Elizabeth and their daughter Elizabeth from Amawalk Monthly Meeting in New York; one for Oliver Matthews and his wife Phebe from Gunpowder Monthly Meeting held at Little Falls; and, one for Samuel Naylor and his wife Rebecca from the same place.

On 11th day of 7th month, 1799, the following certificates were produced: one for Mary Perine from Gunpowder Monthly Meeting; one for James Neal and one for Thomas Sherwood, both from Third Haven Montly Meeting; one for George Harris, his wife Susanna, and their four children, Mary, Beulah, Ann, and George, from Warrington Monthly Meeting; and, one for Samuel Jackson (a minor) from New Garden Monthly Meeting of Chester County, Pennsylvania. Elizabeth Webster (wife of Isaac) requested a certificate of removal to Deer Creek Monthly Meeting.

On 8th day of 8th month, 1799, Elias Ellicott was released from station of Overseer and Ennion Williams was appointed to serve in his stead. Hannah Underwood (wife of Abraham) produced a certificate for herself and two children, Jane and Elihu, from Warrington Monthly Meeting, and Massey Webb also produced one from Deer Creek Monthly Meeting.

On 12th day of 9th month, 1799, the following certificates were produced: one for Benjamin Fell, his wife Jane, and their two children, Mary and Leah, from New Garden Monthly Meeting in Chester County, Pennsylvania; one for John Dillon and one for Thomas Brown, both from Gunpowder Monthly Meeting; one for James Fisher from York Monthly Meeting; and, one for Dennis Read from Indian Spring Monthly Meeting. William Amos, Jr. and Elizabeth Hugo declared their intention to marry. Izak Proctor requested a certificate in order to marry Rebecca Farquhar, a member of Falls Monthly Meeting in Bucks County, Pennsylvania. Winston Smith Dallam charged with "deviating in plainess in dress and address and that he hath joined himself to a military company to learn the art of war."

On 10th day of 10th month, 1799, the following certificates were produced: one for John Harlan from Nottingham Monthly Meeting at Little Britain; one for Rachel Reynolds (wife of Joshua) from the same place; one for William Hayward, Jr., his wife Kezia, and their five minor children, Isaac, John, Elizabeth, Jonathan, and Maryann, from Indian Spring Monthly Meeting; and, one for Thomas Micmillan [McMillen], his wife Jane, and their two minor children, Edith and Deborah, from Deer Creek Monthly Meeting. William Amos, Jr. produced a certificate from Gunpowder Monthly Meeting with his parents consent to marry Elizabeth Hugo. Nathan Johns, Jr. and Joseph Wilson requested certificates of removal to Westland Monthly Meeting in Pennsylvania. Reported that Samuel G. Jones had his marriage accomplished "by the assistance of a hireling teacher to a woman not of our society." Abigail Medcalf requested to be taken under care of Friends. Eunice Starr (formerly Fisher) had married contrary to the good order.

On 14th day of 11th month, 1799, the following certificates were produced: one for Jared Price from Gunpowder Monthly Meeting; and, one for Stephen Cook, Jr. from London Grove Monthly Meeting in Pennsylvania. Marriage of William Amoss, Jr. and Elizabeth Hugo reported to have been orderly accomplished. George England of Gunpowder Monthly Meeting, and Catharine Hooker, declared their intention to marry. Isaac Brooks and Sarah Haywood declared their intention to marry. Thomas McMillen requested a certificate of removal to Warrington Monthly Meeting for himself, his wife Jane, and their two minor children, Edith and Deborah. Certificate recently forwarded to Deer Creek Monthly Meeting for Elizabeth Webster "it appears did not reach there until the decease of her husband and she being since returned amongst us the same was produced and she considered a member of this meeting."

On 12th day of 12th month, 1799, the following certificates were produced: one for Isaac Kinsey, his wife Rachel, and their seven minor children: Isaac, Mary, Hannh, Jacob, Joseph, Oliver, and Thomas; and, one for Daniel Larabee and his wife Ann from New York Monthly Meeting. "A copy of a minute from Indian Spring Monthly Meeting held the 15th of the last month was produced and read, informing that the last Quarterly Meeting had directed that monthly meeting to furnish this with a correct list of the members constituting Elk Ridge Preparative Meeting in order for them to become a branch of this monthly meeting, and the aforementioned list being produced is as follows and they received accordingly: William Hayward, a minister, and his wife Sidney Hayward, in the station of an elder and overseer, and their three children, John Hayward, Rachel Hayward, and Rebecca Hayward; Priscilla Plummer (widow) and her two children, Thomas Plummer and James Plummer; Judith Ellicott (widow) and her two children, Joseph Ellicott and Benjamin Ellicott; John Pierpoint and his sister Ann Pierpoint and her daughter Deborah Pierpoint; Jonathan Ellicott, in the station of an overseer, and his wife Sarah Ellicott and their six children, Samuel Ellicott, Elizabeth Ellicott, Nathaniel Ellicott, William Ellicott, Sarah Ellicott, and Frances Ellicott; George Ellicott and his wife Elizabeth Ellicott and their four children, James Ellicott, Elizabeth Ellicott, Martha Ellicott, and George Ellicott; Benjamin Rich, in the station of an overseer, and his wife Sarah Rich and their two children, Ann Rich and John Rich; Samuel Smith and his wife Hannah Smith and their three children, Elias Smith, George Smith, and Esther Smith; Joseph Atkinson and his wife Rachel Atkinson and their six children, Sarah Atkinson, Rachel Atkinson, Ruth Atkinson, Isaac Atkinson, Mary Atkinson, and Joseph Atkinson; Joseph Heston and his wife Ann Heston and their five children, Samuel Heston, Joseph Heston, Phebe Heston, Letitia Heston, and William Heston; James Gillingham and his wife Elizabeth Gillingham in the station of an overseer, and their four [sic] children, John Gillingham, William Gillingham, George Gillingham, Elizabeth Gillingham, and Ezra Gillingham; Ann Read (wife of Jacob Read) and her three children, Mary Brown, Charles Read, and Joseph Read; Hannah Pierpoint (widow) and her two children, Walter Pierpoint and Mary Pierpoint. Single women: Sarah Atkinson (widow),

Abigail Atkinson, Sarah Brelsford. Single men: Joseph Pierpoint (a minister), Misael Pierpoint, Joshua Stewart, John Ellicott, Samuel Godfrey, Elias Allibone, Amos Gillingham." George England produced a certificate with "the consent of the surviving parents being had" for his marriage to Catharine Hooker. James Naylor of Gunpowder Monthly Meeting and Margaret Marsh declared their intention to marry. Certificate produced for Mary Stokely from Motherkiln Monthly Meeting in Delaware "with information that she was now returned, but as it appears that she lived some considerable time amongst us." Marriage of George England and Catherine Hooker reported accomplished in an orderly manner. Complaint against Grace Knox (formerly Coats) for "marrying contrary to the rules of our discipline," and also against Mary Brown (formerly Read) for marrying in the same manner. Elizabeth Amoss requested a certificate for herself and her son Samuel Hugo to Gunpowder Monthly Meeting. William Copeland (a minor) requested a certificate of removal to Western Branch in Isle of Wight County, Virginia.

On 13th day of 2nd month, 1800, the following certificates were produced: one for Elisha Tolbot (a minor) and one for Jacob Janney (a minor), both from Fairfax Monthly Meeting; one for Willing Underwood (a minor) from Deer Creek Monthly Meeting; one for Hannah Brown from Philadelphia Monthly Meeting; and, one for Edward Wilson from Knarsborough [?] Monthly Meeting in Yorkshire, Great Britain, directed to friends of Boston Monthly Meeting "but it appearing that there is no monthly meeting held in that place was reason of its being produced here." Baltimore Preparative Meeting brings complaint against George Hussey "for having his marriage accomplished by the assistance of a hireling teacher to a woman who there is reason to believe has a former husband still living - he is also publickly charged with having by her two children in his late wife's time which he neither denies nor takes pains to clear himself of." Also complaint made against William Marsh and James Hill for having their marriages "accomplished by the assistance of a hireling teacher."

On 13th day of 3rd month, 1800, Joseph Hews produced a certificate from Wilmington Monthly Meeting, and Ann Sheppard (wife of Thomas) produced one from Gunpowder Monthly Meeting. Gideon Hughes requested to be taken into membership with friends.

On 10th day of 4th month, 1800, the following certificates were produced: one for Rebecca Proctor (wife of Izak) from Falls Monthly Meeting in Bucks

County, Pennsylvania; one for Eli Plummer, his wife Alice, and their son James, from New Garden Monthly Meeting in Pennsylvania; one for Jacob Norbury from York Monthly Meeting in Pennsylvania; one for Caleb Bonsall from London Grove Monthly Meeting; and, one for John D. Sutton from Fairfax Monthly Meeting in Virginia. Samuel G. Jones was disowned for "marrying by assistance of a hireling teacher to a woman not of our society." Complaint made against Aaron Packer for "not attending meeting, deviating in dress and address, and joining himself to a military company to learn the art of war." Complaint made against Joseph Ford for "retailing spiritous liquors and making use of same to excess." Complaint made against Joseph Aborn for having "engaged in business beyond his ability to manage and conveying his property to one of his creditors, to the inury of the others, and also leaving the parts for a time without their consent." John Webster Wilson, Jr., of Deer Creek Monthly Meeting, and Lucretia Tyson declared their intention to marry. Benjamin Amoss and Elizabeth Cornthwait declared their intention to marry.

On 8th day of 5th month, 1800, the following certificates were produced: one for Thomas Jewett from Deer Creek Monthly Meeting; one for Gravener and Samuel Jefferies (minors), and Phebe Carr, all from Gunpowder Monthly Meeting; and, one for David Houlton (a minor) from Northern District of Philadelphia. Reported that Winston Smith Dallam had left these parts, so no opportunity to present copy of testimony against him for joining the military to learn the art of war, and he was disowned. Daniel Hanson requested a certificate to Black Water Monthly Meeting in Virginia. Oliver Matthews (son of William) requested a certificate for himself, his wife Phebe, and their son Joel, to Gunpowder Monthly Meeting.

On 12th day of 6th month, 1800, Samuel Cookson produced a certificate for himself and his wife Olive and their two minor children, Mary and Joseph, from Nottingham Monthly Meeting, and Evan Harry produced one from Kennett Monthly Meeting. Marriage of Benjamin Amos and Elizabeth Cornthwait was reportedly accomplished orderly. Reported that Thomas Mecteer, Jr. "having been placed an apprentice to a friend, hath left his service in a clandestine manner." Robert Bartlett requested a certificate to Third Haven Monthly Meeting.

On 10th day of 7th month, 1800, the marriage of John W. Wilson and Lurcetia Tyson reported orderly accomplished. Sarah Belford [Brelsford?] requested a certificate to Falls Monthly Meeting in Bucks County, Pennsylvania. Certificate produced for Joshua Stapleton, his wife Susanna, and their two minor children, Samuel and Susanna, from Gunpowder Monthly Meeting, and also one for Mary Jewel from Wrightstown Monthly Meeting in Bucks County.

On 14th day of 8th month, 1800, Aaron Packer was disowned for "enlisting on board a ship of war," and Joseph Aborn was disowned for "entering into contracts beyond his ability to comply.. [causing].. injury to his creditors." Jaspar Cope requested a certificate to Northern District of Philadelphia in order to marry Rebecca Shoemaker, a member thereof. Complaint made against Henry Hopkins for "attending a dancing school as a scholar." Nathan Johns requested a certificate for himself, his wife Elizabeth and their minor daughter, Mary, to Westland Monthly Meeting in Pennsylvania, and also one for Ann Johns to the same place. The following certificates were produced: one for Samuel Canby and his wife Elizabeth from Darby Monthly Meeting; one for Joseph Hopkins (a minor) from Indian Spring Monthly Meeting; one for Robert Cornthwait from Gunpowder Monthly Meeting; one for Mary Helms from Crooked Run Monthly Meeting; one for Pricilla Morgan from Gunpowder Monthly Meeting; and, one for Mary Jackson from Third Haven Monthly Meeting.

On 11th day of 9th month, 1800, reported that Robert Cornthwait had deceased. Ann Johns produced a certificate from Concord Monthly Meeting.

On 9th day of 10th month, 1800, Richard Carter requested a certificate to Westland Monthly Meeting in Pennsylvania.

On 13th day of 11th month, 1800, the following certificates were produced: one for Peter Pollard, his wife Elizabeth and their four minor children, Eunice, Mary, David, and Sarah, from Nantucket Monthly Meeting; one for Israel Pleasants, his wife Ann and their eight minor children, Samuel, Thomas, Franklin, Mary, Elizabeth, Ann, Israel Pemberton, and Hannah; one for Joseph Pleasants from the same place; and, one for William Hambleton, his wife Mary, and their seven minor children, Benjamin, James, Charles, Rachel, Joseph, Mary, and William, from New Garden Monthly Meeting in Chester County, Pennsylvania. Joseph Husband requested a certificate to Deer Creek Monthly Meeting to marry Sarah Brown, a member thereof. Martha Hill requested a certificate to Gunpowder Monthly Meeting. Complaint made against Elizabeth Webster (formerly Thornburgh) for marrying with assistance of a hireling. Certificate produced for Marsha Bond from Horsham Monthly Meeting in Pennsylvania, but since she had since removed within the verge of Deer Creek Monthly Meeting, it was forwarded to that meeting.

On 11th day of 12th month, 1800, complaints made against James Fisher and Joseph Hughes for having their marriages accomplished contrary to the good order amongst friends.

LITTLE FALLS MONTHLY MEETING, BIRTHS AND DEATHS, 1738-1800

"Record of Membership of Little Falls Monthly Meeting, Maryland, 1738 to 1848 = 110 years. The earliest date found is that of the birth of Israel Morris in 1738 and the latest is the death of Mary Hollingsworth in 1848. Little Falls Monthly Meeting was established in 1815, which should therefore be the date of the commencement of this book. The next book of membership was opened in 1846 by Benjamin Ferris, and the third one, now in use, in 1881---signed, Edwin Blackburn, the 26th day of 6th month, 1884."

"The following transcript of Joel Carter's memorandum of the births of his family is made from an apprehension that it is not recorded at the meeting from whence they came: Hannah Carter, daughter of Joel and Margaret Carter, b. 23rd day of 9th month, 1799; Isabel Carter, her sister, b. 23rd day of 11th month, 1800; Sarah Carter, her sister, b. 28th day of 6th month, 1802; John Carter, her brother, b. 1st day of 8th month, 1803; Kirwin[?] Carter, his brother, b. 14th day of 4th month, 1805; Joel Carter, his brother, b, 31st day of 12th month, 1806; Edith Carter, his sister, b. 25th day of 9th month, 1808; Enos Carter, her brother, b. 24th day of 4th month, 1810; Ellis Carter, his brother, b. 28th day of 12th month, 1811; Mercy Carter, his sister, b. 5th day of 7th month, 1813; Levi Carter, her brother, b. 25th day of 8th month, 1814; Margaret A. Carter, his sister, b. 10th day of 6th month, 1816; and, James Carter, her brother, b. 12th day of 3rd month, 1819."

William Amos, b. 20th day of 8th month, 1750; his wife Elizabeth Amos, b. 15th day of 3rd month, 1753; his son William H. Amos, b. 26th day of 2nd month, 1782; his dau. Susanna Amos, b. 3rd day of 6th month, 1789; his dau. Elizabeth Amos, b. 8th day of 6th month, 1791; his son Lemuel H. Amos, b. 21st day of 2nd month, 1793. [Note: A later entry in the records states that the first wife of William Amos was Susanna and his second wife was Elizabeth. Additional notes in the 1846 register on the children of William and Susanna Amoss [sic]: Sarah Amoss married Thomas Morgan in Baltimore; Benjamin H. Amoss was buried in Baltimore in 1800; Ann Amoss married Daniel Cunningham in Baltimore; Hannah Amoss married John Harlan; Martha Amoss married Moses Dillon; Thomas Amoss was buried in or near Henrico Co., Virginia; Susanna Amoss married William Wood of Smithfield, Ohio].

James Amos, b. 31st day of 1st month, 1764; his wife Hannah Amos, b. 19th day of 11th month, 1770; their son William Lee Amos, b. 26th day of 7th month, 1796; their son Elias Ellicott Amos, b. 13th day of 10th month, 1799; their son Olver Huff Amos, b. 18th day of 9th month, 1801.

Elihu Brown, b. in 2nd month, 1754; his wife Margaret Brown, b. in 8th month, 1760; their dau. Hannah Brown, b. in 5th month, 1783; their dau. Amy Brown, b. in 12th month, 1785; their son Stephen Brown, b. 13th day of 6th month, 1787; their dau. Lydia Brown, b. in 7th month, 1791; their dau. Rachel Brown, b. in 9th month, 1796; their son Jehu Brown, b. in 7th month, 1799.

Stephen Brown, b. 13th day of 6th month, 1787; his wife Achsah Brown, b. 10th day of 12th month, 1792.

Amos Benson, b. 12th day of 12th month, 1779; his wife Margaret Benson, b. 16th day of 7th month, 1784.

Levi Benson, b. 9th day of 2nd month, 1783; his wife Mary Benson, b. 22nd day of 6th month, 1781.

Benjamin Benson, b. 16th day of 3rd month, 1785.

Jesse Benson, b. 11th day of 7th month, 1790.

Edward Brinton, b. 4th day of 11th month, 1780.

Rebecca Beans, b. 21st day of 8th month, 1786.

Isaac Beans, b. 3rd day of 9th month, 1776; his wife Hannah Beans, b. 23rd day of 10th month, 1784.

George Davis, b. 16th day of 9th month, 1776.

George England, b. 3rd day of 9th month, 1752; his wife Catharine England, b. 21st day of 1st month, 1764; their dau. Sarah Hooker England, b. 3rd day of 10th month, 1800; their son Thomas Hooker England, b. 5th day of 1st month, 1803; their dau. Elizabeth Dutton England, b. 16th day of 4th month, 1805.

Virgil Eachus, b, 7th day of 9th month, 1765; his wife Mary Eachus, b. 13th day of 8th month, 1780; his son Joseph Eachus, b. 4th day of 11th month, 1793; his son Obed Eachus, b. 18th day of 9th month, 1795; his dau. Mahalah Eachus, b. 5th day of 11th month, 1802; his son Abner Eachus, b. 21st day of 10th month, 1804; his son Preston Eachus, b. 5th day of 2nd month, 1807; their son Vanleer Eachus, b. 29th day of 6th month, 1808; their dau. Bathsheba Eachus, b. 17th day of 12th month, 1809; their son Minshall Eachus, b. 1st day of 6th month, 1811; their dau. Sarah Eachus, b. 18th day of 2nd month, 1813; their son Virgil Eachus, b. 12th day of 7th month, 1815.

Hannah Ely, b. 1st day of 1st month, 1758.

Hugh Ely, b. 11th day of 9th month, 1783.

Thomas Ely, b. 10th day of 1st month, 1791.

David Ely, b. 23rd day of 11th month, 1793.

Bartholomew Fussell, b. 20th day of 9th month, 1754; his wife Rebecca Fussell, b. 9th day of 10th month, 1751; their dau. Esther Fussell, b. 18th day of 3rd month, 1782; their son Solomon Fussell, b. 28th day of 6th month, 1789; their son Bartholomew Fussell, b. 9th day of 1st month, 1794; their dau. Rebecca Fussell, b. 21st day of 4th month, 1796.

Joseph Fussell, b. 26th day of 4th month, 1787 [Ed. Note: He was listed separately from the above family, but he was probably another son of Bartholomew Fussell]; his wife Elizabeth Fussell, b. 19th day of 2nd month, 1790.

Martha Forwood, b. 29th day of 6th month, 1762.

Esther Garrett, wife of Jonah Garrett, b. 18th day of 6th month, 1770; their children were Eliza Garrett, Jesse Garrett, and Abigail Garrett [no birth dates given].

Nathaniel Hollingsworth, b. 4th day of 8th month, 1755; his wife Abigail Hollingsworth, b. 6th day of 4th month, 1759; their son Robert Hollingsworth, b. 17th day of 5th month, 1784; their dau. Hannah Hollingsworth, b. 31st day of 3rd month, 1786; their son Thomas Hollingsworth, b. 5th day of 8th month, 1791; their son Eli Hollingsworth, b. 1st day of 9th month, 1793; their son Jesse Hollingsworth, b. 22nd day of 10th month, 1796; their dau. Abigail Hollingsworth, b. 12th day of 2nd month, 1799; their son Nathaniel Hollingsworth, b. 20th day of 2nd month, 1801; their son John Hollingsworth, b. 11th day of 1st month, 1805.

Robert Hollingsworth, b. 17th day of 5th month, 1784; his wife Elizabeth Hollingsworth, b. 17th day of 4th month, 1792.

John Harlan, b. 20th day of 11th month, 1777; his wife Hannah Harlan, b. 21st day of 5th month, 1779.

John Hutton, b. 19th day of 12th month, 1760; his wife Sarah Hutton, b. 16th day of 10th month, 1772.

Mary Harry, b. 19th day of 2nd month, 1756.

Abraham Huff, b. 25th day of 11th month, 1779; his wife Mercy Huff, b. 30th day of 4th month, 1780.

Nathaniel Hoskins, son of William and Martha Hoskins, b. 17th day of 5th month, 1774.

Elizabeth Hoskins, dau. of John Hoskins and Elizabeth Cheyney Hoskins, b. 26th day of 2nd month, 1784.

Abner Jones, b. 16th day of 9th month, 1762; his wife Maria Jones [no birth date given]; his son Yearsly Jones, b. 23rd day of 8th month, 1792; their dau. Hannah Jones, b. 5th day of 12th month, 1814.

Rebecca James, wife of Frederick James, b. 1st day of 3rd month, 1776.

Jesse Lancaster, b. 1st day of 3rd month, 1751; his wife Elizabeth Lancaster, b. 29th day of 7th month, 1768; his dau. Rachel Lancaster, b. 27th day of 5th month, 1790; their son Joseph Lancaster, b. 10th day of 9th month, 1798; their dau. Esther Lancaster, b. 2nd day of 5th month, 1802; their son John Lancaster, b. 28th day of 6th month, 1804; their dau. Julia Lancaster, b. 14th day of 2nd month, 1807; their dau. Hannah Lancaster, b. 22nd day of 3rd month, 1810.

David Lee, b. in 11th month, 1740.

Ralph S. Lee, son of David Lee, b. 14th day of 4th month, 1780.

Elizabeth Lee, dau. of William and Margaret, b. ---- [blank].

Israel Morris, b. 16th day of 6th month, 1738.

Sarah Morris, b. in 1768.

David Malsby, b. 14th day of 6th month, 1750.

Sarah Malsby, b. 1st day of 10th month, 1752.

Frances Malsby, b. 11th day of 12th month, 1794.

Samuel McConnell, b. 13th day of 2nd month, 1763; his wife Frances McConnell, b. 10th day of 1st month, 1762; their dau. Mary McConnell, b. 24th day of 1st month, 1799; their son James McConnell, b. 14th day of 10th month, 1801.

Frances Mechem, b. 11th day of 6th month, 1764; his wife Naomi Mechem, b. 22nd day of 4th month, 1771; their son John Mechem, b. 23rd day of 6th month, 1792; their dau. Lydia Mechem, b. 26th day of 2nd month, 1795; their son Richard Mechem, b. 29th day of 5th month, 1798; their son Isaac Mechem, b. 8th day of 4th month, 1800; their son George Mechem, b. 4th day of 3rd month, 1804; their son William Mechem, b. 8th day of 6th month, 1807.

Ann Mason, wife of John Mason, b. 6th day of 6th month, 1759; their son Howard Mason, b. 12th day of 10th month, 1789; their dau. Susan Mason, b. 2nd day of 2nd month, 1792.

Mary Malsby, wife of Morris Malsby, b. ---- [blank]; their son David Lee Malsby, b. ---- [blank].

Sarah McComas, wife of James McComas, b. 10th day of 3rd month, 1774.

David Preston, b. 20th day of 9th month, 1774; his wife Judith Preston, b. 21st day of 12th month, 1776; their son Isaac Hollingsworth Preston, b. 10th day of 1st month, 1798; their dau. Hannah Preston, b. 3rd day of 11th month, 1801; their son Silvester Bills Preston, b. 23rd day of 8th month, 1804; their dau. Rachel Preston, b. 12th day of 5th month, 1807; their son Edmond Preston, b. 25th day of 9th month, 1814.

Children of Abner Parsons: Elizabeth D. Parsons, b. 5th day of 2nd month, 1791; Joseph Dyer Parsons, b. 1st day of 2nd month, 1793; Abraham Parsons, b. 1st day of 2nd month, 1795.

Samuel Reed, b. 2nd day of 4th month, 1771.

Matilda Reed, b. 17th day of 3rd month, 1797.

Amos Smith, son of Samuel and Rachel Smith, b. 18th day of 8th month, 1779; his wife Rebecca Smith, b. 26th day of 8th month, 1784.

Aquila Starr, b. 29th day of 7th month, 1771; his wife Abigail Starr, b. 29th day of 10th month, 1776; their dau. Sidney Starr, b. 3rd day of 3rd month, 1797; their son Engle Starr, b. 17th day of 3rd month, 1798; their son James Starr, b. 31st day of 7th month, 1799; their dau. Molly Starr, b. 29th day of

9th month, 1803; their son Joseph Starr, b. 23rd day of 12th month, 1807; their dau. Sally Ann Starr, b. 13th day of 5th month, 1811.

John Slogdon, b. 11th day of 9th month, 1749.

Sarah Spencer, b. 24th day of 5th month, 1745.

Mahlon Spencer, b. 23rd day of 2nd month, 1771; his wife Elenor Spencer, b. 11th day of 3rd month, 1780; their dau. Ann Spencer, b. 11th day of 5th month, 1800; their son William Lee Spencer, b. 13th day of 9th month, 1803; their dau. Mahalah Spencer, b. 23rd day of 10th month, 1805; their son Enoch Spencer, b. 15th day of 1st month, 1808; their dau. Elizabeth Spencer, b. 9th day of 9th month, 1810; their son Mahlon Spencer, b. 1st day of 2nd month, 1812; their twin daughters, Hannah and Eliza Spencer, b. 29th day of 7th month, 1814.

Elizabeth Spencer (widow), b. 3rd day of 11th month, 1778.

Hannah Spencer, b. 14th day of 12th month, 1798.

William Trego, b. 16th day of 3rd month, 1744.

Thomas Trego, son of William Trego, b. 15th day of 7th month, 1769; his wife Sarah Trego, b. 9th day of 1st month, 1768; their son Samuel Trego, b. 6th day of 4th month, 1792; their son William Trego, b. 19th day of 6th month, 1796; their dau. Harriet Trego, b. 30th day of 3rd month, 1798; their dau. Francenia Trego, b. 19th day of 4th month, 1800; their son Albert David Trego, b. 16th day of 4th month, 1802; their dau. Sarah Trego, b. 7th day of 8th month, 1805; their dau. Hannah Trego, b. 6th day of 5th month, 1807; their son James D. Trego, b. 9th day of 12th month, 1810.

David Tucker, b. in 12th month, 1760; his wife Elizabeth Tucker, b. in 10th month, 1763; their son James Tucker, b. in 7th month, 1791; their dau. Hannah Tucker, b. in 2nd month, 1793; their dau. Elizabeth Tucker, b. in 6th month, 1798; their son David Tucker, b. in 12th month, 1800; their son Samuel Tucker, b. in 9th month, 1802; their dau. Ann Tucker, b. in 11th month, 1804.

James Tucker, son of David and Elizabeth Tucker, b. in 7th month, 1791; his wife Rachel Tucker Tucker [sic], b. in 6th month, 1794.

Children of John Trimble: Elizabeth Sims Trimble, b. 26th day of 10th month, 1799; Thomas Brogden Trimble, b. 31st day of 1st month, 1806.

Jacob Vore, b. 25th day of 3rd month, 1787; his wife Elisabeth Vore, b. 23rd day of 4th month, 1796.

Jonathan Vanhorn, b. in 9th month, 1792.

Thomas West, b. 10th day of 10th month, 1757.

Enos West, son of Thomas, b. 23rd day of 12th month, 1777; his wife, Rebecca West, b. 3rd day of 1st month, 1773.

Mahlon H. West, son of Thomas and Elizabeth West, b. 24th day of 7th month, 1789; his wife Mary West, b. 3rd day of 10th month, 1788.

Jonathan Warner, b. 27th day of 1st month, 1789; his wife Sarah Warner, b. 20th day of 1st month, 1788.

William Whitson, b. 16th day of 5th month, 1780.

John White, b. 5th day of 5th month, 1781.

Jonathan Pugh, b. 16th day of 3rd month, 1763; his wife Esther Pugh, b. 30th day of 11th month, 1770; their son Eli Pugh, b. 13th day of 5th month, 1793; their dau. Jane Pugh, b. 12th day of 11th month, 1794; their dau. Rachel Pugh, b. 10th day of 6th month, 1796; their dau. Abigail Pugh, b. 12th day of 12th month, 1797; their dau. Alice Pugh, b. 16th day of 5th month, 1799; their dau. Lydia Pugh, b. 3rd day of 2nd month, 1801; their dau. Hannah Pugh, b. 2nd day of 10th month, 1802; their son Job Pugh, b. 13th day of 5th month, 1805; their son Jonathan Pugh, b. 28th day of 1st month, 1809; their son Stephen Pugh, b. 8th day of 10th month, 1810; their son Levi Pugh, b. 14th day of 11th month, 1812; their son Louis D. Pugh, b. 16th day of 3rd month, 1816.

"List of Members of Little Falls Monthly Meeting" [Compiled between 1846 and 1884 by the clerks of the meeting, only those born in, or prior to, 1800 have been copied here]:

William Lee Amoss, b. 26th day of 7th month, 1796.

William H. Amoss, b. 26th day of 3rd month, 1782.

David Ambler, b. 3rd day of 6th month, 1790.

Margaret Ambler, b. 25th day of 11th month, 1795.

Amos Benson, b. 12th day of 12th month, 1779.

Margaret Benson, b. 16th day of 7th month, 1784.

Benjamin Benson, b. 16th day of 3rd month, 1785.

Jonathan Beans, b. 19th day of 12th month, 1791.

Elizabeth Beans (his wife), b. 15th day of 1st month, 1793.

Joel Carter, b. 15th day of 9th month, 1774.
Hannah Carter, b. 31st day of 3rd month, 1786.
Mary Caldwell, b. 2nd day of 3rd month, 1792.
Elizabeth A. Hoskins, b. 6th day of 6th month, 1792.
Abigail Hollingsworth, Jr., b. 13th day of 12th month, 1798.
Alice Hendon, d. in 1871 in the 72nd year of her age.
Robert Hollingsworth, b. 7th day of 5th month, 1784.
Elizabeth W. Hollingsworth, b. 17th day of 4th month, 1792.
Eli Hollingsworth, b. 1st day of 9th month, 1791.
Asahel Haviland, b. 15th day of 8th month, 1786.
Esther Haviland, b. 18th day of 3rd month, 1794.
Rebecca James, b. 1st day of 3rd month, 1776.
Elizabeth Lancaster, b. 29th day of 7th month, 1768.
Ralph S. Lee, b. 14th day of 4th month, 1780.
Abraham Merritt, b. 4th day of 9th month, 1790.
Ann P. Merritt, b. 22nd day of 3rd month, 1798.
Benjamin P. Moore, b. 6th day of 12th month, 1791.
Naomi Mechem, b. 22nd day of 4th month, 1771.
Lydia Mechem, b. 26th day of 2nd month, 1795.
William H. Morgan, b. 10th day of 7th month, 1796.
Mary Maulsby, b. 9th day of 8th month, 1774.
Lloyd Norris, b. 29th day of 11th month, 1800.
Mary Ann Norris, b. 4th day of 10th month, 1793.
David Preston, b. 9th day of 2nd month, 1774.
Isaac H. Preston, b. 10th day of 1st month, 1798.
Daniel Pope, b. 11th day of 11th month, 1787.
Lois K. Pope, b. 22nd day of 3rd month, 1795.
Harmon Pyle, b. 30th day of 1st month, 1789.
Eliza Parker, d. in 1882 in her 88th year.
Hannah Spencer, b. 14th day of 12th month, 1798.

Amos Smith, b. 18th day of 8th month, 1779.

Rebecca Smith, b. 26th day of 8th month, 1784.

Nathan Tyson, b. 4th day of 11th month, 1787.

Martha Tyson, b. 13th day of 9th month, 1795.

Joseph Trimble, b. 19th day of 6th month, 1772.

Elizabeth Tucker, b. 15th day of 10th month, 1763.

Jonathan Warner, b. 27th day of 1st month, 1790. [Note: The year "1790" is lined out and "1789" written over it].

Sarah Warner, b. 20th day of 1st month, 1788. [Note: The year "1788" is lined out and "1791" written over it].

PIPE CREEK MONTHLY MEETING - WOMEN'S MINUTES

From the beginning meetings were held at Pipe Creek and Bush Creek and known as Pipe Creek Monthly Meeting. The first meeting was held at Bush Creek Meeting House the 19th of 12th month 1772. On that day Samuel Cooksen and Mary Haines announced intentions to marry.

On 20th day of 2nd month, 1773, it was announced that the marriage of Samuel Cookson and Mary Haines had been accomplished. Ann Farquhar appointed overseer of Pipe Creek and Ellen Plummer of Bush Creek. Joseph Talbott and Anna his wife produced certificate from West River Monthly Meeting.

On 17th day of 4th month, 1773, Cassandra Ballenger appointed overseer of Bush Creek.

On 19th day of 6th month, 1773, Ruth Holland and Rachel Farquhar appointed overseers.

On 21st day of 8th month, 1773, George Pusey and Sarah his wife presented a certificate for themselves and son William from Deer Creek Monthly Meeting.

On 18th day of 9th month, 1773, John Moore produced a certificate from Gunpowder Monthly Meeting for himself, Rebecca his wife and his children, John, John, Mary, Hannah and Francis. A certificate was produced for Zipporah Maynard from Gunpowder Monthly Meeting with an endorsement from --- Fairfax Monthly Meeting.

On 20th day of 11th month, 1773, Phebe Farquhar junr produced a certificate from Goshen Monthly Meeting.

On 15th day of 12th month, 1773, Ann Everitt requested a certificate to Fairfax Monthly Meeting.

On 21st day of 5th month, 1774, Ruth Holland produced a certificate from Quarterly Meeting, Little River in Perquimans County, North Carolina.

On 16th day, 7th month, 1774, David Cumming and Rachel Miller announced their intentions to marry. Samuel Hutton and Mary his wife produced a certificate for themselves and children, John, Joseph, William, Benjamin, Joel and Jonathan, from Warrington Monthly Meeting. Sarah Hewitt produced a certificate from New Garden Monthly Meeting, Pennsylvania.

On 17th day, 9th month, 1774, Joseph Everit and Sarah Hewitt announced intentions to marry. Mary Chamberlain produced a certificate from Chester Monthly Meeting. Rachel Cummins requested a certificate to Philadelphia.

On 15th day of 10th month, 1774, Samuel Hutton and Mary his wife produced a certificate for themselves and six children, John, Joseph, William, Benjamin, Joel and Jonathan, from Warrington Monthly Meeting.

On 19th day of 11th month, 1774, it was announced that the marriage of J.E. and S. H. had been accomplished. A complaint was made against Sarah Colvon formerly Ellis a young woman at Pipe Creek for having gone out in marriage.

On 18th day of 2nd month, 1775, Sarah Plummer produced a certificate from West River Monthly Meeting for herself, daus. Ursula and Susanna and granddau. Sarah Harris.

On 15th day of 4th month, 1775, Yate Plummer produced a certificate from West River Monthly Meeting for himself, Artrige his wife and dau. Sarah.

On 17th day of 6th month, 1775, a certificate was produced from Abraham Plummer, Sarah his wife and three children, Samuel, John and Robert, from West River Monthly Meeting.

On 20th day of 5th month, 1775, Mary Plummer produced certificate from Fairfax Monthly Meeting.

On 16th day of 9th month, 1775, Rachel Cookson having been under the care of Friends.

On 18th day of 11th month, 1775, Application for a certificate was made by Eleanor Ellis to Exeter Monthly Meeting. A certificate was produced from Hopewell Monthly Meeting for Deborah Ellis but she being removed within the verge of Exeter Monthly Meeting, Friends think it best to undersign and send it there.

On 11th day of 9th month, 1776, a certificate was produced for Hannah Bucher from Richland Monthly Meeting, Pennsylvania.

On 19th day of 10th month, 1776, Robert Hunt produced a certificate from Evesham Monthly Meeting in West New Jersey for himself, Abigail his wife, and children, Mary, Joshua, William and Samuel.

On 17th day of 4th month, 1777, Moses Farquhar and Sarah Poultney announced their intentions to marry. Anthony Poultney and Susanna Plummer announced their intentions to marry.

On 17th day of 7th month, 1777, Isaac Brown and Sarah Ballinger announced their intentions to marry. William Morsel, wife and two children, Rachel and Rebekah, were received into the meeting. Samuel Coale produced a certificate for himself and Lydia his wife, from Deer Creek Monthly Meeting.

On 18th day of 9th month, 1777 it was announced that the marriage of Isaac Brown and Sarah Ballinger was accomplished. Sarah Brown requested certificate to Hopewell Monthly Meeting.

On 16th day of 10th month, 1777, Susanna Wright requested certificate with her husband and children to Warrington Monthly Meeting.

On 18th day of 12th month, 1777, Jonah Hollingsworth and Hannah Miller announced intentions to marry.

On 12th day of 3rd month, 1778, it was announced that the marriage of Jonah Hollingsworth and Hannah Miller had been accomplished. Hannah Hollingsworth requested a certificate to Hopewell Monthly Meeting. Cassandra Wood produced a certificate from New Garden Monthly Meeting, Pennsylvania.

On 16th day of 4th month, 1778, Hannah Dorsey produced certificate from Nottingham Monthly Meeting, Pennsylvania. Mary Talbott with her husband, produced certificate from Monthly Meeting held at Indian Spring, for themselves and children, Benjamin, Joseph, John, Elizabeth, Susanna, Anne, Samuel, Rachel and Peggy Talbott.

On 14th day of 5th month, 1778, Joanna Diar requested certificate with her husband and children to Gunpowder Monthly Meeting.

On 16th(?) day of 7th month, 1778, Mary Rees produced a certificate from Goshen Monthly Meeting.

On 12th day of 11th month, 1778, Mary Elliot produced a certificate from New Garden Monthly Meeting for himself, wife and children, Eli(?) and Hannah Elliot.

On 17th day of 12th month, 1778, Joseph Haines and Rachel Cookson announced intentions to marry. Elizabeth Cookson having requested to come under the care of Friends. Rachel Scoffield requested certificate to Fairfax Monthly Meeting. Susanna Belts produced certificate from Wrights Town Monthly Meeting.

On 14th day of 1st month, 1779, a certificate was produced for Rachel Scoffield and children, Samuel, John, Enoch, Benjamin and Jane Scofield.

On 11th day of 2nd month, 1779, it was announced that the marriage of Joseph Haines and Rachel Cookson had been accomplished.

On 6th month, 1779, a memorial to William Farquhar who died at Pipe Creek on 21st day of 9th month, 1778, aged near 78(?) years, husband of Ann Farquhar who also gave testimonial. Testimonial was given for Rachel Farquhar who died on 19th day, 4th month, 1777, aged 40 years.

On 18th day of 7th month, 1779, Sarah Yarnall produced a certificate from Warrington, Monthly Meeting. John and Hannah Russell produced certificate from Kenet Monthly Meeting for themselves and children, Thomas, Sarah, Jesse, Mary, Rachel and James Russel.

On 16th day of 9th month, 1779, Solomon Shepherd and Susanna Farquhar announced intentions to marry. Robert Miller and Cassandra Wood announced intentions to marry. Susanna Belts requested certificate to Wrights Town Monthly Meeting in Bucks County, Pennsylvania.

On 18th day of 11th month, 1779, it was announced that the marriage of Solomon Shepherd and Susanna Farquhar was accomplished. Also the marriage of Robert Miller and Cassandra Wood.

On 17th day of 2nd month, 1780, Elisha Kirk and Ruth Miller announced intentions to marry.

On 16th day of 3rd month, 1780, a certificate was produced from Cedar Creek Monthly Meeting, Virginia, for Sarah Harris dau of Moses Harris.

On 13th day of 4th month it was announced that the marriage of Elisha Kirk and Ruth Miller had been accomplished. A certificate for Phebe Maynard was produced from Warrington Monthly Meeting.

On 18th day of 5th month, 1780, Rachel Pidgeon requested a certificate to remove with husband and children to Fairfax Monthly Meeting. Ruth Kirk, about to remove with her husband within the verge of Warrington Monthly Meeting requested certificate.

On 6th month, 1780, Stephen Howel produced a certificate for himself and Sarah his wife from New Garden Monthly Meeting, Chester County, Pennsylvania.

On 13th day of 7th month, 1780, Israel Janney and Anne Plummer announced intentions to marry.

On 14th day of 9th month, 1780, Jacob Janney and Sarah Harris announced intentions to marry. It was announced that the marriage of Israel Janney and Ann Plummer had been accomplished.

On 18th day of 10th month, 1780, Mary Starr produced a certificate from New Garden Monthly Meeting. Grace Taylor produced a certificate from Uwchland Monthly Meeting. Anna Janney requested certificate to --- Monthly Meeting.

On 16th of 11th month, 1780 it was announced that the marriage of Jacob Janney and Sarah Harris had been accomplished. Mary Hutton requested certificate to remove with her husband and children to the verge of Fairfax Monthly Meeting. Sarah Janney, formerly Harris, requested certificate to Fairfax Monthly Meeting. Elizabeth Hughes produced certificate from Nottingham Monthly Meeting.

On 13th day of 12th month, 1780, a paper from Susanna Galloway was produced here condemning her outgoing in marriage.

On 13th day of 3rd month, 1781 it was announced that the marriage of Samuel Waters and Sarah Unckles had been accomplished. Also the marriage of John Maulsby and Mary Starr had been accomplished. Hannah Bucher requested certificate to Richland Monthly Meeting. Abigail Moore produced certificate from Gunpowder Monthly Meeting.

On 17th day of 5th month, 1781, Mary Cookson requested certificate to remove with her husband and family within verge of Menallen Monthly Meeting. Elizabeth Cookson requested certificate to Menallen Monthly Meeting.

On 14th day of 6th month, 1781, a complaint was made against Sarah Farquhar daughter of Allen, in standing up in a publick meeting at Pipe Creek with a man not of our Society saying over a marriage ceremony which has a tendency greatly to interrupt the solemnity thereof.

On 13th day of 7th month, 1781, a certificate from Menallen Monthly Meeting for Mary Blackburn and family was read.

On 16th day of 1st month, 1781, a certificate was received for William Chandley, his wife Mary and daughter Susanna, from Warrington Monthly Meeting.

On 13th day of 9th month, 1781, a complaint was made against Sarah Everitt for neglecting attendance of meetings.

On 18th day of 10th month, 1781, Mary Wood produced certificate from monthly meeting held at Little Falls.

On 15th day of 11th month, 1781, Abigail Dower produced a certificate from Chester Monthly Meeting.

On 17th day of 1st month, 1782, a certificate was produced from Benjamin Benson and Hannah his wife and 5 children from Uwchland Monthly Meeting.

On 14th day of 2nd month, 1782, a certificate was produced from Warrington Monthly Meeting for Isaac Fisher, Eliza. his wife and daughter Deborah.

On 4th month, 1782, Mary Blackburn joins her husband in requesting certificate to Menallen Monthly Meeting for themselves and children.

On 20th day of 7th month, 1782, William Shepherd and Phebe Hay announced intentions to marry. Ann Taylor produced certificate from New Garden Monthly Meeting.

On 11th day of 8th month, 1782, Abigail Duer requested certificate to Northern District, Philadelphia.

On 12th day of 9th month, 1782, it was announced that the marriage of William Shepherd and Phebe Hay had been accomplished.

On 19th day of 10th month, 1782, Elizabeth Webb produced certificate from New Garden.

On 16th day of 11th month, 1782, Bush Creek Preparative Meeting reported that Miriam Plummer had removed within the verge of Fairfax Monthly Meeting with consent of her father.

On 14th day of 12th month, 1782, a complaint was made by Pipe Creek Preparative Meeting against Mary Stevenson, formerly Chamberlain, for marrying a man not of our Society.

On 18th day of 1st month, 1783, Mary Hay produced a certificate from Warrington Monthly Meeting.

On 19th day of 4th month, 1783, Friends were appointed in the case of Mary Stevenson previously Moore [sic], report they performed the service.

On 17th day of 5th month, 1783, certificate was produced by Francis Mathews and his wife Mary from Gunpowder Monthly Meeting.

On 14th day of 6th month, 1783, a certificate was requested from Sarah Miller to be joined with her husband and children to Warrington Monthly Meeting as also one for their daughter Mary to Crooked Run Monthly Meeting.

On 19th day of 12th month, 1783, Deborah Chandler produced certificate from Fairfax Monthly Meeting. Mary Rees requested certificate to Goshen Monthly Meeting.

On 18th day of 3rd month, 1784, Hannah Russel requested certificate to be joined with her husband and children to Indian Spring. Mary Elliot requested certificate to join with her husband and children to Indian Spring Monthly Meeting.

On 17th day of 4th month, 1784, Ruth Wood produced certificate from New Garden Monthly Meeting.

On 19th day of 6th month, 1784, Bush Creek Preparative Meeting informed that Elizabeth Fisher requested certificate to be joined with her husband and children to Warrington Monthly Meeting.

On 14th day of 8th month, 1784, William Farquhar and Elizabeth Talbott announced intentions to marry. A certificate was produced for Joseph Gamble and Elizabeth his wife from Indian Spring Monthly Meeting.

On 16th day of 9th month, 1784, Ann Taylor requested certificate to New Garden Monthly Meeting. A certificate was produced for George Yarnall and his wife Lydia and their children from Goshen Monthly Meeting. A complaint was made against Mary Plummer for some misconduct to her husband's brother and making use of unbecoming expressions.

On 16th day of 10th month, 1784, it was announced that the marriage of William Farquhar and Elizabeth Talbott had been accomplished. Henry Robert and Ann Farquhar announced intentions to marry. Mary Way requested certificate to Warrington Monthly Meeting, Pennsylvania. Phebe Shepherd requested certificate to remove with her husband to Warrington Monthly Meeting, Pennsylvania.

On 20th day of 11th month, 1784, Ruth Wood requested certificate to New Garden Monthly Meeting.

On 18th day of 12th month, 1784, it was announced that the marriage of Henry Robert and Ann Farquhar had been accomplished. On 13th day of 1st month, 1785, Deborah Chandler requested to be joined with her husband and child in a certificate to Indian Spring Monthly Meeting. Sarah Pusey was appointed clerk.

On 19th day, 2nd month, 1785, Sarah Elliot requested certificate to be joined with her husband and children to Indian Spring Monthly Meeting. Mary Wood requested a certificate to be joined with her husband and child to Gunpowder Monthly Meeting.

On 16th day of 4th month, 1785, Isaac Plummer and Grace Taylor announced intentions to marry. Rebeccah Moore requested certificate for herself and children to Gunpowder Monthly Meeting.

On 17th day of 5th month, 1785, a certificate was produced for Jane Hibberd jointly with her husband and children from Goshens Monthly Meeting. A certificate was requested for Lydia Yarnal jointly with her husband and children to Gunpowder Monthly Meeting.

On 18th day of 6th month, 1785, it was announced that the marriage of Isaac Plummer and Grace Taylor had been accomplished. A certificate was produced from Fairfax Monthly Meeting for Mariam Plummer.

On 7th month, 1785, a certificate was produced from Warrington Monthly Meeting for Rebeckah Day.

On 20th day of 8th month, 1785, Benjamin Talbott and Susanna Chandlee announced intentions to marry. Elizabeth Hardorker acknowledged misconduct.

On 15th day of 9th month, 1785, Moses Plummer and Elizabeth Webb announced intentions to marry. It was reported that Rachel Richardson formerly Farquhar has accomplished her marriage contrary to rules of our Discipline. It was announced that the marriage of Benjamin Talbott and Susanna Chandlee had been accomplished. Abigail Moore requested certificate to Gunpowder Monthly Meeting. Abigail Rusel requested certificate jointly with her husband and children to Crooked Run Monthly Meeting.

On 10th day, 1st month, 1786, Jeremiah Cook and Rachel Farquhar announced intentions to marry.

On 16th day of 3rd month, 1786, it was announced that the marriage of Jeremiah Cook and Rachel Farquhar had been accomplished.

On 18th day of 4th month, 1786, Ann Taylor requested certificate jointly with her husband and children to Fairfax Monthly Meeting, Virginia.

On 20th day of 5th month, 1786, Hannah Farquhar produced certificate from Warrington Monthly Meeting.

On 18th day of 8th month, 1786, Mary, wife of Francis Matthews, requested certificate to Gunpowder Monthly Meeting.

On 14th day of 9th month, 1786, Joseph Talbott and Mary Farquhar announced intentions to marry.

On 14th day of 10th month, 1786, a certificate was produced from Sarah Safthill and she having lived for some time within the verge of this meeting and not attending.

On 18th day of 11th month, 1786, it was announced that the marriage of Joseph Talbott and Mary Farquhar had been accomplished. Friends appointed to visit Sarah Pancost report that it would be best not to be hasty in receiving her.

On 10th day of 1st month, 1787, Mary Ducket produced certificate from Warrington Monthly Meeting. Sarah Williams produced certificate from Warrington Monthly Meeting.

On 17th day of 2nd month, 1787, Sarah Saltkill produced certificate from Chester Monthly Meeting held at Providence, Pennsylvania. Mary Stevenson (formerly Moore) having condemned her misconduct in going out in marriage is received into membership again and requests certificate to Gunpowder Monthly Meeting.

On 14th day of 4th month, 1787, complaint was made against Meriam Bowlin formerly Plummer who has accomplished her marriage contrary to the rules of our Discipline with a man not of our Society.

On 16th day of 6th month, 1787, a certificate was produced from Haverford Monthly Meeting for Martha and Tacy Jones.

On 18th of 8th month, 1787, Rachel Cook requested certificate jointly with her husband and child to Westland Monthly Meeting.

On 20th day of 10th month, 1787, Susanna Talbott requested certificate jointly with her husband and child to Menallen Monthly Meeting.

On 17th day of 11th month, 1787, Phebe Farquhar appointed overseer of Pipe Creek Meeting in the room of Jane Hibberd.

On 15th day of 12th month, 1787, a certificate was produced for Meriam Harrison with her husband and children from Upper Springfield, New Jersey.

On 19th day of 1st month, 1788, Joseph Everitt requested certificate for his minor daughter to Fairfax Monthly Meeting.

On 15th day of 3rd month, 1788, Cassandra Miller requested certificate jointly with her husband and children to Hopewell Monthly Meeting. Sarah Elis having offered to this meeting a few lines condemning her misconduct in trying to accomplish her marriage in an unsuitable manner, a committee was appointed to visit her and report to the meeting.

On 19th day of 4th month, 1788, Rebeckah Roberts produced a certificate from Fairfax Monthly Meeting.

On 20th day of 9th month, 1788, Jane Williams produced a certificate from Menallen Monthly Meeting.

On 18th day of 10th month, 1788, Robert Miller and Jane Williams announced their intentions to marry. Elizabeth Hughes produced a certificate from New Garden Monthly Meeting, Pennsylvania.

On 21st day of 11th month, 1788, Elizabeth Hendricks produced a certificate from Menallen Monthly Meeting.

On 20th day of 12th month, 1788, it was announced that the marriage of Robert Miller and Jane Williams had been accomplished.

On 14th day of 2nd month, 1789, a complaint was made against Meriam Swamly formerly Roberts from accomplishing a marriage with the assistance of a hireling preacher to a man not of our Society.

On 16th day of 5th month, 1789, Mary Ducket requested a certificate to Warrington Monthly Meeting.

On 20th day of 6th month, 1789, Elizabeth Roberts, formerly Hendricks, has been guilty of having accomplished her marriage by a hireling preacher with a man not of our Society.

On 18th day of 7th month, 1789, Martha Jones requested a certificate to Westland Monthly Meeting.

On 19th day of 9th month, 1789, Rachel Richardson produced a paper condemning her misconduct in her outgoing in marriage.

On 17th day of 10th month, 1789, Pipe Creek Particular Meeting informs that Ann Norris requested to come under the care of this meeting jointly with her husband and children.

On 19th day of 12th month, 1789, Mary Wood produced a certificate jointly with her husband and children from Gunpowder Monthly Meeting.

On 20th day of 3rd month, 1790, a complaint was made against Sarah Williams for being guilty of fornication, which is become manifest.

On 15th day of 5th month, 1790, Hannah Farquhar requested a certificate jointly with her husband and child to Westland Monthly Meeting. Elizabeth Farquhar requested a certificate jointly with her husband to Westland Monthly Meeting.

On 19th day of 6th month, 1790, a certificate was produced from Warrington Monthly Meeting for Mary Husey.

On 17th day of 7th month, 1790, Mary Cordery produced a certificate from Motherkill Monthly Meeting.

On 14th day of 8th month, 1790, Sarah Farquhar requested a certificate to Westland Monthly Meeting.

On 13th day of 11th month, 1790, John Talbot and Elizabeth Plummer announced their intentions to marry. Mary Fowler produced a certificate with her husband and children from Chesterfield Monthly Meeting.

On 15th day of 1st month, 1791, it was announced that the marriage of John Talbot and Elizabeth Plummer had been accomplished.

On 19th day of 2nd month, 1791, Mary Balinger was appointed clerk in the room of Sarah Husey.

On 16th day of 4th month, 1791, Elizabeth Wright was appointed overseer of Pipe Creek Particular Meeting in the room of Rachel Willits.

On 16th day of 7th month, 1791, a certificate was produced from Exeter Monthly Meeting for Elenor Wright with her husband and children, Esther and Mary.

On 13th day of 10th month, 1791, William Harrison and Ruth Farquhar announced their intentions to marry.

On 19th day of 12th month, 1791, it was announced that the marriage of William Harrison and Ruth Farquhar had been accomplished. A certificate was produced for Rebeccah Kenworthy with her husband from Goose Creek Monthly Meeting.

On 18th day of 2nd month, 1792, Ann Wright requested a certificate to Wilmington Monthly Meeting. A certificate was produced for Patience Buntin and her husband and children, four daughters, Sarah, Lucy, Patience and Rebekah, from Chesterfield Monthly Meeting. Mary Plummer appointed overseer of Bush Creek Preparative Meeting in the room of Sarah Waters. A certificate was produced for Mary Buntin from Chesterfield Monthly Meeting.

On 17th day of 3rd month, 1792, Hannah Benson requested certificate with her husband and children to York Monthly Meeting.

On 19th day of 5th month, 1792, Bush Creek Preparative Meeting informs that Mary Harrison formerly Bunting has accomplished her marriage by the assistance of a hireling teacher to a man not of our Society. Bush Creek also informs that Sarah Harrison formerly Bunting has accomplished her marriage by a hireling teacher to a man not of our Society.

On ? day of 6th month, 1792, a certificate was produced from Indian Spring Monthly Meeting for Sarah Elliott with her husband and children.

On 18th day of 8th month, 1792, Mary and Sarah Harrison produced papers condemning their misconduct and were received into membership.

On 13th day of 9th month, 1792, William Plummer and Rachel Morsel announced their intentions to marry. Esther Haines produced a certificate from Warrington Monthly Meeting.

On 2nd day of 10th month, 1792, Mary Wood was appointed overseer in room of Sarah Howel.

On 17th day of 11th month, 1792, it was announced that the marriage of William Plummer and Rachel Morsel had been accomplished. Pipe Creek Preparative Meeting informs that Mary Stoner formerly Pusey hath accomplished her marriage by the assistance of a hireling with a man not of our society. Ann Wright produced a certificate from Wilmington Monthly Meeting.

On 15th day of 12th month, 1792, Pipe Creek Preparative Meeting informs that Rachel Willits requested a certificate for herself and children to Westland Monthly Meeting.

On 19th day of 1st month, 1793, the meeting was informed that Ruth Harrison hath been guilty of unchastity before marriage.

On 16th day of 2nd month, 1793, Bush Creek Meeting informs that Elizabeth Clay formerly Hardaker hath accomplished her marriage by a hireling teacher with a man not of our Society. A certificate was produced for Rachel Willits.

On 16th day of 3rd month, 1793, William Farquhar and Esther Wright announced their intentions to marry.

On 20th day of 4th month, 1793, Mary Talbot requested a certificate for herself and children jointly with her husband to Westland Monthly Meeting. Mary Hussey requested a certificate to Warrington Monthly Meeting.

On 18th day of 5th month, 1893 Mary Kenworthy requested a certificate with her husband and children to Menallen Monthly Meeting.

On 17th day of 8th month, 1793, Robert Plummer and Rachel Talbot announced their intentions to marry.

On 14th day of 9th month, 1793, Thomas Russel and Sarah Roberts announced their intentions to marry.

On 19th day of 10th month, 1793, it was announced that the marriage of Robert Plummer and Rachel Talbot had been accomplished. Thomas Russel and Sarah Roberts announced their intentions to marry. A certificate was received from Menallen Monthly Meeting for John Pidgeon, his wife Susanna and their two children.

On 16th day of 11th month, 1793, it was announced that the marriage of Thomas Russel and Sarah Roberts had been accomplished.

On 14th day of 12th month, 1793, a certificate was received from Fairfax monthly Meeting for Thomas Tylor(?), Sarah his wife and their five children.

On 18th day of 1st month, 1794, a complaint was made against Esther Farquhar for being guilty of unchastity before marriage.

On 15th day of 2nd month, 1794, the mens meeting informs that Joseph Everitt requested a certificate for his wife Sarah to Menallen Monthly Meeting.

On 19th day of 4th month, 1794, Jane Miller requested a certificate with her husband and children to Menallen Monthly Meeting.

On 14th day of 6th month, 1794, this meeting unites with Men Friends in receiving a certificate for Margaret Rush with her husband and children from Exeter Monthly Meeting.

On 19th day of 7th month, 1794, Mary Farquhar produced a certificate from Menallen Monthly Meeting. Rachel Farquhar produced a certificate from Menallen Monthly Meeting. This Meeting unites with Men Friends in receiving a certificate from Menallen Monthly Meeting for Margaret Elgar with her husband and children.

On 14th day of 2nd month, 1795, Elizabeth Plummer requested certificate with her husband and children to Fairfax Monthly Meeting.

On 14th day of 3rd month, 1795, Pipe Creek informs that Ann Richardson formerly Wright accomplished her marriage with a man not of our Society by the assistance of a hireling teacher.

On 18th day of 4th month, 1795, a certificate for Elizabeth Plummer is being prepared.

On 20th day of 6th month, 1795, a certificate was produced from Menallen Monthly meeting for Susanna Wright with her husband and children. A certificate was produced from Indian Spring Monthly Meeting for Hannah Russel and her husband and children. A certificate was produced for Sarah and Mary Russel from Indian Spring Monthly Meeting.

On 15th day of 8th month, 1795, Sarah Pusey was appointed overseer of Pipe Creek Preparative Meeting in room of Elizabeth Wright.

On 19th day of 9th month, 1795, Israel Plummer and Rebecca Morsel announced their intentions to marry.

On the 17th day of the 10th month, 1795, Susanna Wright requested a certificate with her husband and children to Menallen Monthly Meeting.

On 19th day of 11th month, 1795, Elizabeth Gamble requested a certificate with her husband to Westland Monthly Meeting. It was announced that the marriage of Israel Plummer and Rebecca Morsel had been accomplished. Mary Red(?) produced a certificate from Indian Spring Monthly Meeting.

On 16th day of 1st month, 1796, Bush Creek Preparative Meeting informs that Sarah Salthill hath neglected attendance of meetings and encourages fiddling and dancing in her house.

On 13th day of 2nd month, 1796, Jehu Moore and Hannah Hibberd announced their intentions to marry. Hannah Russel was appointed overseer of Bush Creek Preparative Meeting in the place of Mary Plummer. A certificate was produced from Indian Spring Monthly Meeting for Mary Elliott with her husband and children. A certificate was produced from Indian Spring Monthly Meeting for Margaret Elliott.

On 19th day of 3rd month, 1796, Jane Hibberd was appointed clerk in the room of Mary Ballinger.

On 16th day of 4th month, 1796, it was announced that the marriage of Jehu Moore and Hannah Hibberd had been accomplished. Mary Read produced a certificate from Indian Spring Monthly Meeting.

Sarah Harrison requested a certificate to Redstone Monthly Meeting.

On 14th day of 5th month, 1796, a certificate was produced for Mary Parvain with her husband and daughter Mary from Exeter Monthly Meeting.

On 10th day of 7th month, 1796, Bush Creek Preparative Meeting informs that Mary Pope requested to come under the care of Friends.

On 13th day of 8th month, 1796, Lydia Smith produced a certificate from New Garden Monthly Meeting.

On 17th day of 9th month, 1796, Ann and Abigail Parvain produced a certificate from Exeter Monthly Meeting. A certificate for Elizabeth Plummer and family was approved. Bush Creek Preparative Meeting informs that Ann Waters formerly Ballinger had accomplished her marriage with a man not of our Society.

On 19th day of 5th month, 1797, Lydia Farquhar produced a certificate from York Monthly Meeting.

On 17th day of 6th month, 1797, William Ballinger and Lydia Smith announced their intentions to marry.

On 15th day of 7th month, 1797, Moses Given and Ann French announced their intentions to marry.

On 19th of 8th month, 1797, it was announced that the marriage of William Ballinger and Lydia Smith had been accomplished.

On 16th, 9th month, 1797, it was announced that the marriage of Moses Given and Ann French had been accomplished.

On 19th day of 5th month, 1798, Bush Creek Preparative Meeting made a complaint against Mary Saltkill for frequenting places of diversion and dancing.

On 16th day of 6th month, 1798, a certificate was produced from New Garden Monthly Meeting, Pennsylvania, for Susanna Wood with her husband and six minor children. Lydia Wood produced a certificate from New Garden Monthly Meeting.

On 19th day of 7th month, 1798, Martha Hibberd produced a certificate from Hopewell Monthly Meeting.

On 18th day of 8th month, 1798, Eli Eliott and Margaret Hughes announced their intentions to marry.

On 15th day of 9th month, 1798, Sarah Taylor requested a certificate with her husband and children to York Monthly Meeting.

On 15th day of 12th month, 1798, Mary Salthill appeared with a paper condemning her misconduct and was received into the meeting. Esther Starr produced a certificate from Exeter Monthly Meeting.

On 19th day of 1st month, 1799, Lydia Farquhar was appointed overseer of Pipe Creek Preparative Meeting. Ann, Abigail and Mary Parvain Junr, requested to be disowned from being members of our Society.

On 20th day of 4th month, 1799, New Market Friends requested to hold a meeting ...

On 15th day of 6th month, 1799, Mary Eliott was appointed overseer in place of Hannah Russell. Phebe Starr produced a certificate from London Grove Monthly Meeting.

PIPE CREEK MONTHLY MEETING 263

On 17th day of 8th month, 1799, William Ward and Sarah Plummer announced their intentions to marry. Mary Pancoast produced a certificate from Fairfax Monthly Meeting.

On 14th day of 9th month, 1799, Rebeccah Kenworthy requested a certificate to be joined with her husband to Fairfax Monthly Meeting.

On 19th day of 10th month, 1799, it was announced that the marriage of William Ward and Sarah Plummer had been accomplished. The Bush Creek Preparative Meeting informs that Margaret Baily requested to come under the care of Friends. Sarah Ward requested a certificate to Indian Spring Monthly Meeting.

On 15th day of 2nd month, 1800, it was reported that An Norris was prevented from attending last meeting by indisposition.

On 19th day of 4th month, 1800, Esther Starr requested a certificate for Southland Monthly Meeting, Virginia.

On 14th day of 6th month, 1800, Thomas Plummer and Susanna Talbott announced intentions to marry.

On 19th day of 7th month, 1800, Kinsey Talbott and Deborah Plummer announced intentions to marry. Susannah Wood was appointed overseer of Bush Creek Preparative Meeting in place of Susanna Poultney. Kitturah Parish produced a certificate from Gunpowder Monthly Meeting.

On 15th day of 8th month, 1800, it was announced that the marriage of Thomas Plummer and Susanna Talbott had been accomplished.

On 20th day of 9th month, 1800, it was announced that the marriage of Kinsey Talbott and Deborah Plummer had been accomplished.

On 18th day of 10th month, 1800, Jonah Updegraff and Hannah Farquhar announced intentions to marry.

On 10th day, 12th month, 1800, it was announced that the marriage of Jonah Updegraff and Hannah Farquhar had been accomplished. Joseph Elgar junr and Ann Wright announced intentions to marry. Lydia Howel requested a certificate to Kennet Monthly Meeting, Pennsylvania. Lydia Hussey produced a certificate from Wilmington Monthly Meeting. Nathan Wood and Margaret Waters announced intentions to marry.

Marriages

Samuel Cookson, Westminster Town, Frederick Co. and Mary Haines of Pipe Creek, 20th day of 1st month, 1773 at Pipe Creek Meeting House. Witnesses: Mordica Price, Samuel Price, Sophia Haines, Nathan Haines, Thomas Price, Rebekah Moore, Mary Carmack, Elizabeth Cookson, Rachel Cookson, Rachel Miller, Hannah Miller, Mordecca Haines, Joseph Haines, Cornelius Carmack, Robert Miller, Daniel Matthews, Sarah Miller, Sarah Poultney, John Chamberlin, John Moore, Richard Griffee, Jacob Braselton, John Richards, William Farquhar, George Ashman, William Pidgeon, Rachel Pidgeon, Morris Ellis, Nancy Ashman, Elizabeth Haines, Allen Farquhar, junr., William Farquhar, Ann Farquhar, Rachel Farquhar, Sarah Ellis, Joseph Wright, Joel Wright, Elizabeth Wright, Phebe Farquhar, Sarah Unckles, Eleaner Shelmerdine.

David Cumming of the City of Philadelphia, son of David Cumming and Sarah his wife, dec'd, of same place and Rachel Miller, dau of Solomon and Sarah Miller of Frederick County, 24th day of 8th month, 1774. Witnesses: Solomon Miller, Sarah Miller, Hannah Miller, Elizabeth Miller, Rebeccah Cumming, Sarah Dorsey, Tho. Matthews, William Matthews, Robert Miller, William Bentley, Anthony Poultney, Wm. Roberts, junr, Margaret Bentley, Ann Farquhar, Phebe Farquhar, Ann Moore, Rachel Farquhar, Mary Wright, Sarah Farquhar, Elizabeth Wright, Sarah Poultney, Susanna Farquhar, Rachel Pidgeon, William Farquhar, Allen Farquhar, junr., William Farquhar, Nathan Haines, Arthur Howel, Joseph Wright, Joel Wright, William Farquhar, William Pidgeon.

Joseph Everett of Pipe Creek, Frederick County, and Sarah Hewes of the same place, 26th day of 10th month, 1774. Witnesses: Rachel Scholefield, Phebe Farquhar, junr., Sarah Ellis, junr., Elliner Ellis, Susanna Wright, Rachel Willets, Sarah Poultney, Ruth Miller, Ruth Bicket, Ann Moore, Ann Farquhar, Sarah Farquhar, Mary Wright, Sarah Ellis, Elizabeth Wright, Rachel Farquhar, Phebe Farquhar, Sarah Unckles, Susanna Farquhar, Moses Farquhar, Thomas Ellis, William Pidgeon, William Kenworthy, William Farquhar, Joseph Wright, Jonathan Wright, Allen Farquhar, Charles Pidgeon, William Farquhar, Samuel Farquhar, Morris Ellis.

Anthony Poultney, Bush Creek, Frederick County, Maryland, son of John Poultney and Eleanor his wife, and Susanna Plummer of the same place, dau of Samuel and Sarah Plummer, 22nd day of 5th month, 1777. Witnesses:

Allen Farquhar, Joel Wright, Robert Hunt, Abigail Hunt, Wm. Morsel, Mary Morsel, Samuel Peach, Samuel Plummer, Jonathan Plummer, Mary Plummer, Daniel Ballinger, William Ballenger, Isaac Plummer, Samuel Plummer, Jesse Plummer, Moses Farquhar, Hannah Ballinger, Samuel Gover, Susanna Farquhar, Deborah Brooke, Richd. Holland, Sarah Plummer, Mahlon Janney, William Ballinger, Mary Plummer, Joseph Talbott, Samuel Waters, Yate Plummer, Susannah Waters, Sarah Ballinger, Joseph Vo.(?) Plummer, Mary Ballinger, Ann Plummer, Sarah Plummer, Ellen Plummer, Ruth Holland, Thomas Plummer, Joseph Plummer, Samuel Plummer, Cassandra Ballinger, Sarah Janney, Abram Plummer, Ursula Plummer, Anna Talbott, Sarah Poultney, Mary Poultney.

Moses Farquhar son of William and Ann Farquhar of Pipe Creek, Frederick Co., and Sarah Poultney of Bush Creek, Frederick Co., dau of John and Ellianor Poultney, 5th day of 6th month, 1777. Witnesses: Richd. Holland, Richd. Roberts, Joseph Wood, Gideon Gipson, Saml. Peach, Abram Plummer, Robert Hunt, Wm. Plummer, Joshua Hunt, Saml. Plummer, --- Taylor, --- Shephard, ---1 Plummer, Rachel Cookson, Abigail Hunt, Hannah Dorsey, Cassandra Wood, Susanna Belts, Mary Ballinger, Saml. Gover, Rachel Taylor, Henry Roberts, John Roberts, Jos. Talbott, Jesse Hughes, Thos. Taylor, junr., Joseph Haines, Thos. Plummer, junr., Sarah Farquhar, Jesse Plummer, Ruth Plummer, Eliza. Farquhar, Ruth Holland, Casendra Ballinger, William Ballinger, Jos. Plummer, Anne Plummer, Mary Plummer, Sarah Plummer, Anna Talbott, Ursula Plummer, Sarah Plummer, Jos. Farquhar, Elleanor Plummer, Ann Farquhar, William Farquhar, Allen Farquhar, Mary Wright, Samuel Farquhar, Elizh. Wright, Susanna Farquhar, Anthy. Poultney, Mary Poultney, Sarah Poultney, Joseph Wright, Phebe Farquhar, Phebe Farquhar, Sarah Farquhar, Hannah Farquhar, Wm. Farquhar, Isaac Plummer, Joel Wright.

Isaac Brown of Frederick Co., Virginia, son of Daniel and Susanna Brown and Sarah Ballinger, dau of William and Cassandra Ballinger, Frederick Co., Maryland, 14th day of 8th month, 1777. Witnesses: Mary Roberts, Eliz. Wright, Robert Hunt, Allen Farquhar, junr., Jos. Wright, Lydia Miller, Richd. Roberts, Saml. Waters, Joel Wright, --- Janney, Sarah Miller, Sarah Janney, Henry Ballinger, Saml. Ballinger, Thos. Plummer, Sarah Plummer, Hannah Miller, Jesse Plummer, Saml. Plummer, Yate Plummer, Saml. Plummer, Abigail Hunt, Phebe Farquhar, Sarah Farquhar, Susanna Farquhar, Ursula Plummer, Jos. Talbott, Achsah Worthington, Mary Plummer,

Eliz: Brooke, Ann Ballinger, John Talbott, Wm. Worthington, Mahlon Janney, Solomon Miller, Anne Plummer, Ruth Miller, Wm. Farquhar, Ruth Holland, William Ba---, Cassandra B--, Daniel Brown, Susanna Brown, Sarah Brown, Mary Ballinger, Daniel Ballinger, Wm. Ballinger, Sarah Plummer, Hannah Ballinger, Rachel Ballinger, Saml. Plummer, Ellin Plummer, Anthoy. Poulltney, Susanna Poultney, Anna Talbot, Abram. Plummer, Sarah P---.

Jonah Hollingsworth, son of Rachel Hollingsworth, widow of Frederick County, Virginia, and Hannah Miller, dau of Solomon and Sarah Miller of Frederick Co., Maryland, 15th day of 1st month, 1778. Witnesses: William Farquhar, Isaac Lane, Isaac Jackson, William Jackson, Junr., Thomas Milhous, Mary Townsend, John Hough, Wm. Williams, Joseph Janney, John Berry, John Parrish, Allen Farquhar, Junr., Benj. Wright, Jesse Hughes, Edward Benson (Beason?), Benjamin Farquhar, Amos Farquhar, Joel Wright, Thomas Taylor, junr., Sarah Janney, Sidney Wright, Hannah Janney, Eliza. Wright, David Lupton, John James, Rachel Willits, Thomas Ellis, Anthony Poultney, Susanna Poultney, Ursula Plummer, Moses Farquhar, Sarah Farquhar, Susanna Farquhar, Moses Ellis, Anthoney Lee, John Willits, William Pidgeon, Isaac Steer(?), Solomon Miller, Rachel Hollingsworth, Sarah Miller, Lydia Hough, Ruth Miller, Robert Miller, Elizabeth Miller, Lydia Miller, Mordi. Matthews, Saml. Matthews, William Farquhar, Junr, Ann Farquhar Junr., Elizabeth Farquhar.

Joseph Haines, son of Nathan and Sophia Haines of Pipe Creek, Frederick Co., Maryland, and Rachel Cookson, dau of Samuel and Jane Cookson of same co., 20th day of 1st month, 1779. Witnesses: Allen(?) Farquhar, Junr., ---l Wright, Samuel Farquhar, William Farquhar, --- se Hughes, Thomas Ellis, William Roberts, junr., --- Willits, ---es Farquhar, Thomas Farquhar, ---m Molendore, Sarah Farquhar, Rachel Pidgeon, Phebe Farquhar, junr., Phebe Farquhar, Elizabeth Wright, Susanna Farquhar, Sarah Farquhar, Ann Farquhar, Lydia Miller, Rachel Farquhar, Mary Miller, Sarah Farquhar, Joseph Wright, William Farquhar, Samuel Matthews, Mordicai Matthews, William Pidgeon, Robert Miller, Joseph Miller, James Brown, Moses Farquhar, Rachel Willets, Samuel Cookson, Mary Cookson, Nathan Haines, Sophia Haines, Elizabeth Haines, Mary Moore, Samuel Cookson, Ruben Haines, William Haines.

Robert Miller son of Solomon and Sarah Miller of Pipe Creek, Frederick Co., and Cassandra Wood dau. of William and Margaret Wood, 21st day of

10th month, 1779. Witnesses: Mary Morsel, Rachel Ballinger, Hannah Ballinger, Mary Poultney, William Ballinger, junr., Stephen Howel, Isaac Plummer, Yate Plummer, Anne Plummer, Jesse Hughes, Anthony Poultney, Susanna Poultney, John Maulsby, Richard Roberts, Levi Woodrow, Abigail Hunt, Hannah Gipson, John Talbott, Mary Talbott, Mordecai Miller, Sarah Plummer, William Ballinger, Thomas Plummer, Ellen Plummer, Cassandra Balinger, Samuel Plummer, Anna Talbott, Mercy Roberts, Ursula Plummer, Abram. Plummer, Sarah Miller, Elizabeth Wood(?), Richd. Holla---, Wm. Wood, Ruth Holland, Ruth Miller, Elizabeth Mil---, Mary Miller, Solomon Shepherd, Isaac Haines, Samuel Waters.

Solomon Shepherd son of William and Richmond Shepherd of Menallen, York Co., Pennsylvania, deceased, and Susannah Farquhar dau of William Farquhar of Pipe Creek, Frederick Co., and his wife, Ann, 27th day of 10th month, 1779. Witnesses: Hannah Russell, Rachel Willits, Sarah Elliot, Sarah Yarnall, Mary Ellot, Thos. Carson, Wm. Elliot, Mary Kenworthy, Mary Cookson, Elizabeth Miller, Lydia Miller, Ann Farquhar, Rachel Farquhar, Ruth Farquhar, Rachel Farquhar, Mary Farquhar, Robert Farquhar, Saml. Farqr. of Allen Snr., James Farquhar, Abigail Hunt, Mary Poultney, Sarah Harris, Rachel Pidgeon, Jesse Hughes, Lydia Coale, Sarah Farquhar, Hannah Owings, Mary Owings, Joseph Wright, Joel Wright, Mary Owings, Solomon Miller, Wm. Farquhar, Wm. Wood, Thos. Farquhar, John Elliot, Samuel Peach, Robert Miller, Eli Farquhar, Ann Farquhar, Hannah Owings, William Farquhar, Allen Farquhar, junr., Mary Wright, Saml. Farquhar, Eliz: Wright, Moses Farquhar, Wm. Shepherd, Sarah Farquhar, Phebe Farquhar, Sarah Farquhar, Thomas Ellis, Jesse Plummer, John Clemson, Isaac Plummer, Thos. Matthews, Gidion Gipson, Wm. Kenworthy, Wm. Kenworthy, Samuel Coale, Thoms. Plummer, Saml. Hutton, John Maulsby, Robert Hunt, Wm. Ballinger, junr., John Willits, Mary Miller, Sarah Miller, junr., Nathan Haines, Samuel Cookson, William Pidgeon.

Elisha Kirk of New Garden, Chester Co., Pennsylvania, son of Caleb and Elizabeth Kirk (the former dec'd) and Ruth Miller dau of Solomon and Sarah Miller of Pipe Creek, Frederick Co., 5th day of 4th month, 1780. Witnesses: Allen Farquhar, junr., Joel Wright, Moses Farquhar, John Maulsby, Samuel Coale, Jesse Hughes, Solomon Shepherd, Thomas Farquhar, John Willits, Joseph Wright, John Russell, Robert Hunt, John Elliot, Mary Hutton, Sarah Farquhar, Ann Farquhar, William Farquhar, Susanna Shepherd, Sarah Elliot, Sarah Farquhar, Ann Farquhar, Mary Elliot, Mary

Rees, Elizabeth Farquhar, Phebe Way, Rachel Farquhar, Hannah Russell, Ruth Farquhar, Solomon Miller, Elizabeth Kirk, Sarah Miller, Isaac Coates, Robert Miller, Elizabeth Miller, Lydia Miller, Mary Miller, Rebekah Miller, Casandra Miller, Joseph Miller, Mary Wright, Rachel Willits, Abigail Hunt.

Israel Janney son of Jacob Janney and Hannah his wife of Loudon Co., Virginia, and Anna Plummer dau of Joseph Plummer and Sarah his wife, Frederick Co., Maryland, 17th day of 8th month, 1780. Witnesses: Ruth Plummer, Mary Wright, Mary(Marcy?) Roberts, Hannah Gibson, Anthony Poultney, William Farquhar, Joseph Talbott, William Balenger, junr., Yate Plummer, Saml. Gover, Joel Wright, Joseph Wright, Henry Roberts, Saml. Plummer, Casandra Balenger, Abram. Plummer, Ursula Plummer, Samuel Waters, Anna Talbott, Susanna Poultney, Mahlon Janney, William Balenger, Mary Balenger, Sarah Harris, Hannah Balenger, Mary Poultney, Isaac Pluer, Jacob Janney, Joseph Plummer, Hannah Janney, Sarah Plummer, Rebekah Gregg, Samuel Plummer, Mary Plummer, Aquila Janney, Mosses Plummer, Aaron Plummer, Meream(?) Plummer, Thos. Plummer, Ellen Plummer, Sarah Janney.

Jacob Janney son of Jacob Janney and Hannah his wife, Loudon Co., Virginia, and Sarah Harris dau of Moses Harris and Elizabeth his wife, Frederick Co., Maryland, 14th day of 10th month, 1780. Witnesses: Mary Roberts, Hannah Gipson, Rachel Balinger, Ann Balinger, Mary Randal, Delilah Plummer, Miriam Plummer, Henry Roberts, Samuel Talbott, Anthony Poultney, Ursula Plummer, Aquila Janney, Hannah Janney, junr., Sarah Plummer, Samuel Waters, John Talbott, Mary Ballenger, Mary Poultney, Saml. Plummer, Ruth Plummer, Isaac Plummer, William Balenger, junr., Jesse Plummer, Jacob Janney, senr, Hannah Janney, senr, Sarah Plummer, senr, Ruth Holland, Thos. Plummer, Joseph Plummer, Casandra Ballenger, Anna Talbott, Richd. Holland, Ellenor Plummer, William Ballinger.

Samuel Waters of Bush Creek, Frederick County, Maryland, and Sarah Unkles of Pipe Creek, Frederick Co., Maryland, 21st day of 2nd month, 1781. Witnesses: Anthony Poultney, Rachel Haines, Samuel Wright, William Wright, John Elliot, Jonathan Carson, James Farquhar, William Webb, Thomas Ellis, Jesse Plummer, Samuel Gover, Isaac Miller, Samuel Coale, George Chandlee, Jehu Moore, Jesse Hughes, Mord. Churchman, Ann Farquhar, Ann Farquhar, Sarah Farquhar, Elizabeth Farquhar, Samuel Plummer, Junr, Yate Plummer, Rachel Farquhar, Ruth Holland, Margaret

Wood, Moses Farquhar, Sarah Farquhar, Thomas Farquhar, Mary Farquhar, Ruth Farquhar, Ruth Farquhar, John Russell, Hannah Russell, Mary Rees, Eliza. Cookson, Joel Wright, Samuel Ellis, Ann Farquhar, snr., Allen Farquhar, Sarah Farquhar, Hannah Gipson, Allen Farquhar, junr., Joseph Wright, William Farquhar, Mary Wright, Phebe Farquhar, Elizabeth Wright, Solomon Miller, Susanna Shepherd, Sophia Haines, Samuel Farquhar, Phebe Farquhar Junr.

John Maulsby of Pipe Creek in Frederick Co., Maryland, son of David and Mary Maulsby and Mary Starr of same co., dau of John and Mary Starr, dec'd., 21st day of 2nd month, 1781. Witnesses: Robert Hunt, Mary Ballinger, Mary Smith, Lydia Coale, Lydia Miller, Sarah Miller, Robert Miller, Wm. Balinger, junr., William Pusey, Allen Farquhar, junr., Joseph Wright, William Farquhar, Israel Cox, Solomon Miller, Sarah Miller, Hannah Gipson, Mary Wright, Eliza. Miller, Phebe Farquhar, Elizabeth Wright, Susanna Shepherd, Ann Farquhar, Sarah Farquhar, Elizabeth Farquhar, Eliza. Cookson, Rachel Farquhar, Ruth Holland, Sophia Haines, Sophia Haines, William Wright, Jonathan Cookson, Anthony Poultney, John Elliot, Sarah Elliot, Samuel Coale, George Chandlee, Jehu Moore, Mary Farquhar, Ruth Farquhar, Rachel Farquhar, John Russell, Samuel Wright, Joel Wright, George Pusey, Richard Richardson, Iscointia Richardson, Joseph Miller, Margret Wood, Yate Plummer, Thomas Farquhar, Joshua Smith, Moses Farquhar, Jesse Hughes, Sarah Farquhar, Mord. Churchman.

William Shepherd, son of William and Richmond Shepherd of Menallen, York Co., Pennsylvania, and Phebe Way, dau of William and Mary Way of York Co., Pennsylvania, the former dec'd., 21st day of 8th month, 1782. Witnesses: Elizabeth Farquhar, Ann Farquhar, Rachel Farquhar, Ruth Farquhar, William Farquhar, Sarah Farquhar, Mary Maulsby, Lydia Coale, Mary Rees, Joseph Wright, Thomas Farquhar, William Farquhar, Joel Wright, Hanneh Russell, Moses Farquhar, Allen Farquhar, junr, John Willits, John Maulsby, Sarah Farquhar, Mary Poultney, James Hartey, Robert Miller, William Farquhar, Mary Farquhar, John Elliot, Sarah Elliot, Mary Elliot, William Shepherd, Phebe Shepherd

[separated by a line]

Mary Way, Solomon Shepherd, Susanna Shepherd, Joseph Way, William Way, Jesse Hughes, Elizabeth Hughes.

William Farquhar and Elizabeth Talbott, 13th day of 9th month, 1784. Witnesses: Benjamin Talbott senr. William Hobbs, Mary Ballinger, Isaac

Plummer, Abram. Plummer, Eliza. Hobbs, Ann Ballinger, Meriam Plummer, Henry Roberts, Morris Ellis, Ruth Holland, Saml. Waters, Sarah Waters, Anthony Poultney, Samuel Farquhar, Joseph Talbott Senr., Anna Talbott, Mary Morsell, Ann Benton, Willm. Morsell, James Brooke, Joseph Benton, Cassy Ballinger, Elizath. Brooke, Susanna Chandlee, Jos. Cowman of John, James Dobson, John Talbott, Mary Talbott, Sarah Farquhar, Thomas Farquhar, Sarah Ellis, Rachel Farquhar, Mary Farquhar, Benjamin Talbott, junr, Joseph Talbott, Junr., Amos Ellis, John Talbott, Junr, Robert Farquhar, Samuel Talbott.

Henry Roberts, son of Richard and Mersey Roberts of Frederick Co., Maryland and Ann Farquhar, dau of William and Rachel Farquhar of Frederick Co., Maryland, the latter decd, at Pipe Creek, 24th day 11th month, 1784. Witnesses: Allen Farquhar, Sarah Farquhar, Sarah Pusey, Jonathan Wright, Joel Wright, Elizath. Wright, Solo. Shepherd, Phebe Farquhar, Junr., Rachel Farquhar, Ruth Farquhar, John Roberts, William Farquhar, William Roberts, Mary Wright, Joseph Wright, Moses Farquhar, Richard Roberts, Marcy Roberts, William Farquhar, Mary Farquhar, Elizabeth Farquhar, James Farquhar, Sarah Farquhar, Samuel Wright, William Farquhar, Thos. S.(?) Pleasants, James Bates, Thomas W. Pleasants, William Haines, Sarah Yarnall, Samuel Haines, Cary Pleasants, James Brooke, Jesse Plummer, John Willits, Elizabeth Webb, Ruth Webster, Hannah Gipson, Sarah Elliot, Ann Wright, Elizabeth Farquhar, Mary Farquhar, Rachel Farquhar, Thomas Farquhar, Jeremiah Cook, William Webster, Joseph Hutton, Susanna Shepherd, John Milhouse, John Elliot, Isaac Webster, Sarah Farquhar, Jesse Hughes, William Wright, Amos Farquhar, George Pusey, Mary Poultney, Ruth Plummer.

Isaac Plummer of Frederick Co., Maryland, son of Thomas Plummer and Eleanor his wife, and Grace Taylor of same place, dau of Israel and Elizabeth Taylor, 25th day of 5th month, 1785. Witnesses: Mary Wright, Phebe Farquhar, Abigail Moore, George Pusey, Jesse Hughes, Sarah Pusey, Solo. Shepherd, Susanna Shepherd, Rachel Farquhar, Eliza. Farquhar, Sarah Farquhar, snr., Thomas Farquhar, Jane Hibberd, Sarah Spencer, Hannah Hibberd, Rebekah Day, Jno. Richardson, Abraham Moore, Sarah Bentley, William Bentley, Ann Roberts, Wm. Ballinger, junr., Joseph Hibberd, John Clemson, Elizabeth Clemson, Jeremiah Cook, Thomas Ellis, Nathan Haines, William Farquhar, Mary Farquhar, Allen Farquhar, junr, Joel Wright, Henry Roberts, Elizabeth Webb, Joseph Wright, Joseph Miller,

Elizabeth Miller, Jesse Plummer, Sarah Farquhar, Mary Poultney, Ruth Plummer, Ursula Plummer, Moses Farquhar, Moses Plummer, Richard Holland, Elizabeth Miller, William Plummer, Ruth Farquhar.

Benjamin Talbot son of John Talbot and Mary his wife, and Susanna Chandlee dau of William Chandlee and Mary his wife, both of Bush Creek, Frederick Co., Maryland, 6th day of 10th month, 1785. Witnesses: Edward Stewart, Rebekah Day, Jane Way, Hezekiah Ford, Jesse Plummer, Miriam Roberts, Sarah Roberts, Sarah Taylor, Samuel Waters, Sarah Waters, Eliza. Hardacre, William Roberts, Miriam Plummer, Benjamin Talbott, Anna Talbott, Samuel Talbott, Joseph Talbott, Elizabeth Webb, Ellen Plummer, Ruth Plummer, Rachel Morsell, Jno. Roberts, Elizabeth Gamble, Yate Plummer, Gidion Gipson, William Plummer, Nicholas Watkins, Jesse Hughes, William Chandlee, Mary Chandlee, George Chandlee, Deborah Chandlee, John Talbott, Mary Talbott, Joseph Talbott, Junr, Susanna Talbott, Ann Talbott, Rachel Talbott, John Talbott, junr, Joseph Talbott, Mary Morsell, Willm. Morsell.

Moses Plummer of Joseph and Sarah Plummer of Pipe Creek in Frederick Co., Maryland and Elizabeth Webb of same place dau of George and Ann Webb of Lancaster Co., Pennsylvania, 3rd day of 11th month, 1785. Witnesses: Elizabeth Miller, Margret Waters, Anthony Poultney, Mary Talbott, Elizabeth Gamble, Willm. Morsell, Samuel Plummer, Sarah Macklefresh, John Talbott, John Ducket, Jonathan Plummer, Mary Morsell, Hezekiah Ford, Asa Plummer, James Steward, Stephen Howell, Sarah Howell, Sarah Waters, William Balinger, Ellen Plummer, Mary Poultney, Ruth Plummer, Samuel Waters, Sarah Waters, Isaac Plummer, Grace Plummer, Jesse Plummer, Mercy Roberts, Richard Holland, Jesse Hughes, William Webb, Joseph Plummer, Ezra Plummer, Mary Webb, Miriam Plummer, Abrahm. Plummer, Ruth Holland, Ursula Plummer, Anna Talbott, Susanna Poultney, Joseph Talbott, Yate Plummer, Benjamin Talbot.

Jeremiah Cook, late of Pipe Creek, Frederick Co., Maryland, son of Stephen Cook and Hannah his wife, and Rachel Farquhar, dau of Allen and Sarah Farquhar of same co., 22nd day of 2nd month, 1786. Witnesses: Sarah Farquhar, Margret Cook, Hannah Owings, Elizabeth Gamble, Eliz. Dorsey of Eliz., Samuel Wright, Ann Wright, Jane Hibberd, George Pusey, Sarah Pusey, Jesse Hughes, Rachel Willits, Richard Condon, Hannah Hibberd, Joseph Jackson, Polly Warfield, Morris Ellis, Moses Farquhar, Elizabeth Farquhar, Ruth Farquhar, William Farquhar, Joseph Wright, Mary Wright,

Joel Wright, Solo. Shepherd, William Wright, Joseph Talbott junr, Joseph Hibberd, John Roberts, Elizabeth Norris, Ruth Holland, Mary Rees, Sarah Dorsey, Thomas Farquhar, Hannah Farquhar, William Farquhar, Elizabeth Farquhar, Robert Farquhar, Sarah Ellis, Amos Ellis, Mary Farquhar, Mordeca Price, Abrm. Griffith, Rachel Price, Allen Farquhar, Phebe Farquhar, Sarah Farquhar.

Joseph Talbott of Bush Creek, Frederick Co., son of John and Mary Talbott, and Mary Farquhar of Pipe Creek, dau of Allen and Sarah Farquhar, 1st day of 7th month, 1786. Witnesses: Wm. Farquhar of Allen, Jno. Roberts, Solo. Shepherd, Hezekiah Ford, Mary Farquhar, Amos Farquhar, William Farquhar, Mary Poultney, Sarah Roberts, William Farquhar, Samuel Wright, Mary Wright, Phebe Farquhar, Moses Farquhar, Sarah Farquhar, Jehu Moore, William Wright, Henry Roberts, Ann Roberts, Ruth Farquhar, John Talbott, Mary Talbott, Sarah Farquhar, Thomas Farquhar, Hannah Farquhar, Sarah Ellis, Elizabeth Farquhar, William Farquhar, Susanna Talbott, Robert Farquhar, Samuel Farquhar, Benjamin Talbott, Susanna Talbott, John Talbott, Rachel Talbott, Elizabeth Farquhar, Susanna Shepherd, Ann Wright.

Robert Miller of Pipe Creek, Frederick Co., Maryland, son of Robert Miller and Sarah his wife of Newbury Township, York Co., Pennsylvania, and Jane Williams of Pipe Creek, dau of Jacob Williams and Ruth his wife of Warrington Township, York Co., Pennsylvania, 26th day of 11th month, 1788. Witnesses: John Willets, Solo. Shepherd, Susanna Shepherd, Samuel Farquhar, John Penrose, William Roberts, Ittai Everitt, William Kenworthy, Wm. Kenworthy junr., Mary Kenworthy, Hannah Kenworthy, Moses Farquhar, William Farquhar, Benja. Farquhar, Eliza. Farquhar, Ann Roberts, Geo: Pusey, John Pidgeon, Joseph Everitt, Sarah Farquhar, Wm. Farquhar (of A.), Ruth Plummer, Robert Miller, Jacob Williams, Ruth Williams, Samuel Miller, Hannah Jordan, James Miller, Israel Williams, Sarah Williams, Hannah Miller, Allen Farquhar junr, Jehu Moore, Mary Farquhar.

John Talbott, Bush Creek, Frederick Co., Maryland, son of John and Mary his wife, and Elizabeth Plummer of the same place, dau of Samuel and Mary Plummer, 30th day of 12th month, 1790. Witnesses: Sarah Waters, Margaret Waters, Sarah Waters, Junr, Ann French, William Hunt, Yate Plummer, Emme French, Mary Hussey, Sarah French, Saml. Gipson, Elizabeth Gamble, William Morsell, Samuel Poultney, Anthony Poultney, Mercy Roberts, Elizh. Hughes, Jesse Hughes, Mary Wood, Sarah Howel, David

Barnes, Thomas Russel, Samuel Waters, Samuel Talbott, Wm. Plummer, Ursula Plummer, Jno. Poultney, Joseph Talbott, Ruth Plummer, Elizabeth Plummer, Rebeckah Morsell, Rachel Morsell, Robert Plummer, Willm. Morsell, John Talbot, Mary Talbott, Joseph Talbott, Susannah Talbott, Sarah Plummer, Rachel Plummer, Rachel Talbott, Samuel Talbott, Israel Plummer, Ruth Holland, Evan Plummer, Moses Plummer.

William Harrison of Frederick Co., Maryland, son of Thomas and Elizabeth Harrison (the latter dec'd.) and Ruth Farquhar, dau of William and Rachel Farquhar (the latter dec'd), 20th(?) day of 11th month, 1791. Witnesses: Hannah Farquhar, Solo. Shepherd, Susanna Farquhar, Mary Cordray, Elianor Vore, John Wright, Benjn. Norris, Ann Norris, Jane Hibberd, Elenor Plummer, Sarah Ogleon (Ogbon?), William Kenworthy, Benjamin Benson, Joseph Wright, Isaac Wright junr, Thos. Parvin junr, William Farquhar, Ruth Harrison, Susanna Harrison, Ann Wright, Peter Harrison, Henry Roberts, Allen Farquhar, Phebe Farquhar, Moses Farquhar, Rachel Richardson, Elizabeth Wright, Sarah Farquhar, Susanna Shepherd, Benja. Farquhar, Amos Farquhar, William Farquhar (of Allen), Mary Farquhar, William Farquhar, Mary Farquhar, Benjamin Harrison, Myriam Harrison, Eliza. Farquhar, James Farquhar, William Farquhar, Sarah Farquhar, junr, Sarah Harrison, Daniel Harrison.

William Plummer of Bush Creek, Frederick Co., Maryland, son of Thomas Plummer and Elen his wife, and Rachel Morsel of the same place, dau of William and Mary Morsel, 1st day of 11th month, 1792. Witnesses: Christopher Hussey, Sarah Poultney, Israel Plummer, Stephen Howell, Sarah Howell, Samuel Waters, Sarah Waters, Margaret Waters, Sarah Plummer, Rachel Plummer, Yate Plummer, Moses Given, Grace Plummer, Moses Farquhar, Sarah Farquhar, Anthony Poultney, Susanna Poultney, Moses Plummer, Elizabeth Plummer, Henry Ballenger, Ann Ballenger, Hannah Ballenger, Israel Plummer, Robert Plummer, William Morsell, Mary Morsell, Ellen Plummer, Rebekah Morsell, Isaac Plummer, Jesse Plummer, Ruth Plummer, Mary Poultney, William Morsell, junr, Casandra Ballenger, John Talbott, Mary Talbott, Elizabeth Morsell, Ruth Plummer, senr, Ruth Holland, Abner Williams, Hanson Waters, John Poultney, William Farquhar, Samuel Poultney, James Barnes, John Barnes, William Hunt, Israel French, Gulielma Maria Waters, Rachel Talbott, Rebecca Roberts, Sarah Roberts, Elizabeth Gamble, Mercy Roberts, Elizabeth Randal, Harriott Richardson, Charles Jones, Mary Carrick, Tacey Johns, Mary Pope, Joseph

Miller, Jesse Hughes, Thomas Russel, Benjamin Boyd, Richard Roberts, William Flint.

William Farquhar son of William and Rachel Farquhar of Frederick Co., the latter dec'd, and Ester Wright dau of Isaac and Eleanor Wright, 24th day of 4th month, 1793. Witnesses: Ann Wright, Eliza. Wright, junr, Esther Haines, Sarah Pusey, Ittai Everitt, John Hosler, Joseph Hibberd, Hannah Hibberd, William Haines, Joseph Wright, James Farquhar junr, Hannah Farquhar, Mahlon Farquhar, Jonah Farquhar, Moses Farquhar, Rachel Wright, Elizabeth Wright, Betsy (Betey?), Wright of Joel, Allen Farquhar, William Farquhar of A., Solo. Shepherd, Susanna Shepherd, Benj. Farquhar, Amos Farquhar, Wm. Wright, Caleb Windle, Joseph Elgar, junr, John Wright, Aaron Hibberd, Mark Parvin, Caleb Farquhar, William Farquhar, Isaac Wright, Eleanor Wright, Mary Farquhar, Ann Roberts, Rachel Richardson, Isaac Vore, Elanor Vore, James Farquhar, Sarah Farquhar, Ann Wright, junr, Isaac Wright, junr, Henry Roberts, Ruth Kirk, Moses Farquhar, Sarah Farquhar, Elizabeth Wright, Thomas Parvin, George Pusey, William Farquhar, Polly Farquhar.

Robert Plummer of Frederick Co., Maryland, son of Abraham Plummer and Sarah Plummer his wife, and Rachel Talbott of Frederick Co., Maryland, dau of John Talbott and Mary Talbott his wife, 3rd day of 10th month, 1793. Witnesses: Ann French, Mary Russell, Sarah Roberts, Margaret Waters, Hannah Elliott, Emma French, Elizabeth Miller, John Elliott, Joseph Gamble, Elizabeth Gamble, Elizabeth Ballenger, John Barnes, Thomas Russell, Joseph Miller, Richard Roberts, junr, Hanson Waters, Israel French, John Bissett, Joseph Ford, Richard Roberts, Sarah Elliott, Rachel Wayman, Ann Wayman, Edward Warfield, Beal Warfield, Prissilla Williams, Stephen Howell, Rachel Plummer, Anthony Poultney, Ruth Holland, Elizabeth Hughes, Rebekah Stanley, Jesse Hughes, Mary Poultney, Yate P)lummer, Jesse Russel, Israel Plummer, John Talbott, Mary Talbott, Susanna Talbott, John Plummer, Benjamin Talbott, Joseph Benton, junr, Ann Benton, Willm. Morsell, Mary Morsell, Samuel Talbott, Jonathan Plummer, Elizabeth Talbott, Rebekah Morsell, Sarah Plummer, Rachel Plummer, Ellen Plummer, Wm. Wood, Samuel Polney, William Plummer.

Thomas Russell of Frederick Co., Maryland, son of John and Hannah Russell, and Sarah Roberts of the same place, dau of Richard Roberts and Mary Roberts his wife, 31st day of 10th month, 1793. Witnesses: William Plummer, Joseph Miller, John Pidgeon, Ruth Holland, John Talbott, Mary

Talbott, John Russell, Richard Roberts, Mercy Roberts, Henry Roberts, Ann Roberts, Zachariah Roberts, Israel Plummer, Emma French, Stephen Howell, Abner Williams, Samuel Poultney, Otho French, Anthony Poultney, Mary Ballenger, Ruth Plummer, Israel Plummer, Rebekah Morsell, Sarah Plummer, Ann French, Elizabeth Miller, Rachel Plummer, Hannah Elliott, Miriam Swamley, Sarah Russell, Mary Russell, Jesse Russell, Hannah Gibson, William Morsell, Yate Plummer, Mary Poultney.

Israel Plummer of Frederick Co., Maryland, son of Samuel and Mary Plummer, and Rebeckah of the same place, dau of William and Mary Morsel, 29th day of 10th month, 1795. Witnesses: Sarah Russell, Anthony Poultney, Jesse Hughes, John Elliott, Zachariah Roberts, Stephen Howel, Israel French, Wm. Murphy, junr, Moses Given, John Roberts, Wm. Wood, Ellenor Bennett, Grace Plummer, John Plummer, John Pancoast, Jno. Poultney, Jesse Plummer, Richard Roberts, junr, Otho French, Ann Plummer, Margaret Waters, Kinsey Talbott, Mary Poultney, Philip Mackelfresh, Jane Mackelfresh, Elizabeth Hughes, Mary Roberts, Polly Parvin, Eliza: Wright, Hannah Elliott, Lydia Mackelfresh, Ann Duckett, Ann French, Emma French, Lucy Smith, Mary Plummer, Willm. Morsell, Mary Morsell, Rachel Plummer, Sarah Plummer, Elizabeth Morsell, Peggy Talbott, Rachel Plummer, junr, William Morsell, Jonathan Plummer, William Plummer, John Talbott, junr, Elizabeth Talbott, Sarah Poultney, Samuel Talbott, John Talbott, Ursula Plummer, Ruth Plummer, Rachel Ballinger, Sarah Waters, Ellen Plummer.

John Moore of Frederick Co., Maryland, son of John and Hannah Moore, dec'd., and Hannah Hibberd, dau of Joseph Hibberd and Jane his wife of Pipe Creek, 23rd day of 3rd month, 1796. Witnesses: Joseph Elgar, Margaret Elgar, Moses Farquhar, Sarah Farquhar, Isaac Atler, Joseph Ogborn, Sarah Ogborn, Joseph Haines, Mordecai Price, junr, Isaac Wright, junr, Daniel Haines, Allen Farquhar, junr, Wm. Farquhar (of A.), William Farquhar, Joseph Wright, Joel Wright, Ann Roberts, Mary Wright, Elizabeth Wright, Ann Wright, Rachel Richardson, Eliza. Wright, junr, Amos Farquhar, Mary Farquhar, Benjn. Farquhar, Rachel Farquhar, Ann Shepherd, Joseph Hibberd, Jane Hibberd, James Fowler, Allen Farquhar, Aaron Hibberd, Thomas Moore, Allen Hibberd, Phebe Farquhar, Jane Hibberd, Sarah Hibberd, Joseph Hibberd, Silas Hibberd, Hannah Farquhar.

William Ballinger of Frederick Co., Maryland, son of William Ballinger of Frederick Co., Maryland and Cassandra his wife, the former dec'd., and

Lydia Smith dau of John Smith, late of Harford Co., Maryland and Elizabeth his wife, the latter dec'd., 20th day of 7th month, 1797. Witnesses: Sarah Waters, Margaret Waters, Sarah Plummer, Rachel Plummer, Joel Wright, Jesse Hughes, Jesse Plummer, Rebekah Roberts, Solo. Shepherd, Elizabeth Hughes, Lydia Pusey, Ann Shepherd, Sarah Poultney, Joel Wood, Samuel Harlan, Thomas Poultney, William Poultney, Ann French, Moses Given, Wm. Hobbs (of Saml.), Henry Wayman, Jonathan Plummer, Belt Brashear, Ely Brashear, Wm. Murphy, junr, Henry McEl...(?), Anthony Poultney, Stephen Howel, Richard Roberts, junr, Anne Brashear, Zacah. Roberts, Elizabeth Hall, Peggy Talbott, Elizabeth Morsell, Ann French, Casandra Ballinger, Mary Wood, Mary Ballinger, Rachel Ballinger, Elizabeth Ballinger, William Wood, Daniel Ballinger, Henry Ballinger, Anna Norris, Ellen Plummer, Sarah Elliot, Margaret Baily, George Pusey, Silas Smith, Elizabeth Poultney, Mary Griffith, Ruth Plummer.

Moses Given, Frederick Co., Maryland, son of James Given and Isabella his wife (the former dec'd) and Ann French of the same place, dau of Israel French and Margaret his wife (the latter dec'd), 31st day of 8th month, 1797. Witnesses: Susanna Pidgeon, Mary Eliott, Margaret Eliott, Mary Russell, Elizabeth Poultney, Mary Poultney, Lydia Howel, Priscilla Plummer, Jesse Russell, Willm. Morsell, Samuel Luke, William Eliott, Emma Phelps, Jno. Pancoast, Mary Pope, Sarah Uncles, Sarah Russell, Anna Norris, Ruth Holland, Casandra Ballinger, Ellen Plummer, Mersey Roberts, Mary Poultney, Ursula Plummer, Anthony Poultney, Susanna Poultney, Mary Wood, Hannah Eliott, Achsah Harrison, Hannah Russell, Sarah Russell, Hannah Gipson, Israel French, George Phelps, Emma French, Sarah Plummer, William Wood, John Given, Israel French, junr, Samuel French, Otho French, Wm. Ballinger, Jno. Athn. Hall, John Talbott, Benjn. Norris, Jesse Hughes, John Russell.

Eli Elliott of Frederick Co., Maryland, son of John Elliott and Sarah his wife, and Margaret Hughes of the same place, dau of Jesse Hughes and Elizabeth his wife (the latter dec'd.), 20th day of 9th month, 1798. Witnesses: Thos. Russell, Sarah Russell, John Pidgeon, Willm. Morsell, Henry Roberts, Mary Talbott, Asenath Hobbs, Rachl. Plummer, Abraham B. Wooward [Woodward?], Isaac Plummer, Grace Plummer, Emma French, Elizabeth Pearce, Ann Given, John Roberts, Richard Roberts, Stephen Howell, Richd. Roberts, junr, Anna Hobbs, Priscilla McKinstry, Lydia Howel, Sarah Elliott, Mary Elliott, Samuel Gibson, Hannah Gibson, Susanna Poultney, Susanna

Wood, Nathan Wood, John Talbott, John Russell, Yate Plummer, Thos. Maynard, Moses Given, Anthony Poultney, Ruth Holland, Ann Roberts, Sarah Russell, Margaret Bailey (Bayley), John Elliott, Sarah Elliott, Jesse Hughes, Elizabeth Hughes, William Elliott, Hannah Elliott, Mary Elliott, Rachel Hughes, Amos Elliott, Ruth Elliott, Thos. Wood, Margaret Elliott, Lydia Wood, Jno. Wood, Thomas Elliott, Samuel Hughes, William Gipson, Joel Wood, Israel Howel.

William Ward of Herring Creek, Anne Arundel Co., Maryland, son of Robert Ward and Elizabeth his wife, dec'd., and Sarah Plummer of Frederick Co., Maryland, dau of Yate Plummer and Artridg his wife, 19th day of 9th month, 1799. Witnesses: John Talbott, junr, Kinsey Talbott, Moses Given, Ann Ward, Ruth Holland, Robert Plummer, Yate Plummer, Artridge Plummer, Priscilla Plummer, Sarah Waters, Ann Plummer, Margaret Waters, Emma French, Elizabeth Talbott, John Elliott, Sarah Elliott, John Talbott, Mary Talbott, Thomas Plummer, Richard Roberts, Ruth Plummer, Ursula Plummer, Hannah Russell, Sarah Russell, Sarah Plummer, Isaac Iiams, Israel French, Isaac Plummer, Wm. C. Anderson, Otho French, Richard Roberts, junr, John Pidgeon.

Thomas Plummer of Frederick Co. son of Joseph West Plummer and Mary his wife and Susanna Talbott of the county afsd, dau of John Talbott and Mary his wife, 24th day of 7th month, 1800. Witnesses: Elizabeth Welsh, Ellen Plummer, Hannah Elliott, Ann Roberts, Margaret Elliott, Ruth Meredith, Anna Norris, Emma French, Priscilla Plummer, Silas Baily, Julia Breashear, Mary Breashear, Rachel Plummer, Sarah Waters, Margaret Waters, Elizabeth Morsell, Lydia Pusey, Thomas Benton, John Pidgeon, Susanna Pidgeon, William Morsell, junr, Benjn. Talbott, John Williams, Sarah Elliott, Jos. W. Plummer, Mary Talbott, Mary Plummer, John Talbott, Kinsey Talbott, Mary Talbott, Deborah Plummer, Peggy Talbott, Sally Plummer, Mahala Plummer, Robt. Plummer, Rachel Plummer, Yate Plummer, Wm. Morsell, Jesse Hughes, John Talbott, junr, Nathan Pusey, Anthony Poultney, Susanna Poultney, Otho French, Rebecca Roberts, John Roberts, Wm. P. Richardson, Susanna Wood, Fielder Richardson, John Dilworth.

Kinsey Talbott, Frederick Co., Maryland, son of John Talbott and Mary his wife and Deborah Plummer of co afsd, dau of Joseph West Plummer and Mary his wife, 21st day of 8th month, 1800. Witnesses: Jesse Hughes, Sarah Poultney, Anne Plummer, Joel Wood, Otho French, George Pusey, Jane

Mackelfresh, Lydia Adams, Eliza: Anderson, Dorcas Anderson, Mary Wood, Lydia Wood, Margaret Wood, William Elliott, Nathan Wood, Richard Plummer, Caleb Plummer, John Musseter, Isaac Plummer, Grace Plummer, Margaret Waters, Sarah Russell, Mary Russell, Benjamin Benton, Benjamin Talbott, Thomas Parvin, John Russell, Elizabeth Hughes, Ursly Plummer, Phebe Starr, Ann Roberts, Mary Poultney, Mary P. Poultney, John Talbott, Mary Talbott, Mary Plummer, John Talbott, junr, Deborah Talbott, Thomas Plummer, Susanna Plummer, Peggy Talbott, Robert Plummer, Rachel Plummer, Betsy Plummer, Ann Plummer, Sally Plummer, Elizabeth Talbott, Thos. Wood, Thos. Russell, Wm. C. Anderson.

Josiah Updegraf of York Co., Pennsylvania, son of Joseph Updegraf of same place, and Mary his wife, and Hannah Farquhar dau of Allen Farquhar and Phebe his wife, both late of Frederick Co., dec'd., 19th day, 11th month, 1800. Witnesses: Sarah Hibberd, Hannah Shepherd, Rachel Wright, Phebe Hibberd, Lydia Willis, Sarah Russell, Joseph Wright, Benjn. Farquhar, junr, Silas Hibberd, Gideon Gibson, Isaac Wright, Moses Wright, Joseph Hibberd, junr, Susan Wright, Jonathan Wright, Mary Wright (of Isaac), Mary Richardson, Joseph Worley, Enoch Farquhar, Wm. Farquhar, Allen Hibberd, Jehu Moore, Jonathan Roberts, Joseph Hibberd, Aaron Hibberd, Jane Hibberd, Phebe Farquhar, Sarah Sheward, Timothy Kirk, Anna Potts, Moses Farquhar, Wm. Farquhar, junr, Esther Farquhar, Joel Wright, Ann Shepherd, Martha Hibberd, Rachel Richardson, Hannah Moore, Jane Farquhar, Lydia Farquhar, Benjn. Hibberd, Solo. Shepherd, Allen Wright, Susanna Shepherd, Eliza: Wright, Mary Wright, Benjn. Farquhar, Wm. Farquhar (of A.), Rachel Farquhar, Amos Farquhar, Susanna Jessop, Sarah Updegraff, Mary Updegraff, Sarah Welch, Allen Farquhar, Isrl. Updegraff, Mary Farquhar, Sarah Farquhar, Caleb Farquhar, Jonah Farquhar, Mahlon Farquhar, James Farquhar, Jane Sheward, Caleb Sheward, Jane Hibberd, junr, William Farquhar, senr, Geor: Chandlee, Margaret Elgar, Elizabeth Wright.

Joseph Elgar, junr. of Montgomery Co., Maryland son of Joseph Elgar of Frederick Co., Maryland, and Margaret his wife, and Ann Wright, dau of Joel Wright of Frederick Co., Maryland, and Elizabeth his wife, 19th day of 11th month, 1800. Witnesses: Wm. P. Farquhar, Allen Hibberd, Jonah Farquhar, Joseph Hibberd, Caleb Sheward, Aron Hibberd, Hannah Shepherd, Rachel Wright, Lydia Willis, Joseph Wright, Jane Farquhar, Silas Hibberd, James Farquhar, Benjn. Hibberd, Polly Wright, Jos: Ogborn,

Lydia Farquhar, Sarah Russell, Sarah Ogborn, Moses Farquhar, Wm. Farquhar (of A.), Isaac Wright, Susanna Shepherd, Ann Shepherd, Rachel Richardson, Solo. Shepherd, Eliza: Wright, Mary Wright, Moses Wright, Susan Wright, Wm. Farquhar, junr, Esther Farquhar, Jane Hibberd, jr., Sarah Sheward, Jane Sheward, Sarah Welch, Jehu Moore, Hannah Moore, Jos. Hibberd, jr., Caleb Farquhar, Joseph Elgar, Margaret Elgar, Joel Wright, Elizabeth Wright, Amos Farquhar, Mary Farquhar, Allen Wright, Rachel Wright, Jonathan Wright, Nathan Elgar, John Elgar, Israel Wright, George Chandlee, Gainer Chandlee, Hannah Churchman, Elizabeth Wright, Geo: Pusey, Wm. Farquhar, senr, Rachel Farquhar, Benjn. Farquhar, Polly Richardson.

Births

Allen Farquhar son of William and Ann Farquhar b. 16th day of 10th month, 1737, d. 15th day of 10th month, 1790(1793?).

Phebe Farquhar dau of Benjn. and Phebe Hibberd, b. 16th) day of 2nd month, 1745, d. 7th day of 1st month, 1795(?).

Their children: Benjamin Farquhar b. 8th day, 5th month, 1766; Amos b. 5th day, 7th month, 1768, William b. 15th day, 11th month, 1770; a son not named b. 10th day, 9th month, 1772, d. 5th day, 11th month, year(?); Allen b. 15th day, 9th month, 1773; Caleb b. 26th day, 3rd month, 1776; Jonah b. 13th day, 3rd month, 1778; Hannah b. 10th day, 3rd month, 1780; Mahlon b. 27th day, 6th month, 1782, d. 21st day, 12th month, ? year; James b. 29th day, 7th month, 1786.

Children of Thomas and Ellen Plummer: Isaac b. 15th day, 2nd month, 1762; Jesse b. 28th day, 10th month, 1763; Ruth b. 24th day, 12th month, 1765; William b. 27th day, 11th month, 1770.

Children of John Willits and Rachel his wife: Samuel Willits b. 28th day, 11th month, 1773; Sarah b. 29th day, 1st month, 1776; Ellis b. 1st day, 5th, 1778; Elizabeth b. 21st day, 3rd month, 1781; Jesse b. 15th, 10th month, 1784.

Children of William Pidgeon and Rachel his wife: Mary b. 13th day, 7th month, 1761, d. 4th day, 1st month, 1773; John b. 21st day, 3rd month, 1763; Elizabeth b. 16th day, 9th month, 1764; d. 13th day, 12th month, 1772; Rachel b. 22nd day, 5th month, 1766; William b. 24th day, 12th month, 1767; Isaac b. 24th day, 9th month, 1769; Ruth b. 15th day, 7th month, 1771, Charles b. 13th day, 3rd month, 1773; Hannah b. 30th day, 11th month, 1774.

Children of Samuel Waters and Susanna his wife: Sarah b. 20th day, 12th month, 1773; Margret b. 3rd day, 9th month, 1776.

Joel Wright (b. 4th day of 4th month, 1750, son of John and Eliza. Wright and Eliza. Wright (b. 24th day of 6th month, 1748, d. 24th day of 6th month, 18--, dau of Wm. and Ann Farquhar, who had children as follows: A son not named b. 12th day, 4th month, 1774; Ann Wright, b. 25th day of 1st month, 1776, Allen Wright b. 14th day of 12th month, 1777.

Children of Daniel Haines and Mary his wife
Samuel b. 25/4/1763
Jesse Haines b. 15/8/1765, d. 15/9/1769
Isaac b. 3/5/1767
Deborah b. 16/6/1769

Children of Samuel Cookson and Mary his wife:
Daniel Cookson, b. 8/3/1774

Samuel Plummer son of Thos. and Eliz: Plummer b. 9/12/1691 and Sarah his wife dau of Thos. and Ruth Miles, b. 17/1/1705, d. 3/8/1788

John Poultney son of Richd. and Mary Poultney b. 12/4/1715 and Ellen his wife dau of Wm. and Sarah Walker b. 3/5/1720

Richard Roberts son of Henry Roberts and Mary his wife b. 8/4/1730.
Mary Roberts dau of Thomas and Susanna Belts b. 2/13/1733.
Their children:
Henry Roberts, b. 5/6/1760
John Roberts, b. 12/5/1763, d. 20/5/1807
Miriam Roberts, b. 20/10/1765
William Roberts, b. 4/10/1767
Sarah Roberts, b. 10/7/1770
Richard Roberts, b. 14/7/1773
Zachariah Roberts, b. 30/6/1775

Children of Samuel Hutton and Mary his wife, who d. 25/4/1782. Sarah Hutton, b. 21/5/1754, d. 10/9/178-.
John Hutton, b. 12/1/1755
Levy Hutton, b. 12/8/1757, d. 18/8/1767
Joseph Hutton, b. 9/11/1759
William Hutton, b. 17/3/1762, d. 31/8/1781
Joel Hutton, b. 31/3/1764, d. 18/10/1766
Benjamin Hutton, b. 22/4/1766

Joel Hutton, b. 8/2/1769
Jonathan Hutton, b. 29/12/1771, b. 31/8/1781
Mary Hutton, b. 12/2/1775
Thomas Hutton, b. 15/3/1776
Levi Hutton, b. 10/10/1778

Children of Robert Hunt and Abigail his wife.
Samuel Hunt, b. 9/10/1766
Mary Hunt, b. 25/7/1768
Joshua Hunt, b. 20/8/1770
William Hunt, b. 21/1/1773
Samuel Hunt, b. 13/4/1775
Joseph Hunt, b. 9/11/1777
Abigail Hunt, b. 24/1/1781
John Hunt, b. 21/8/1784

Children of Yate and Arltridge Plummer. (Arthridge Plummer d. 17/10/1823 in 75th year of her age.)
Sarah Plummer, b. 9/4/1773
Precilla Plummer, b. 13/7/1775
Samuel Plummer, b. 13/8/1777, removed to Ohio and there died.
Richard Plummer, b. 12/2/1780
Rachel Plummer, b. 21/7/1782
Yate Plummer, b. 22/12/1784, d. 2/10/1795
Gule: Plummer, b. 18/4/1787
Rebeckah Plummer, b. 9/8/1791

William Morsel, b. 22/11/1745, d.11/8/1813
Mary his wife b. 12/12/1740
Their children: Rachel Morsel, b. 22/5/1771
Rebeckah Morsel, b. 9/5/1774
William Morsel, b. 13/4/1778
Elizabeth Morsel, b. 20/10/1780

Anthony Poultney son of John and Ellen Poultney b. 31/3/1752, d. 25/7/1805(?).
Susanna Poultney dau of Saml. and Sarah Plummer, b. 16/12/1751, d. 9/5/181-.
Their children:
John Poultney, b. 15/8/1778
Samuel Poultney, b. 18/1/1780

Sarah Poultney, b. 1/3/1781
Elizabeth Poultney, b. 2/12/1782
Mary Poultney, b. 15/7/1784
Thomas Poultney, b. 27/4/1786
William Poultney, b. 12/8/1788, d. 5/8/1800
James Poultney, b. 26/11/1790, d. 15/5/1813
Rachel Poultney, b. 24/8/1793, d. 24/2/1809
Jesse Poultney, b. 16/2/1796, d. 187-.

Children of George Pusey and Sarah his wife
William b. 6/1/1771
Nathan b. 20/1/1774
George b. 31/4/1776
Mary b. 15/8/1778
Lydia b. 15/4/1781

John Elliot son of Wm. and Mary Elliot b. 22/4/1742
Sarah Elliot dau of John and Margret Milhous, b 31/5/1751.
Their children:
Eli Elliot b. 1/11/1773
Hannah b. 7/9/1776, d. 27/8/1804
Amos b. 27/12/1778, d. 6/6/1803
William, b. 14/12/1780, d. 23/9/1786
Ruth b. 9/12/1783
Mary b. 16/4/1786
Joanna b. 21/4/1788
John b. 4/3/1792

Joseph Wright son of John and Elizabeth b. 13/1/1735, d. 21/11/1816
Mary Farquhar dau of Wm. and Ann Farquhar, b. 22/11/1739.
Their children: Ann b. 5/3/1762, d. 14/9/1764
William, b. 27/1/1764
Samuel b. 21/7/1766
Jonathan b. 16/11/1768, d. 12/4/1769
Ann b. 18/8/1770
Elizabeth b. 2/3/1773
Nameless child b. -/7/1775
Moses Wright b. 25/11/1776, d. 15/4/1812
Mary b. 12/2/1779

Rachel b. 3/2/1782
Susanna b. 15/9/1784

Gidion Gipson, b. 24/11/1733
Hannah his wife b. 10/10/1739
Their children:
two nameless children b. 24/6/1771, d. 24/6/1771
William b. 6/11/1772
Ann b. 28/9/1774
Gidion b. 10/12/1776
Hannah b. 8/2/1779
Samuel b. 17/6/1781
Mahlon b. 12/5/1784

Israel French b. 16/9/1746.
Marget French his wife b. 16/1/1746, d. 7/1/1785.
Their children: Ann b. 7/3/1772
Emma b. 6/10/1773
Joanna b. 29/6/1775, d. -/7/1779
Otho b. 2/5/1777
Israel b. 21/10/1779

Jesse Hughes, b. 3/8/1752, d. 19/9/1812.
Elizabeth his first wife b. 8/1/1760, d. 16/9/1784.
Their children: Margaret b. 16/2/1781
Rachel b. 1/5/1782
Samuel b. 20/3/1784 Children of Jesse Hughes and Elizabeth his second wife (latter decd) d. 17/12/1818.
Lydia b. 1/6/1794, d. 7/10/1867
George b. 20/3/1797, d. 1859
Wm. b. 17/5/1799, d. 7/3/1866.

William Kenworthy b. 18/8/1743 and Mary Kenworthy, dau of John and Elizabeth Everitt, b. 18/2/1749. Their children:
William Kenworthy, b. 18/6/1766
Benjamin Kenworthy, b. 5/7/1768
Mary Kenworthy, b. 20/1/1770
Hannah Kenworthy, b. 23/12/1774
Amy Kenworthy, b. 11/12/1776
Lydia and Ruth Kenworthy, b. 5/4/1779
Jesse Kenworthy, b. 20/6/1781
Isaac Kenworthy, b. 3/4/1786
Amos Kenworthy, b. 12/7/1789

Phebe Kenworthy, b. 5/9/1791.
Removed to Dunnings Creek and from thence to Redstone.
Joseph Everitt b. 23/7/1742.
Sarah his wife b.1/1/1749
Their children:
Isaac b. 21/9/1775
John b. 13/8/1777
Elizabeth b. 22/9/1780

Children of Stephen Howell and Sarah his wife who d. 14/2/1793
Israel b.1/1/1781
Lydia b. 4/11/1782
Mary b. 31/3/1786
David b. 6/12/1788
Hannah b.12/6/1791

Children of Robert and Jane Miller:
Ruth b. 26/12/1789
Sarah b. 23/11/1791
Samuel b. 27/8/1793

Caleb Farquhar b. 26/3/1776.
Sarah Farquhar dau of A. Paultney, b. 1/3/1781.
Their son James b. 26/6/1808.

Children of Wm. Elliott and Mary his wife:
Joel b.10/2/1775
Margaret b. 20/10/1776
Thomas b.13/12/1778
John b. 14/11/1780
Sarah b. 11/5/1783
Lydia b. 5/9/1785
Rachel b. 27/3/1788
Elizabeth b. 31/3/1790
Mary b. 27/7/1792
William b.4/9/1794, d. 13/12/1817
Ruth b. 17/10/1796
Evan b. 21/1/1800

William Ballinger son of Wm. and Cassandra, b. 22/7/1758.
Lydia Ballinger dau of John and C.S. b. 3/3/1775.

Their children:
Edith b.11/4/1799
Cassandra b. 21/10/1802
William b. 7/3/1805, d. 3/3/1811
Elizabeth b. 13/6/1807, d. 9/2/1811
Samuel b. 1/10/1809
Mary b. 17/12/1811
Rebecca b. 22/3/1814

Thomas Russell son of John and Hannah Russell b. 16/9/1768, d. 6/9/1811. Sarah Russell his wife dau of R. and Mary Roberts b. 10/7/1770. Their children:
Joshua Russell b. 12/8/1794 d. "Record of 1881."
Elizabeth b. 18/2/1796
Jonathan [middle name inserted but unreadable] b. 10/1/1792, d.26/1/1799
Susanna b. 10/11/1799
John b. 2/10/1801
Caleb b.12/3/1804
Anna b. 16/5/1806
Mariam b. 27/3/1808, removed to Goose Creek
Jesse b. 5/3/1810
Thomas b. 9/3/1812

Wm. Ballinger son Henry Ballinger b. 11/7/1730, d. 7/1/1787.
Cassandra Ballinger b. 3/5/1732, d.12/7/1820.
Their children:
Sarah b. 8/11/1752
Mary b. 16/6/1754
Daniel b. 25/6/1756
William b. 22/7/1758
Hannah b. 7/10/1761
Rachel b. 28/9/1763
Henry b. 29/9/1765
Ann b. 28/9/1767, d. 18/3/1803
Samuel b.10/2/1770, d. 15/11/1808
Elizabeth b. 19/10/1772

Amos Farquhar son of Allen and P.F., b. 5/7/1768.
Mary Farquhar dau of J. and M. Engor b. 3/9/1772.
Their children:

Annoymous son, b. 17/1/1797, d. 17/1/1797
Margret E. b. 19/8/1798, d. 1/5/1875
Charles b. 31/7/1800, d. 10/12/1844
Edmund b. 9/5/1803, d. 23/10/1805
Phebe b. 26/1/1805
Ann b. 13/7/1807
Granville b. 18/7/1810
William Henry b. 14/6/1813 (born at York)

William Wood son of Wm. and M. Wood b. 11/4/1758.
Mary Wood dau of John and E Smith b. 29/9/1761.
Their children:
Joel b. 1/9/1782
Elizabeth b.19/2/1788
Joshua b. 9/4/1790
Richard Wood b. 16/2/1792
William b. 8/9/1794
Thomas b. 6/4/1797
Mary b. 29/6/1799
Lydia b. 9/6/1805.
"Removed to Smithfield Ohio."

Benjamin Hibberd son of Joseph and Jane Hibberd b. 15/11/1786

Wm. Morsell junr, son of Wm. and Mary Morsel b. 13/4/1778.
Mary Morsell, dau of Thos. Edmundson b. 11/1/1774, d. 21/6/1842
Their child: Rachel Morsell b.11/12/1809

Eli Elliott b. 1/11/1773.
Margaret Elliott his wife b. 16/2/1781.
Their children: Jesse b. 22/6/1799
George b. 10/4/1801
Sarah b. 19/6/1803
Eli b. 7/7/1805
Ruben b. 12/8/1807

Children of John Talbott and Elizabeth his wife.
Susanna b. 12/11/1791
Ruth b. 25/7/1793, d. 4/7/1843
Samuel b. 1/4/1797
John b. 8/1/1802

Nathan Wood of Thos. b. 7/2/1781
Margaret Wood his wife b. 3/9/1776
Their children (remvoed to Ohio) follow:
Samuel b. 19/2/1802
Susanna b.5/1/1805
Joel b. 16/5/1807
Sarah b. 22/9/1810

Joseph Hibberd son of Joseph and Jane Hibberd b. 18/4/1779.
Rachel Hibberd his wife, dau of Joel and Elizabeth Wright, b. 28/9/1780.
Their children: Israel b.1/4/1807
Joel b.28/9/1809, d. 23/9/1815
William b. 26/9/1811
Samuel b. 19/7/1814
James b. 4/11/1816
Elizabeth b. 9/5/1819, d. -/4/183-
Joseph b. 25/7/1822, d. 5/8/184-.

Benjamin Hibberd son of Joseph and Jane Hibberd b. 15/11/1786.
Charity Hibberd his wife dau of Edward and Jane Beeson, b. 31/12/1782.
Their children (Removed to Indiana?).
Jane Sarah b. 24/8/1812
Alice Ann b. 25/9/1821

Thomas Wood b. 1785, d. 15/5/1843 and Mary his wife b. 29/1/1791, d. 7/10/1875.

William Coale son of Saml. and Lydia Coale b. 13/1/1779

Anna Coale, dau of Joseph and Ann Talbott, b. 31/1/1786.

Israel Howell son of Stephen Howell and Mary b. 1/1/1781.
His wife Mary Howell dau of John Smith and Mary b. 8/8/1785.

Jazer Garretson son of Garrit Garretson and Margaret his wife b. 5/11/1787.
His wife Sarah Garretson dau of Anthony Poultney and Susan his wife b 1/3/1787.
Their dau Mary b. 3/4/1814

Allen Hibberd son of Joseph and Jane Hibberd b.29/7/1771, d. 28/7/1838.
Rachel Hibbard dau of Nathan and Sophia Haines b. 23/11/1775, d. 24/4/1855.

Silas Hibberd son of Joseph and Jane Hibberd, b. 3/3/1782, d. 18/9/1850.
Elizabeth Hibberd dau of Joseph and Rachel Haines b. 29/8/1781.

Wm. Farquhar son of Wm. and Ann Farquhar and Rachel Farquhar dau of Jno. and Elith. Wright, b.1737, d. 19/4/177-
Their children:
Elizabeth b. 16/12/1760
Ann b. 30/6/1762
Samuel b. 24/11/1763
Rachel b. 12/6/1765
Ruth b. 28/2/1767
William b. 20/7/1770
John b. 9/9/1772
Wm. Farquhar and (2nd wife) Mary Farquhar had children as follows:
Mary b. 3/12/1783
Susanna b. 18/2/1786
Richard b. 18/1/1788
Moses b. 12/4/1789, d. 1/11/187-
Wm. Farquhar and Lydia Farquhar (3d wife) had children as follows:
Joel b. 14/9/1797, d. 30/11/1865(?)
Hannah (Hughes) b. 31/8/1799, d. 3/5/183-
Deborah b. 4/1/1801, d. 19/2/85--

Joel Farquhar son of Wm. and Lydia Farquhar, b. 14/9/1797, d. 30/11/1865.
Ruth Farquhar dau of Wm. and Catharine Wright, b. 27/11/1795, d. 16/6/187-
.

INDEX

-A-

ABORN,
 Joseph, 196, 229, 237, 238
ABRAHAM, 69
ADAIR, Elizabeth, 65
ADAMS, Lydia, 278
ADDY, Robert, 198
AISQUITH,
 Elizabeth, 51
 William, 51
ALBERTSUM,
 Chalkly, 97
ALBION,
 Elias, 163
 Phebe, 163
ALEXANDER, Mark, 49
ALIBONE, Elizabeth, 95
ALLEN,
 Jane, 110
 Robert, 126
 Sarah, 161
ALLEY,
 Amos, 210
 Enos, 214
ALLIBONE,
 Benjamin, 227
 Elias, 205, 227, 236
 Elizabeth, 187, 223
 Phebe, 193, 227
 William, 85, 184, 221, 223
ALLISON, Ann, 226
AMBLER, David, 245
 Margaret, 245
AMBROSE, Ann, 54

Mary, 53, 66
William, 54
AMOS,
 Ann, 9, 35, 48, 50, 56
 Anna, 46
 Anne, 47
 Benjamin, 9, 48, 50, 52, 55, 96, 98, 163, 177, 237
 Catherine, 55
 David, 96
 Eleanor, 52, 64
 Elias Ellicott, 240
 Elisabeth, 49
 Elizabeth, 35, 50, 62, 173, 239
 Ellener, 49, 50
 Hannah, 9, 35, 48, 54, 96, 240
 James, 9, 48, 50, 55, 89, 96, 240
 Joseph, 163
 Joshua, 48
 Lemuel H., 239
 Luke, 9, 95
 Martha, 48, 49, 50, 52, 53, 55
 Mary, 52, 53, 54, 68, 96, 170
 Maulden, 57, 60, 55
 Mauldon, 52
 Oliver Huff, 240
 Priscilla, 54, 56
 Rachel, 52, 55, 163
 Sarah, 48, 50, 97
 Susanna, 54, 55, 239
 Thomas, 48, 50
 William, 9, 35, 36, 42, 48, 49, 50, 52, 53, 54, 55,
 56, 57, 60, 64, 68, 69, 70, 83, 89, 96, 98, 100, 118, 234, 239, 55, 56
 William H., 239
 William Lee, 240
AMOSS,
 Ann, 11, 97, 240
 Benjamin, 11, 12, 99, 190, 215, 217, 224, 237
 Benjamin H., 240
 David, 190, 225
 David Lee, 22
 Elias Ellicott, 22
 Elizabeth, 12, 236
 Hannah, 11, 22, 46, 171, 190, 215, 216, 225, 240
 James, 22, 99, 171, 190, 225
 John, 12
 Lee, 171
 Lemuel Howard, 12
 Martha, 12, 217, 240
 Mary, 171, 190, 225
 Mary Ann, 22
 Mordecai, 215
 Oliver Hough, 22
 Sarah, 11, 225, 240
 Susanna, 11, 12, 217, 240
 Thomas, 12, 240
 William, 11, 12, 46, 99, 193, 215, 217, 225, 227, 234
 William H., 245
 William Lee, 22, 245
AMUS,
 Hannah, 47
 William, 47, 49
ANDERSON,

Dorcas, 278
Elizabeth, 278
William C., 277, 278
ANDREWS,
  Charlot, 112
  Isaac, 39
  Thomas, 114
ANTHONY, 69
ARCHER, Robert, 126
ARMSTRONG,
  David, 57
  George, 57
ARNOLD, Richard, 169
ASHMAN,
  George, 27, 264
  John, 27
  Nancy, 264
  Patiance, 27
ASKEW, Elisabeth, 52
ATKINSON,
  Abigail, 205, 236
  Isaac, 204, 235
  Joseph, 163, 204, 205, 235
  Mary, 163, 204, 235
  Rachel, 163, 204, 235
  Ruth, 204, 235
  Sarah, 204, 205, 235
ATLER, Isaac, 275

-B-
BAILEY,
  Caleb, 149
  Margaret, 277
BAILY,
  Margaret, 263, 276
  Silas, 277

BAKER,
  Charles, 48, 54
  Elexander, 31
  Nichles, 37
  Norton Groves, 27
  Zeporah, 29, 36
  Zepporiah, 31
BALDERSON,
  Ely, 151
  Hugh, 151
  Isaiah, 139, 150, 151
  Jacob, 135
  Jonathan, 151
  Martha, 139, 150
  Mary, 135
  Parthenia, 151
  Sarah, 150
BALDERSTON,
  Eli, 176
  Elizabeth, 197
  Ely, 105, 184, 197, 208, 212, 213, 221, 229
  Esther, 197, 208, 215, 217
  Hugh, 105, 184, 213, 215, 221
  Isaiah, 105, 113, 115, 118, 119, 120, 121, 122, 184, 211, 212, 213, 215, 216, 221
  Jacob, 105, 115, 117, 118, 119, 120, 122, 123, 124, 125, 126, 127, 156, 162
  Jonathan, 105, 184, 212, 213, 215, 221
  Mark, 213
  Marth, 122

  Martha, 105, 113, 115, 118, 119, 120, 121, 122, 184, 208, 211, 212, 213, 214, 215, 216, 221
  Mary, 113, 115, 118, 119, 120, 122, 123, 125, 126
  Parthenia, 211, 227
  Pathenia, 184, 221
  Perthenia, 105
  Sarah, 105, 113, 115, 121
  Sary, 112
BALDW[?], William, 56
BALENGER,
  Casandra, 268
  Hannah, 268
  Mary, 268
  William, 268
BALINGER,
  Ann, 268
  Rachel, 268
  William, 269, 271
BALL,
  Amos, 69, 71
  Catharine, 83
  Elizabeth, 89, 212
  Jaminna, 64
  John, 215
  Joseph, 57, 65, 66, 67
  Mary, 57, 65, 66
  Peter, 41
  William, 212, 215
BALLENGER,
  Ann, 273
  Casandra, 268, 273
  Cassandra, 247
  Elizabeth, 274

Hannah, 273
Henry, 273
Mary, 268, 275
BALLINGER,
  Ann, 266, 270, 285
  C. S., 284
  Casandra, 276
  Casendra, 265
  Cassandra, 265, 267, 275, 284, 285
  Cassy, 270
  Daniel, 265, 266, 276, 285
  Edith, 285
  Elizabeth, 276, 285
  Hannah, 265, 266, 267, 285
  Henry, 265, 276, 285
  John, 284
  Lydia, 284
  Mary, 258, 261, 265, 266, 269, 276, 285
  Rachel, 266, 267, 275, 276, 285
  Rebecca, 285
  Samuel, 265, 285
  Sarah, 249, 265, 285
  William, 262, 265, 266, 267, 268, 270, 275, 276, 284, 285
BANKSON, Mary, 51
BARCLAY,
  James, 122
  John, 122
  John Gill, 122
  Sarah, 122
BARKER, Elizabeth, 136
BARNABY, Rachel, 85

BARNES,
  David, 273
  James, 273
  John, 273, 274
BARNETT, Hannah, 87
BARNEY, Sarah, 132, 214
BARR, Elizabeth, 122
BARRET, Edward, 53
BARRY,
  Jane, 82
  Lavalin, 82
  Mary, 183, 213, 215, 220
  Standish, 83
BARTLETT,
  John, 175
  Robert, 173, 193, 226, 237
  Susanna, 84
BARTON, Susanna, 86, 126
BASEY, Sarah, 50
BATEMAN, Henry, 36
BATES, James, 270
BAUSLY, Joseph, 31
BAUZLEY,
  Elizabeth, 27
  James, 27
BAYLES,
  Cassa, 121
  Cassandra, 124, 125
  Samuel, 125
BAYLEY,
  Cassandra, 147
  Margaret, 277
BEAL,
  Ann, 184, 220, 223

Grace, 163, 184, 220
Jesse, 163
Joseph, 163, 184, 220, 223
Ruthy, 163
Samuel, 163, 184, 220
Thomas, 163, 184, 220, 223
BEALE,
  Alice, 87
  Thomas, 87
BEANS,
  Elizabeth, 245
  Hannah, 240
  Isaac, 240
  Jonathan, 245
  Rebecca, 240
BEARD, James, 56
BEASON, Edward, 266
BEAVER, Elisabeth, 52
BEESON,
  Charity, 287
  Edward, 287
  Jane, 287
BELFORD, Sarah, 237
BELINDA, 137
BELT,
  --illh., 57
  Benoni, 48
  Jeremiah, 44, 45, 48, 53
  John, 2, 36, 47, 48, 51, 53, 56, 57, 62, 81
  Joseph, 2, 95
  Keturah, 19
  Leod., 53
  Leonard, 42
  Lucey, 2

Lucy, 62
Mary, 2, 90, 94
Milcah, 19, 62
Milkah, 94
Nathan, 48
Rachel, 81
Rebecca, 72
Rebeckah, 57, 72
Rebekah, 53, 54
Richard, 19, 37, 44, 47, 51, 53, 56, 57, 81
BELTS,
  Mary, 280
  Susanna, 250, 265, 280
  Thomas, 280
BENIRE, John, 55
BENNET,
  Joshua, 119, 120, 121, 126, 148
  Mary, 119, 120, 121, 126
BENNETT, 137
  Ellenor, 275
  Hannah, 105
  Joshua, 105, 124, 126, 156
  Mary, 105, 124, 126
  Rebeckah, 105
  Sarah, 105
BENSON,
  Amos, 25, 240, 245
  Benjamin, 25, 240, 245, 252, 273
  Edward, 266
  Elijah, 25
  Elizabeth, 25
  Hannah, 252, 258
  James, 25, 93, 95

Jesse, 240
John, 25
Levi, 240
Margaret, 240, 245
Mary, 240
Mordecai, 25
Rachel, 25
Reuben, 25
Sarah Ann, 25
William, 25
BENTLEY,
  Caleb, 162
  Margaret, 264
  Sarah, 270
  William, 264, 270
BENTON,
  Ann, 270, 274
  Benjamin, 278
  Joseph, 270, 274
  Thomas, 277
BERRY,
  James, 175
  Jane, 72
  John, 266
  Joseph, 175
BICKET, Ruth, 264
BIGGER, Sarah, 91
BILLINGSLEA,
  Aseth., 57
  Sarah, 57
BISHOP,
  Margaret, 128
  Thomas, 128, 140, 128
BISSETT, John, 274
BLACKBURN,
  Edwin, 171, 239
  Mary, 252

BLAGDON,
  Ann, 77
  Tabitha, 77
BLEAKER, Judith, 165
BLEANY, John, 57
BOLMAN, Elizabeth, 36
BOLTON,
  Isaac, 118, 127
  Joseph, 108
  Sarah, 116, 118
BOND,
  Alasana, 110
  Alasanna, 48, 110
  Alesanna, 49
  Alley, 52
  Alsann, 48
  Amelia, 69
  Ann, 50, 52, 57
  Anne, 46
  Benjamin, 147, 126
  Buckler, 55
  Bukler, 52
  Cathe., 55
  Charity, 49
  Daniel, 54, 55, 56
  Elisabeth, 54, 55
  Elizabeth, 50, 52, 147, 55
  Francis, 46
  Hannah, 39, 46
  J., 46
  Jacob, 54
  James, 46
  Jea., 46
  John, 32, 39, 42, 46, 48, 49, 50, 52, 53, 57, 60, 62, 83, 89, 110, 112, 50
  John Churchman, 70

INDEX

Josa., 46
Marsha, 239
Martha, 46, 48, 54, 55, 124, 126, 147, 159, 173
Mary, 51, 87, 126, 147, 162
Nathan, 68
Patience, 54, 55
Rebecca, 52
Richard, 49
Ruth, 53, 147
Samuel, 39, 57, 89, 98
Sarah, 48, 50, 54, 57, 70, 73
Silas, 147
Susanna, 52, 60
Thomas, 31, 32, 35, 42, 46, 52, 54, 55, 62
William, 62, 70, 98
BONSALL, Caleb, 207, 237
  Catharine, 201, 233
  Mary, 226
  Sarah, 201, 233
  Vincent, 201, 233
  William, 201, 233
BORAM,
  Aaron, 124, 150, 154, 162
  Ann, 124, 154, 162
  Elizabeth, 162
  John, 124, 154
BOREING,
  Ann, 36
  Martha, 29
BOSLEY,
  Eligah, 48
  Greenberry, 61
  James, 54
  Susanna, 81
  Thomas, 37, 38
BOSON CLARK, 71
BOULTON,
  Isaac, 108
  Sarah, 108
BOWEN,
  Aquila, 33
  Beniamin, 27, 29
  Benjamin, 27, 30, 33, 58
  Catharine, 76
  Elizabeth, 33, 67, 92
  Joshua, 33
  Josias, 28, 84
  M., 29
  Mary, 33, 69
  Nathan, 28
  Rees, 27, 28, 29, 30, 31, 32, 35, 36, 42, 47, 48
  Solomon, 28
  Tabitha, 27
BOWLIN, Meriam, 256
BOYD,
  Andrew, 219
  Benjamin, 274
  James P., 211
  Mary, 180, 211, 215, 219
BOZLEY,
  Bellenda, 49
  Green, 48
  Joseph, 36, 49
  Thomas, 48
  Walter, 47
BRADFORD,
  Margaret, 142, 147
  Margaret Hill, 138
  Margret Hill, 118
BRASELTON, Jacob, 264
BRASHEAR,
  Anne, 276
  Belt, 276
  Ely, 276
BREASHEAR,
  Julia, 277
  Mary, 277
BRELSFORD, Sarah, 173, 205, 236, 237
BRICE, John, 111
BRIGGS,
  George, 42, 131
  William, 56, 66
BRIGS, Fanney, 49
BRINTON,
  Edward, 240
  Eliner, 142
  Elinor, 116
  Joseph, 116, 125, 142
  Moses, 116, 142
  Susanna, 142
BROOKE,
  Deborah, 265
  Dorothy, 166
  Elizabeth, 266, 270
  James, 270
BROOKES,
  Hannah, 216
  Isaac, 176, 189, 216, 224
BROOKS,
  Isaac, 209, 234
  John, 209, 216
  Sarah, 209
BROWN, Achsah, 240

Amos, 205
Amy, 240
Ann, 13, 104, 139, 176, 212, 218
Anne, 213
Benajah, 91
Benjamin, 36, 63, 65
Catharine, 206
Daniel, 40, 265, 266
David, 8, 42, 54, 56, 66, 67, 73, 75, 83, 163, 176, 211, 212, 213, 215, 216, 218
Dianna, 163
Dorothea, 163
Dorothy, 180, 187, 201, 211, 214, 217, 220
Eleazor, 139
Elihu, 240
Elizabeth, 8, 13, 56, 67, 163, 165, 176, 194, 212, 213, 215, 218, 230
Esther, 13, 176, 212, 218, 229
Fanny, 212, 213, 216
Fillah, 120
Frances, 8, 13, 42, 54, 176, 213, 215, 218
Freeborn, 117, 162
George, 8, 35, 36, 46, 176, 201, 213, 215, 218
Hanah, 31
Hannah, 13, 53, 162, 176, 187, 206, 212, 218, 228, 236, 240
Hephzibah, 188
Hepzibah, 95, 223, 224
Isaac, 249, 265

James, 12, 42, 54, 77, 124, 176, 179, 206, 213, 214, 215, 216, 218, 230, 233, 266
Jehosheba, 215, 216
Jehu, 240
Jesse, 90, 180, 187, 201, 211, 212, 213, 214, 215, 220
John, 8, 12, 13, 54, 89, 176, 201, 206, 211, 212, 213, 214, 215, 216, 217, 218
Joseph, 13, 53, 62, 139, 176, 212, 213, 218
Joshua, 31, 122, 162, 163
Joshua R., 163
Josiah, 216
Leah, 165
Lydia, 240
Margaret, 130, 139, 240
Mary, 8, 12, 13, 35, 42, 49, 54, 55, 75, 76, 85, 120, 162, 176, 205, 206, 211, 212, 213, 214, 215, 217, 218, 235, 236
Mary Baines, 138
Mercer, 163
Rachel, 240
Ruth, 187
Sarah, 29, 104, 139, 142, 162, 194, 238, 249, 266
Sarah B., 163
Sillah, 120
Stephen, 240
Susanna, 57, 85, 90, 174, 265, 266
Susannah, 75

Thomas, 12, 13, 54, 85, 102, 139, 202, 234
William, 8, 13, 53, 56, 57, 62, 65, 70, 75, 86, 163, 174, 176, 211, 212, 213, 214, 215, 216, 217, 218
BROWNE,
George, 5
John, 59
Mary, 5
BRUCE,
Ann, 121, 127, 159
Anna, 115, 125
John, 111, 112, 113, 114, 115, 116, 125, 127, 136
Joseph, 109
Robert, 125
BUCHANAN,
Margaret, 54
Sidney, 54
BUCHER, Hannah, 249, 251
BUCKINGHAM,
Thomas, 79, 182, 220, 221
BUCKLEY,
Lawrence, 92
BUFFINGTON,
Ann, 223
Susanna, 222
BUFFINTON,
Benjaman, 38
BULL,
Abraham, 56
Anna, 144
Anne, 123
Billingsley, 97
Edward, 50

Eleanor, 64
Elenar, 55
Elener, 53
Eliner, 56
Hannah, 52, 50, 55
Jacob, 55
John, 61, 90
Martha, 49
Nancy, 123
Rachal, 52
Rachel, 49, 53, 55, 56, 57, 216
Richard, 123
Rinnis, 50, 55
Sarah, 50, 52, 53, 54, 56, 57, 61, 65
Thomas, 78
Walter, 52, 56, 57
William, 55, 56, 57, 61, 66, 67, 90, 52
BUNTIN,
  Lucy, 258
  Mary, 258
  Patience, 258
  Rebekah, 258
  Sarah, 258
BUNTING,
  Mary, 258
  Sarah, 258
BURGES,
  Daniel, 119, 125
  Deborah, 119, 125
  Deborough, 119
  Grace, 119
  Henry, 46
  Hugh, 41, 49
  John, 119, 121, 125, 49
  Joseph, 51, 119, 122, 125
  Letishe, 119
  Martha, 93, 119, 125, 126
  Sarah, 49, 119
  Tacey, 125
  Thomas, 119
BURGESS,
  Ann, 80, 101, 148, 156, 157, 159
  Anne, 81
  Daniel, 65, 137, 151
  Deborah, 65, 114, 137, 156
  Drusilla, 156
  Elizabeth, 65, 114, 137
  Grace, 65, 151
  Hugh, 46
  Jesse, 65, 114, 137
  John, 65, 88, 101, 137, 148, 151, 155, 156, 157, 159
  Jonathan, 65, 137
  Joseph, 54, 65, 68, 73, 101, 114, 137, 146, 148, 151, 156, 157
  Leticia, 65, 137
  Letitia, 151
  Martha, 65, 151, 183, 220, 232
  Mary, 54, 74, 163, 183, 220
  Nathan, 137
  Sarah, 65, 117, 137, 146
  Tacey, 65, 114, 118, 119, 137, 145, 216
  Tacy, 85, 183, 220
  Thomas, 65, 137, 151, 158
  Ura, 63
BURK, Hannah, 89
BURSON, Catharine, 82
BUSSEY,
  Anne, 81
  Edward, 50
BUTLER,
  Ann, 192, 212, 213, 226, 230
  John, 192, 226
  Joseph, 192, 226
  Ura, 63
BYE, Ann, 165
BYFIELD, Mercy, 145
BYRNES,
  Betsy, 207
  Caleb, 194
  Daniel, 194, 213, 228
  Hannah, 194, 207, 214, 228
  Mary, 84
  Ruth, 194, 200, 228, 232
  Samuel, 194, 207, 228
  Thomas, 85, 88

-C-
CADDY, Robert, 164
CALDWELL, Mary, 246
CANBY,
  Elizabeth, 164, 208, 238
  Joseph, 164, 208
  Samuel, 164, 208, 238
CAREY,
  George, 209
  Hannah, 190
  James, 81, 82, 178, 186, 190, 197, 209, 213, 218

John E., 213
John Ellicott, 178, 218
Margaret, 197
Martha, 178, 186, 190, 197, 209, 214, 217, 218
Samuel, 178, 218
CARLILE, Lancelot, 52
CARLISLE, David, 48
CARMACK,
  Cornelius, 264
  Mary, 264
CARNAN, R. N., 53
CARPENTER,
  George, 171, 188, 223, 227
  Hannah, 171, 188, 223, 227
  John, 171, 188, 223, 227
  Joseph, 171, 188, 227
  Lydia, 171, 188, 223, 227
  Rachel, 171, 188, 223, 227
  William, 171, 188, 223, 227
CARR,
  Ann, 86, 93
  Aquila, 27, 28, 29, 30, 35, 36, 46, 47, 51, 58, 61, 82
  Aquilia, 26, 29
  Aquilla, 30
  Benjamin, 30
  Elizabeth, 30, 34, 58, 93
  James, 77, 93
  Jesse, 15, 93
  Joshua, 45
  Mary, 27, 54, 70
  Mordica, 31
  Phebe, 85, 102, 207, 237
  Priscilla, 89, 93
  Rachel, 30, 58
  Samuel, 93
  Sarah, 15, 93
  Susan, 30
  Susana, 36, 47
  Susanah, 30
  Susanna, 35
  Thomas, 27, 28, 29, 30, 31, 32, 34, 75
  Tulatha, 31
  William, 15, 91, 93
CARRICK, Mary, 273
CARROLL, Sophia, 215
CARSON,
  Jonathan, 268
  Thomas, 267
CARTER,
  Agner, 154
  Ann, 127, 154
  Edith, 239
  Ellis, 239
  Enos, 239
  Francis, 31
  Hannah, 127, 154, 239, 246
  Isabel, 239
  James, 239
  Jeremiah, 154
  Joel, 127, 147, 154, 239, 246
  John, 31, 127, 148, 151, 159, 239
  Kirwin, 239
  Levi, 239
  Margaret, 239
  Margaret A., 239
  Mercy, 239
  Rachel, 154
  Richard, 201, 232, 238
  Rith, 154
  Ruth, 117, 120, 121, 143
  Samuel, 118, 127, 141, 154
  Sarah, 154, 239
CASLANG, Francis, 126
CATES,
  Elizabeth, 87
  Grace, 87
  Jane, 70, 87
  Jonathan, 87
CATO, 139
CATS, Jane, 100
CATTS,
  Jane, 98
  Mary, 217
CEATH, Michael, 56
CHALK,
  Joshua, 54
  Mary, 46
CHALKE,
  Elizabeth, 34
  George, 34
  John, 34, 36
  Joshua, 34
  Margret, 34
  Margrett, 46
  Martha, 34
  Mary, 34
  Sarah, 34
  Tudor, 34
CHAMBERLAIN,
  Mary, 248, 253

CHAMBERLIN, John, 264
CHAMBERS, Rebekah, 120
CHANDLEE,
  Deborah, 271
  Gainer, 279
  George, 268, 269, 278, 279, 271
  Mary, 271
  Susanna, 254, 255, 270, 271
  William, 271
CHANDLER,
  Deborah, 253, 254
  Mary, 135
CHANDLEY,
  Mary, 252
  Susanna, 252
  William, 252
CHANDLY, Benjamin, 58
CHANNEL, Edmund, 213
CHANY, Greenbury, 52
CHAPMAN,
  Mary, 124
  William, 122, 124, 154
CHARITY, 137
CHENOWTH, Cashiah, 27
  Richard, 27, 28
CHEW,
  Ann, 169
  Ann C., 169
  Elizabeth, 111, 133
  Joseph, 111, 133
  Mary, 169
  Mas?, 122
  Samuel, 169
  Sarah, 111, 119, 133
  Susanna, 52, 114
  Susannah, 51
  Thomas, 111, 114
CHINOATH, Richard, 32
CHINOUTH,
  Art., 31
  Sufirah, 31
CHINOWTH, Richard, 30
CHOAKE,
  George, 61
  Mary, 48, 67
CHOALK, Mary, 40
CHOCKE, John, 46, 48
CHOLK,
  Joshua, 52
  Tuder, 52
CHRISTIE,
  James, 110
  Robert, 110
CHURCHMAN,
  Dianna, 163
  Gainer, 117
  Hannah, 163, 174, 279
  John, 163, 174
  Margret, 117
  Mary, 127
  Micajah, 117
  Mordecai, 118, 268
  Mordica, 269
  Polly, 124
CLARK, Abraham, 82, 85, 92
  Ann, 85, 92
  Elizabeth, 85, 92
  Hannah, 92
  Joseph, 85, 92
  Mary, 85, 92, 217
  Mathew, 126
  Sarah, 85, 92
CLAUSY, John, 29
CLAY, Elizabeth, 259
CLEAVER, Peter, 175
CLEMSON,
  Elizabeth, 270
  John, 267, 270
CLENDININ,
  Adam, 125
  David, 125
CLOENDININ, A., 126
COAL,
  Denis Garrot, 27
  Elizabeth, 34
  Rachel, 34
  Salahiel, 34
  Sarah, 34, 111
  Skipwith, 111
  Sophia, 34
  Thomas, 34
  William, 35
COALE,
  Amelias, 110
  Ann, 104, 111, 113, 115, 116, 117, 120, 121, 122, 123, 124, 125, 126, 152, 154, 161, 206
  Anna, 116, 287
  Cassandra, 104, 108, 109, 110, 117, 120, 121, 123, 124, 125, 128, 157

Dennis, 36
Elisabeth, 112
Eliza, 127
Elizabeth, 3, 103, 105, 111, 113, 114, 115, 116, 117, 118, 121, 123, 124, 125, 127, 163, 169
Ellis P., 107
Frances, 104, 117, 119, 120, 121, 123, 154
Grace, 115
Hannah, 163, 164
Henry, 51
Hester, 163
Isaac, 103, 115, 116, 117, 118, 119, 120, 121, 122, 123, 124, 126, 127, 143
Isack, 113
John, 103
Joseph, 107
Joshua, 78, 84, 107
Lewis, 107
Lidia, 77
Lydia, 84, 107, 119, 120, 121, 123, 125, 127, 249, 267, 269, 287
Margaret, 84, 108, 109, 119, 137, 146
Margarett, 107
Margret, 110, 113, 118
Mary, 77, 84, 107, 120, 124, 169
Mordecai, 57
Philip, 104, 105, 108, 109, 110, 111, 112, 113, 114, 115, 116, 117, 118, 120, 121, 123, 124, 125, 131, 152, 154, 155, 156, 174, 195
Rachel, 36, 57, 118, 124
Richard, 104, 123, 124, 125, 154
Rigbie, 103
Samuel, 40, 41, 77, 83, 84, 107, 110, 113, 118, 119, 120, 121, 122, 123, 124, 125, 126, 127, 137, 146, 154, 155, 159, 249, 267, 268, 287, 269
Samuel Robertson, 3
Sarah, 3, 36, 50, 103, 104, 108, 109, 110, 111, 113, 115, 116, 117, 119, 120, 123, 126, 143, 146, 152, 174
Sarah W., 109
Sary, 109, 110, 113
Sary W., 109, 110
Skipwith, 50, 77, 84, 107, 108, 109, 110, 111, 112, 113, 114, 115, 116, 117, 118, 119, 120, 121, 122, 123, 124, 125, 128, 133, 137, 138, 141, 146, 157, 159, 200
Skipworth, 113
Sophia, 59
Susan, 110, 113
Susanna, 111, 124, 125
Susannah, 109, 113, 119, 120, 123
Thomas, 36
William, 3, 36, 47, 49, 51, 77, 84, 103, 105, 107, 108, 109, 110, 111, 112, 113, 115, 116, 117, 118, 120, 121, 123, 124, 125, 126, 127, 128, 131, 133, 138, 143, 155, 161, 163, 164, 169, 174, 287
William L., 119
COALSON, Henry, 109
COATES,
  Ann, 179, 219, 224
  Elizabeth, 179, 219
  Grace, 179, 211, 213, 214, 219
  Hannah, 179, 219
  Isaac, 268
  Jane, 164, 179, 216, 219
  Jonathan, 87, 120, 164, 179, 219, 220
  Keziah, 90
  Phebe, 89, 179, 216, 217, 219
  Rachel, 222
  Susannah, 93
COATS,
  Ann, 88
  Grace, 236
  Jane, 164
  Jonathan, 164
  Kezia, 88
COCKEY,
  Achsah, 51
  Joshua, 36
  Penelope Deye, 52
COGAL,
  Alice, 136
  Catherine, 135
  Henry, 136
COHOON, Alexander, 55
COLE, Abraham, 29
  Christofer, 29

Denis, 27, 32
Denis Garrott, 27
Dennis, 37
John, 32, 53
Mary, 53, 57
Mordecai, 66
Mordica, 51
Philip, 228
Rachel, 53, 62
S., 176
Sarah, 47, 49
Thomas, 29, 31, 40, 47, 48, 49, 62
Ureth, 27
Urith, 32
Vensent, 53
William, 31, 32, 47, 212
COLEGATE, Ann, 50
Asaph, 51, 56
Charlote Deye, 52
Colegate, 47
Eliz., 50
Elizabeth, 52, 56, 62, 63, 76
Honner, 35
Honnour, 36
Honour, 46
John, 27, 35, 37, 40, 46, 67
Rachel, 63
Rebecca, 62
Rebeckah, 50
Thomas, 26, 27, 29, 30, 32, 36
COLGATE, Ann, 47
Casa. Cockey, 47
Elizabeth, 51

John, 47
Rachel, 51
Richard, 47, 51
COLLEY, Thomas, 118
COLLINS, Stevens, 41
COLVIN, Daniel, 212
COLVON, Sarah, 248
COMELY, Charity, 97
COMFORT, 137
COMLEY,
Jacob, 48, 59
James, 44, 48, 59, 49
John, 66
Mary, 48, 49, 59, 92
Rachel, 59
COMLY,
David, 39
Jacob, 39, 42
James, 39
John, 39
Jonathan, 39
Joseph, 39, 46
Mary, 39
Rachel, 39
Sarah, 39, 211
CONDON, Richard, 271
CONLEY, James, 43
CONNARD,
Abigail, 71
Edward, 68
COOK,
Hannah, 271
Jeremiah, 255, 270, 271
Margaret, 81
Margret, 271
Rachel, 256
Sarah, 120

Stephen, 203, 216, 234, 271
COOKSEN, Samuel, 247
COOKSON,
Daniel, 280
Elizabeth, 250, 252, 264, 269
Jane, 266
Jonathan, 269
Joseph, 208, 237
Mary, 208, 237, 252, 266, 267, 280
Olive, 208, 237
Rachel, 248, 250, 264, 265, 266
Samuel, 208, 237, 264, 266, 267, 280
COOPE, Jasper, 217
COOPER,
Alice, 122
Duckett, 122
Ecey, 122
Elizabeth, 162
Hannah, 122
Hugh, 122
Isaiah, 162
Margret, 114
Martha, 162
Mary, 122
Nicholas, 121, 122, 127, 150, 162
Parthenia, 162
Sarah, 121, 150, 162
Stephen, 122
William, 114, 122
COOTS, Samuel, 190
COOX, James, 49
COPE, Israel, 196, 229

Jaspar, 238
Jasper, 196, 229
COPELAND,
  William, 173, 196, 229, 236
CORDERY, Mary, 257
CORDRAY, Mary, 273
CORKIN, Grace, 89
CORNELL, Arnaud, 217
CORNTHWAIT,
  Deborah, 82, 177, 212, 214, 217, 218
  Elizabeth, 52, 54, 70, 82, 85, 177, 212, 214, 217, 218, 237
  Grace, 70, 82, 177, 214, 217, 218
  Hannah, 10, 164
  Isaac, 218
  Isaac Granton, 164
  John, 10, 52, 54, 63, 66, 101, 164, 177, 180, 197, 212, 213, 214, 215, 216, 217, 218, 230
  Mary, 10, 54, 57, 82, 177, 217, 218
  Mary M., 164
  Robert, 10, 70, 82, 102, 164, 177, 208, 211, 214, 217, 218, 227, 238, 215
  Robert, 217
  Thomas, 52, 82, 177, 217, 218
  William, 82, 177, 214, 217, 218
CORNTHWAITE,
  John, 58
CORSE, Cassandra, 116
  John, 116
  Sarah, 116
CORSEY, 69
COSLEY, Mary, 205
COULSON, David, 85, 220
COURSE, John, 134
COUSINS,
  John, 114, 131, 140
  Sarah, 114, 131
  Susanna, 131
COUZENS, John, 114
COWGIL,
  Henry, 129
  Ruth, 129
COWGILL,
  Alice, 132
  Ellen, 132
  Henry, 104, 132
  James, 104
  John, 132
  Lydia, 132
  Mary, 104
  Rachel, 104
  Ruth, 104
COWMAN,
  Gerard, 164
  John, 270
  Joseph, 164, 270
COX, Baines, 130, 131
  Dinah, 85
  Elisabeth, 111
  Elizabeth, 81, 112
  Israel, 117, 122, 269
  Jacob, 36
  James, 51
  Jane, 85, 88
  John, 85, 111, 112, 117, 118, 119, 120, 124, 126, 133, 146, 153, 110, 118, 162, 184, 221
  Jonah, 85
  Lawrence, 85
  Mary, 51, 109, 110, 111, 112, 113, 114, 115, 116, 117, 118, 119, 120, 122, 124, 134, 143, 146, 148, 174, 111, 115, 118
  Mary Baines, 138
  Mary Banes, 112
  Mercy, 117
  Rachel, 113, 115, 117, 143
  Robert, 85, 164, 183, 220
  Sarah, 111, 133, 134
  Sary, 110, 112, 110
  Thomas, 85, 184, 221
  William, 108, 109, 110, 111, 112, 113, 115, 117, 118, 122, 123, 124, 125, 128, 134, 140, 141, 143, 154, 161, 174
CRAFFORD,
  Frances, 154
CRAWFORD,
  Ann, 145, 146
  Frances, 124, 125, 147, 154
  James, 130, 131, 137
  Mordica, 124
  Ruth, 124
CRIPPLE, Edward, 49, 52
CROCKETT,
  Ann, 129, 131
  Samuel, 131

INDEX

CROMWELL,
  A., 29
  Henry, 53
  John, 53
  Thomas, 53
CROSS,
  Jane, 61
  John, 32
  Richard, 28, 29
CROXALL, Richard, 26
CUMMING,
  David, 248, 264
  Rebeccah, 264
  Sarah, 264
CUMMINS, Rachel, 248
CUNARD,
  Edward, 57
  Judith, 57
CUNNARD,
  Abigail, 82
  Ann, 78
  Edward, 54, 55, 61, 63, 75, 76, 78
  Henry, 64, 76
  Judith, 54, 55, 78
  Pamela, 78
  Sarah, 78
CUNNINGHAM,
  Daniel, 240

-D-
DAFFIN,
  George, 51
  Joseph, 51
DALLAM,
  Cassandra, 122, 123, 156
  Elizabeth, 109, 122, 124, 156
  Frances, 110, 111, 119, 129, 135, 150
  Francis, 109, 112, 122
  John, 112, 113, 116, 117, 119, 120, 124, 125, 126, 153
  Joseph, 125
  Joseph Wilson, 124
  Margaret, 117, 119, 123, 125, 150, 152
  Margarett, 116
  Margret, 112, 115, 117
  Mary, 120, 123, 125, 126, 140, 151
  Richard, 109, 111, 114, 115, 116, 129, 135
  Samuel, 119
  Susanna, 111, 123, 126, 127
  Susannah, 162
  Winstant Smith, 135
  Winston, 112
  Winston Smith, 111, 199, 231, 234, 237
DARBY, Deborah, 222
DARE,
  Elizabeth, 80
  Gideon, 164
DAUGHADAY,
  Francis, 27
  John, 37
  Joseph, 33, 37
  Rachel, 33, 36
  Richard, 33, 37, 40

DAUGHDY,
  Catharine, 200, 214, 215, 232
DAVENPORT,
  Elizabeth, 164, 180, 189, 219, 224
  Jonathan, 164, 179, 189, 212, 219
  Joseph, 179, 219
  Margaret, 179, 212, 219
DAVIS,
  ---, 182
  Frances, 213
  Francis, 214
  George, 240
  John, 92, 220
  Joseph, 68, 79
  Martha, 54, 67, 213, 215
  Mary, 76, 213, 215
  Sarah, 158
  William, 68, 78, 79, 80
DAWES,
  ---, 166
  Abraham, 90
  Benjamin, 57
  Eda, 220
  Elizabeth, 57
  Francis, 220
  Isaac, 49, 50, 57, 83, 94
  Mareb, 80
  Mary, 57, 83, 220
  Mordecai, 57
DAWS,
  Abraham, 96
  Benjamin, 55
  Elizabeth, 53
  Francis, 45, 50

Isaac, 43, 52, 53, 55, 74
Mary, 49, 50, 52, 55, 58
Mordecai, 55
DAY,
  Hannah, 48, 110
  John, 146, 185
  Rebeckah, 254
  Rebekah, 270, 271
  Samuel, 43, 46, 62
  Sarah, 117, 118, 119, 146, 152, 185, 221
DEAN, Susana, 36
DEAVER,
  Abraham, 35
  Basel, 35, 43
  Basil, 30, 43
  Bassel, 41
  Bazel, 74
  Chew, 31, 35, 41
  John, 49
  Jonah, 74
  Margaret, 74
  Mary, 35
  Misael, 74
  Misal, 35
  Tue, 74
DEAVOR,
  Jonas, 53
  Margaret, 53
DEAVR, Basel, 31
DELWORTH,
  William, 189, 224
DEUR, John, 214
DEVENPORT,
  Elizabeth, 90
  Jonathan, 88
DEVER, Basel, 29
DEWIT, Ann, 135
DEYE, Thomas Cockey, 48, 52
DIAH,
  Esther, 43
  Josiah, 43
  Pheby, 43
  Rachel, 43
DIAR, Joanna, 250
DICKENSON,
  David, 96
  John, 101
  Ruth, 101, 198, 231
DICKINSON,
  John, 81, 83, 98
  Sarah, 97
DILLON,
  Ann, 11
  Elizabeth, 11, 89
  Hannah, 11, 57
  Isaac, 11
  John, 11, 102, 202, 212, 214, 215, 234
  Loyd, 11
  Martha, 11
  Mary, 11, 214, 215
  Moses, 11, 54, 55, 57, 72, 78, 118, 162, 240
  Rebecka, 11
DILWORTH,
  John, 277
  William, 78, 79
DIMMET, Mary, 52, 55
DIMMIT, Mary, 53
DIXON,
  Mary, 110
  William, 110
DOBSON, James, 270
DONEY, Clementine, 212
DORAN, Thomas, 121
DORSEY,
  Elizabeth, 271
  Hannah, 249, 265
  Henry, 47
  John Hammond, 26
  Priscilla, 29
  Rebeca, 29
  Rebecca, 47
  Sarah, 264, 272
DOVE, Joseph, 112
DOVES,
  James, 126
  Rachel, 126
DOWER, Abigail, 252
DOWNING, Richard, 113
DUBRY,
  Joseph, 56
  Mary, 56
DUCKET,
  John, 271
  Mary, 255, 257
DUCKETT, Ann, 275
DUER, Abigail, 252
DUKEHART,
  Catharine, 2, 82, 179, 212, 213, 214, 215, 219, 233
  Elizabeth, 1, 82, 89, 212, 216
  John, 2, 82, 179, 184, 196, 202, 211, 213, 214, 215, 216, 219, 227, 216

Margaret, 1, 2, 60, 82, 88, 164, 179, 202, 211, 212, 214, 215, 216, 219
Martha, 196
Mary, 54
Parthenia, 196, 202, 212, 213
Sarah, 1
V., 195
Valerius, 179
Volerisus, 82
Volerius, 1, 2, 211, 212, 214, 215, 216, 217, 219, 217
DULERY,
  Joseph, 56
  Mary, 56
DULTON, Hannah, 231
DUN, John, 115
DUNGAN, Mary, 152
DUNKIN,
  Benjaman, 42
  James, 42, 62
  Jane, 61
  Jean, 42
  Margaret, 60
  Margreat, 42
  Patrick, 42
DURBIN,
  Cassandra, 119
  Mary, 131
DUTTAN, Susanna, 127
DUTTON,
  Anne, 5
  Benjamin, 199
  Elizabeth, 50, 60
  Hannah, 199, 214, 231

John, 5, 52, 54, 88
Mary, 45, 46, 49
Robert, 5, 36, 38, 46, 49, 50, 52, 54, 60, 73, 75
Sarah, 5
Susanna, 5, 48
DYE, Thomas Cockey, 29
DYER,
  Aaron, 57, 83, 182, 220, 225
  Benjamin, 182, 220, 225
  Elizabeth, 58, 61, 83, 182, 220, 225
  Ester, 50
  Esther, 77
  Hester, 50, 64, 77
  Joanna, 57, 58
  John, 50, 58, 85
  Joseph, 57, 58, 91, 182, 220, 225
  Josiah, 43, 45, 50, 64, 182, 220, 225
  Mary, 58, 182, 220, 225
  Phebe, 45, 50, 58, 85
  Rachel, 51, 52, 64, 88
  Ureth, 50

-E-
EACHUS,
  Abner, 241
  Bathsheba, 241
  Joseph, 241
  Mahalah, 241
  Mary, 241
  Minshall, 241
  Obed, 241
  Preston, 241
  Sarah, 241
  Vanleer, 241
  Virgil, 241
EATON,
  David, 126
  Rachel, 119, 126, 157
ECKSON, Nicholas, 117
EDMUNDSON,
  Mary, 286
  Thomas, 286
ELGAR,
  John, 279
  Joseph, 52, 263, 274, 275, 278, 279
  Margaret, 260, 275, 278, 279
  Nathan, 279
ELICOTT,
  Andrew, 165
  Ann, 165
  Benjamin, 81
  David, 81
  Elias, 165
  Elizabeth, 165
  Evan Thomas, 165
  Frances, 165
  John, 165, 178
  Jonathan, 165
  Joseph, 81
  Judith, 81
  Mary, 81
  Nathaniel, 165
  Rachel, 81
ELIOTT,
  Eli, 262
  Hannah, 276
  Margaret, 276

Mary, 262, 276
William, 276
ELIS, Sarah, 256
ELLICOT,
  Ann, 71
  Benjamin, 71
  David, 71
  Elias, 73
  Joseph, 71
  Judith, 71
  Latitia, 71
  Mary, 71
  Rachel, 71
ELLICOTT,
  Andrew, 195, 196, 213, 214, 215, 217, 228, 229
  Andrew T., 210
  Ann, 199
  Benjamin, 189, 194, 204, 214, 217, 224, 235
  Cassandra, 90
  Cassandria, 231
  Elias, 6, 83, 178, 186, 189, 194, 199, 210, 211, 212, 213, 214, 218, 226, 233
  Eliza, 213
  Elizabeth, 6, 178, 204, 218, 235
  Esther, 195, 228
  Evan T., 6
  Evan Thomas, 6, 186
  Frances, 204, 235
  George, 162, 204, 235
  James, 192, 204, 210, 213, 214, 217, 226, 235
  John, 74, 90, 195, 205, 210, 213, 228, 236
  Jonathan, 204, 235
  Joseph, 165, 204, 235
  Judith, 204, 235
  Martha, 204, 235
  Mary, 6, 83, 178, 186, 189, 194, 199, 210, 213, 218
  Nathaniel, 204, 235
  Rachel, 6, 178, 218
  Samuel, 204, 210, 235
  Sarah, 204, 235
  Tacy, 189
  Thomas, 203, 210, 217
  William, 204, 235
ELLIOT,
  Amos, 282
  Eli, 250, 282
  Hannah, 250, 282
  Joanna, 282
  John, 267, 268, 269, 270, 282
  Mary, 250, 253, 267, 269, 282
  Ruth, 282
  Sarah, 254, 267, 269, 270, 276, 282
  William, 267, 282
ELLIOTT,
  Amos, 277
  Eli, 276, 286
  Elizabeth, 284
  Evan, 284
  George, 286
  Hannah, 274, 275, 277
  Jesse, 286
  Joel, 284
  John, 118, 274, 275, 276, 277, 284
  Jonathan, 204, 235
  Lydia, 284
  Margaret, 261, 277, 284, 286
  Margarett, 88
  Mary, 261, 276, 277, 284
  Rachel, 284
  Ruben, 286
  Ruth, 277, 284
  Sarah, 258, 274, 276, 277, 284, 286
  Thomas, 277, 284
  William, 277, 278, 284
ELLIS,
  Amos, 270, 272
  Ann, 117, 143
  Benjamin, 117, 143
  Deborah, 249
  Eleanor, 249
  Elliner, 264
  Mary, 144
  Mercy, 117, 144
  Morris, 264, 270, 271
  Moses, 266
  Samuel, 269
  Sarah, 248, 264, 270, 272
  Thomas, 264, 266, 267, 268, 270
  William, 112, 115, 116, 117, 139, 143, 144, 146
ELLOT, Mary, 267
ELY,
  Amoss, 88, 147
  Ann, 119, 121, 122, 124, 146
  David, 241
  Elizabeth, 88, 147
  George, 88, 147

Hannah, 88, 121, 241
Hugh, 88, 112, 113, 115, 120, 122, 123, 124, 125, 127, 147, 158, 161, 162, 241
Joseph, 112, 113, 115, 119, 121, 124, 127, 146, 147
Mahlon, 112, 113, 115, 156, 195, 229
Martha, 125, 126
Mary, 88, 115, 147
Rachel, 112, 113, 115, 119, 124, 125
Ruth, 113, 135
Sarah, 115, 119, 120, 122, 123, 124, 125, 127, 135, 154, 162
Thomas, 88, 112, 113, 115, 122, 124, 136, 147, 154, 241
William, 115, 119, 124, 125, 154
EMLIN, Samuel, 73
ENGLAND,
  Catharine, 23, 173, 216, 240
  David, 44
  Elisabeth, 52
  Elisebeth, 46
  Elizabeth, 1, 38, 44, 48, 50, 216
  Elizabeth Dutton, 23, 240
  George, 23, 38, 117, 199, 216, 234, 236, 240
  Hannah, 38, 83
  John, 38, 54

Joseph, 1, 37, 38, 44, 46, 47, 48, 61, 216
Lewis, 1
Robert, 38, 46, 48, 49, 56
Samuel, 1, 38, 83
Sarah, 1
Sarah Hooker, 23, 240
Thomas Hooker, 23, 240
ENGLE, Joseph, 82, 92
ENGOR,
  Ann, 286
  Charles, 286
  Edmund, 286
  Granville, 286
  J., 285
  M., 285
  Margret E., 286
  Mary, 285
  Phebe, 286
  William Henry, 286
ENSOR,
  George, 51
  John, 50
ERWIN,
  Jane, 84
  Mary, 84
ESTHER, 71, 140
EVANS,
  Alice, 213
  Amos, 126, 155, 157, 188, 224
  Amoss, 151, 153
  Cadwallader, 78
  Catharine, 168
  Elenor, 73, 78
  Elizabeth, 57
  Griffith, 57, 126, 157

Isaac, 201, 232
Jane, 126
Joel, 121, 126
Lukins, 153
EVERETT, Joseph, 264
EVERIT,
  Ittai, 274
  Joseph, 248
  Rachel, 57
  Richard, 48
  William, 43
EVERITT,
  Ann, 248
  Elizabeth, 283, 284
  Frances, 57
  Isaac, 284
  Ittai, 272
  John, 283, 284
  Joseph, 256, 260, 272, 284
  Mary, 283
  Sarah, 252, 260, 284

-F-
FANNEY, 72
FARIS, Ziba, 113
FARQUER, Allen, 47, 48
FARQUHAR, --es, 266
  A., 272, 274, 275, 278, 279
  Allen, 49, 252, 264, 265, 266, 267, 269, 270, 271, 272, 273, 274, 275, 278, 279, 285
  Amos, 266, 270, 272, 273, 274, 275, 278, 279, 285

Ann, 247, 250, 254, 264, 265, 266, 267, 268, 269, 270, 279, 280, 282, 288
Benjamin, 266, 272, 273, 274, 275, 278, 279
Caleb, 274, 278, 279, 284
Deborah, 288
Eli, 267
Elizabeth, 257, 265, 266, 268, 269, 270, 271, 272, 273, 280, 288
Enoch, 278
Esther, 260, 278, 279
Hannah, 255, 257, 263, 265, 272, 273, 274, 275, 278, 279, 288
James, 267, 268, 270, 273, 274, 278, 279, 284
Jane, 278
Joel, 288
John, 288
Jonah, 274, 278, 279
Joseph, 265
Lydia, 261, 262, 278, 279, 288
Mahlon, 274, 278, 279
Mary, 255, 260, 267, 269, 270, 272, 273, 274, 275, 278, 279, 282, 285, 288
Moses, 249, 264, 265, 266, 267, 269, 270, 271, 272, 273, 274, 275, 278, 279, 288
P. F., 285
Phebe, 248, 256, 264, 265, 266, 267, 269, 270, 272, 273, 275, 278, 279
Polly, 274
Rachel, 247, 250, 255, 260, 264, 266, 267, 268, 269, 270, 271, 273, 274, 275, 278, 279, 288
Rebecca, 234
Richard, 288
Robert, 267, 270, 272
Ruth, 258, 267, 268, 269, 270, 271, 272, 273, 288
Samuel, 264, 265, 266, 267, 269, 270, 272, 288
Sarah, 252, 257, 264, 265, 266, 267, 268, 269, 270, 271, 272, 273, 274, 275, 278, 284
Susanna, 250, 264, 265, 266, 273, 288
Susannah, 267
Thomas, 266, 267, 269, 270, 272
William, 250, 253, 254, 259, 264, 265, 266, 267, 268, 269, 270, 271, 272, 273, 274, 275, 278, 279, 280, 282, 288
William P., 278
FELL,
 Ann, 110
 Benjamin, 202, 234
 Edward, 26
 Jane, 202, 234
 Leah, 202, 234
 Mary, 202, 234
 Sarah, 27
FENLEY, Joseph, 50
FERRIS, Benjamin, 239
FIELD,
 ---, 191
 George, 225
 George W., 172, 230
FISHER,
 Deborah, 252
 Eliza, 252
 Elizabeth, 253
 Eunice, 180, 220, 234
 Hannah, 180, 220, 222
 Isaac, 252
 James, 202, 234, 239
 Joseph, 65
 Josiah, 65, 180, 220, 221
 Margaret, 65, 180, 220
 Mary, 165
 Ruth, 65, 90
 Samuel, 65, 180, 220, 221, 223
 Sarah, 115
 Thomas, 91, 117, 171, 184, 211, 221, 227
 Unice, 65
FITZWATER,
 Abel, 56
 Hannah, 55
FLINT, William, 274
FLOYD,
 Ana, 68
 Ann, 69
 Caleb, 185, 221
 John, 36
 Joseph, 77
 Mary, 183, 220, 224
 Rachel, 49, 67, 68, 69
 Richard, 81
 Thomas, 36, 49, 51, 83
 William, 183, 220
FOARD,
 Beniamin, 28

Benimin, 29
Mary, 27
FORD,
  Charcila, 47
  Edward, 165, 194
  Frances, 155, 165, 189, 190, 194, 198, 225
  Harriott, 198
  Hezekiah, 271, 272
  John, 124
  Joseph, 123, 153, 154, 155, 165, 189, 190, 194, 198, 225, 237, 274
  Mary, 32
  Philip, 155, 165, 189, 190, 225
  Rosanna, 123, 154
  Thomas, 55
  William, 123, 154
FOREMAN,
  Mary, 51
  Robart, 51
  Robert, 44, 51, 52, 62
FORMAN,
  Elizabeth, 50
  John, 1, 50
  Mary, 1
  Robert, 1, 50
FORSYTHE, John, 127
FORTUNE, 137
FORWOOD,
  Hannah, 112, 115
  Jacob, 141
  Joh, 108
  John, 112, 114, 117, 124, 125, 137
  Martha, 241

Mary, 155
Samuel, 141
FOWLER,
  James, 275
  Mary, 257
FOX, George, 231
FRAISOR, John, 32
FRAZER,
  Francis, 57
  Mary, 49
  Sarah, 51
FREDD, Mary, 77
FREELAND, Elizabeth, 121
FRENCH,
  Ann, 262, 272, 274, 275, 276, 283
  Emma, 274, 275, 276, 277, 283
  Emme, 272
  Israel, 207, 273, 274, 275, 276, 277, 283
  Joanna, 283
  Margaret, 276
  Margret, 283
  Otho, 275, 276, 277, 283
  Samuel, 276
  Sarah, 272
FRINAL, Anne, 158
FULLER, Oliver, 200, 232
FULTON,
  Cassandra, 54, 55
  Hannah, 50, 55
FUSSELL,
  Bartholomew, 241
  Esther, 241

Joseph, 241
Rebecca, 241
Solomon, 241

-G-
GALLAWAY,
  David, 58
  Susanna, 58
GALLION, Joseph, 159
GALLOWAY,
  Abraham, 28
  David, 74
  Elizabeth, 67
  Moses, 27
  Susanna, 251
  Susannah, 74
GAMBLE,
  Elizabeth, 253, 261, 271, 272, 273, 274
  Joseph, 253, 274
GARRETSON,
  Garrit, 287
  Jazer, 287
  Margaret, 287
  Mary, 287
  Sarah, 287
GARRETT,
  Abigail, 241
  Eliza, 241
  Esther, 241
  Jesse, 241
  John, 57
  Jonah, 241
GARRISON,
  James, 56
  Samuel, 56
GASH, Rachel, 69

GASSAWAY,
  Margaret, 55
  Margret, 35, 36, 47
  Nicholas, 29, 31, 35, 47, 53, 55, 60, 61
  Rachel, 35, 47, 53, 55, 68
  Richard, 36
GATCHEL, Hannah, 163
GEORGE, Elizabeth, 217
GIBBONS,
  Ann, 44
  John, 44, 45
  Joseph, 44
  Martha, 44
GIBSON,
  Deborah, 92
  Eliza, 92, 96, 99
  Gideon, 278
  Hannah, 92, 96, 99, 268, 275, 276
  John, 92, 96, 99
  John Lee, 122
  Joshua, 92, 96, 99
  Lydia, 92, 96, 99
  Mary, 92, 96, 99
  Mary Ann, 122
  Samuel, 276
  Susannah, 92, 96, 99
GIELETT, Stephen, 173
GILBERT,
  Elisabeth, 55
  Ruth, 90
GILES,
  Anna, 105, 136
  Aquilla, 103, 132
  Casandro, 27
  Edward, 103, 132
  Elisabeth, 110
  Elizabeth, 27, 103, 105, 112
  Hannah, 113, 114
  Hester, 136
  Jacob, 103, 105, 132, 134, 138
  James, 50, 51, 103, 132, 134
  Johannah, 103
  John, 166
  Nathaniel, 110
  Sarah, 26, 166
  Sarah S., 166
  Thomas, 103, 132
GILL,
  Cassandry, 53
  Catherine, 54
  Edward, 53
  John, 53
  Leah, 59
  Stephen, 53
GILLINGHAM,
  Amos, 205, 236
  Elizabeth, 205, 235
  Ezra, 205, 235
  George, 205, 235
  James, 59, 205, 235
  John, 205, 235
  Mary, 205
  William, 205, 235
GILPIN,
  Alban, 122
  Margery, 121
  Samuel, 91
GIPSON,
  Ann, 283
  Gideon, 265
  Gidion, 267, 271, 283
  Hannah, 267, 268, 269, 270, 276, 283
  Mahlon, 283
  Samuel, 272, 283
  William, 277, 283
GIVEN,
  Ann, 276
  Isabella, 276
  James, 276
  John, 276
  Moses, 262, 273, 275, 276, 277
GODFREY, Samuel, 205, 236
GORSUCH,
  Charles, 31, 47, 48, 49
  John, 48, 49
  Mary, 52
  Rachel, 47
  Sarah, 47
GOTHROP, Thomas, 45
GOTT,
  Anthony, 32
  Casa., 32
  El., 29
  Elizabeth, 28
  Hanah, 32
  Rebecca, 36
  Richard, 26, 29
  Samuel, 27, 29
GOUGH, Caleb, 54
  P., 215

GOVER,
  Ann, 123
  Betsy, 109
  Cassander, 50
  Cassandra, 111, 114, 116, 117, 143
  Cassandry, 111, 112
  Cassy, 109
  Elisabeth, 112
  Elizabeth, 111, 112, 116, 117, 122, 133, 135, 143, 151, 110
  Ephraim, 109, 110, 111, 112, 117, 122, 133, 135, 143
  Gerrard, 122
  Gittings, 112, 115, 116, 117
  Margarett, 135
  Margret, 110, 111, 112
  Mary, 109, 112, 121, 122, 133, 150, 110
  Nathaniel, 122, 127
  Philip, 111, 116, 122, 126, 128, 150, 151
  Philiph, 112, 113
  Pricila, 109
  Prisala, 122
  Priscilla, 50, 111, 114, 116, 114
  Priss., 113
  Prissila, 112
  Rachel, 110, 111, 112
  Robert, 114, 115, 116, 117, 122, 138
  Samuel, 109, 112, 113, 116, 117, 122, 123, 150, 265, 268, 114

GOWSRY, John, 36
GRACE, 69
GRANT, Ann, 32
GRAY, Samuel, 75
GREEN,
  Hannah, 228
  John, 29, 68
  Lydia, 200, 232
  Mary, 46
  Sarah, 85
GREENLAND,
  Ann, 110
  Flour, 109
  Flower, 130
  Naomi, 109, 130
  Naomy, 109
  Richard, 110
  Sarah, 109
  Sary, 110
GREGG, Rebekah, 268
GRELETT, Stephen, 173
GRIFFEE, Richard, 264
GRIFFITH,
  Abraham, 9, 10, 21, 51, 56, 57, 59, 86, 87, 272
  Ann, 9, 10, 51, 52, 57, 59, 88
  Anne, 59
  Beng., 51
  Benjamin, 49
  Catharine, 82
  Eleoner, 96
  Elizabeth, 51, 59, 73
  Evan, 75, 95, 99
  Even, 44
  Hannah, 51, 52, 59, 60

  Isaac, 9, 10, 51, 52, 57, 59, 64, 66, 77
  James, 59, 77
  John, 52, 59, 77, 83
  Joseph, 52, 59, 74, 82
  Martha, 59, 66
  Mary, 9, 10, 21, 51, 52, 56, 57, 59, 95, 99, 276
  Miriam, 10
  Nathan, 51
  Rachel, 21, 87
  Rebecca, 95, 99
  Rebecckah, 44
  Reuben, 10, 98
  Sarah, 21, 59, 63, 95, 99
  Sophia, 10
  Thomas Taylor, 21
GRILSE, Jaminna, 64

-H-
HAGAR, 139
HAILE, R., 29
HAINES,
  Ann, 209
  Daniel, 48, 49, 275, 280
  Deborah, 280
  Elisabeth, 48
  Elizabeth, 264, 266, 287
  Esther, 258, 274
  Isaac, 267, 280
  Jane, 49
  Jesse, 280
  Joseph, 48, 49, 250, 264, 265, 266, 275, 287
  Lydia, 49
  Mary, 49, 247, 264, 280
  Mordecca, 264

Nathan, 49, 264, 266, 267, 270, 287
Rachel, 268, 287
Ruben, 266
Samuel, 270, 280
Sophia, 264, 266, 269, 287
William, 49, 266, 270, 274
HAINS,
　Daniel, 41, 47
　Deborah, 47
　Elizabeth, 47
　Jacob, 47
　Joseph, 46, 47, 58
　Lydia, 47
　Nathan, 37, 46
　William, 47
HAIR,
　Elennor, 25
　Elizabeth, 24, 25
　Hannah, 25
　Jemima, 91
　Jeminah, 24
　John, 24, 25, 53, 70, 78, 97
　Mary, 25
　Phebe, 25
　Rachel, 25
　Rebekah, 25
　Sarah, 25
　Tamar, 25
HALE, Thomas, 53
HALL,
　Catherine, 114, 119
　Christopher, 123
　Edward, 53

Elihu, 50, 114, 116
Elizabeth, 276
J., 115
Jacob, 117
John, 172, 173
John Athn., 276
Joseph, 50
Joseph Harris, 123
Mary, 117, 165
Sarah, 164
Sophia, 110
Susanna, 114
HAMBLETON,
　Benjamin, 209, 238
　Charles, 238
　James, 209, 238
　Joseph, 209, 238
　Mary, 209, 238
　Rachel, 209, 238
　William, 209, 238
HAMMOND,
　Sarah, 27
　Sary, 108
　William, 26
HANAWAY, Ruth, 76
HANES, Nathan, 38
HANNAH, 69, 137, 139
　Mary, 80
HANSON,
　Alisana, 49
　Daniel, 173, 201, 233, 237
　Hollis, 112
　Mary, 27, 28
HANWAY,
　Elizabeth, 93, 94, 167
　Samuel, 99

HARBERT,
　Ann, 41, 93
　Sarah, 91
HARDACRE,
　Elizabeth, 271
HARDAKER,
　Elizabeth, 259
HARDEN, Lydia, 212
HARDESTY,
　Charles, 89
HARDING,
　Charles, 19, 92, 99
　David, 19
　Elizabeth, 19
　George, 19
　Lydia, 19
　Mary, 19
　Thomas, 19
HARDORKER,
　Elizabeth, 254
HARGROVE,
　Hannah, 216
　John, 216
HARGUER,
　Allin, 31
　William, 31
HARKLEE,
　Elisabeth, 52
HARLAN,
　Alice, 157, 160, 162
　Ezekiel, 172, 194, 206, 228
　Hannah, 242
　John, 203, 234, 240, 242
　Rebecca, 157
　Rebeccah, 159
　Samuel, 200, 231, 276

INDEX

Susanna, 81, 183, 217, 220
HARLAND,
  Alice, 127
  David, 127
  Hannah, 127
  Jeremiah, 127
  Lewis, 127
  Rebecca, 127
HARPLY, Nathaniel, 126
HARRIS,
  ---, 177
  Ann, 105, 111, 112, 113, 114, 115, 116, 117, 144, 202, 233
  Benjamin, 105, 117, 144
  Beulah, 4, 177, 202, 218, 221, 233
  Cassandra, 144
  Elizabeth, 51, 105, 114, 115, 116, 117, 144, 166, 268
  George, 4, 86, 87, 105, 117, 121, 122, 125, 202, 208, 218, 221, 233
  James, 112
  Jane, 208
  John, 105, 114, 115, 116, 117
  Joseph, 105, 112, 113, 116, 117, 118, 119, 122
  Margaret, 108, 109, 116, 117, 136, 143, 144
  Margarett, 105, 116
  Margret, 110, 111, 112, 113, 114, 115, 117
  Mary, 4, 105, 136, 177, 202, 218, 221, 233
  Moses, 250, 268
  Rachel, 166
  Samuel, 50, 51, 61, 105, 108, 111, 112, 113, 115, 116, 117, 136, 139, 141, 143, 144, 166, 177
  Sarah, 105, 144, 248, 250, 251, 267, 268
  Susanna, 4, 177, 202, 208, 218, 221, 233
  Thomas, 105, 144
  William, 50, 89, 105, 144, 214
HARRISHALL, Joseph, 123
HARRISON,
  Achsah, 276
  Benjamin, 273
  Daniel, 273
  Elizabeth, 273
  Mary, 258
  Meriam, 256
  Myriam, 273
  Peter, 273
  Ruth, 259, 273
  Sarah, 88, 169, 258, 261, 273
  Susanna, 273
  Thomas, 273
  William, 258, 273
HARRISS, Peggy, 109
HARRY, 139
  David, 18, 92, 96, 97
  Evan, 208, 237
  Mary, 242
HARTEY, James, 269
HARVEY,
  Amos, 114
  Hannah, 114
  Sarah, 165
  William, 57
HASTINGS, Mary, 98
HAVILAND,
  Asahel, 246
  Esther, 246
HAWARD,
  Ann, 109
  Betty, 109
  Joseph, 109
  Rebecah, 109
HAWKINS,
  Augustine, 27, 31
  Benjamin, 128
  Elizabeth, 120, 122
  Sarah, 128
HAWLEY, William, 83
HAWOOD, Ann, 109
HAY,
  Mary, 253
  Phebe, 252
HAYES, John, 211
HAYHURST,
  Ann, 56, 140
  David, 84
  Elisabeth, 54
  Elizabeth, 56, 71
  Ely, 88
  Hannah, 88, 89
  James, 56, 88, 115, 140
  Job, 88
  John, 115
  Mary, 74, 88, 140
  Rachel, 88
  Ruth, 54, 56, 75, 76, 115
  Sarah, 56, 75, 88

Tamer, 54
HAYWARD,
  Ann, 41, 46, 109, 129
  Elisabeth, 53
  Elizabeth, 31, 42, 46, 47, 55, 128, 203, 234
  Hannah, 80
  Harman, 208
  Isaac, 203, 234
  John, 52, 55, 203, 234, 235
  Jonathan, 203, 234
  Josep, 51
  Joseph, 31, 38, 40, 46, 47, 53, 108, 120, 148, 180, 216, 220
  Joshua, 166, 194
  Kezia, 203, 234
  Mary, 52, 89, 148, 166, 180, 187, 194, 198, 208, 220
  Mary Ann, 203
  Maryann, 234
  Molley, 55
  Rachel, 14, 53, 55, 74, 203, 235
  Rebecca, 53, 78, 120, 203, 216, 235
  Rebecka, 148
  Rebeckah, 55
  Samuel, 166, 180, 220
  Sarah, 120, 176, 213, 216, 218
  Sidney, 55, 203, 235
  Thomas, 198
  William, 37, 39, 46, 47, 53, 55, 70, 90, 120, 148, 166, 180, 187, 194, 198, 203, 208, 215, 216, 220, 228, 234, 235
HAYWART,
  Ann, 41
  Joseph, 40
  William, 39
HAYWOOD,
  Joseph, 36
  Sarah, 234
  William, 36
HEATON,
  Abner, 144, 153
  Elizabeth, 126, 144, 155, 158
  Isaiah, 144
  Jeremiah, 118, 119
  Joseph, 144, 155
  Levan, 144
  Leven, 162
  William, 118
HEDDINTON,
  Hannah, 94
HELM,
  Leonard, 219
  Mary,, 180, 219, 224
HELMS, Mary, 91, 208, 238
HENDERSON,
  Esther, 77
HENDON, Alice, 246
HENDRICKS,
  Elizabeth, 256, 257
HERBERT,
  Charles, 54
  William, 57
HERCULES, 139
HERVEY, Mary, 52
HESSELIUS, M., 215
HESTER, 137, 139
HESTINGS, Mary, 98
HESTON,
  Ann, 204, 235
  Joseph, 204, 235
  Letitia, 204
  Mary, 100
  Phebe, 204
  Samuel, 204, 235
  William, 204, 235
HEWES,
  Joseph, 207
  Sarah, 264
HEWITT, Sarah, 248
HEWS, Joseph, 236
HIBBARD, Joseph, 192
HIBBERD,
  Aaron, 274, 275, 278
  Alice Ann, 287
  Allen, 275, 278, 287
  Aron, 278
  Benjamin, 278, 279, 286, 287
  Charity, 287
  Elizabeth, 287
  Hannah, 261, 270, 271, 274, 275
  Israel, 287
  James, 287
  Jane, 254, 256, 261, 270, 271, 273, 275, 278, 279, 286, 287
  Jane Sarah, 287
  Joel, 287
  Joseph, 213, 217, 226, 270, 272, 274, 275, 278, 279, 286, 287

INDEX

Lydia M., 164
Martha, 262, 278
Phebe, 278, 279
Rachel, 287
Samuel, 287
Sarah, 275, 278
Silas, 275, 278, 287
William, 287
HICCOTT, Judith, 81
HICKS,
---, 179
  Ann, 6, 179, 213, 214, 215, 217, 219
  Bathshe, 179
  Bathsheba, 7, 219
  David, 7, 89
  Henry, 7, 179, 219
  James, 6, 7, 53, 56, 67, 70, 179, 219
  Jane, 7, 179, 219, 222
  Mary, 6, 7, 179, 214, 215, 219, 222
  Susanna, 6, 77
  Tamer, 179, 219
HIGHAT, William, 45
HILL,
  Elizabeth, 110, 112
  James, 137, 151, 156, 199, 231, 236
  Margaret, 109, 110
  Martha, 153, 173, 188, 212, 223, 238
  Mary, 112, 113, 135, 139, 146, 147, 166, 183, 212, 215, 220
  Moses, 129
  Rachel, 112, 135
  Sarah, 137, 157
  Shem, 113, 139
  William, 112, 135, 139, 156, 157
HILLEN, John, 211, 212, 216
HOBBS,
  Anna, 276
  Asenath, 276
  Elizabeth, 270
  Samuel, 276
  William, 269, 276
HOEG, Comfort, 132
HOFFMAN, Jacob, 217
HOKER,
  Barney, 37
  Benjamin, 47
  Thomas, 49
HOLLA--, Richard, 267
HOLLAND,
  Frances, 169
  Richard, 265, 268, 271
  Ruth, 247, 248, 265, 266, 267, 268, 269, 270, 271, 272, 273, 274, 276, 277
HOLLINGSWORTH,
  Abigail, 241, 246
  Eli, 241, 246
  Elizabeth, 242
  Elizabeth W., 246
  Hannah, 241, 249
  Isaac, 91
  Jesse, 241
  John, 241
  Jonah, 249, 266
  Mary, 54, 239
  Nathaniel, 241
  Rachel, 266
  Robert, 241, 242, 246
  Thomas, 241
HOLTON, David, 90
HOOF, Michael, 38
HOOKER,
  Aquila, 28, 70
  Barney, 40
  Barny, 28
  Benimin, 29
  Benjaman, 47
  Benjamin, 51
  Catharine, 91, 199, 211, 216, 231, 234, 236
  Catherine, 101, 236
  Charity, 28
  Eurath, 28
  Hanah, 27
  Hannah, 216
  John, 28, 47
  Love, 31
  Lovely, 29, 35
  Margaret, 28
  Margret, 30
  Mary, 28
  Rachel, 59, 81
  Richard, 27, 28, 29, 31, 32, 35, 37, 40, 69, 70
  Ruth, 35
  Samuel, 29, 31, 35, 41, 42
  Sarah, 28, 29, 31, 35
  Susannah, 35
  Thomas, 27, 29, 31, 35, 37, 40, 41, 42, 45, 47, 216
  Urith, 31
HOOPES, Esther, 124
  Joseph, 124
  Lydia, 124, 127

Thomas, 124
HOOPS,
David, 124, 154
Esther, 124, 154
Jesse, 119, 124, 154
Sarah, 155
HOPKINS,
Agnes, 128
Amelia, 105, 127
Ann, 50, 108, 110, 111, 112, 113, 115, 116, 122, 133, 138, 144, 150
Anna, 119, 121
Anne, 109
Cassandra, 3, 51, 165
Catharine, 33, 75, 83
Charles, 113, 114, 115, 116, 117, 119, 121, 122
Deborah, 209
Dorothy, 193, 196, 200, 209, 212, 213, 227
Edward, 166, 200
Elenor, 108
Elisabeth, 111, 113
Eliza, 108, 122, 127
Elizabeth, 4, 33, 51, 52, 81, 110, 111, 112, 113, 114, 115, 116, 117, 119, 120, 122, 123, 124, 125, 126, 127, 131, 133, 134, 150, 157, 158, 181, 196, 210, 212, 214, 220, 229, 233
Ephraim, 127
Ephraim Gover, 155
Frances, 105, 119, 120, 121, 124, 125, 157, 158, 196, 230

Francis, 79, 81, 122, 229
Garrard, 33, 39, 51, 113
Gerard, 69, 105, 127, 165
Gerard T., 166
Gerrard, 4, 33, 68, 72, 109, 110, 111, 114, 115, 116, 117, 118, 119, 121, 125, 127, 128, 131, 136, 137, 177, 212, 214, 218, 227
Gerrard T., 193, 196, 200, 209, 212, 213, 214, 215, 217, 230
Grace Jacob, 105
Hannah, 114, 115
Hannah Moore, 114, 115, 116, 141
Henry, 108, 177, 214, 218, 238
J., 125, 127
James, 70
Joel, 124, 158, 196, 229
John, 33, 49, 50, 51, 52, 92, 105, 108, 111, 114, 116, 117, 119, 121, 122, 127, 133, 159, 181, 210, 214, 220
John Wallace, 193, 227
John Wallas, 152
Johns, 65, 72, 166, 181, 220, 227, 229
Joseph, 3, 4, 50, 73, 108, 109, 110, 111, 112, 113, 114, 116, 117, 118, 119, 120, 122, 126, 127, 133, 138, 150, 158, 160, 208, 238
Katherine, 4
Leavin, 138

Levan, 155
Leven, 105, 111, 112
Leven Hill, 71, 72, 115, 116
Levin Hill, 114, 139, 141
Lewis, 184, 220, 222
Margaret, 51, 61, 84, 111, 165, 170
Margreat, 49
Margret, 33
Mary, 50, 59, 109, 112, 116, 128, 131, 132, 196
Miriam, 51
Nancy, 117
Nicholas, 4, 51, 52, 111, 214
Nicholos, 33
P., 184
Philip, 33, 43, 65, 69, 110, 128, 133, 159, 220, 222
Priscilla, 108, 177, 215, 218
Rachel, 4, 27, 33, 49, 51, 52, 75, 83, 108, 110, 111, 112, 114, 115, 116, 120, 121, 122, 136, 139, 141, 149, 177, 214, 218
Richard, 3, 4, 33, 36, 44, 49, 51, 54, 63, 69, 72, 83, 110, 177, 218
Samuel, 3, 4, 26, 27, 29, 30, 33, 36, 37, 39, 40, 43, 44, 49, 68, 70, 72, 73, 108, 110, 111, 112, 113, 114, 115, 116, 117, 118, 119, 120, 121, 122, 123, 124, 125, 126, 127, 128, 133,

148, 150, 156, 158, 166, 214, 218
 Sarah, 3, 4, 28, 33, 46, 49, 51, 63, 70, 83, 92, 105, 111, 114, 119, 121, 122, 123, 124, 126, 133, 137, 166, 181, 201, 214, 215, 216, 220, 232
 Sarah W., 124, 125, 126, 127
 Susanna, 110, 111, 114, 123, 124, 127
 Susannah, 105, 110, 139, 162
 Thomas, 166, 181, 220
 W., 124, 126
 William, 3, 27, 70, 105, 109, 110, 111, 112, 114, 115, 116, 117, 121, 124, 127, 131, 136, 138, 139, 141, 148
HORSEMAN,
 Charles, 80
 John, 80
 Mary, 80
HOSKINS,
 Elizabeth, 242
 Elizabeth A., 246
 Elizabeth Cheyney, 242
 John, 242
 Martha, 242
 Nathaniel, 242
 William, 242
HOSLER, John, 274
HOUGH,
 Abraham, 68
 Frances, 201
 James Carey, 201
 John, 213, 266
 Joseph, 213
 Lydia, 266
 Mary, 213
 Michael, 59
 Rebecca, 213
 Robert, 183, 192, 201, 213, 226, 230
HOULTON, David, 83, 208, 237
HOUSTMAN, Mary, 91
HOWARD,
 Ann, 46, 49, 54, 68, 109
 Anne, 4, 5, 52
 B., 50, 55, 57
 Benjaman, 49
 Benjamin, 5, 40, 45, 52, 53, 54, 55, 56, 63, 69, 70
 Elizabeth, 5
 Hannah, 61
 John, 32, 35
 Joseph, 60, 109
 Lamuel, 49
 Lemuel, 4, 5, 35, 46, 49, 52, 54
 Limuel, 32
 M. W., 215
 Martha, 52
 Mary, 5, 50, 52, 54, 55, 61, 96, 168
 Rachel, 61
 Rebecca, 60
 Ruth, 52
 Sarah, 5, 54, 95
 Susanna, 5, 46, 52, 64
 Suse, 38
 Sussa, 38
 Sussy, 38
 William, 61
HOWEL,
 Arthur, 264
 Israel, 277
 Lydia, 263, 276
 Sarah, 251, 259, 272
 Stephen, 251, 267, 275, 276
HOWELL,
 David, 284
 Hannah, 284
 Israel, 284, 287
 Lydia, 284
 Mary, 284, 287
 Samuel, 57
 Sarah, 271, 273, 284
 Stephen, 271, 273, 274, 275, 276, 284, 287
HUCHINS, Francis, 169
 Mary, 169
HUDSON, Jonathan, 129, 130
HUFF,
 Abraham, 44, 242
 Jennat, 31
 Jennet, 30
 Mercy, 242
 Michel, 30, 31, 35
 Thomas, 30
HUGH, Elizabeth, 221
HUGHES,
 --se, 266
 Elizabeth, 251, 256, 269, 272, 274, 275, 276, 277, 278, 283
 George, 283

Gideon, 208, 236
Hannah, 91, 182, 220, 288
Jesse, 265, 266, 267, 268, 269, 270, 271, 272, 274, 275, 276, 277, 283
Joseph, 239
Lydia, 283
Margaret, 262, 276, 283
Rachel, 277, 283
Samuel, 277, 283
Scott, 120
Thomas, 55
William, 283
HUGHS, Thomas, 67, 71
HUGO, Elizabeth, 151, 186, 191, 214, 215, 226, 234
Guli, 191
Gulie, 226
Julia, 214, 232
Samuel, 191, 226, 236
Samuel B., 215
Thomas B., 186
HULL, Henry, 160
HULTON,
David, 212
Margaret, 216
HUMPHREY,
Ann, 51
Anna, 41
Catharener, 41
David, 41, 44, 49, 58, 165, 166
Elenn, 165, 166
Elenor, 41, 183, 220
Elizabeth, 41, 49, 92
Jeane, 41
Jonathan, 49
Joshua, 41
Margaret, 41
Robert, 41
HUMPHREYS,
Elizabeth, 54
Jane, 54
Natl., 54
Robert, 64
HUMPHRIES,
Ann, 66
David, 46
HUMPHRY, Eleanor, 57
HUNT, Abigail, 249, 265, 267, 268, 281
Eleaser, 30
Elisha, 199
John, 129, 281
Joseph, 281
Joshua, 249, 265, 281
Margaret, 61, 72
Mary, 249, 281
Robert, 249, 265, 267, 269, 281
Samuel, 249, 281
William, 249, 272, 273, 281
HURFORD,
Elisabeth, 110
Hannah, 109, 130
Isaac, 110
John, 109, 110, 130
Joseph, 109, 130
Samuel, 110
HURST, Judith, 61, 63
HUSBAND, Anna, 108
Elizabeth, 105, 114, 115, 116, 120, 121, 123, 131, 195, 212, 213, 214, 216, 228
Hannah, 105
Herman, 108
John Jewett, 108
Joseph, 105, 107, 111, 112, 114, 115, 116, 117, 120, 121, 122, 123, 129, 133, 147, 148, 149, 162, 197, 216, 230, 238
Joshua, 78, 81, 105, 107, 108, 115, 117, 118, 120, 121, 122, 124, 125, 133
Lydia, 105, 196, 214, 216, 229
Margaret, 107, 108, 123, 125
Mary, 105, 107, 111, 112, 113, 114, 115, 116, 117, 118, 119, 120, 121, 122, 123, 133, 143, 147, 148, 149, 162
Polley, 114
Rachel, 114, 115, 116, 120, 122
Samuel, 105, 196, 229
Sarah, 105, 117, 119, 120, 121, 149
Susanna, 105, 114, 116, 147, 196, 216, 229
William, 89, 105, 111, 120, 121, 147, 184, 199, 212, 213, 214, 216, 217, 221, 226, 231
HUSBANDS, Eliza, 122
Joseph, 110, 137, 152, 158
Joshua, 127, 152

Mary, 110, 152
HUSEY,
  Mary, 257
  Sarah, 258
HUSSEY,
  Christopher, 273
  Ennion, 15, 181, 219
  George, 14, 15, 73, 74, 165, 166, 181, 187, 194, 219, 236
  Hannah, 194
  Isaac, 187
  John, 15, 165, 166, 181
  Joseph, 14, 181, 219
  Lydia, 263
  Mary, 95, 98, 101, 102, 199, 214, 217, 231, 259, 272
  Miriam, 183, 220, 222
  Rachel, 14, 15, 165, 166, 181, 187, 194, 216, 219
  Rebecca, 15, 181, 219
  Ruth, 79, 84, 86
  William, 15, 181, 219
HUTCHENS, John, 50
HUTCHINS,
  Elizabeth, 55, 169
  Francis, 169
  Jacob, 56
  Mary, 169, 170
  Thomas, 49, 50, 55
  William, 55
HUTCHONS, Thomas, 55
HUTTON,
  Benjamin, 248, 280
  Joel, 248, 280, 281
  John, 242, 248, 280
  Jonathan, 248, 281
  Joseph, 248, 270, 280
  Levi, 281
  Levy, 280
  Mary, 248, 251, 267, 280, 281
  Samuel, 248, 267, 280
  Sarah, 242, 280
  Thomas, 281
  William, 248, 280
HYATT,
  George, 36
  Mary, 36

-I-

IIAMS, Isaac, 277
INGLAND,
  Elizabeth, 35
  Joseph, 35, 36

-J-

JACK, 137
JACKSON,
  Ann, 3, 179, 219, 223
  Elizabeth, 46
  Frances, 3, 180, 219
  Isaac, 166, 167, 266
  Isaiah, 3, 56, 179, 219, 227, 233
  John, 3, 180, 184, 219, 220
  Joseph, 93, 166, 184, 220, 229, 271
  Margaret, 3, 166, 167, 179, 219
  Mary, 3, 180, 208, 219, 233, 238
  Philip, 46
  Rachel, 184, 220, 222
  Samuel, 166, 202, 233
  Sarah, 3, 167, 179, 219, 231
  Susanna, 184, 220
  Susannah, 93, 224
  Thomas, 93, 232, 233
  Thomas Lewis, 3, 180, 219
  William, 266
JACOB, 72, 137
  Cassandra, 115
  Grace, 114
  Jane, 215
  William, 216
JAMES, 139
  Amos, 57, 90, 102, 178, 188, 189, 195, 206, 212, 213, 214, 217, 219, 223
  Ann, 178, 219
  Elizabeth, 51, 206
  Frederick, 242
  Jane, 222
  John, 266
  Mary, 178, 189, 195, 206, 214, 219
  Miriam, 188, 223
  Mordecai, 163
  Rebecca, 242, 246
  Thomas, 38, 43, 48, 50
  William, 57, 74, 91, 189
JAMISON, Ann, 223
JANE, 137
JANNEY,
  ---, 265
  Anna, 251
  Aquila, 268

Benjamin Say, 193, 227
Elizabeth, 193, 227
George Fox, 193, 227
Hannah, 266, 268
Israel, 193, 227, 251, 268
Jacob, 206, 236, 251, 268
Joseph, 266
Levis, 193, 216, 227
Mahlon, 265, 266, 268
Mary, 193, 227
Moses, 198, 231
Sarah, 161, 251, 265, 266, 268
JARRETT, Ellen, 52
JAY, Elizabeth, 113, 125, 126, 149, 151
Hannah, 113, 116, 126, 129, 137, 145, 157
John, 137
Joseph, 190, 224, 227
Martha, 126, 127
Samuel, 151, 152
Soffy, 113
Sophia, 113, 136, 137
Stephen, 113, 126, 145, 157
Thomas, 126, 137, 157
JEFFEREIS, William, 76
JEFFERIES,
 Gravener, 237
 Samuel, 237
JEFFERIS,
 Gravener, 11, 96, 207, 215
 Gravenor, 92
 Priscilla, 11, 92, 96
 Samuel, 11, 92, 96, 176, 207, 215, 217
William, 11
JEFFERYS,
 Gravener, 102
 Samuel, 102
JENKINS,
 John Clark, 116
 Mary, 119
 Sarah, 119
 William, 120
JERVIS, Charles, 128
JESS, 137
JESSOP, Susanna, 278
JEWEL,
 Alice, 74
 George, 74, 93, 101
 Mary, 74, 101, 238
JEWELL,
 Alice, 86
 George, 102, 206
 John, 206
 Joseph, 206
 Mary, 102, 206
 Sarah, 206
 William, 206
JEWET,
 Ann, 122, 123, 144
 John, 123, 144, 159
 Margaret, 122, 144
 Thadeus, 122
 Thomas, 123, 144
JEWETT,
 Ann, 118, 119, 124, 138
 Dr., 138
 John, 119, 198, 214, 216
 Margret, 119
 Thomas, 207, 237
JEWIT, Ann, 135, 152
Margaret, 152
Thadeus, 152
JEWITT, John, 231
JINKINS,
 Jonathan, 53, 55, 57
 Margaret, 53, 55
 William, 53, 55, 57
JOHN, 69, 72
 Ann, 209, 216
JOHNS,
 Alesanna, 52
 Ann, 108, 109, 128, 129, 146, 173, 197, 230, 238
 Aquila, 46, 129
 Cassandra, 147
 Elizabeth, 50, 119, 120, 121, 122, 123, 124, 125, 146, 154, 166, 173, 197, 213, 214, 215, 216, 217, 230, 238
 Frances, 147
 Hannah, 15, 42, 48, 63, 108, 109, 113, 129, 164
 Henry, 138
 Hosea, 119
 Hosier, 108, 109
 Margaret, 165
 Mary, 109, 129, 131, 146, 173, 197, 230, 238
 Nathan, 108, 109, 116, 122, 124, 125, 129, 146, 147, 154, 166, 172, 173, 197, 200, 230, 232, 234, 238
 Philip, 130
 Richard, 109, 110, 115, 123, 125, 129, 140, 147, 154, 160, 165

Sarah, 160
Skipwith, 116, 132
Tacey, 273
JOHNSON,
  Ann, 69, 132, 134
  Benjamin, 132, 134
  Ephraim, 132
  Hannah, 56
  Isaac, 172, 184, 221, 229
  Jacob, 3, 52, 56, 57, 63
  Mareb, 80
  Mary, 27, 132
  Merab, 213
  Sarah, 148
  Thomas, 47
JONES,
  Abner, 242
  Ann, 118, 119, 142, 146
  Anna, 118, 215
  Anne, 195, 228
  Anthony, 118, 142
  Antony, 162
  Aquila, 15, 86, 89, 146, 178, 219, 222
  Asa, 108, 160
  Charles, 273
  Deborah, 195, 228
  Elisabeth, 52
  Elizabeth, 15, 90, 97, 108, 153, 160, 178, 219, 222
  Ezekiel, 94, 95, 99, 118, 119, 123, 142, 152, 155
  Febe, 156
  Hannah, 15, 222, 242
  Isaac, 108, 118, 119, 126, 142, 150, 152, 153, 160
  John, 108, 160, 212
  Jonathan, 142
  Joseph, 42, 48, 50, 108, 109, 110, 111, 118, 121, 131, 142, 147, 149, 152
  Joshua, 51
  Maria, 242
  Martha, 256, 257
  Mary, 74, 108, 160, 182, 195, 212, 213, 215, 220, 228
  Morgan, 80, 82
  Nathan, 112
  Nicholas S., 176
  Phebe, 121, 126, 149, 156, 159
  Rebeckah, 142, 158
  Richard, 112
  Robinson, 195, 220, 228
  Samuel, 86
  Samuel G., 194, 228, 234, 237
  Susanna B., 178
  Susanna Buffington, 219
  Susannah, 15
  Tacy, 256
  Thomas, 108, 160
  William, 90, 195, 214, 215, 228
  Yearsly, 242
JONSON, Sarah, 122
JONSTON, James, 122
JORDAN,
  Hannah, 272
  Lewis, 80
JUIT, John, 159
JUITT, Thomas, 161

-K-

KALL, Joseph, 65
KEEN, Timothy, 110, 112
KELSO,
  John, 220
  Mary, 90, 182, 220
KENDALL, Henry, 172, 193, 226, 232
KENNARD,
  Ann, 124, 126
  Anthony, 126
  Eli, 158
  Elizabeth, 124, 126
  Hannah, 135, 161
  Joseph, 115, 119, 124, 158, 161
  Levi, 115, 124, 126
  Priscilla, 119, 124
  Thomas, 124, 126, 158
  William, 158
KENWORTHY,
  Amos, 283
  Amy, 283
  Benjamin, 283
  Hannah, 272, 283
  Isaac, 283
  Jesse, 283
  Lydia, 283
  Mary, 259, 267, 272, 283
  Phebe, 284
  Rebeccah, 258, 263
  Ruth, 283
  William, 264, 267, 272, 273, 283
KEY, Robert, 110

KINNARD, Anthony, 149
  Elizabeth, 149
  Ely, 161
KINSEY,
  Alice, 19
  Elizabeth, 165, 209
  Hannah, 203, 235
  Isaac, 203, 209, 235
  Isaiah, 167
  Jacob, 167, 203, 235
  Joseph, 203, 235
  Mary, 203, 235
  Oliver, 203, 235
  Rachel, 101, 167, 203, 209, 217, 235
  Thomas, 203, 235
KIRK,
  Caleb, 267
  Elisha, 175, 250, 251, 267
  Elizabeth, 267, 268
  Ruth, 251, 274
  Samson, 64
  Timothy, 278
KNOX,
  ---, 179
  Grace, 236

-L-
LABAR, D., 127
LACEY,
  Amos, 52, 53
  Ann, 53, 56, 57, 80
  David, 53, 69
  Elizabeth, 52
  Ephraim, 82
  Esther, 53, 56, 80, 83
  Ralph, 83
  Samuel, 53, 56
  Thomas, 52, 53, 56, 83, 91
  William, 53
LACY,
  Amoss, 75
  Ann, 58, 168
  David, 58
  Elizabeth, 53, 58, 65
  Ephraim, 58
  Esther, 58
  Ralph, 58
  Samuel, 58
  Thomas, 54, 58, 71
  William, 58
LAMB, Puree, 115
LANCASTER,
  Ann, 56, 134, 137
  B., 54
  Benjamin, 16, 53, 54, 55, 56, 57, 61, 75, 76, 83, 134
  Elizabeth, 16, 17, 242, 246
  Esther, 16, 242
  Hannah, 242
  Isaiah, 16, 83, 101, 196, 229
  James, 53
  Jesse, 16, 17, 53, 54, 55, 56, 57, 61, 68, 83, 101, 242
  Joannah, 16
  John, 16, 83, 94, 242
  Joseph, 16, 53, 55, 57, 61, 68, 242
  Julia, 17, 242
  Mary, 16, 55, 57, 83
  Nathan, 61, 76
  Nathl., 55
  Phebe, 16
  Rachel, 16, 52, 56, 57, 61, 134, 242
  Stanchy, 52
LANCSTER, Mary, 82
LANE,
  Cherity, 31
  Dutto, 35
  Dutton, 30, 35, 37
  Isaac, 266
  John, 31
  Margret, 31
  Mary, 35
LARABEE,
  Ann, 235
  Anna, 203
  Daniel, 203, 235
  Hannah, 203
LARD, Joshua, 39
LARRABEE,
  Ann, 210
  Daniel, 210
LAVERLY, Elizabeth, 86
LAWLER, James, 51
LAWSON, Dorothy, 27
LEE,
  Amos, 92
  Anthoney, 266
  Casandry, 112
  Cassander, 50
  Cassandra, 109, 110, 134
  David, 54, 55, 72, 76, 82, 96, 242
  Elener, 76
  Elenor, 196

Elenora, 167
Elisabeth, 113
Elizabeth, 108, 109, 110, 111, 112, 137, 141, 190, 242
Ellener, 76
Hannah, 82, 89
Isaac, 131
Isabella, 167
James, 110, 113, 131
Jesse Thomas, 167, 188
John, 77, 89, 127, 167, 178, 186, 188, 190, 196, 219, 232
Josey, 113
Margaret, 242
Margaret Ann, 97
Mary, 50, 76, 77, 82, 90, 109, 111, 136, 137, 167, 186
Rachel, 77, 92, 109, 110
Ralph, 82
Ralph S., 242, 246
Rebecca, 82
Rebekah, 54, 55
Samuel, 77, 89, 113
Sebella, 178, 186, 188, 190, 196, 219
Sebellah, 89
Sebile, 76
Thomas, 98, 100
William, 76, 87, 97, 242
LEMMON, Elextious, 52
LEMOND, Elexeious, 27
LESTER, William, 57
LETITIA, Joseph, 235
LETTER, Nathan, 98
Thomas, 212

LEWEN, William, 54
LEWIN, William, 53
LEWIS, Betty, 27
LINDLEY, James, 114
LINTON, Jacob, 62
Sarah, 66
William, 55
LIPPINCOTT, Samuel, 214
LITLER, Nathan, 100
LITTON, Hannah, 115
LLOYD, John, 72
LOID, John, 40
LONEY, Elizabth, 115
Thomas, 115
LOVE,
James, 189, 211, 224
Mary, 185, 211, 225
William, 211
LOW, Deborah, 134
LOWDEN, Elizabeth, 233
LOWDON, Elijah, 99
Elizabeth, 95
LOYD, John, 40
LUKE, Samuel, 276
LUKENS, Alice, 78, 118, 123, 126, 148
Benjamin, 78, 118, 119, 121, 123, 126, 146, 148
Charles, 118, 121, 123, 198, 231
Edith, 86
Gaynor, 121
Jacob, 118
Magdalen, 118
Mahdalen, 121

Mary, 118, 121
Moses, 118, 123, 126, 148
Phebe, 118
Sarah, 118, 121, 123, 126, 149, 198, 231
LUKING, Moses, 95
LUKINS,
Alice, 121, 142, 152, 161
Ann, 142
Benjamin, 16, 100, 121, 152, 156
Charles, 142, 152, 158
Gainer, 142, 159
Jacob, 96, 142, 154
Lydea, 152
Lydia, 94, 100, 156
Magdalen, 142
Mary, 142, 152
Moses, 16, 94, 100, 121, 142, 152, 156, 159
Phebe, 142
Rachel, 16, 100, 156
Sarah, 16, 94, 100, 124, 142, 152, 156, 158
LUNDY, Sarah, 222
LUNGAN, Ganer, 78
LUPTON, David, 266
LYELL, Thomas, 217

-M-
MCATEER,
Mercey, 206
Thomas, 198, 206
MCCASKEY,
Alexander, 115
Hannah, 115, 116, 117
Mary, 135

Mary Ann, 115, 116, 117, 119, 122
William, 115, 116
MCCAY, Andrew, 227
Joseph, 227
MCCKIM, John, 90
MCCLASKEY,
  Alice, 86
  Patience, 78
MCCLERY,
  Elizabeth, 126
MACCOMAS,
  Daniel, 48
MCCOMAS,
  James, 243
  John, 52
MACCOMAS, Moses, 48
MCCOMAS,
  Moses, 52, 55
  Sarah, 95, 96, 243
MACCOMAS,
  Solomon, 48
  William, 46, 48
MCCOMAS, William, 55
MCCONNEL, Samuel, 92
MCCONNELL,
  Frances, 23, 243
  James, 243
  James Orr, 23
  Mary, 23, 243
  Samuel, 23, 97, 243
  William, 114
MCCORMICK, James, 178
MCCOY, Andrew, 156, 193, 227

Cassandra, 158
Joseph, 156, 179, 193, 227
Martha, 193, 227
Mary, 135
Priscilla, 143
Robert, 138
William, 126, 138, 143, 146
MACCUBINS, Rlear, 30
MCDERMOT, Grace, 85, 180
MCDERMOTT,
  Grace, 219, 222
  John, 219
MCEL---, Henry, 276
MCFADDEN, Hugh, 114
MCGOUGH, John, 121
MCHINSTRY, Evan, 216
MCILSEY, Thomas, 214
MACKELFRESH,
  Jane, 275, 278
  Lydia, 275
  Philip, 275
MCKEY, Margaret, 60
MCKIM,
  Alexander, 211
  Charine, 211
  Eliza, 211
  Isabella, 211
  John, 92, 185, 211, 212, 213, 214, 215, 216, 217, 218, 225, 226, 228
  Margaret, 211
  Mary, 212, 213, 215, 216, 217, 230
  Robert, 211
  Samuel, 211

William Duncan, 218
MCKINSTRY,
  [See McHinstry]
  Priscilla, 276
MACKLEFRESH,
  Sarah, 271
MCMILLAN,
  Deborah, 203
  Edith, 156, 203
  Jane, 156, 203
  Thomas, 156, 203
MCMILLEN,
  Deberough, 160
  Deborah, 172, 234
  Edith, 160, 172, 234
  Jane, 126, 160, 172, 234
  Thomas, 126, 160, 172, 234
MCWILLIAMS,
  Elizabeth, 113
MADCALF, Jesse, 231
MAILOR, Jane, 56
MALENEE, John, 45
MALENY, John, 45
MALLONE,
  Cassandry, 54
  Dennis, 54
  John, 53, 54
  Peter, 53
MALLONEE,
  John, 48
  Rachel, 57
MALLONEY, Rachel, 66
MALONE, Edif, 53
  John, 53
  Rachel, 53

MALSBEY,
 David, 53
 John, 53, 54
MALSBY, Angelina, 76
 Angeline, 86
 Ann, 70, 82
 Benjamin, 85
 Daniel, 70
 David, 24, 52, 54, 57, 71, 242
 David Lee, 243
 Elenor, 82
 Frances, 24, 76, 242
 John, 1, 24, 52, 55, 57, 70, 77, 82, 167, 174
 Katharine, 24
 Lydia, 70, 82
 Mary, 1, 24, 77, 148, 243
 Morris, 24, 243
 Pamala, 24
 Rachel, 1
 Rose, 85
 Sarah, 24, 70, 82, 242
 Susanna, 70, 82
 Wheeler, 56
 William, 70, 82
MANIFOLD, Elinor, 124
 Ellin, 119
 Lydia, 150
MANTLE,
 Rebekah, 121
 William, 126
MANYFOLD,
 Bilinder, 126
 Eleanor, 135
 Ellen, 132
 Lydia, 132
MARGARET, 72
MARIS, Mathias, 215
MARRYMAN,
 Jane, 27
 Samuel, 27
MARSH,
 Ann, 102, 167, 195, 208
 Eliza, 201
 Elizabeth, 196, 229
 Hannah, 89, 178, 187, 201, 211, 213, 217, 219, 212
 John, 89, 167, 178, 187, 201, 211, 213, 216, 217, 219
 Jonathan, 199, 231
 Margaret, 195, 216, 229, 236
 Marian, 167
 Mary, 167, 208
 Miriam, 178, 219
 Rebecca, 178, 219
 William, 167, 195, 208, 229, 236
MARSHAL, Edward, 99
MARSHALL,
 Edward, 91, 95
MARTIN,
 Athenatius, 198
 Frances, 89, 183, 213, 220, 230
 Francis, 211
 John, 213
 Margaret, 213
 Rachel, 212
 Samuel, 213
 Susanna, 198, 212, 213, 214, 215, 231
 William, 213
MARY, 139
MARYMAN, Rachel, 47
MASON,
 Ann, 10, 11, 55, 56, 57, 243
 Benjamin, 10, 54, 114
 Elizabeth, 89
 G., 111
 George, 10, 46, 54, 58, 114, 139, 167, 191, 217, 225, 230
 Grace, 46, 54, 79, 88, 89, 114, 116
 Howard, 11, 243
 James, 11, 46, 54, 70, 73, 76, 114
 Jane, 54, 114, 139
 Jean, 46
 John, 10, 11, 46, 54, 55, 56, 58, 67, 68, 72, 96, 114, 211, 243
 Lemuel, 11
 Mary, 11
 Nancy, 114
 Rachel, 90, 191, 215, 216, 217, 225
 Roberta, 89
 Sarah, 10
 Susan, 243
 Susanna, 11, 167, 191, 211, 212, 214, 225
 Susannah, 118, 139
 William, 167, 191, 225
MASSEY, Ann, 117, 125, 127

Anna, 107, 144
Aquila, 32, 104, 107, 108, 109, 118, 128, 130, 145, 153, 159
Aquila Bolton, 107
Aquilla, 119, 123, 125, 153
Cassandra, 123, 135, 153
Isaac, 104, 107, 110, 113, 115, 116, 117, 118, 121, 123, 126, 127, 145, 149, 158
James R., 107
John, 123, 153, 154
Jonathan, 32, 107, 108, 109, 123, 130, 131, 153
Margaret, 120, 122, 123, 124, 125, 126
Margarett, 120
Rigbie, 107
Sarah, 104, 108, 118, 127, 145
Sarah Bolton, 107
William, 107
MATHEWS,
Daniel, 38, 264
Danil, 30, 31
Edward, 31, 32
Francis, 253
George, 28, 30, 31, 32, 35, 36, 43, 47
Mary, 31, 50, 164, 253
Mordica, 38
Oliver, 31, 32, 45, 164
Rachel, 35, 38
Sarah, 28, 31, 38
Thomas, 28, 29, 30, 31, 32, 35, 36, 38, 48

William, 31, 36
MATTHEWS,
---, 187
Alice, 19
Amos, 20
Ann, 9, 20, 21, 54, 56, 94, 99, 101, 176, 197, 198, 209, 212, 213, 214, 215, 216, 217, 218, 222, 230, 231
Aquila, 16
Ariana, 21
Benjamin, 20, 21
Daniel, 7, 8, 20, 54, 56, 57, 59, 67, 71, 77, 84
Dorothy, 6, 54, 65, 79, 90, 163, 170
Edith, 20
Edward, 20
Eli, 8, 20
Eliza, 20
Elizabeth, 6, 8, 9, 16, 20, 21, 51, 54, 62, 66, 93, 94, 97, 99, 101, 187, 197, 198, 209, 212, 213, 214, 215, 217, 222, 230, 231
Emelia, 167
Emelie, 197
Evan, 21
Frances, 52
Francis, 56, 59, 70, 77, 84, 255
George, 6, 9, 21, 37, 39, 49, 52, 54, 56, 58, 60, 65, 66, 69, 71, 75, 78, 80, 170, 176, 211, 213, 216, 217, 218, 224
Hannah, 7, 9, 15, 20, 37, 46, 47, 48, 49, 52, 56, 57,

94, 96, 99, 167, 175, 187, 190, 214, 215, 222, 224, 229
Hanway, 230
Jesse, 8, 19, 20, 56, 81, 94
Joel, 237
Joh., 29
John, 8, 15, 16, 19, 20, 89, 95
Joshua, 21, 94, 187, 213, 215, 222
Leah, 15, 16
Lydia, 197, 230
Mariah, 20
Martha, 16, 19, 95
Mary, 6, 9, 20, 37, 47, 49, 52, 65, 84, 97, 100, 101, 170, 172, 192, 198, 212, 214, 226, 230, 231, 255
Matilda, 15
Meriam, 99
Milcah, 19, 20
Miriam, 9, 197, 230
Mordecai, 8, 20, 53, 54, 55, 56, 78, 86, 90, 92
Mordica, 51, 266
Mordicai, 266
Oliver, 7, 9, 15, 37, 47, 48, 49, 52, 54, 56, 57, 59, 63, 77, 99, 102, 173, 175, 202, 213, 214, 233, 237
Phebe, 102, 173, 202, 233, 237
Rachel, 8, 9, 19, 20, 22, 48, 49, 54, 56, 69
Rebecca, 9, 20, 21, 22, 197, 230
Rebeckah, 99

INDEX

Rhoda, 20, 21
Richard, 20
Rodger, 116
Ruth, 9, 20, 87
Samuel, 6, 56, 58, 97, 101, 198, 209, 230, 231, 266
Samuel Hanway, 16, 197
Sarah, 8, 9, 19, 52, 54, 55, 56, 99, 176, 197, 211, 212, 213, 216, 218, 230
Sophia, 101, 198, 231
Susanna, 20
Thomas, 7, 8, 15, 19, 20, 21, 37, 41, 46, 47, 48, 49, 52, 56, 57, 66, 79, 84, 94, 96, 187, 222, 264, 267
Uriah, 19
William, 6, 8, 9, 16, 21, 22, 37, 52, 53, 54, 56, 57, 58, 59, 63, 66, 78, 94, 97, 99, 101, 167, 173, 175, 197, 209, 213, 214, 226, 230, 231, 237, 264
MATTHEWSS, Rachel, 47
MAULE,
 Caleb, 100
 Ebenezer, 84, 92, 120
 Elizabeth, 100
 Margaret, 86
 Margarett, 100
 Thomas, 86, 100
MAULSBY,
 David, 139, 269
 Elinor, 93
 John, 77, 251, 267, 269
 Mary, 87, 246, 269

William, 98
MAYNARD,
 Phebe, 251
 Thomas, 277
 Zipporah, 247
MEARS, John, 169
MECHEM,
 Frances, 243
 George, 243
 Isaac, 243
 John, 243
 Lydia, 243, 246
 Naomi, 243, 246
 Richard, 243
 William, 243
MECTEER,
 Mercy, 216
 Thomas, 213, 216, 231, 237
MEDCALF,
 Abigail, 210, 215, 234
 Jesse, 172, 212, 231
 Rebecca, 212, 214, 215, 216
 William, 215
MELEIN, Joseph, 51
MELINDA, 137
MELLONEE, John, 32
MENDENHALL,
 Eleanor, 185, 221, 222
 Hannah, 185, 221, 222
 John Wilson, 185, 221, 222
 Martha, 175
 Sarah, 185, 221, 222
 Thomas, 185, 221, 222
MERCER, Ann, 163

MEREDITH, Ruth, 277
MERIMON, Nicholas, 49
MERRICK,
 Anna, 73
 Anne, 69
 Elizabeth, 69
 George, 69
 James, 69
 Jason, 73
 Robert, 69, 73
 Ruth, 69
MERRITT,
 Abraham, 246
 Ann P., 246
MERRYMAN,
 Mary, 92
 Moses, 27, 29
 Nicholas, 27, 32
 Samuel, 27, 51
MERYMAN,
 Nich:, 48
 Samuel, 48
 Sarah, 52
MICMILLAN,
 Deborah, 234
 Edith, 234
 Jane, 234
 Thomas, 234
MIDDHIFF, Ann Buffington, 187
MIDHIFF,
 Abraham, 187, 223
 David, 187, 223
 Jesse, 187, 223
 Joshua, 187, 223
 Rebecca, 187, 223
 William, 187, 223

MIFFLIN,
  Daniel, 120, 147
  Elizabeth, 147
  Lydia, 147
  Mary, 120, 147, 196, 212, 213, 214, 215, 216, 217, 229
  Samuel, 147
MIL--, Elizabeth, 267
MILES,
  Hannah, 50, 62
  Peter, 35, 46, 50, 58
  Petter, 48
  Ruth, 280
  Sarah, 280
  Thomas, 35, 217, 280
MILHOUS,
  John, 282
  Margret, 282
  Sarah, 282
  Thomas, 266
MILHOUSE, John, 270
MILLER,
  ---, 181
  Casandra, 268
  Cassandra, 256
  Dorthy, 31
  Elizabeth, 264, 266, 267, 268, 269, 271, 274, 275
  Emelie, 181, 220, 225
  Emilie, 82
  Frances, 143
  Hannah, 249, 264, 265, 266, 272
  Isaac, 268
  Israel, 79, 82, 181, 220, 225

Jacob, 49
James, 79, 82, 89, 220, 225, 272
Jane, 260, 284
Joseph, 114, 116, 117, 118, 127, 266, 268, 269, 270, 274
Lydia, 265, 266, 267, 268, 269
Margaret, 127
Mary, 133, 253, 266, 267, 268
Mordecai, 267
Priscilla, 127
Rachel, 79, 82, 181, 220, 225, 248, 264
Rebekah, 268
Robert, 31, 49, 250, 256, 264, 266, 267, 268, 269, 272, 284
Ruth, 31, 49, 250, 251, 264, 266, 267, 284
Samuel, 272, 284
Sarah, 49, 253, 264, 265, 266, 267, 268, 269, 272, 284
Solomon, 31, 47, 49, 264, 266, 267, 268, 269
Thomas, 79, 82, 181, 220, 225
Warrick, 49
William, 133
MILLS, Rachel, 200
MILNER, Isaac, 48
MITCHEL,
  John, 81, 178, 211, 214, 217, 218
  Joseph, 213

Mary, 81, 178, 211, 213, 214, 215, 216, 217, 218
Tacy, 81, 178, 211, 213, 214, 215, 217, 218
MITCHELL, John, 162
MOLENDORE, ---m, 266
MONEY, Isaac, 112
MOOBERRY,
  Ann, 138
  Phebe, 138
  Robert, 138
MOOBREY,
  Ann, 130
  Mary, 130
  Phebe, 130, 140
  Robert, 130, 140
  William, 130
MOOR,
  Abigail, 74
  Ann, 34, 36, 37, 46, 47
  Elizabeth, 34, 46, 47
  Rachel, 34, 47
  Walter, 47
MOORE,
  Abigail, 86, 251, 255, 270
  Abigal, 43
  Abraham, 270
  Ailce, 49
  Amelia, 69
  Ann, 9, 33, 34, 36, 47, 48, 49, 50, 52, 53, 54, 56, 57, 71, 80, 87, 88, 167, 174, 264
  Anne, 48
  Benjamin P., 246
  David, 43, 63, 67, 68
  Elizabeth, 33, 36, 86

INDEX

Frances, 80, 95
Francis, 247
Hannah, 80, 93, 94, 247, 275, 278, 279
Jehu, 43, 53, 91, 182, 220, 222, 261, 268, 269, 272, 278, 279
John, 33, 34, 43, 45, 46, 49, 50, 51, 63, 64, 90, 247, 264, 275
Keturah, 80, 194
Keturak, 228
Kitturah, 98, 100
Mary, 9, 34, 43, 49, 51, 116, 247, 253, 255, 266
P---, 73
Phebe, 64, 88
Rachel, 33, 36, 47, 214
Rebecca, 80, 100, 172, 194, 228, 232, 247
Rebeccah, 254
Rebeckah, 98
Rebekah, 264
Robert, 116
Samuel, 51
Stephen, 66
Thomas, 50, 51, 94, 275
Walter, 9, 36, 47, 48, 63
William, 46, 49, 51, 59, 68, 80, 90
MORE, Ailse, 49
John, 47
MORFORD,
Stephen, 115
Thomas, 51, 52, 57
MORG--, Ann, 221
MORGAIN, Edward, 127

Hugh, 127
MORGAN,
Achsah, 121, 148
Ann, 125, 136, 148, 156, 185, 206, 215, 216
Armfield, 125
Cassandra, 134
Drusilla, 121, 125, 156
Elizabeth, 113, 114, 216
Hannah, 229
Hosea, 214, 215
Hugh, 121, 123, 124, 125, 127
Jesse, 117, 151, 187, 214, 215, 222, 226
Joel, 121, 214, 216, 217
John, 102, 121, 125, 148, 156, 194, 206, 208, 214, 215, 216, 217, 226, 227, 231
Lydia, 138, 142
Margaret, 154
Mary, 121, 206, 210, 214, 227
Pricilla, 238
Priscilla, 102, 208, 215, 217
Robert, 138
Sarah, 90, 97, 100, 117, 121, 142, 146, 152, 192, 206, 210, 214, 215, 226
Susanna, 210
Thomas, 50, 97, 190, 192, 206, 210, 212, 214, 215, 222, 225, 226, 240
William, 90, 112, 114, 117, 123, 151, 187, 190, 206, 210, 214, 215, 216, 222

William H., 246
MORRAY,
---, 29
Mary, 31
Ruth, 27, 31
Shedrick, 31
MORRIS,
Amos, 97
Ann, 100, 156, 158, 161
Benjamin, 97, 100, 156, 158
Enoch, 97, 100, 156, 158
Isaac, 97, 100, 156, 158
Israel, 57, 239, 242
John, 100, 156, 158
Martha, 97, 100, 156, 158
Mary, 97, 100, 156, 158
Nathan, 97
Nehemiah, 97, 100, 156, 158
Sarah, 242
Susanna, 57, 80, 100, 156, 158
Susannah, 97
MORRISON, Jane, 90, 101
MORRISS,
Ann, 84
Benjamin, 84
Isaac, 84
Martha, 84
Mary, 84
Susanna, 84
MORSEL,
Elizabeth, 281
Mary, 265, 267, 273, 275, 281, 286

Rachel, 249, 258, 259, 273, 281
Rebecca, 260, 261
Rebeckah, 275, 281
Rebekah, 249
William, 249, 265, 273, 275, 281, 286
MORSELL,
　Elizabeth, 215, 275, 276, 273, 277
　Mary, 27, 270, 273, 274, 275, 286
　Rachel, 271, 273, 286
　Rebeckah, 273
　Rebekah, 273, 274, 275
　William, 270, 271, 272, 273, 274, 275, 276, 277, 286
MORTHLAND,
　Samuel, 185, 221, 222
　Sarah, 192, 217, 226
　Susanna, 211
MOSELY, James, 80
MURPHEY, william, 115
MURPHY,
　Alice, 126
　William, 275, 276
MURRA, John, 141
MURRAY,
　Alexander, 128
　Archibald, 149, 155
　Jane, 128
　John, 141
　Mary, 155
　Rebecca, 62
MURREY,
　Jane, 135
　Mary, 135

MURRIER, 139
MUSSETER, John, 278
MUTCHNER,
　Christn., 55
　Sarah, 55

-N-
NAILOR,
　Abraham, 94
　Ann, 41
　Elizabeth, 56, 96, 100
　Hannah, 90, 93
　Jane, 56, 65, 70
　John, 56, 57, 62
　Mary, 44, 57, 62, 94
　Rachel, 56, 67, 88
　Samuel, 56, 96
　Sarah, 56, 71
　William, 94
NALOR, Jane, 50
　John, 42, 50
　Mary, 51
　Sarah, 50
NAYLOR,
　Abraham, 7
　Ann, 7, 46, 48
　Charles, 210
　Elizabeth, 7, 97, 167, 172, 182, 192, 200, 210, 217, 220, 223, 226, 230, 232
　Hannah, 186, 221, 228
　Isaac, 7
　James, 7, 52, 102, 195, 206, 216, 236
　Jane, 7, 46, 47, 48, 50, 51, 72

John, 7, 39, 46, 48, 50, 51, 167, 182, 207, 210, 216, 217, 220
Joseph, 210
Levinah, 7
Mary, 7, 50, 216
Rachel, 71, 102
Rebecca, 79, 102, 167, 202, 207, 233
Rebecca Ann, 210
Rebeckah, 75
Samuel, 7, 71, 102, 167, 202, 207, 210, 233
Sarah, 52
William, 7
NEAL, James, 202, 233
NEGRO BECKAH, 141
NEGRO DINAH, 141
NEGRO HESTER, 141
NEGRO JACOB, 141
NEGRO JAMES, 141
NEGRO JOHN, 141
NEGRO LYDIA, 141
NEGRO MARISH, 141
NEGRO POLLEY, 141
NEGRO ROBIN, 140
NEGRO SAM, 141
NEGRO SARAH, 141
NEGRO TIMBER, 141
NEGRO TOWER, 141
NEGRO WAPPING, 139
NEGRO WILLIAM, 139
NELLY, 139
NEWBOROUGH,
　Sarah, 75
NICAR, Sarah, 125
NIGAR, Sarah, 127, 152

INDEX

NORBARY, Jacob, 207
NORBURY,
  Jacob, 237
  Js., 183
  Martha, 232
NORRINTON, Rebeckah, 56
NORRIS,
  An, 263
  Ann, 161, 257, 273
  Anna, 276, 277
  Aquila, 52, 57
  Benjamin, 273, 276
  Edward, 50, 52, 55, 57
  Elisabeth, 52, 55
  Elizabeth, 57, 62, 97, 215, 272
  John, 57, 213, 215, 217
  Joseph, 55
  Lloyd, 246
  Martha, 55
  Mary, 57
  Mary Ann, 246
  Sarah, 55, 57
  Susan, 214
  Susanna, 57, 215, 217
  Thomas, 55, 57
  William, 211, 214, 217
NORTON,
  Stephen, 113, 126, 127, 137
  Thomas, 162
NOTT, Burrage, 36

-O-

OARR, James, 161
ODDY, Robert, 230
OGBON, Sarah, 273
OGBORN,
  Joseph, 275, 278
  Sarah, 275, 279
OGLEON, Sarah, 273
OLLEMORE, John, 122
ONION, L., 55
ORR,
  Angelina, 87, 147
  James, 86, 87, 122, 147, 161
ORRICK, John, 116
OSBORN, William, 116
OSBURN, Paul, 45
OSHMORE, John, 122
OWINGS,
  --opocia, 29
  Bale, 51
  Colegate Deye, 53
  Hannah, 267, 271
  John Cockey, 53
  Mary, 267

-P-

PACKER, Aaron, 199, 231, 237, 238
PAIN,
  John, 128
  Martha, 128
PANCOAST,
  Esther, 187, 211, 221, 226
  John, 275, 276
  Mary, 263
PANCOST, Sarah, 255
PANE,
  Mary, 114
  Rachel, 114
PAREPONT, Henry, 113
PARIS, Sarah, 157
PARISH,
  Ann Meryah, 53
  Annmariah, 62
  Aquila, 53
  Keturak, 47
  Kitturah, 263
  Mary, 53, 93
  Mordecai, 88
  Rachel, 58
PARKER,
  Edward, 55
  Eliza, 246
  Robert, 57
PARR, James, 67, 70
PARRISH,
  Ann, 29, 54
  Annmaria, 34
  Aquila, 54, 57, 87
  Aquilla, 4
  Benjamin, 26
  Edieth, 26
  Edward, 28, 30
  Elizabeth, 27, 28, 29
  Hanah, 34
  Hannah, 47
  Isaac, 28, 43
  Jaret, 26
  John, 3, 4, 26, 27, 28, 29, 30, 31, 32, 34, 46, 266
  Joseph, 27, 28, 30, 31, 32, 40
  K., 29
  Ketturah, 48
  Kettutah, 77

Keturah, 2, 27, 28, 30, 31, 36, 46, 47, 48, 102
Kitturah, 57
Kiturah, 49
Leonard, 26
Mary, 3, 4, 26, 27, 28, 30, 31, 34, 36, 46, 47, 48, 57, 66
Mordecai, 4, 26, 34, 57, 66, 96
Mordica, 30, 51
Nicholas, 94
Peter, 26
Rachel, 26
Robert, 28, 30
Susanah, 27, 28, 30
Susanna, 57
Susannah, 28, 34
Uareth, 26
William, 2, 27, 28, 29, 30, 31, 34, 36, 42, 46, 47, 48, 51, 69, 74, 78
PARSON,
  Gainer, 159
  John, 89
  Rebecca, 89
  Susannah, 89
PARSONS,
  Abner, 17, 88, 243
  Abraham, 17, 243
  Benjamin, 99
  Elizabeth, 17
  Elizabeth D., 243
  Gaynor, 159
  Honner, 17
  Jessee, 18
  John, 18, 55
  Joseph Dyer, 17, 243
  Martha, 142
  Rachel, 17
  Rebekah, 55
  Susanna, 18
PARTRIDGE, Ann, 225
PARVAIN,
  Abigail, 261, 262
  Ann, 261, 262
  Mary, 261, 262
PARVIN,
  Mark, 274
  Polly, 275
  Thomas, 273, 274, 278
PATON, Catherine, 37
PATRICK,
  Elizabeth, 211
  George, 56
  J., 111
  Jennet, 54, 56
  John, 55, 56
  L., 113
  Mary, 53, 54, 55, 56, 57, 59, 65, 68, 74
PAUL, John, 54, 55, 60, 72
PAULTNEY,
  A., 284
  Sarah, 284
PAYNE,
  Alice, 137
  George, 137
  Martha, 137
  Rachel, 137
  Sarah, 137
PAYTON, Catheren, 33
PEACH, Samuel, 265, 267
PEARCE,
  Cassandra, 116
  Elizabeth, 276
PEARSE, Casandry, 113
PEARSON,
  Benjamin, 94, 95
  Gideon, 128, 129
PEASLY, Mary, 37
PECKNER, Edmund, 174
PEDDICAOT, Mary, 94
PEIRPOINT, Abraham, 29, 30, 31, 35, 36, 39, 40, 46
  Ann, 29, 31, 37, 47, 52
  Barshaba, 35
  Barsheba, 31, 36
  Bathsheba, 53
  Bershaba, 29, 31
  Bethsheba, 47
  Caleb, 31
  Calib, 29, 30
  Charles, 29, 30, 31, 36, 47, 52, 53, 71, 73
  Chew, 29, 30, 53
  Chue, 53
  Faithfull, 29, 31, 35, 36, 53
  Francis, 29, 30, 31
  Henry, 29, 31, 35, 37, 44, 47, 53
  Johanna, 29, 31, 36, 47
  Johannah, 52
  John, 29, 31, 32, 35, 36, 37, 44, 53, 73
  Joseph, 29, 31, 35, 36, 47, 53
  Margaret, 29

Mary, 29, 31, 35, 36
Miscal, 53
Misel, 30, 31, 36
Misial, 29
Obed, 31
Rachel, 37, 47
Samuel, 31, 35, 36, 37
Samuell, 46, 47
Sarah, 29
Sidney, 29, 30, 31, 35, 36, 39, 46, 47, 53
PEIRPONT, John, 39
PENINGTON,
 Daniel, 56, 70, 98
 David, 70
 Elizabeth, 98
 John, 98
 Josiah, 98
 Josias, 51
 Levi, 98
 Martha, 98
 Paul, 59, 98
PENNINGTON,
 Amos, 58, 90
 Daniel, 15, 53, 58, 94, 100
 Elizabeth, 58, 100
 Harris, 58
 Isaiah, 100
 Israel, 58, 102
 John, 15, 100
 Josiah, 15
 Levi, 15
 Levy, 100
 Martha, 15, 58, 100
 Mary, 15
 Paul, 15, 100

Sarah, 15, 85
PENROSE,
 John, 272
 Robert, 57
PERINAH, 137
PERINE,
 Ann, 91, 94, 183, 211, 220, 222
 Hannah, 48, 68, 69, 211
 Hephzibah, 188
 Heppy, 211, 215
 Hepzibah, 216, 224
 Malden, 183, 188, 198, 211, 220, 222
 Margaret, 183, 211, 220
 Mary, 102, 198, 202, 233
 Mauldin H., 168
 Peter, 44, 48, 50, 52, 64, 168, 184, 198, 202, 211, 221, 231
 Simon, 52, 168, 182, 220, 224
 Simon Peter, 168
 William, 50
PERRINE, Simon, 50
PERVAIL,
 Ann, 123, 124, 125, 158
 Gideon, 117, 121, 158
 Mary, 117, 125
PERVALE, John, 127
PERVEIL,
 Gideon, 119
 Mary, 119
PESELEY, Mary, 33
PETERS,
 George, 185, 213
 Mary, 213, 227, 228

PHARRIS, Zachariah, 62
PHEBE, 71, 140
 Joseph, 235
PHELPS,
 Emma, 276
 George, 276
PIDGEON,
 Charles, 264, 279
 Elizabeth, 279
 Hannah, 279
 Isaac, 279
 John, 259, 272, 274, 276, 277, 279
 Mary, 279
 Rachel, 251, 264, 266, 267, 279
 Ruth, 279
 Susanna, 259, 276, 277
 William, 264, 266, 267, 279
PIERPOINT,
 Ann, 55, 61, 64, 204, 235
 Charles, 68
 Deborah, 204, 235
 Eli, 55
 Francis, 55
 Hannah, 205, 235
 Henry, 55
 John, 55, 70, 204, 235
 Joseph, 55, 182, 205, 220, 225, 236
 Margaret, 223
 Mary, 205, 235
 Misael, 205, 236
 Thomas, 87, 182, 220, 223
 Walter, 87, 183, 205, 220, 224, 235

PILLAR, William, 73, 81
PINNIX, Sarah, 126
PITS, Rebecca, 94
PITTS, Rebeka, 63
PLEASANTS,
  Ann, 209, 238
  Ann P., 209
  Cary, 270
  Elizabeth, 118, 209, 238
  Franklin, 238
  Hannah, 209, 238
  Israel, 209, 238
  Israel Pemberton, 209, 238
  Joseph, 238
  Margaret, 110
  Mary, 209, 238
  Robert, 110
  Samuel, 209, 238
  Sarah, 209
  Thomas, 238
  Thomas Franklin, 209
  Thomas S., 270
  Thomas W., 270
PLUER, Isaac, 268
PLUMMER,
  ---, 265
  Aaron, 268
  Abraham, 248, 266, 267, 268, 270, 271, 274
  Abram, 265
  Alice, 207, 237
  Ann, 162, 251, 265, 275, 277, 278
  Anna, 268
  Anne, 251, 265, 266, 267, 277
  Arltridge, 281
  Artridg, 277
  Artridge, 277, 281
  Artrige, 248
  Asa, 271
  Betsy, 278
  Caleb, 278
  Deborah, 263, 277
  Delilah, 268
  Eleanor, 270
  Elen, 273
  Elenor, 273
  Eli, 207, 237
  Elizabeth, 257, 260, 261, 272, 273, 280
  Elleanor, 265
  Ellen, 247, 265, 267, 268, 271, 273, 274, 275, 276, 277, 279
  Ellenor, 268
  Ellin, 266
  Evan, 273
  Ezra, 271
  Grace, 271, 273, 275, 276, 278
  Gule:, 281
  Isaac, 254, 265, 267, 268, 270, 271, 273, 276, 277, 278, 279
  Israel, 260, 261, 273, 274, 275
  James, 203, 207, 235, 237
  Jesse, 265, 267, 268, 270, 271, 273, 275, 276, 279
  John, 248, 274, 275
  Jonathan, 265, 271, 274, 275, 276
  Joseph, 211, 265, 268, 271
  Joseph Vo.(?), 265
  Joseph W., 277
  Joseph West, 277
  Mahala, 277
  Mariam, 254
  Mary, 248, 254, 258, 261, 265, 268, 272, 275, 277, 278
  Meream, 268
  Meriam, 256, 270
  Miriam, 253, 268, 271
  Moses, 255, 271, 273
  Mosses, 268
  Precilla, 281
  Priscilla, 203, 235, 276, 277
  Rachel, 273, 274, 275, 276, 277, 278, 281
  Rebeckah, 281
  Richard, 278, 281
  Robert, 248, 259, 273, 274, 277, 278
  Ruth, 265, 268, 270, 271, 272, 273, 275, 276, 277, 279
  Sally, 277, 278
  Samuel, 248, 264, 265, 266, 267, 268, 271, 272, 275, 280, 281
  Sarah, 248, 263, 264, 265, 266, 267, 268, 271, 273, 274, 275, 276, 277, 280, 281
  Sinah, 207
  Susanna, 196, 211, 248, 249, 264, 278

Thomas, 203, 235, 263, 265, 267, 268, 270, 273, 277, 278, 279, 280
Ursly, 278
Ursula, 265, 266, 267, 268, 271, 273, 275, 276, 277,
William, 258, 259, 265, 271, 273, 274, 275, 279
Yate, 248, 265, 267, 268, 269, 271, 272, 273, 274, 275, 277, 281
POLLARD,
  David, 209, 238
  Elizabeth, 209, 238
  Eunice, 209, 238
  Mary, 209, 238
  Peter, 209, 238
  Sarah, 209, 238
POLNEY, Samuel, 274
POLTON, Elizabeth, 61, 76
POPE,
  Daniel, 246
  Lois K., 246
  Mary, 261, 273, 276
POTEET, Ann Buffington, 187
POTTER, Elizabeth, 199
POTTS, Anna, 278
POULTNEY, Ann, 91, 178, 186, 190, 209, 210, 219
  Anthony, 249, 264, 265, 266, 267, 268, 269, 270, 271, 272, 273, 274, 275, 276, 277, 281, 287
  Eleanor, 264
  Elizabeth, 186, 276, 282
  Ellen, 280, 281
  Ellianor, 265
  Evan Thomas, 190
  James, 282
  Jesse, 282
  John, 264, 265, 273, 275, 280, 281
  Mary, 265, 267, 268, 269, 270, 271, 272, 273, 274, 275, 276, 278, 280, 282
  Mary P., 278
  Philip, 209
  Rachel, 282
  Rachel Thomas, 210
  Richard, 280
  Samuel, 209, 272, 273, 275, 281
  Sarah, 249, 264, 265, 273, 275, 276, 277, 281, 282, 287
  Susan, 287
  Susanna, 263, 266, 267, 268, 271, 273, 276, 277, 281
  Thomas, 91, 178, 186, 190, 209, 210, 211, 217, 219, 276, 282
  William, 276, 282
POWEL,
  Benjaman, 47
  Benjamin, 42, 51, 53
  Mary, 47, 51, 53
POWELL,
  Beniamin, 36
  Benjamin, 46, 47, 55
  Mary, 47, 52
POYD, John, 31
POYEL, John, 31
PRALL, Edward, 122
PRESTON,
  David, 243, 246
  Edmond, 243
  Hannah, 243
  Henry, 124, 154
  Isaac H., 246
  Isaac Hollingsworth, 243
  Joseph, 154
  Judith, 243
  Martha, 124, 150, 154
  Rachel, 124, 154, 243
  Silvester Bills, 243
PREVAIL, John, 161
PREVALE,
  Ann, 107
  Elizabeth, 107
  Gideon, 107
  John, 107
  Margret, 107
  Mary, 107
  Samuel, 107
PRICE, ---, 29
  Aggnis, 48
  Agness, 34
  Amos, 24
  Ann, 2, 5, 7, 8, 23, 24, 48, 49, 50, 52, 56, 57, 167, 168, 197, 210, 212, 231
  Anna, 51
  Anne, 101, 198
  Aquila, 14, 28, 30, 32, 36, 37, 43, 46, 47, 48, 49, 50, 51, 52, 57, 63
  Aquilla, 5
  Beal, 17

Beniamin, 27, 31, 36
Benjamin, 14, 17, 26, 29, 34, 45, 47, 48, 49, 50, 51, 52, 53, 57, 62
Betty, 12
Caleb, 12
Charity, 24
Constant, 52
Daniel, 7, 12, 56, 79, 92, 212
David, 24
David E., 120, 121, 127
Edith, 12
Eli, 24
Elijah, 23
Elizabeth, 7, 13, 14, 17, 23, 27, 28, 34, 47, 48, 49, 56, 95, 206
Esther, 2, 51, 53, 65
Frances, 24
George, 12
Hannah, 168, 197, 213, 214
Isabel, 13, 47, 48, 50, 51, 52, 53, 57, 58
Isabela, 47
Isabella, 46
Isable, 49, 51
Israel, 7, 101, 168, 184, 197, 206, 212, 213, 214, 221, 228
J., 50, 52
James, 17, 56
Jane, 168, 189
Jared, 24, 234
Jarred, 203
Jarrett, 17, 102
Jehu, 24

Jesse, 2, 12, 53
Joel, 12
John, 2, 5, 8, 14, 24, 26, 27, 28, 29, 30, 31, 32, 34, 36, 43, 45, 46, 47, 48, 51, 52, 53, 54, 56, 57, 62, 65, 73, 79, 94
John Hussey, 12
Jonathan, 168, 191
Joseph, 23
Joshua, 13, 17, 79
Joshua C., 24
Js., 176
Keturah, 17, 27, 28, 32, 36, 46, 47
Kiturah, 14
Leah, 5, 15, 27, 34, 59, 89
Levi, 23, 24
M., 31
Mahlon, 24
Mary, 2, 3, 5, 7, 12, 24, 27, 34, 36, 41, 46, 47, 48, 53, 85, 212
Mordeca, 46, 47, 48, 272
Mordecai, 2, 5, 7, 8, 13, 14, 23, 24, 34, 43, 48, 53, 54, 56, 57, 70, 79, 97, 98, 212, 275
Mordica, 27, 28, 29, 30, 31, 32, 36, 48, 49, 50, 51, 52, 264
Nathan, 12
Phebe, 2
Rachel, 2, 13, 14, 23, 24, 27, 28, 29, 30, 31, 34, 48, 49, 50, 51, 52, 54, 272
Rebecah, 43
Rebecca, 7, 14, 17, 32, 34, 47, 48, 49, 51

Rebeccah, 30, 49, 51
Rebecka, 63
Rebeckah, 27, 28, 34, 50, 51, 57
Rebecker, 28
Rebekah, 46, 47
Rebh., 30
Richard, 8, 99, 190, 212, 216, 217, 225
Ruth, 2, 7, 51
S., 29
Samuel, 7, 8, 12, 24, 31, 34, 36, 37, 40, 47, 48, 49, 50, 51, 52, 56, 61, 65, 69, 70, 95, 99, 168, 188, 212, 225, 264, 212
Sarah, 23, 27, 28, 29, 90
Sophia, 23, 34, 37, 46, 56
Stephen, 32, 57
Sufiah, 31
Susann, 47
Susanna, 81, 168, 182, 188, 189, 191, 206, 210, 211, 212, 216, 220
Susannah, 49
Tabitha, 13, 14, 51, 54
Temperance, 17, 26
Temperence, 48
Thomas, 13, 17, 26, 36, 47, 48, 49, 51, 53, 56, 61, 264
Urath, 2
Ureth, 51
Urith, 26, 34, 36
Warrick, 93, 168, 182, 188, 189, 191, 210, 212, 220
Warwick, 99

INDEX

William, 14, 30, 50, 210
Worrick, 7
PRICHARD,
  Jonathan, 115
  Joseh, 111
PRION, Ann, 94
PRISCILLA, 71
PRITCHERT,
  Margaret, 60
PROCTER,
  Izak, 193, 207, 226
  Rebecca, 207, 216
  Rebeckah, 216
  Sarah, 212, 216
  William, 195, 228
PROCTOR,
  Izak, 234, 236
  Rebecca, 236
  Richard, 138, 140, 144
  William, 193
PROSER, Elizabeth, 76
PROSSER, Elizabeth, 94
PUGH,
  Abigail, 245
  Alice, 245
  Eli, 245
  Elizabeth, 214
  Esther, 245
  Hannah, 245
  Jacob, 189, 214, 223, 232
  Jane, 245
  Job, 245
  Jonathan, 245
  Levi, 245
  Louis D., 245
  Lydia, 245
  Rachel, 245
  Stephen, 245
PURVEAL, Gideon, 136, 141
PUSEY,
  Catherine, 111, 133
  Elizabeth, 120, 146, 151
  Ellis, 120
  George, 111, 133, 247, 269, 270, 271, 272, 274, 276, 277, 279, 282
  Hannah, 120
  John, 111, 133
  Joshua, 113, 120, 129, 137
  Lewis, 114
  Lydia, 113, 134, 137, 276, 277, 282
  Mary, 114, 129, 137, 259, 282
  Nathan, 277, 282
  Sarah, 247, 254, 260, 270, 271, 274, 282
  William, 247, 269, 282
PYCRAFT, Thomas, 108, 110
PYLE, Harmon, 246

-Q-

QUARELL, Lydia, 152
QUINLAN, Jane, 88

-R-

RACHEL, 69, 141
RADD, Jacob, 52
RAKER, Mercy, 145
RALLINGS, Daniel, 48
RALPH, 137
RAMSAY, Edward Mitchell, 132
RANDAL,
  Elizabeth, 273
  Mary, 268
RANDALL,
  Ann, 86
  Catharine, 83
  Christofer, 27
  John, 213
  Margaret, 213, 214, 215
  Mary, 213
  Robert, 122
  Roger, 31
RANSOME,
  Elizabeth, 202, 233
  John, 202, 233
RATCLIFF, Isaiah, 54, 55, 67, 71
RAWLINGS,
  Aaron, 36
  Daniel, 27, 40, 43, 48
  Danil, 36
  Dorothy, 27
  Mary, 27
REA,
  Benjamin 77
  Joseph, 77
  Mary, 81
READ,
  Ann, 205, 235
  Charles, 205, 235
  Dennis, 203, 234
  Ephraim, 112
  Jacob, 52, 55, 70, 205, 235
  Joseph, 205, 235

Larkin, 191, 225, 227, 229
Mary, 236, 261
RED,
  Jacob, 64
  Mary, 261
REDGELY,
  John, 27
  Pleasents, 27
REED,
  Anna, 22
  Deborah, 22
  Elizabeth, 22, 101, 201, 217, 232
  Eveline, 22
  Harriett, 22
  John Wilson, 22
  Matilda, 22, 102, 201, 232, 243
  Samuel, 22, 97, 101, 201, 232, 243
  William, 22
REES,
  Ann, 84, 178, 186, 188, 219
  Catharine, 79
  Daniel, 79
  David, 86
  Esther, 188
  John, 74, 84, 186, 188
  John E., 77, 213, 232
  John Evan, 80, 178, 219
  Joseph, 81
  Maria, 178, 219
  Mary, 250, 253, 268, 269, 272
  Thomas, 178, 219
REESE, Ann, 207, 212
  Daniel, 98
  John, 168, 207
  John E., 212, 214
  John Evans, 168
  Margaret, 154
  Solomon, 112
  William, 207
REESS, Solomon, 112
RESSKEY, Mary, 224
REYNOLDS,
  Betty, 29
  John, 66
  Joshua, 203, 232, 234
  Rachel, 203, 216, 234
  Richard, 29
RHEA,
  Benjamin, 81
  Joseph, 78
RHOADS,
  Richard, 48
  Sarah, 48
RIBGY, N., 109
RICE,
  Ann, 79, 172, 181, 220, 227
  Elizabeth, 224
  George, 79, 181, 220, 224
  Joseph, 79, 83
  Lawrence, 172, 220, 227
  Sarah, 79, 91
RICH,
  Ann, 204, 235
  Benjamin, 204, 235
  John, 204, 235
  Sarah, 204, 235
RICHARD, 69
  Jonathan, 115
RICHARDS,
  Jane, 163
  John, 264
RICHARDSON,
  Ann, 260
  Betey, 122
  Daniel, 110, 116
  Elizabeth, 158
  Fielder, 102, 277
  Hannah, 108, 109, 110, 114, 118, 119, 120, 122, 138, 139, 145
  Harriott, 273
  Iscointia, 269
  John, 270
  Joseph, 169
  Margaret, 110
  Margaret Hill, 138
  Margret, 29
  Mary, 52, 55, 278
  Miriam, 102
  Nathan, 27, 118, 138, 145
  Polly, 279
  Rachel, 255, 257, 273, 274, 275, 278, 279
  Rebecca, 136
  Richard, 27, 32, 269
  Samuel, 109, 110, 129
  Sarah, 117, 118, 145
  William P., 277
RICHMORE, Elenor, 227
RICKETTS,
  Catharine, 54
RIDGWAY,
  Mary, 29

Richard, 29
RIGBIE, Ann, 108, 109, 122, 123, 129, 133, 113
  Anna, 104, 109, 116, 117, 118, 119, 120, 122, 123, 130, 153, 115
  Anne, 110
  Cassandra, 104, 108, 109, 110, 111, 129, 132, 133, 134, 108
  Cassy, 109
  Elizabeth, 104, 110, 113, 115, 133, 142
  Hannah, 110, 111, 112, 136, 112, 113
  James, 104, 108, 109, 110, 111, 112, 113, 114, 115, 116, 119, 123, 127, 129, 131, 133, 134, 136, 141, 142, 153, 174, 109, 114
  Mary, 116
  Massey, 104, 116
  Mercy, 104, 118
  N., 108, 109, 110, 111, 113, 110, 112
  Nathan, 104, 108, 127, 129, 130, 132, 133, 138, 174
  Natt, 108
  Philip, 108
  Sarah, 104, 108, 109, 110, 111, 112, 113, 115, 123, 132, 133, 136, 141, 142, 153, 113, 114, 115
  Sary, 109, 110, 112
  Skipwith, 138
  Susan, 110
  Susanna, 142

  Susannah, 116
RIGBY,
  James, 116
  Sary, 109, 110
RIGHT, Sarah, 97
RILEY,
  Ann, 3, 177, 214, 215, 219
  Benjamin, 3, 177, 212, 219
  Hannah, 3
  John, 215
  John Smith, 186
  Joshua, 205
  Nicholas, 210
  Samuel, 194
  Sarah, 3, 85, 177, 186, 194, 205, 210, 212, 215, 219, 213
  Volerius, 219
  William, 3, 85, 177, 186, 194, 205, 210, 211, 212, 213, 214, 215, 216, 217, 219, 230
RISSETT,
  Catherine, 69
  Nicholas, 69
  Rachel, 85
RISSITT, Rachel, 69
ROACH,
  Barbary, 225
  Hannah, 225
  Mary, 225
  Rachel, 225
ROADES,
  Richard, 50
  Sarah, 50
ROADS, Hannah, 46

Richard, 35
ROBERS,
  Henry, 276
  Stephen, 35
ROBERSON,
  John, 29
  Temperence, 48
ROBERT, 139
  Henry, 254
ROBERTS, Ann, 270, 272, 274, 275, 277, 278, 272, 277
  Elizabeth, 165, 166, 257
  Henry, 265, 268, 270, 272, 273, 274, 275, 280
  John, 265, 270, 271, 272, 276, 277, 280, 275
  Jonathan, 216, 278
  Marcy, 268, 270
  Mary, 265, 268, 274, 275, 280, 285
  Mercy, 267, 271, 272, 273, 275
  Meriam, 257
  Mersey, 270, 276
  Miriam, 271, 280
  R., 285
  Rebecca, 273, 277
  Rebeckah, 256
  Rebekah, 276
  Richard, 265, 267, 270, 274, 275, 276, 277, 280
  Sarah, 259, 271, 272, 273, 274, 280, 285
  Stephen, 32, 48, 70
  William, 264, 266, 270, 271, 272, 280
  Zachariah, 275, 276, 280

ROBERTSON,
  Daniel, 39, 104, 110, 118, 120, 123, 124, 130, 133, 144, 161
  David, 138
  Elizabeth, 3, 104, 118, 119, 123, 124, 144, 145
  Hannah, 104
  Isaac, 104, 123
  James, 119
  Margaret, 104
  Mary, 104
  Peggy, 119, 123
  Samuel, 3, 104, 119, 152
  Sarah, 3
ROBETSON, Daniel, 47
ROBINET, James, 122
ROBINETT, Prissilla, 150
ROBINSON,
  Daniel, 133, 161
  Elizabeth, 145
  George, 128, 133
  Hannah, 133
  Margaret, 49
  Samuel, 94
RODES, Sarah, 49
RODGERS,
  Margaret, 117
  Susannah, 123, 144
  Thomas, 117
ROGERS,
  Elizabeth, 27
  Enos, 72
  Evan, 85
  John, 72, 77
  Levi, 85
  Lewis, 72
  Margaret, 72
  Margrett, 87
  Mordecai, 72, 76, 82
  Rachel, 72
  Sarah, 72, 87
  Susanna, 87
  Susannah, 116, 118, 119, 125
ROLLS, Hezekiah, 115
ROSS, Richard, 46
ROWLS, Mary, 114
ROWS, Richard, 113
RUCKMAN,
  Sarah, 134
  Sary, 112
  Thomas, 134, 112
RUFF,
  Henry, 122
  Mary, 122
  Richard, 122
RULLAY, Samuel, 36
RUMSEY, Joseph, 118
RUSEL, Abigail, 255
RUSH, Margaret, 260
RUSK,
  David, 51
  Mary, 51
RUSSEL, Hannah, 253, 260, 261
  James, 250
  Jesse, 250, 274
  Mary, 250, 260
  Rachel, 250
  Sarah, 250, 260
  Thomas, 250, 259, 273, 274
RUSSELL,
  Anna, 285
  Caleb, 285
  Elizabeth, 285
  Hannah, 250, 262, 267, 268, 269, 274, 276, 277, 285
  Hanneh, 269
  Jesse, 275, 276, 285
  John, 250, 267, 269, 274, 275, 276, 277, 278, 285
  Jonathan, 285
  Joshua, 285
  Mariam, 285
  Mary, 274, 275, 276, 278
  Sarah, 275, 276, 277, 278, 279, 285
  Susanna, 285
  Thomas, 274, 276, 278, 285
RYAN, Sarah, 63, 75
RYON, Sarah, 56, 70, 102

-S-

SAFTHILL, Sarah, 255
SALTHILL,
  Mary, 262
  Sarah, 261
SALTKILL,
  Mary, 262
  Sarah, 255
SAM, 137
SAMUEL, 71
SANDERSON,
  Ann, 210
  Catharine, 210
  F., 214

INDEX

Margaret, 84, 97, 194, 227
Margarett, 100
Mayerel, 210
Rachel, 210
Sarah, 210
Thomas, 194
SAUNDERS,
Edward, 128
Lemuel, 47
Thomas, 128
SCARBOROUGH,
John, 139
Sarah, 139
SCHOFIELD,
Andrew, 6
Ann, 5
David, 133
Enoch, 133
Issachar, 6
John, 43, 133
Joseph Leonard, 6
Mahlen, 6
Rachel, 133
Samuel, 133
William, 5
SCHOLEFIELD,
Rachel, 264
SCHOLFIELD,
Benjamin, 61
David, 61
Enoch, 61
Issachar, 75
Issacher, 84
John, 48, 61
Mahlon, 80
Rachel, 48, 49, 61

Samuel, 61
William 75
SCOFFIELD, Rachel, 250
SCOFIELD,
Benjamin, 250
Enoch, 250
Jane, 250
John, 250
Samuel, 250
SCOGGIN, John, 75
SCOLFIELD,
William, 74
SCOOLY, Reuben, 80
SCOT,
Hannah, 129
Jacob, 129
Joseph, 129
SCOTT,
Abraham, 18, 21, 57, 62, 63, 76, 83, 90, 168, 180, 220
Amos, 18, 19, 53, 56, 57, 62
Ann, 71, 91, 129, 168, 186, 211, 213, 216, 221
Anna, 91
Edith, 168, 180, 196, 203, 214, 220
Eli, 13
Eliza 13
Elizabeth, 13, 18, 21, 51, 53, 62, 71
Esther, 18, 93
George Dent, 13
Granville, 203
Hannah, 46, 60, 76, 82, 109, 216, 217

Heather, 62
Isaac, 91, 186, 216, 217, 221
Jacob, 1, 42, 46, 47, 48, 50, 53, 71, 91, 109, 168, 186, 221
Jane, 21
Jesse, 56, 62, 85, 168, 180, 220
Jessee, 21
John, 13, 185
Jonathan, 88
Jonathan Jones, 21
Joseph, 41, 46, 47, 70, 71, 91, 109, 129, 168, 186, 192, 217, 221, 224, 226
Levi, 18
Mary, 45, 86, 88, 109
Mordecai, 18
Rachel, 13, 18, 19, 53, 56, 58, 62, 73, 91, 101, 168, 186, 221
Rebecca, 38, 85
Rebeckah, 46
Rebekah, 21
Roserter, 62
Rositer, 56
Rossiter, 86, 168, 180, 196, 203, 220
Sarah, 46, 87, 91, 168, 183, 186, 196, 216, 220, 221
Thomas, 13, 62, 93
William, 18, 80, 84
SCOTTEN, Abraham, 62
Jane, 161
William, 113

SELLMON, Eliza., 29
SHARP,
  Charlotte, 126
  James, 94
  John, 76, 125, 150, 155
  Susanna, 86, 155
  Susannah, 48, 125
  Thomas, 38, 90, 92, 94, 125, 126, 155
  William, 56, 75
SHARPLESS,
  Benjamin, 113, 115, 136, 141
  Edith, 113
  Elizabeth, 115
  Isaac, 113
  Rebecky, 113
  Sarah, 136, 141
SHAW,
  Ann, 73
  Benjamin, 149
  Catharine, 221
  Catherine, 149, 152, 185
  David, 73
  George, 73
  Joseph, 51, 64
  Rachel, 73
  Samuel, 73
SHEEPHERD, John, 32
SHELMERDINE,
  Eleaner, 264
SHEPHARD, ---, 265
SHEPHERD, Ann, 97, 102, 181, 275, 278, 279, 276
  Hannah, 278
  Moses, 182, 211
  Phebe, 254, 269
  Richmond, 267, 269
  Sarah, 181
  Solomon, 250, 267, 269, 270, 272, 273, 274, 278, 279
  Susanna, 267, 269, 270, 272, 273, 274, 278, 279, 270
  Thomas, 181
  William, 252, 267, 269
SHEPPARD,
  Ann, 168, 207, 214, 220, 226, 236
  Moses, 214, 217, 220
  Sarah, 168, 220
  Thomas, 207, 214, 220, 226, 236
SHEREDINE,
  Cassandra, 132
  Daniel, 118
SHERIDINE,
  Casandry, 111, 113
  Thomas, 48
SHERWOOD, Thomas, 202, 216, 233
SHEWARD,
  Caleb, 278
  Jane, 278, 279
  Sarah, 278, 279
SHIELDS,
  David, 49, 211
  Jane, 211
  Mary, 211
SHOEMAKER,
  Esther, 170
  Isaac, 170
  Rebecca, 238

SHUMAKER,
  Margaret, 124
SIMMONS, Mary, 217
SIMON, 69
SINCLAIR,
  Esther, 226
  Hetty, 216
  R., 187
  Robert, 216
SKINNER, Mary, 117
SLADE,
  Elizabeth, 55
  William, 71
SLOAN, James W., 196, 229
SLOGDON, John, 244
SMITH,
  Amos, 191, 225, 243, 247
  Ann, 53
  Cassandra, 166
  Cylas, 87
  David, 53, 56
  Dotty, 118
  E., 286
  Elias, 204, 235
  Elisabeth, 52
  Elizabeth, 46, 55, 57, 60, 80, 114, 129, 276
  Esther, 204, 235
  Frances, 150
  George, 204, 235
  Hannah, 204, 235
  John, 46, 50, 56, 57, 75, 76, 80, 112, 115, 116, 117, 122, 129, 130, 276, 286, 287
  Joshua, 46, 56, 57, 70, 115, 129, 269

INDEX

Lucy, 275
Lydia, 80, 261, 262, 276
Mary, 46, 54, 56, 57, 74, 129, 269, 286, 287
Peter, 46
Rachel, 216, 243
Ralph, 116
Rebecca, 243, 247
Robert, 53, 55, 60, 69
Sally, 118
Samuel, 53, 204, 235, 243
Samuel S., 176
Silas, 276
Susanna, 80
SMITSON, William, 52
SNOWDEN,
  Elizabeth, 116, 141
  Hannah Moore, 142
  Mary, 116, 170
  Mary C., 169
  Richard, 116, 141, 169, 170
  Samuel, 116, 141
SOLLERS, John, 27
SOPHIA, 137
SOTT, Elizabeth, 51
SPARROW,
  Elizabeth, 165
SPAVOLD, James, 132
SPENCER,
  Abel, 74, 90, 105, 115, 126, 149, 150, 158, 159, 168, 199, 231, 124
  Ann, 22, 244
  Eleanor, 22, 23
  Elenor, 244
  Eliza, 244
  Elizabeth, 23, 74, 90, 105, 126, 149, 158, 199, 231, 244
  Enoch, 56, 64, 78, 83, 244
  Enoch Lucas, 22
  Hannah, 64, 86, 87, 244, 246
  Job, 56, 64, 68, 70, 73
  Joseph, 107, 158, 199, 231
  Mahala, 22
  Mahalah, 244
  Mahlon, 22, 23, 64, 244
  Makton Atkinson, 23
  Rebecca, 168, 199, 231
  Rebeccah, 90, 149, 150, 158
  Rebeckah, 74, 105
  Rebekah, 105
  Reuben, 90, 107, 149, 199, 231
  Rubin, 158
  Sarah, 22, 56, 64, 90, 105, 149, 158, 199, 231, 244, 270
  Townsend, Josh
  William, 22, 90, 105, 149, 158, 199, 231
  William Lee, 22, 244
SPICER,
  Ann, 59
  Elizabeth, 55, 66
  Gulim, 59
  Isaiah, 25
  James, 25, 55, 59, 68, 76
  John, 59, 92
  Rachel, 59, 92
  Sarah, 59, 63
  Uriah, 59
  Yeaman, 59, 68
STANER, Sarah, 117
STANLEY, Rebekah, 274
STANSBURY, Danil, 27
STAPLETON,
  Joshua, 102, 125, 158, 208, 238
  Lydia, 125
  Mary, 188, 223, 226
  Rachel, 216
  Robert, 158
  Samuel, 102, 158, 208, 238
  Susanna, 102, 125, 158, 208, 238
  Susannah, 124
  Thomas, 113
STARR, Abigail, 243
  Aquila, 243
  Engle, 243
  Esther, 262, 263
  Eunice, 234
  Isaac, 119
  James, 243
  John, 269
  Joseph, 244
  Mary, 167, 174, 251, 269
  Molly, 243
  Phebe, 262, 278
  Sally Ann, 244
  Sidney, 243
STEDMAN,
  Ann, 111
  John, 111

STEER, Isaac, 266
STEVENSON,
  Abigail, 86
  Charles, 53
  Henry, 216
  Mary, 84, 181, 220, 225, 253, 255
  Nicholas, 220
STEWARD, Ann, 161
  James, 271
STEWART,
  Ann, 55, 161
  Edward, 271
  Hannah, 69
  Joshua, 205, 236
  Josiah, 168
  Sarah, 214
STOCKDALE,
  John, 6, 91, 94
  Mary, 6
  Thomas, 6, 54, 55, 68, 70, 78, 94
  William, 6, 55, 94
STOKELEY, Mary, 173
STOKELY, Mary, 236
STOKES,
  David, 162
  Hannah, 115
  Joseph, 115, 134
STONER, Mary, 259
STORER, John, 40
STORES, John, 40
STORY, Enoch, 119
STRAWBRIDGE,
  Abraham, 126
  Isaac, 121
  Rebeccah, 126

STUART,
  Ann, 134, 161
  George, 109
  Hannah, 211
STUMP,
  Cassandra, 73, 118, 119, 120, 121, 122
  Easther, 127
  Hannah, 159, 168
  Henry, 117, 127
  Herman, 118, 120, 121, 123
  John, 118, 121, 122, 124, 168
  Reuben, 125
  William, 118
SULIVAN, Jemima, 91
SUTTON, John D., 207, 237
SWAMLEY, Miriam, 275
SWAMLY, Meriam, 257
SWANEY, Harriet, 127

-T-
TALBERD, John, 46
TALBOT,
  Anna, 266
  Benjamin, 271
  Edward, 169
  Elisha, 206
  Elizabeth, 169
  John, 108, 109, 138, 257, 271, 273
  Margaret, 108, 109, 142, 147
  Mary, 259, 271
  Rachel, 259
  Richard, 169

TALBOTT,
  Ann, 271, 287
  Anna, 247, 265, 267, 268, 270, 271, 287
  Anne, 249
  Benjamin, 249, 254, 255, 269, 270, 271, 272, 274, 277, 278
  Cassandrew, 30
  Deborah, 278
  Edward, 27, 28, 29, 35, 36, 60, 169
  Eliza., 29
  Elizabeth, 249, 253, 254, 269, 274, 275, 277, 278, 286
  Jeremiah, 36, 47
  John, 103, 110, 111, 249, 266, 267, 268, 270, 271, 272, 273, 274, 275, 276, 277, 278, 286
  Joseph, 247, 249, 255, 265, 268, 270, 271, 272, 273, 287
  Kinsey, 263, 275, 277
  Margaret, 103, 135
  Mary, 47, 103, 141, 249, 267, 270, 271, 272, 273, 274, 275, 276, 277, 278
  Mathew, 52
  Peggy, 249, 275, 276, 277, 278
  Rachel, 249, 271, 272, 273, 274
  Richard, 36, 47
  Ruth, 286
  Samuel, 249, 268, 270, 271, 273, 274, 275, 286

Susanna, 249, 256, 263, 271, 272, 274, 277, 286
Susannah, 273
TAMER, 72
TANNER, George, 60
Hannah, 60
TASKER,
James, 145
Mercy, 145
TAYLER,
Joh., 29
Joseph, 27, 28, 29, 30, 32, 33, 36, 37
Mary, 32
Rachel, 29
Richard, 33, 36, 37
Sarah, 32, 36
Thomas, 31
TAYLOR,
---, 265
Ann, 98, 101, 252, 253, 255
Calip, 21
Elizabeth, 48, 270
Grace, 251, 254, 270
Israel, 270
John, 52, 55
Joseph, 26, 27
Rachel, 21, 86, 265
Samuel, 151
Sarah, 262, 271
Susanna, 57
Thomas, 21, 265, 266
THACKER,
Barker, 171, 191, 225, 227, 230
William, 171

THOMAS, 69
Abel, 92
Ann, 50
Ann C., 169
Benjamin, 155, 178, 219
Cartt?, 122
Daniel, 56, 57
Elizabeth, 169, 170, 229, 215
Grace, 110
Isaac, 155
J., 110
Jehu, 155
John, 31, 56, 57, 56
John Chew, 116
Jonah, 178, 186, 219, 225, 228
Jonathan, 79
Josiah, 186
Martha, 169
Mary, 165, 169
Mary C., 169
Mordecai, 155
P., 217
P. E., 217
Philip, 169, 170, 191, 213
Philip E., 225
Rachel, 155
Rebecca, 178, 186, 219
Richard, 110
Richard S., 122
Richard Snow, 116
Samuel, 92, 169, 170, 184, 221, 227, 228
Sarah, 155, 157, 169
Susanna, 155

THOMPSON, Aquila, 48, 70
Hannah, 126, 145
James, 126
William, 91, 93
THOMSON,
Aquila, 55
Catron, 56
Elizabeth, 55
Hannah, 62
Mary, 40
Natl., 55
THORN, Tabitha, 53
THORNBURGH,
---, 215
Cassandra, 214, 217, 232
Cassandria, 201
Deborah, 210, 211, 217, 230
Elizabeth, 210, 230, 238
Joseph, 192, 201, 211, 217, 226, 230, 231, 232
Margaret, 210, 215, 230
Phebe, 211
Sarah, 210, 215, 230
Thomas, 211
THYSEY, Meriam, 88
TIPTON,
Angelica, 14
Angilico, 51
Anjalico, 36
Anjillico, 53
Ann, 53
Aquila, 51, 52, 57
Elizebeth, 27
Esther, 14
Jabus M:y, 51

John, 14, 27, 32, 51
Jonathan, 51
Joshua, 53, 57
Luke, 14, 51
Mary, 14, 51, 98
Micajah, 14, 98
Mordica, 29, 32
Nicholas, 14, 15, 51, 53, 57, 65
Rebecca, 14, 72
Rebeckah, 72
Rebekah, 53
Sarah, 14
Tabitha, 51, 62
William, 14, 15, 27, 30, 31, 32, 35, 47, 48, 51, 52, 53, 57, 62, 36, 37, 47, 51
TOACH,
  Barbary, 190
  Hannah, 190
  Henry, 190
  Mary, 190
  Rachel, 190
TODD,
  Elinor, 29
  Frances, 29
TOLBOT, Elisha, 236
TOMKINS,
  Ann, 121, 124, 126, 145
  Benjamin, 119, 121, 124, 126, 145, 156, 157, 161, 121
  John, 119, 121, 124, 126, 147, 152, 125
  Joseph, 152
  Martha, 125
  Mary, 119, 121, 124, 126, 145, 157
  Rachel, 119, 121, 124, 126, 145, 157, 125
  Sarah, 121, 124, 125, 126, 147
TOMPKINS, Benjamin, 148
  Elizabeth, 145, 146
  John, 146
  Mary, 146, 148
  Sarah, 147, 148
TORRENCE,
  Ann, 212
  Eliza, 212
  Elizabeth, 212
TOWNSEND,
  Granville, 189
  Granville S., 216
  Hannah, 76
  Hannah P., 211, 213, 214, 215, 216
  Hannah Painter, 176, 218
  James Pemberton, 170, 201
  John England, 170
  Joseph, 76, 78, 89, 170, 176, 184, 189, 194, 195, 201, 211, 212, 214, 215, 216, 218, 217
  Joseph England, 194
  Mary, 170, 176, 184, 189, 194, 201, 213, 218, 266
  Mary Martha, 170
  Mary Matthews, 194, 195
  Nicholas Waln, 176, 218
  Sarah, 194, 228
  William Mathews, 184
TOWSEND, Granville S., 216
  Hannah P., 216
  Hannah Painter, 13
  Joseph, 13, 216
  Mary, 13
  Nicholas Waln, 13
TOWSON, Thomas, 51
TRACEY,
  Jemina, 32
  Teague, 29
  Tego, 48
TRAGO, Sarah, 127
TRAPNALL, James, 57
TREADAWAY, Daniel, 36
TREADWAY, Daniel, 72
TREDAWAY, Daniel, 32, 46
TREDWAY,
  Daniel, 15, 48
  John, 48
  Mary, 48, 110
  Sarah, 48
  Thomas, 48
TREGO,
  Albert David, 244
  Francenia, 244
  Hannah, 244
  Harriet, 244
  James D., 244
  Samuel, 244
  Sarah, 244
  Thomas, 244
  William, 244

INDEX

TRIMBLE,
  Ann, 89, 189, 221, 224
  Elizabeth, 143, 201, 213
  Elizabeth Sims, 244
  Hannah, 10, 176, 216, 218
  Isaac, 93, 143, 150, 153, 185, 187, 212, 213, 214, 21, 222
  James, 10, 77, 93, 143, 150, 176, 185, 213, 218, 221
  Jane, 93, 143, 150, 185, 212, 213, 215, 221
  John, 10, 93, 143, 150, 176, 185, 201, 211, 212, 213, 215, 218, 221, 230, 244
  Joseph, 93, 143, 150, 185, 221, 247
  Julia, 232
  Mary, 93, 143, 150, 185, 201, 221, 227, 228
  Sarah, 10, 176, 218
  Thomas Brogden, 244
  William, 10, 84, 92, 176, 211, 212, 215, 216, 218, 225, 230, 231
TRIPPE, Elizabeth, 214
TRUMP, Jesse, 66, 67
TRY, Henry, 217
TUCKER,
  Abraham, 114
  Ann, 244
  David, 87, 244
  Elizabeth, 41, 114, 244, 247
  Esther Shoemaker, 170
  Hannah, 244
  Isaac, 170
  James, 244
  Joseph, 114, 140
  Mary, 80, 89, 91, 170, 183, 220
  Matthias, 170
  Mry, 41
  Nicholas, 41, 63
  Rachel Tucker, 244
  Robert, 41
  Sally, 114
  Samuel, 244
TUDER,
  Ann, 98
  Elizabeth, 98
  Isaac, 98
  John, 98
  Joshua, 98
  Martha, 98
  William, 98
TUDOR,
  Abraham, 26
  Hannah, 26
  Martha, 26, 78
  Ruth, 26
  William, 26
TURNER,
  Daniel, 122
  Thomas, 122
TYE, George, 47, 51
TYLOR, Sarah, 260
  Thomas, 260
TYSON,
  ---, 177
  Ann, 18, 96, 223
  Deborah, 197
  Dorothy, 78, 95
  Elisha, 54, 57, 68, 78, 170, 186, 191, 197, 211, 212, 215, 217, 218, 228
  Elizabeth, 95, 99, 189, 201, 202, 224, 232
  Enos, 55
  Esther, 54, 96, 99, 170, 190, 192, 211, 225
  George, 18, 96
  Isaac, 54, 95, 99, 170, 177, 189, 201, 202, 211, 215, 217, 218, 224, 229, 211, 232
  Jacob, 18, 55, 65, 74, 94, 96, 211, 222, 223
  Jesse, 78, 79, 95, 99, 189, 192, 197, 224, 217
  John, 65
  John Shoemaker, 197
  Jonathan, 18
  Lucrecia, 161
  Lucretia, 177, 211, 213, 214, 215, 217, 218, 237
  Margaret, 18, 89, 95, 99, 189, 192, 197, 211, 214, 217, 224, 211
  Martha, 247
  Mary, 55, 57, 177, 186, 191, 197, 214, 215, 217, 218
  N---, 167
  Nathan, 66, 177, 211, 213, 215, 217, 218, 247, 214
  Philip Thomas, 202
  Rachel, 217
  Sarah, 18, 186, 214, 231
  Tacy, 55, 65, 55
  Thomas, 95, 99, 189, 224

William, 177, 204, 217, 218
William Amos, 18

-U-
UNCKLES, Sarah, 251, 264
UNCLES, Sarah, 276
UNDERHILL, Ann, 1
UNDERWOOD,
  Abraham, 202, 233
  Ann, 170, 201, 233
  Barbary, 190
  Benjamin, 76, 88, 149, 154, 161, 201, 233
  Elihu, 202, 234
  Elizabeth, 27
  Elizebeth, 27
  Enoch, 80, 82, 149, 170, 190, 201, 233
  Hannah, 202, 233
  James, 201, 233
  Jane, 202, 234
  Mary, 88, 126, 149, 160, 170, 190, 201, 222, 225, 233
  Nehemiah, 76, 79, 83, 85, 88, 149, 160
  Rachel, 76, 88, 149
  Samuel, 27, 28
  Sarah, 76, 88, 126, 149, 153, 161
  William, 160, 175
  Willin, 88
  Willing, 76, 149, 206, 236
UNKLES, Sarah, 268
UPDEGRAF,
  Joseph, 278
  Josiah, 278
  Mary, 278
UPDEGRAFF,
  Isrl., 278
  Jonah, 263
  Mary, 278
  Rachel, 203
  Sarah, 278

-V-
VANBIBER, Isaac, 124
VANCE, Agnes, 132
VANCLEAVE,
  Rachel, 131
VANHORN,
  Gabriel, 70
  Jonathan, 245
VANWYCK,
  Elizabeth, 212
VICKERS, Amos, 206
VORE,
  Benjamin, 200, 232
  Elanor, 274
  Elianor, 273
  Elisabeth, 244
  Hannah, 149
  Isaac, 200, 232, 274
  Jacob, 200, 232, 244
  Jessee, 149
  Rachel, 200, 232
  Rebecca, 200, 232
  Sarah, 200, 232
  Thomas, 149

-W-
WAGSTAFF,
  Richard, 1, 42
  Sarah, 1, 42
WAINRIGHT, James, 215
WAINWRIGHT,
  James, 198
WALKER,
  Agness, 28
  Ellen, 280
  Mary, 28
  Sarah, 280
  William, 280
WALL, Ned, 141
WALLACE,
  Cassandra, 134
  Elizabeth, 157
  Grace, 110, 157
  John, 134
  John Lukins, 157
  Joseph, 157
  Ruth, 117
  Samuel, 141
  Sarah, 141, 157
WALLER, Caleb, 215
WALLICE,
  Ann, 162
  Grace, 109
WALLIS,
  Ann, 143, 155
  Casandrew, 113
  Edward, 109, 129
  Elizabeth, 114, 115, 116, 141, 142, 144
  Frances, 113, 114, 115, 139
  Francis, 109, 112
  Gainor Lukins, 142

Grace, 108, 109, 110, 111, 112, 113, 114, 115, 132, 136, 139, 141
Jo. Joseph, 113
John, 108, 109, 128
John Lukens, 141
Joseph, 115, 144
Joseph Jacob, 128, 141, 142
Margaret, 143
Mary, 144
Randal, 121, 123, 155
Randel, 118
Richard, 215
Samuel, 109, 115, 117, 118, 119, 123, 128, 131, 136, 139, 141, 143, 144
Sarah, 109, 111, 117, 120, 123, 125, 136, 141, 143
Sary, 113
Thomas, 117, 132, 142, 144
WALSH, Richard, 80, 182, 220, 224
WALTON,
 Alice, 101
 Ann, 101
 Benjamin, 148, 160
 Elisha, 119, 126, 146
 Elizabeth, 101, 119, 124, 125, 126, 148, 149, 153, 155
 Hannah, 121, 126, 148
 James, 121, 126, 148, 160
 Joseph, 126, 148, 149, 160
 Lukens, 101, 187, 223
 Sarah, 101, 153, 187, 223
 William, 101, 125, 153, 155, 187, 223
WARD,
 Ann, 277
 Casandrew, 112
 Edward, 113
 Elizabeth, 277
 John, 44, 68, 70
 Rachel, 44, 68, 70
 Richard, 126, 127
 Robert, 277
 Sarah, 263
 William, 263, 277
WARFIELD,
 Beal, 274
 Edward, 274
 Polly, 271
WARNER,
 Aaron, 60, 64, 115, 118, 121, 148
 Agness, 64, 121, 125
 Agness Crosdale, 127
 Amelia, 127
 Amos, 60, 64, 127
 Ann, 125, 127
 Anne, 115
 Aran, 127
 Asa, 125, 127, 159
 Aseph, 56, 113, 115, 121, 123, 139, 143
 Benjamin, 112, 115, 135, 140, 141, 144
 Corasdel, 135
 Croasdal, 60, 149
 Croasdel, 113, 121, 125, 136
 Crosdal, 148
 Crosdale, 63, 121
 Crosedale, 64, 113
 Cuthbert, 112, 113, 135
 Hannah, 60, 64, 112, 113, 136
 Hezekiah, 113, 115
 Jane, 222
 John, 127, 152
 Jonathan, 245, 247
 Joseph, 112, 113, 115, 120, 121, 122, 123, 124, 127, 134, 135, 138, 144, 150
 Martha, 113, 115, 139, 141
 Mary, 60, 64, 112, 113, 115, 121, 127, 135, 140, 142, 148
 Mordecai, 117
 Rachel, 144
 Ruth, 112, 113, 121, 122, 123, 125, 134, 135, 143
 Sarah, 60, 64, 115, 117, 118, 125, 127, 135, 140, 245, 247
 Silas, 121, 123, 125, 156
WATERHOUSE,
 Ann, 192
 Elizabeth, 213
 Joshua, 213
 William, 188, 192, 213, 215, 230
WATERS,
 Ann, 261
 Gulielma Maria, 273
 Hanson, 273, 274

Margaret, 263, 272, 273, 274, 275, 276, 277, 278
Margret, 271, 280
Samuel, 251, 265, 267, 268, 270, 271, 273, 280
Sarah, 258, 270, 271, 272, 273, 275, 276, 277, 280
Susanna, 280
Susannah, 265
WATKINS, Nicholas, 271
WATSON, William, 127
WATTERS, Edward, 129
WAY, Jane, 271
  Joseph, 213, 269
  Mary, 254, 269
  Phebe, 268, 269
  William, 269
WAYBLE, Mary, 211
WAYMAN,
  Ann, 274
  Henry, 276
  Rachel, 274
WEBB,
  Alisanna, 130
  Ann, 271
  David, 148
  Elizabeth, 107, 143, 253, 255, 270, 271
  George, 271
  Hannah, 128, 136
  James, 107, 111, 114, 128, 136, 137, 155
  Jesse, 107
  John, 107, 114, 118, 128
  Joseph, 107
  Mary, 107, 114, 121, 124, 126, 137, 148, 159, 160, 271
  Massa, 126
  Massey, 160, 234
  Mercy, 107, 202, 216
  Moses, 107, 154, 162
  Richard, 87, 107, 114, 118, 119, 121, 126, 128, 143, 147, 151
  Sarah, 114, 128
  W., 112, 113
  William, 111, 268, 271
WEBSTER, Alasanna, 109, 110
  Ann, 109, 110, 111, 144
  Cassandra, 109, 116, 119, 130, 160
  Dolly, 214
  Dorithy, 101
  Dority, 160
  Dorothy, 95, 201, 233
  Elizabeth, 109, 110, 120, 133, 160, 172, 217, 233, 235, 238
  Isaac, 103, 108, 109, 110, 116, 118, 119, 122, 124, 128, 130, 131, 138, 144, 145, 154, 160, 172, 214, 233, 270
  J., 181
  James, 103, 109, 119, 122, 123, 214
  John, 160
  John L., 124, 217
  John Lee, 103, 119, 120, 123, 131, 132, 154, 171, 189, 224
  John S., 123, 214
  John Skinner, 118
  Joseph, 103, 119, 151
  Lee, 118, 119, 160
  Margaret, 103, 108, 109, 110, 131, 135, 138, 145, 160, 161
  Margret, 110, 118
  Mary, 109
  Peggy, 118, 124, 125
  Polley, 124
  Polly, 123
  Robert, 103, 119, 155, 170, 191, 226
  Ruth, 270
  Samuel, 103, 109, 110, 119, 123, 131, 154, 160
  Sarah, 103, 108, 118, 120, 128, 130, 145
  Susan, 123, 124
  Susanna, 124
  Susannah, 125
  Thomas, 119, 123, 154, 200, 214, 232
  William, 82, 103, 119, 160, 270
WEEKS,
  Ann, 56, 57, 70, 72, 137
  Benjamin, 96
  Daniel, 56, 57
  Ezekiel, 57
  Lydia, 96
  Rachel, 101, 195, 228
WELCH, Sarah, 278, 279
WELLS,
  Ann, 55, 86, 179, 219, 226
  James, 127
  John, 55, 66, 68, 219

Lydia, 216
Margaret, 86, 179, 219, 223
Nancy, 52
Rachel, 86, 90, 179, 219, 224, 227
Susanna, 55
William, 55
WELSH, Elizabeth, 277
WEST, Amos, 18, 101, 179, 196, 212, 229
Eli, 18
Elizabeth, 18, 245
Enos, 18, 73, 245
George, 114, 118, 119, 121, 143, 148, 158
Hannah, 118, 143, 197, 217
James, 95
Jesse, 171, 200, 232
Jonathan, 114
Joseph, 171
Mahlon H., 245
Martha, 36
Mary, 245
N., 180
Priscilla, 114, 119, 161
Rachel, 114
Rebecca, 18, 245
Stacey, 73
Stacy, 18, 187, 222
Thomas, 18, 73, 94, 95, 101, 222, 245
WETHERED, L., 178
WHEELER,
Agness, 33
Beniamin, 31
Benjaman, 49

Benjamin, 29
Constant, 35
Elizabeth, 60, 97, 98
H., 29
Hannah, 29
Joseph, 116
Martha, 28
Mary Ann, 114
Monica, 114
Moses, 29
Rachel, 33
Samuel, 29
Sarahanna, 33
Solomon, 29, 33
Susan, 1
Tabitha, 33
Thomas, 29
William, 1, 27, 29, 35
WHITE,
Jane, 135
John, 245
Joseph, 198
WHITSON, William, 245
WICKS,
Ann, 72
Benjamin, 72
John Lancaster, 72
Lydia, 72
Matthew, 72
Rachel, 72
WIGGANS, Bazaleel, 155
WIGGINS,
Bazeleel, 153
Bezleel, 127
Cuthbert, 145
Elizabeth, 127

John, 127, 159
Joseph, 121, 127, 135, 138, 145, 159
Margret, 127
Sarah, 127, 135
Tacey, 151
Tracey, 119, 120, 121
WIGHAM, John, 225
WILES, John, 56
WILEY,
Cumfort, 55
Luke, 49
Susanna, 171
WILLETS,
Ann, 105, 110, 118
Cassandra, 105
John, 272
Rachel, 264, 266
Samuel, 105, 110
Sarah, 105
WILLETTS, Samuel, 111
WILLIAMS,
Abner, 273, 275
Ann, 18
Catharine, 163
Elizabeth, 86, 88, 128
Ellen, 18
Ellenor, 56
Enion, 120
Ennion, 80, 200, 216, 232, 233
Enoch, 18, 55, 56, 57, 68
George, 128
Hannah, 120, 200, 215, 216, 232
Isaac, 78, 86, 100, 171, 191, 211, 225

Israel, 57, 272
Jacob, 272
Jane, 256, 272
John, 277
Lydia, 191
Mary, 135
Peter, 57
Prissilla, 274
Rebecca, 171, 176, 215, 216, 218
Ruth, 272
Sarah, 255, 257, 272
William, 56, 86, 266
WILLIS,
Lydia, 278
Samuel, 116
WILLITS,
---, 266
Ann, 115, 116, 117, 120, 140
Cassandra, 123, 140
Elizabeth, 279
Ellis, 279
Henry, 133
Jesse, 279
John, 266, 267, 269, 270, 279
Rachel, 258, 259, 266, 267, 268, 271, 279
Samuel, 117, 133, 140, 279
Sarah, 133, 279
WILLMOT,
Elizabeth, 111
Mary, 111
WILLMOTT,
John, 27

Mary, 116
Sarah, 56
WILLSON,
Ben Kid, 38, 51
Benjamin, 50
Cassand., 50
Cassander, 50
Elizabeth, 35, 50, 51
Gittings, 51
Gover, 35
Henry, 32, 35, 36, 41, 50, 51
John, 35, 36, 50, 51
Johnkid, 51
Kid, 34
Margaret, 51
Mary, 49, 50
Presilla, 35
Priscilla, 50
Prisilla, 46, 51
Rachal, 46
Rachel, 34, 35, 49, 50
Samuel, 35, 50
William, 32, 35, 40, 50, 51
WILMOTH, Elizabeth, 55
WILMOTT,
Averilla, 27
Elizabeth, 56, 110
John, 28
Mary, 112
Richard, 109
WILSON,
Alasanna, 117, 121, 124, 146, 150, 155
Alasannah, 119, 120

Alesanna, 118, 125, 127, 162
Aliceanna, 164
Alisana, 111
Alisanna, 118, 119, 120, 122, 124, 144, 154, 217, 127
Alissanna, 116
Alissannah, 117
Ann, 114, 118, 123, 125, 126, 144, 145, 155, 157, 162
Ann Benfield, 118
Anna, 18, 100, 162, 193, 227
Anne, 103
B. Kid, 46
Benjamin, 75, 124, 125, 126, 153, 154, 160, 195, 229
Benjamin Kid, 160
Benkid, 48, 49, 52, 60, 65, 69, 72, 86
Betsey, 229
Betty, 195
Casandrew, 112
Cassandra, 73, 110, 168
Cassandry, 110, 111
Catharine, 97, 193, 212, 214, 215, 227
Cathrine, 100
Charles, 171, 197
Christopher, 103, 110, 115, 118, 119, 120, 121, 122, 123, 125, 126, 129, 130, 136, 146
D., 126
David, 18, 55, 67, 78, 97, 100, 162, 170, 180, 189,

192, 211, 212, 214, 227, 215, 219
Deborah, 17, 18, 53, 54, 100, 171, 193, 215, 227
Drucilla, 123
Edward, 206, 236
Elisabeth, 113
Elizabeth, 17, 48, 65, 125, 149, 150, 154, 164, 180, 215, 75, 219
Frances, 103, 143
Frances Young, 114, 117
Gittings, 67, 112
Grace, 17, 100, 104, 149, 171, 193, 212, 214, 227
Hannah, 103, 114, 118, 120, 125, 126, 129, 153, 159, 212
Henry, 46, 48, 49, 52, 53, 54, 55, 58, 60, 63, 64, 65, 67, 68, 71, 72, 83, 86, 92, 93, 116, 119, 120, 123, 124, 134, 144, 153, 160, 166, 186, 113
Isaac, 103, 115, 120, 125, 126, 127, 150, 153, 162, 195, 229, 127
James, 117, 119, 125, 147, 151, 152, 153, 157, 171, 192, 226, 227
James Hampton, 209
Jane, 97, 100, 170, 180, 189, 192, 212, 213, 214, 215, 216, 217, 219
John, 17, 18, 54, 56, 60, 61, 69, 70, 75, 92, 93, 100, 101, 103, 110, 111, 112, 113, 114, 115, 116, 117, 118, 119, 120, 121, 122, 123, 124, 125, 126, 127, 129, 130, 137, 140, 144, 145, 146, 149, 152, 154, 157, 162, 171, 193, 198, 212, 215, 216, 217, 227, 230, 113, 217
John Kid, 67, 112
John W., 120, 122, 125, 161, 177, 237
John Webster, 152, 159, 217, 237
Joseph, 103, 109, 111, 112, 113, 114, 115, 116, 119, 120, 122, 125, 126, 127, 131, 137, 140, 144, 145, 149, 153, 172, 195, 197, 229, 230, 234, 111
Kathrine, 17
Margaret, 55, 64, 120, 122, 125, 186, 217, 124
Martha, 97, 100, 103, 113, 114, 118, 120, 121, 122, 125, 126, 150, 153, 160
Mary, 59, 97, 100, 113, 114, 119, 120, 121, 125, 136, 140, 141, 171
Massanna, 103
Mercy, 195, 197, 209, 229
Mixon, 217
Nancy, 124, 217
Nargarett, 162
Nixon, 120, 124, 159, 199, 231
Oliver, 195, 229
Peggy, 125, 126
Peter, 118, 119, 120, 121, 122, 124, 125, 126, 127, 138, 145
Precilla, 57
Pricilla, 125
Priscilla, 49, 54, 55, 57, 112, 134
Prisilla, 46, 52
Prissella, 48
Prissilla, 112
Rachal, 48
Rachel, 46, 48, 49, 61, 109, 110, 111, 112, 166
Sally, 114, 120, 122, 123
Samiel, 96
Samuel, 17, 93, 97, 99, 100, 111, 112, 113, 115, 190, 192, 212, 213, 214, 215, 225
Sarah, 110, 118, 120, 121, 122, 123, 124, 125, 126, 130, 136, 144, 145, 149, 154, 157, 161, 118, 127
Stephen, 171, 195, 197, 209, 229
Susanna, 76, 120, 124, 127
Susannah, 150, 162
Thomas, 18, 79, 97, 100, 114, 118, 119, 120, 122, 124, 125, 126, 127, 144, 145, 155, 156, 157, 193, 217, 227
W., 126
William, 18, 46, 52, 54, 75, 79, 92, 93, 100, 103, 110, 112, 114, 116, 120, 123, 153, 157, 171, 175, 193, 212, 227
WINDLE, Caleb, 274
WISE, William, 112

WOLSEY, Joseph, 109
WOOD,
 Cassandra, 249, 250, 265, 266
 Elizabeth, 87, 267, 286
 Joel, 81, 87, 276, 277, 286, 287
 John, 277
 Joseph, 265
 Joshua, 286
 Lydia, 262, 277, 278, 286
 M., 286
 Margaret, 266, 269, 278, 287
 Margret, 269
 Mary, 81, 87, 252, 254, 257, 259, 272, 276, 278, 286, 287
 Nathan, 263, 277, 278, 287
 Richard, 286
 Ruth, 84, 85, 253, 254
 Samuel, 287
 Sarah, 287
 Susanna, 262, 277, 287
 Susannah, 263
 Thomas, 277, 278, 286, 287
 William, 74, 81, 87, 240, 266, 267, 274, 275, 276, 286
WOODCOCK,
 Deborah, 77
 Robert, 77
WOODEN,
 Rachel, 51
 Stepton, 51

WOODLAND, Cassandra, 119, 123
 Jonathan, 123
 Nancy, 119
 William, 123
WOODROW, Levi, 267
WOODSON, Levi, 114
WOODWARD,
 Abraham B., 276
 T., 111
WOOWARD, Abraham B., 276
WORLEY, Joseph, 278
WORTHINGTON,
 Achsah, 265
 Ann, 124, 136, 155
 Cassandra, 105
 Charles, 50, 105, 109, 113, 116, 117, 118, 134, 136, 154, 156, 195, 228
 Eliza, 127
 Elizabeth, 105, 146
 Henry, 86, 105, 117, 146, 183, 221, 231
 J., 116
 John, 50, 59, 105, 108, 111, 112, 113, 114, 117, 118, 122, 126, 127, 134, 138, 153, 156, 158, 188
 Joseph, 120, 122, 127, 134, 147
 Mary, 109, 111, 113, 114, 116, 131, 132, 134, 136, 146
 Pricilla, 158
 Priscilla, 51, 59, 105, 115, 116, 119, 126, 127, 134

Prisey, 119
Prissilla, 126, 150
Rachel, 105, 126, 158
Samuel, 50, 105, 112, 127
Sarah, 105, 109, 116, 117, 119, 143, 144, 147
Sary, 108
Thomas, 105, 127
William, 105, 125, 127, 266
WRIGHT,
 ---l, 266
 Allen, 278, 279, 280
 Ann, 258, 259, 260, 263, 270, 271, 272, 273, 274, 275, 278, 280, 282
 Benjamin, 266
 Betey, 274
 Betsy, 274
 Catharine, 288
 Eleanor, 274
 Elenor, 258
 Elizabeth, 258, 260, 264, 265, 266, 267, 269, 270, 273, 274, 275, 278, 279, 280, 282, 287, 288
 Ester, 274
 Esther, 258, 259
 Isaac, 273, 274, 275, 278, 279
 Israel, 279
 Joel, 264, 265, 266, 267, 268, 269, 270, 272, 274, 275, 276, 278, 279, 280, 287
 John, 273, 274, 280, 282, 288

Jonathan, 264, 270, 278, 279, 282
Joseph, 264, 265, 266, 267, 268, 269, 270, 271, 273, 274, 275, 278, 282
Mary, 258, 264, 265, 267, 268, 269, 270, 271, 272, 275, 278, 279, 282
Moses, 278, 279, 282
Phebe, 204
Polly, 278
Rachel, 274, 278, 279, 283, 287, 288
Ruth, 288
Samuel, 268, 269, 270, 271, 272, 282
Sidney, 266
Susan, 278, 279
Susanna, 249, 260, 264, 283
William, 268, 269, 270, 272, 274, 282, 288
WYLE, John, 55

Sarah, 1
Susanna, 95
Susannah, 99
YARNALL,
Aaron, 81
Amoss, 81
George, 81, 253
Lydia, 81, 254
Martha, 16
Mary, 81
Sarah, 81, 250, 267, 270
Susanna, 81
Thomas, 81
YEATES, Sarah, 111
YELLOTT, Ann, 213
YONG, Rebeca, 50
YOUNG,
Dinah, 85
Rebecca, 222
Robert, 181
Samuel, 50

-Y-
YARNAL,
Aaron, 99
Amos, 95, 99
Ann, 1
Aron, 95
Elizabeth, 95
Ely, 95, 99
George, 95, 99
John, 1
Lydia, 254
Martha, 95
Mary, 95, 99
Mordecai, 95, 99

Other books by the author:

A Closer Look at St. John's Parish Registers [Baltimore County, Maryland], 1701-1801

A Collection of Maryland Church Records

A Guide to Genealogical Research in Maryland: 5th Edition, Revised and Enlarged

Abstracts of the Ledgers and Accounts of the Bush Store and Rock Run Store, 1759-1771

Abstracts of the Orphans Court Proceedings of Harford County, 1778-1800

Abstracts of Wills, Harford County, Maryland, 1800-1805

Baltimore City [Maryland] Deaths and Burials, 1834-1840

Baltimore County, Maryland, Overseers of Roads, 1693-1793

Bastardy Cases in Baltimore County, Maryland, 1673-1783

Bastardy Cases in Harford County, Maryland, 1774-1844

Bible and Family Records of Harford County, Maryland Families: Volume V

Children of Harford County: Indentures and Guardianships, 1801-1830

Colonial Delaware Soldiers and Sailors, 1638-1776

*Colonial Families of the Eastern Shore of Maryland
Volumes 5, 6, 7, 8, 9, 11, 12, 13, 14, and 16*

Colonial Maryland Soldiers and Sailors, 1634-1734

Dr. John Archer's First Medical Ledger, 1767-1769, Annotated Abstracts

Early Anglican Records of Cecil County

*Early Harford Countians, Individuals Living in Harford County, Maryland in Its Formative Years
Volume 1: A to K, Volume 2: L to Z, and Volume 3: Supplement*

Harford County Taxpayers in 1870, 1872 and 1883

Harford County, Maryland Divorce Cases, 1827-1912: An Annotated Index

Heirs and Legatees of Harford County, Maryland, 1774-1802

Heirs and Legatees of Harford County, Maryland, 1802-1846

Inhabitants of Baltimore County, Maryland, 1763-1774

Inhabitants of Cecil County, Maryland, 1649-1774

Inhabitants of Harford County, Maryland, 1791-1800

Inhabitants of Kent County, Maryland, 1637-1787

*Joseph A. Pennington & Co., Havre De Grace, Maryland Funeral Home Records:
Volume II, 1877-1882, 1893-1900*

Maryland Bible Records, Volume 1: Baltimore and Harford Counties

Maryland Bible Records, Volume 2: Baltimore and Harford Counties

Maryland Bible Records, Volume 3: Carroll County

Maryland Bible Records, Volume 4: Eastern Shore

Maryland Deponents, 1634-1799

Maryland Deponents: Volume 3, 1634-1776

*Maryland Public Service Records, 1775-1783: A Compendium of Men and Women of
Maryland Who Rendered Aid in Support of the American Cause against
Great Britain during the Revolutionary War*

*Marylanders to Carolina: Migration of Marylanders to
North Carolina and South Carolina prior to 1800*

Marylanders to Kentucky, 1775-1825

Methodist Records of Baltimore City, Maryland: Volume 1, 1799-1829

Methodist Records of Baltimore City, Maryland: Volume 2, 1830-1839

Methodist Records of Baltimore City, Maryland: Volume 3, 1840-1850 (East City Station)

More Maryland Deponents, 1716-1799

More Marylanders to Carolina: Migration of Marylanders to North Carolina and South Carolina prior to 1800

More Marylanders to Kentucky, 1778-1828

Outpensioners of Harford County, Maryland, 1856-1896

Presbyterian Records of Baltimore City, Maryland, 1765-1840

Quaker Records of Baltimore and Harford Counties, Maryland, 1801-1825

Quaker Records of Northern Maryland, 1716-1800

Quaker Records of Southern Maryland, 1658-1800

Revolutionary Patriots of Anne Arundel County, Maryland

Revolutionary Patriots of Baltimore Town and Baltimore County, 1775-1783

Revolutionary Patriots of Calvert and St. Mary's Counties, Maryland, 1775-1783

Revolutionary Patriots of Caroline County, Maryland, 1775-1783

Revolutionary Patriots of Cecil County, Maryland

Revolutionary Patriots of Charles County, Maryland, 1775-1783

Revolutionary Patriots of Delaware, 1775-1783

Revolutionary Patriots of Dorchester County, Maryland, 1775-1783

Revolutionary Patriots of Frederick County, Maryland, 1775-1783

Revolutionary Patriots of Harford County, Maryland, 1775-1783

Revolutionary Patriots of Kent and Queen Anne's Counties

Revolutionary Patriots of Lancaster County, Pennsylvania

Revolutionary Patriots of Maryland, 1775-1783: A Supplement

Revolutionary Patriots of Maryland, 1775-1783: Second Supplement

Revolutionary Patriots of Montgomery County, Maryland, 1776-1783

Revolutionary Patriots of Prince George's County, Maryland, 1775-1783

Revolutionary Patriots of Talbot County, Maryland, 1775-1783

Revolutionary Patriots of Worcester and Somerset Counties, Maryland, 1775-1783

Revolutionary Patriots of Washington County, Maryland, 1776-1783

St. George's (Old Spesutia) Parish, Harford County, Maryland: Church and Cemetery Records, 1820-1920

St. John's and St. George's Parish Registers, 1696-1851

Survey Field Book of David and William Clark in Harford County, Maryland, 1770-1812

The Crenshaws of Kentucky, 1800-1995

The Delaware Militia in the War of 1812

Union Chapel United Methodist Church Cemetery Tombstone Inscriptions, Wilna, Harford County, Maryland

www.ingramcontent.com/pod-product-compliance
Lightning Source LLC
Chambersburg PA
CBHW071952220426
43662CB00009B/1102